S·O·U·R·C·E·S

NOTABLE SELECTIONS IN

Education

Third Edition

About the Editor

FRED SCHULTZ has been a professor of education at the University of Akron in Akron, Ohio, since 1969. He received his B.S. in social science education in 1962, his M.S. in history and philosophy of education in 1966, and his Ph.D. in history and philosophy of education and American studies in 1969, all from Indiana University in Bloomington, Indiana. His B.A. degree in Spanish was conferred from the University of Akron in 1985. He also likes to study modern languages. Professor Schultz has been the editor of *Annual Editions: Education* (McGraw-Hill/Dushkin) since the 1978/79 edition of that volume, and he also edits *Annual Editions: Multicultural Education,* currently available in its 2001/02 edition. He is coauthor, with James Monroe Hughes, of *Education in America* (Harper & Row, 1976). He is a fellow of the Philosophy of Education Society in the United States and a member of the Philosophy of Education Society of Great Britain. His other professional memberships include the American Educational Research Association and the American Sociological Association. Professor Schultz was also president of the Ohio Valley Philosophy of Education Society in 1976. His articles and papers have appeared in numerous journals, including *Educational Theory, The Journal of Thought, Educational Considerations, Proceedings of the Philosophy of Education Society,* and *Proceedings of the Ohio Valley Philosophy of Education Society* (now *Philosophical Studies in Education*). In the 1970s Professor Schultz did freelance book manuscript editing for New York publishers, in addition to his primary work as a professor. He has also been a visiting professor at Kent State University in Kent, Ohio, and at Oberlin College.

S·O·U·R·C·E·S

NOTABLE SELECTIONS IN

Education

Third Edition

EDITED BY

FRED SCHULTZ
University of Akron

McGraw-Hill/Dushkin

A Division of The McGraw-Hill Companies

30.00

Manufactured in the United States of America

Third Edition

456789FGRFGR4

Library of Congress Cataloging-in-Publication Data
  Main entry under title:
    Sources: notable selections in education/edited by Fred Schultz.—3rd ed.
    Includes bibliographical references and index.
    1. Education—United States. I. Schultz, Fred, *comp.*

                                                                370'.973
  0-07-241398-0   ISSN: 1094-7620

 Printed on Recycled Paper

Preface

The study of education has been approached from several conflicting, and competing, perspectives. This has always been true, although the conflict has become even more pronounced in the past 100 years. The Greek philosopher Aristotle noted in his *Politics* that people in Athens in his time (about 2,350 years ago) could not come to a consensus over what the purposes and content of education should be. This is just as true in industrialized countries today. There are currently several competing ideological perspectives regarding the social and academic purposes of schooling. *Sources: Notable Selections in Education*, 3rd ed., explores and samples some important perspectives and debates on the roles of schools, of teachers, and on the content of school curricula that have emerged over the past several decades. The book also samples important sources regarding the struggle of cultural minorities and women to attain equality of opportunity in the field of education.

The study of education has a rich and compelling legacy, and the 41 selections in this volume are from primary sources, both older and contemporary sources, that have greatly influenced American education since the 1890s. As we begin the twenty-first century, we can see that the literature on American education encompasses the classical humanist tradition in education, the revolutionary ideas concerning what education ought to be about that developed in the United States in the early and middle decades of the twentieth century, and the most current viewpoints and ideas on the psychology of learning that emerged in the 1990s and that have achieved the status of contemporary classics. I have attempted to bring together in one volume a collection of notable selections that uniquely summarizes the conflicting ideological and cultural perspectives that make up the literature in the field of education.

The reader will quickly be able to see the incredible magnitude of the differences between the competing perspectives placed side by side in this volume. For instance, the selections in Part 1 clearly demonstrate the differences in the points of view of the conservative tradition (seen in the selections by E. D. Hirsch, Jr., Diane Ravitch, and Mortimer Adler), the liberal-progressive tradition (represented by John Dewey and William Heard Kilpatrick), and the critical pedagogical perspective (evident in the writings of Henry A. Giroux, Paulo Freire, and Ivan Illich) with regard to the ultimate aims of education. So it is throughout this volume, as competing perspectives on each of the areas of education examined are presented to the reader for his or her own judgment and evaluation.

There were several conceptual parameters that I tried to remain alert to as I went through the process of developing this book of readings. First, I wanted it

i

to sample some highly important sources on education that either have, are, or are going to affect how people respond to the great debates now going on over how to improve the quality of what students learn in school as well as over proposals for new and different sorts of opportunities in the field of education. Second, I wanted the book to reflect the enormous struggle for human dignity and freedom of opportunity in the field of education in American society—in particular, the struggle of racial and ethnic minorities and the struggle of women to attain equal rights in the field of education. Third, I wanted the selections in this volume to accurately and fairly represent the conflicting ideological perspectives now competing for public acceptance in the recent literature on education. Fourth, I sought to sample some of the documentary sources on testing and assessment in American education in recent years. Finally, I wanted to include selections that reflect the great vein of literature that has developed on the inescapable interrelationships between formal educational institutions and the cultures that produce them, as well as the universe of discourse that governs differing conceptions of freedom and culture in the education of persons. I believe that this collection of notable selections does address all of these concerns.

ORGANIZATION OF THE BOOK   The selections are organized topically around the major areas of study within education. Part 1 includes selections on the Foundations of Education; Part 2, Curriculum and Instruction; Part 3, Schools in a Multicultural Society; Part 4, The American Constitutional Tradition and Education; Part 5, Perspectives From the Behavioral Sciences; and Part 6, Society, Culture, and Education. Each selection is preceded by a short introductory headnote that places the selection in the context of its relevance to the literature in the field of education and that provides biographical information on the author.

SUGGESTIONS FOR READING THE SELECTIONS   Student readers of this book are encouraged to read the introductory headnotes prior to reading the selections to which they refer. The headnotes will get you started in the right direction for reading the selections. It is also a good idea to keep in mind—and this is especially true in several of the older selections—that how language is used can and does change over time. The language used in some of the older selections is frequently sexist or nonstandard as compared to current usage. Until the middle of the twentieth century, writers commonly used the terms *he, him,* and *man,* among others, to make generic references to both males and females. Today we are much more sensitive to potentially sexist and racist language. Try to take into account the social contexts in which these older essays were written. Finally, keep in mind that all of the selections in this volume either had or are having notable impact on education and what takes place in the classroom.

ON THE INTERNET   Each part in this book is preceded by an *On the Internet* page. This page provides a list of Internet site addresses that are relevant to the part as well as a description of each site.

A WORD TO THE INSTRUCTOR An *Instructor's Manual With Test Questions* (multiple-choice and essay) is available through the publisher for instructors using *Sources: Notable Selections in Education*, 3rd ed., in the classroom.

ACKNOWLEDGMENTS I was very pleased when I was first contacted about developing this volume. It has been a unique opportunity to place in the hands of readers notable sources that have had great impact on the directions of debate over the social purposes of education in American society. I would like to thank those who reviewed the second edition of *Sources* and responded with specific suggestions for the third edition:

Gilbert Cuevas
University of Miami

John R. Hranitz
Bloomsburg University of
Pennsylvania

Jeffrey Kaplan
University of Central Florida

Robert Kelly
Brooklyn College

Richard Lakes
Georgia State University

Harry Morgan
State University of West Georgia

Laurence Newman
Long Island University

Jody A. Resko
Queens College

During the development of this edition, Theodore Knight, list manager for the Sources series, provided enthusiastic, effective support and encouragement at each step of the publication process. I would also like to thank Irene Brakas, word processing operator, for her fast, accurate, and insightful work in the development of the support material for this volume. My thanks as well to David Brackley, senior developmental editor, and Rose Gleich, administrative assistant for the Sources series. There were many selections by other famous authors that I wanted to include in this volume. However, space limitations prevented inclusion of many equally important selections in this third edition of *Sources: Notable Selections in Education*. I welcome any comments or suggestions you may have about selections for the book. Please write to me in care of SOURCES, McGraw-Hill/Dushkin.

Fred Schultz
University of Akron

Contents

v

"The purpose of education, finally, is to create in a person the ability to look at the world for himself, to make his own decisions, to say to himself this is black or this is white, to decide for himself whether there is a God in heaven or not. To ask questions of the universe, and then learn to live with those questions, is the way he achieves his own identity. But no society is really anxious to have that kind of person around."

"The students' voice should never be sacrificed, since it is the only means through which they make sense of their own experience in the world."

"Powerlessness is a justification for rebellion, but it is not a license for mindlessness. The reality of being without a voice can become part of a good argument, but it is not the same thing as a good argument; it certainly does not exempt the powerless and the voiceless from the obligation to offer good reasons. Indeed, this is precisely why there is both a need and a right to be heard—a right secured only through an education in liberty."

"From the academy the boys of my class went to Union College at Schenectady. When those with whom I had studied and contended for prizes for five years came to bid me good-by, and I learned of the barrier that prevented me from following in their footsteps—'no girls admitted here'—my vexation and mortification knew no bounds. . . . I felt more keenly than ever the humiliation of the distinctions made on the ground of sex."

"I have here shown how the marketplace of childhood promotes highly gender-differentiated constructs of the child in the media and toy industries, and in parenting magazines."

CHAPTER 12   The Cognitive Revolution in Learning   288

PART SIX   *Society, Culture, and Education*   331

CHAPTER 13   Social Change   333

PART ONE

Foundations of Education

On the Internet . . .

Sites appropriate to Part One

This is the home page of the National Paideia Center, the goal of which is to promote and support the efforts of educators who are implementing the long-term systemic school reform known as the Paideia Program.

```
http://www.paideia.org
```

Between the late nineteenth and mid-twentieth centuries, many educational programs grew out of the American reform effort called the progressive movement. This page provides information on the progressive movement and the educational theorists who contributed the most to its philosophies.

```
http://www.ilt.columbia.edu/academic/
   digitexts/notes/prog_education.html
```

This site contains the position statement, key concepts, and practices of the American Montessori Society.

```
http://www.amshq.org
```

This edition of *Philanthropy, Culture and Society* is a condensation of the themes explored in Dr. Gene Edward Veith's new book on the renaissance of classical education. Here he gives a general background on classical education and cites three examples of their use in primary and secondary schools.

```
http://www.capitalresearch.org/pcs/
   pcs-0896.html
```

CHAPTER 1 The Conservative Tradition in Educational Thought

1.1 THEODORE R. SIZER

Horace's Hope: What Works for the American High School

In the selection that follows, Theodore R. Sizer discusses the possibilities for the future of the American public schools. He uses as the vehicle for his discussion the character of Horace Smith, a fictional high school teacher who Sizer first portrayed in *Horace's Compromise: The Dilemma of the American High School* in 1992. In *Horace's Hope: What Works for the American High School* (Houghton Mifflin, 1996), from which the following selection has been taken, Sizer outlines the current debate on school reform and the renewed dialogue on how to improve the public schools.

In his discussion, Sizer notes the obstacles to change in the field of public education. He argues that public schools should be funded primarily at the state level rather than at the local level in order to better equalize the funding of schooling for all students. He further supports "choice" in terms of tax funds for schooling following students into either public or private

3

4

Chapter 1
The
Conservative
Tradition in
Educational
Thought

schools and contends that such a policy is consistent with current public sentiment. Sizer believes that the current dialogue under way regarding how to create alternative visions of academic excellence in schools will lead to great variety in the modes of schooling as well as to higher levels of student achievement. Sizer concludes that Horace Smith has grounds to be hopeful regarding the future of public education.

Sizer served as dean of the Harvard Graduate School of Education for several years. He is a professor at Brown University and one of the founders of the Coalition for Essential Schools, an effort to help schools develop better educational programs based on nine common principles of education. Some of his other books include *Places for Learning, Places for Joy* (Harvard University Press, 1973) and *Horace's School: Redesigning the American High School* (Houghton Mifflin, 1993).

Key Concept: the future of American public education

*H*orace Smith, to the surprise of many of his colleagues, is hopeful about the future of American public education. Horace has hope not because he believes that there will be a return to some purported good old days or that the status quo is fine, bedeviled only by a temporary public relations problem. Quite the contrary. And that is what his colleagues who cannot fathom his optimism do not understand.

I have learned to share Horace's hope, . . . however I absorb the sour messages abroad about schools and schooling, about incompetent teachers, rigid bureaucracies, embarrassing test scores, lazy and indulgent students, and high budgets.

Paradoxically, perhaps, all the public controversy itself provides a cause for hope. It is not that all the criticisms are well taken and all those at work in public education deserve the raking-over they are getting. It is, rather, that the invective, whether accurate or far off the mark, has legitimized a searching rethinking of what schooling is all about. What used to be unsayable now is being said—and listened to. No idea is peremptorily dismissed. The taxing ambiguities have brought a freshening of ideas.

For many, this is a frightening moment. It is also a highly promising one. Out of such turbulence can come better schools—or worse, Horace knows, if we blow the opportunity the times are providing us. To my eye, however, some of the trends are very much in the right direction.

Horace Smith is part of a grass-roots movement for reform, one given increasing running room by those very public authorities who are now so assaulted with criticism. It is not without hassle: the lurches of state legislatures, state departments of education, and school boards are a nuisance and often a barrier to the changes Horace wishes to make. Inappropriate regulations, poorly designed but influential assessment systems, and tighter and more paranoid collective bargaining agreements get in the way.

Nonetheless, school-level reform now has visible momentum. This momentum and the increasing public attention that it is receiving are important.

As the reform quickens, Horace Smith can take its imperatives as much into account as he takes the dictates from above. Pressure to try new ways to do better has its own authority and public approval and is every bit as powerful as the pressure that says, "Do what you are told and toe the line." Horace is getting into the habit of saying that he won't do as he is told if he is told to do something mindless or ill-advised.

Today there is something for Horace to join, something to make cause with, something that is not wholly a creation of government and the corrosive politics that currently infests so much of it, something that speaks directly to the compromises that so dismay him. It is something more than mere talk, something with an edge, something to do. This something may be an identifiable enterprise, such as the Coalition of Essential Schools, or Dr. James Comer's School Development Project, or E. D. Hirsch's Core Knowledge Foundation, or the Accelerated Schools Project, led by Henry Levin, or Harvard Project Zero. Or, more likely, it may be an informal but sustained gathering of earnest friends or a fresh attitude found in a faculty room or at the meetings of a regional professional group. It gives hope, and the energy to tackle persistent compromises that hope inspires. As a veteran teacher told his younger colleagues at a meeting which I recently attended, "I don't have to apologize anymore." Here and there, more and more, the compromises are being addressed from the grass roots, often in spite of the higher-ups.

Horace knows that the stereotype of the teacher is a crabbed one, and that many in his profession, which is devoted to the task of helping young people learn to use their minds well, have little idea what serious intellectual work in fact involves. They have rarely experienced it themselves, having been through an educational system, including college, that rewarded them for merely showing up and passing through, rather than for presenting serious, rigorous academic work. As a result, coming up with demanding intellectual work for the adolescents they teach is difficult, often poignant labor. It starts with the teachers themselves.

Many critics thus protest. Give authority to these school-level people, with all their well-documented limitations? They will botch it. This, however, is a self-fulfilling prophecy. Tell people of any age that they are not to be trusted, and they will soon believe it and act accordingly. Give a job authority and accountability and able people will flock to it. They will especially gravitate to teaching, with its inherent excitement, variety, and legitimate sense of service— a phenomenon long seen in some private schools and prestigious public magnet schools (not all of which serve only well-scrubbed, academically inclined students) and increasingly seen today.

Horace also appreciates what so many far from the neighborhoods and their schools fail to see: the stubborn quality of decency in so many citizens. There are, as always, the complainers and the people who walk away from their responsibilities for their children. However, too much can be made of them: they are good newspaper copy. Many more people rally around in most communities, especially in an emergency.

Take heart from the school's neighbors? Some will think Horace is blind. The people care? Yes, Horace tells me, the parents and many parents by association (most of us older citizens) do give a damn, and if we see a way to help our

6

*Chapter 1
The
Conservative
Tradition in
Educational
Thought*

public schools, we join in. True, if we are patronized or told that we can briefly "advise" and then "come aboard" when we have had little role in shaping a plan, we tune out. I have experienced happy engagement recently with parents and community members starting a regional public charter school. Meetings of its board of trustees, as provided by the state's legislation for all public schools, are open to all, but the engagement at this school is special. Parents—on the board and in the audience—raise issues, shape the agenda, insistently demand to be consulted, heard, involved, put to work, respected. All feel the power that comes with having chosen this school.

A recent meeting dealt with the "tone of decency" (as the agenda put it) of the school, and it eventually spilled into the collective "tone of decency" of the school's larger community, including what happens at home. (Were rap CDs that are contemptuous of and vicious toward women tolerated at home at the same time that they were banned from school? If so, what does this teach?) This kind of involvement, while it leads to long meetings, will surely serve the children well. Of course, it is possible only in human-scale communities, ones that have real authority over their work. Roaring debates at meetings of school boards representing large constituencies are usually led by factions and special-interest groups. The voice of a parent of a particular youngster with a particular problem is rarely heard, and the energy and commitment of that parent is thus rarely energized.

If people of any age are treated with the dignity they deserve, they respond, in community after community. We see it daily. Often it takes a crisis—a flood on the Mississippi or a bombing on Wall Street or in Oklahoma City—to highlight it. It is patently there. It is a cause for hope.

Doomsayers say that democracy is dying. The number of registered voters who cast ballots drops. The pundits suggest to us, persuasively, that Americans are disgusted with their politicians, that they distrust the system and the government that is its agent. However, being disgusted with the status quo does not mean that we are giving up on democracy. Paradoxically, the opposite is true. So many are unhappy precisely because we believe in the system. We know it can work, and we believe that the alternatives are much worse than the system of government we now have, warts and all.

We complain when we see organized forces outside the democratic system seizing excessive influence. We are sick of being manipulated and lied to ("I merely misspoke . . ."), of being the subjects not of respectful persuasion but of an advertising campaign, of being targets of the same sort of sell that gets us to buy a deodorant or cigarettes. We believe that the American way is better than that and that blatant influence-peddling corrupts what we admire.

People do not want to be patronized and manipulated by their government. They want government to work. They want to admire their government. Is this naive, sentimental patriotism? Not entirely, and there is nothing necessarily wrong with patriotism. We should note the extraordinary surge of interest in local action that followed President Clinton's announcement of Ambassador Walter Annenberg's $500 million personal challenge to the nation for school reform. Annenberg's simple idea—that democracy is at risk of destruction through neglect and violence and that local public schools are the necessary and principal bulwark to resist this decay—struck a powerful chord.

Sentimental? Perhaps. Purposeful? Certainly. Realistic? It has to be. What is the alternative, save more decay? People have stepped forward.

There is a host of examples. For instance, I have seen an explosion of energy in parents and local citizens in support of a new district high school in which they will have a respected role and which is designed with their particular children, rather than some stereotype of a child of a certain age (hatched in a remote office building), in mind. A sense of community responsibility is latent in many American neighborhoods, I have found, even those that are racked by poverty and crime or awash in the entitlements of affluence. Too many Americans know that their worlds can be better, that with encouragement those worlds are theirs and they can take charge of them. Give people a cause worth following and the dignity of a necessary role for everyone of every age and they will respond—not quickly or easily, perhaps, but if patiently gathered, they will respond.

I am invited to graduations at Essential schools. Several in communities serving low-income families stick especially in my mind. Most of the young people at these schools have stayed the course, have not dropped out, and have publicly presented their final Exhibitions. Many who never dreamed of going to college are going to college.

Their families know this, and the atmosphere at these gatherings is electric. At one school, student after student gave brief remarks, one coming up after another, spontaneously. Their sustained theme was a poignant and powerful one: "We did what America did not believe we could do." The momentum of this message at this particular gathering—a sad message in its way, as it reminded those assembled that these adolescents knew they were perceived to be people of limited merit—gained force as the long ceremony, some of it colorfully out of control, seemed to burst forth in radiant optimism and determination. Such young people are the fuel of hope. Their schools have made a difference for them, a life-altering difference. Horace has good reason to be hopeful.

The likely shape of a different and useful system of American schools—one created in large part anew—is dimly visible. Key details are still murky and still very much in play, but some outlines are there. The best of these follow.

There will be choice. Every family (not just rich families) will have the ability —indeed, the obligation—to choose among schools for their children. The state will assure that parents do in fact have meaningful choices among schools.

The substance, standard, and culture of each school will be shaped significantly by the families who choose it and the staff who elect to work at it rather than primarily by the deliberations of those families' and the larger communities' elected representatives. Schools will thus differ from one another, often significantly.

Finance will completely or largely be a state (rather than a local) responsibility, and the money will follow the child directly, the full per-pupil allotment going to his or her school. The drift toward state rather than local funding has been under way since the early 1970s. It will continue.

8

Chapter 1
The
Conservative
Tradition in
Educational
Thought

To be a truly public school, worthy of state funding, each school, wherever it is located, will admit every applicant from that state; if there are more applicants than places at the school, it will admit students by lottery. No public policy can more dramatically create the truly common school than this. Civil rights should not and do not need to be weakened by a system of parental choice.

Given general state funding, accountability by and for the schools will be due both to those who chose them—the families, who come first—and to the state. Given the rights of the former, each school should be accountable for the way in which it presents itself and the standard of its work. The state will regularly inspect that school on the basis of the school's own assessment design, objecting only in the most severe cases. The state's essential obligation will be to insist on frequent and public displays by each school of its progress, defined largely by the observable work of its students, which will help provide parents with an accurate picture of the schools. Wise schools will engage outside authorities of their choice to assist in their assessment and public display as they do today with both profit-making and nonprofit agencies, from test publishers to the College Board.

Gradually a spectrum between traditional schooling and formal home schooling will evolve, with what takes place in any one schoolhouse deliberately orchestrated with serious learning activity at home, usually at a computer or book, at a workplace, in an orchestra, as part of a team, as a member of a small neighborhood seminar that is an extension of a larger regional school. "Homework" will change its meaning. Rather than being only studies supplementary to classroom work, it will become activity that is largely independent of the daily, formal school routine, especially for older students. The standard to which the students are held will be met by work at and beyond the formal schoolhouse. The expectation will be that each adolescent will prepare for that standard beyond the immediate shepherding of his teacher in school.

As this configuration of deliberate education emerges, technology—and particularly software—will adapt. Programs will be designed not only to reinforce classroom activity or to entertain in some educational way. They will be freestanding ventures, designed to be used in a variety of ways and organized to prepare a student for an ultimate Exhibition.

In this way students will go to multiple schools, places that in planned combination provide for formal education. For most contemporary adolescents, this will at first appear to call for just a modest change in behavior, as their learning is now influenced powerfully by multiple sources of information. What will be starkly new for them, however, is finding that these sources can and must be taken seriously. Educators, parents, and the media and publishing industries will have to create incentives for students to use all of these sources resolutely —no mean feat. But it will happen, because that is the way the culture increasingly educates itself and because configurations make as much financial as educational sense. Better yet is the fact that these "beyond the schoolhouse" opportunities can at one leap transcend the boundaries of geography and thus of class, ethnicity, and race.

As a practical matter, *systems of schools will emerge,* each representing a particular educational style or opportunity and each governing itself within state authority. For example, one set of schools might emphasize a particular teaching approach, such as that arising from the work of Maria Montessori or from E. D. Hirsch's Core Knowledge Foundation or from the Coalition of Essential Schools. Another might involve a substantial system of computer-driven connected instruction. Others might emphasize, for adolescents, substantial time and formal learning in a workplace other than a traditional school building. The momentum of tradition and expected practice will, at least for a generation, hold these approaches to substantial common ground, as they do today. The temptation of central authorities to micro-manage them, however, will have to be stoutly resisted. These systems of schools would overlap. The options available to families would appear much like those now represented by higher education.

Choice. Variety. Truly open schools. Equitable finance. Power deliberately tilted toward the families of the children served and the professionals who teach them. The deliberate use of various orchestrated configurations of learning, not just the schoolhouse. All of these issues are more or less on the political table today. Over the past decade, interest in them has picked up substantial momentum.

These ideas are consistent with the drift of contemporary public sentiment as expressed in policy or implicitly, by what is happening in practice. They reflect the prevalent view that centralized government is an inept and inappropriate tool to set and shape the substance and standards of school policy and practice. They reflect the view that disproportional authority for these purposes should be given to the families affected and the professionals to whom those families entrust their children. Centralized government is needed as a financier (that is, the dispenser of the people's money), as a documenter, persuader, supporter, advocate for neglected children, truth-teller, but not, except at the extremes, a director.

These ideas reflect the belief that a market—involving competition and real choice among schools—is a better, if not complete or perfect, regulator of schooling than the traditional educational and political authorities and their expert allies in the teaching profession.

They reflect a prominent view loudly expressed today in the context of the debate over national health care: I wish to choose my own doctor rather than be assigned one by the state. In like manner, I wish to pick my children's school rather than have the state do the choosing.

These ideas address reality, however painful or inconvenient that reality is. They are attuned to the extraordinary variety of communities and interests in this country, a variety that is ill served by centralized control, which usually demands standardization. What works well for a small town in northeastern Arizona might be inappropriate for a precinct in Pittsburgh. These ideas recognize and dignify our diversity.

They provide an end run around the *Milliken* decision of the United States Supreme Court, which ruled that the suburbs (usually wealthy and white) have no constitutional responsibility to join in racial integration with the school systems in the central cities (usually poor and disproportionately nonwhite). If the money follows the child and if that child's family can enter him or her in its school of choice, *wherever that may be*—a school that must admit all applicants,

10

*Chapter 1
The
Conservative
Tradition in
Educational
Thought*

using a lottery system if necessary, in order to receive public funding—the opportunity for more class and racial integration, where it is desired, can proceed. Currently it cannot proceed at all, at least for the poor, even if some families —poor and rich—wish that it could. Geographical boundaries, mostly reflecting the demographic and political priorities of the past, dictate current school policy. These boundaries will be pierced.

These ideas address the fact that there are deep and understandable disagreements not only among citizens but among experts on just what an excellent education might be and how we would know it when we saw it. In the emerging public school system, no one point of view dominates; the market of ideas allows both variety and contention among serious positions. This will be untidy, and those who believe that there is a virtue in cultural orderliness will no doubt be unhappy. Unfortunately, our world is untidy, free minds are untidy, and to be genuine and useful, our institutions must reflect that rather than present a spurious uniformity.

They address the compromises that so trouble Horace Smith, by providing channels and incentives for the creation of new schools or the redesign of existing schools that follow more sensible regimens than those now widely in use and largely cemented in place by regulatory practice. This encourages Horace, keeps him at his work, and attracts imaginative and talented people into the school business.

These ideas carry with them important side effects. They imply that school leaders must become more entrepreneurial than exclusively managerial, becoming leaders of schools that have a distinct character rather than agents of someone else's idea of what a school ought to be.

They put an extraordinary responsibility on the profession and the academic community at large to seek out and place before the public evidence of what is working in schools, by a variety of definitions, and what is not, and to define what kinds of investment different goals require, thus pushing into visibility the weaknesses and strengths of the diverse schools that citizens are choosing among. The watchdogs have to be the people themselves, not central governments (except at the extremes, such as when a school gives evidence of appalling neglect or has doctored evidence about its graduates' performance).

These ideas will challenge, directly or by circumvention, the elaborate thickets of educational regulation, certification, and accreditation, which more often than not reflect the vagaries of past academic politics and distrust of local authorities rather than considered and proven practices. They depend on persuasion rather than coercive control.

These systems will be messy, both in their diversity and in the confrontations that will result from their competition. Many will find this aggravating, undercutting the (spurious) spirit of togetherness expressed by main-line education groups.

But these ideas force a test of the proposition that healthy democracy depends on an ultimate trust in and of the people, no matter how small the unit in which the people are gathered for a particular purpose is. Either we trust the people or we don't.

These ideas challenge the notion that the primary purpose of the public schools is to teach a common culture, an American way, American ideals. Di-

Theodore R.
Sizer

versity is centrifugal, some will argue; the common school is the only way to give coherence to what it is to be an American. However, the reality is that we have in the media the most powerful common carrier of mass culture in history. It is so powerful that its existence changes the necessary role for schools from creators of the culture to respectful critics of that culture.

In this regard, the federal government has new and heavy responsibilities. The mass media must be seen as a fundamental piece of public education, a full participant with the schools. Federal responsibility might play out in a number of ways. The financing of useful programming and the maintenance of independent channels devoted to educational purposes is a clear governmental responsibility. Free access by all citizens to the artistic and intellectual treasures of the society must become an absolute right, like free public education itself. The electronic library is the lineal descendant of the public library and is crucial for the support of an intelligent people. Its costs should be wholly met by a tax on those making commercial use of the common good represented by the broadcast channels. There is growing public sentiment for these ideas, only just now powerful enough to affect federal policy.

The outlines of a new kind of public education, then, are visible. One danger is that government will adopt the easy parts and ignore the difficult ones, such as providing fair compensatory funding or access to technology for each poor or handicapped child, or providing access to any publicly financed school in the state, not only those within a historically established district. Another is that the leap from dependence on a rule-driven hierarchical system to trust of families is more than the political system can tolerate and the temptation on the part of the state to keep control will be too strong. Loosening control is always more difficult than tightening it. A third is the danger that removing education from the administrative status it now enjoys within government, weak though that is, will lessen leaders' interest in keeping an eye on the educational needs of its citizens.

All these concerns are real ones. Are they greater than those implicit in going along with the present system? We must always measure the risks of the new against those of the old. The reality is that the currents toward a new sort of American educational system are already flowing. There can be no turning back. The trick will be to understand those new currents and to ride, and thus direct, the best of them.

The traditional American system of schools was in large measure designed exactly a century ago. It has served us well, but times and conditions change. America in 1995 is not the America of 1895. Not surprisingly, a new system of schools is emerging, one that is more complex and potentially more powerful than the one we inherited. If wisely and resolutely shaped, such a system can serve the people and democracy well. Such is a source of Horace's hope....

Public education is an idea not a structure. The idea is that every citizen must have access to the culture and to the means of enriching that culture. It arises from the belief that we are all equal as citizens, and that we all thereby have rights and obligations to serve the community as well as ourselves. To meet

12

*Chapter 1
The
Conservative
Tradition in
Educational
Thought*

those obligations, we must use our informed intelligence. Schools for all assure the intelligence of the people, the necessary equipment of a healthy democracy. A wise democracy invests in that equipment.

Public education, then, is not at all or necessarily the same thing as our current system of schools. Other means to give the people access and intelligence—new configurations of educating institutions—may be better, more appropriate to our time, more respectful of current exigencies. If we are wise, we will consider them, however much they may challenge the conventional ways of doing things.

To the extent that we embrace that challenge and the fundamental American philosophy behind it—that a free and powerful education is the absolute right of every citizen and that this education must be first and foremost seen as the mainspring of a democratic community—we can be hopeful.

For Horace Smith, the hope is also more personal, arise from the particular adolescents all around him—their color and brashness, their gawkiness, their risk-taking, their naiveté about the world, which sucks so many of them into optimism, however unrealistic. The high theater of the school hallway never ceases to amuse him, and the diversions of the kids' little passions tickle his love of fiction, creating tiny comic stories in his head. The dance of youth is timeless and beautiful in its awkwardness.

Most of the young people are resilient in the face of either the lures of affluence or the savagery of neglect. Horace worries more about them than they do about themselves, and he is ashamed when it dawns on his students how little American culture actually values them. Most of the kids, however, sweep this away, not so much with anger as with tacit rejection. *To hell with you, old-timer. We'll go it on our own, and we'll make it.*

Horace knows that some will and many won't. But the energy is there, fueled as much by inexperience as by grit. With all its unreality, it yet insistently radiates the strength and inventiveness of humankind. In dark days, such light brings hope.

Literacy and Cultural Literacy

E. D. (Eric Donald) Hirsch, Jr., is a widely read, conservative scholar concerned with the purposes and content of school curricula. His views reflect a traditionalist consensus on what every student should learn or know.

In the selection that follows, he argues that the standard of literacy required of citizens of advanced modern states has risen in recent years and will continue to rise. He further argues that standards of literacy in American schools have not risen to meet world standards. He wishes to see as much emphasis placed on the information that students are taught as is currently placed on the skills that they are taught. He agrees that all students need higher levels of communications skills than ever before in order to enhance national and cultural unity. He provides some interesting examples to illustrate what he believes has been a major decline in standards of literacy in the United States.

Hirsch (b. 1928) is the Linden Kent Memorial Professor of English at the University of Virginia in Charlottesville, Virginia, and president of the Core Knowledge Foundation. He is coauthor, with Joseph F. Kett and James Trefil, of *The Dictionary of Cultural Literacy* (Houghton Mifflin, 1988) and coeditor, with William G. Rowland, Jr., and Michael Stanford, of *First Dictionary of Cultural Literacy* (Houghton Mifflin, 1989). He is also the author of *The Schools We Need and Why We Don't Have Them* (Doubleday, 1996).

The following selection is from Hirsch's book *Cultural Literacy: What Every American Needs to Know* (Houghton Mifflin, 1987). At the end of that book is an appendix created with Joseph F. Kett and James Trefil that consists of a checklist of what every literate American ought to know.

Key Concept: cultural literacy

THE DECLINE OF LITERATE KNOWLEDGE

This [selection begins to] explain why we need to make some very specific educational changes in order to achieve a higher level of national literacy. It does not anatomize the literacy crisis or devote many pages to Scholastic Aptitude Test scores. It does not document at length what has already been established, that

14

*Chapter 1
The
Conservative
Tradition in
Educational
Thought*

Americans do not read as well as they should. It takes no position about methods of initial reading instruction beyond insisting that content must receive as much emphasis as "skill." It does not discuss teacher training or educational funding or school governance. In fact, one of its major purposes is to break away entirely from what Jeanne S. Chall has called "the great debate" about methods of reading instruction. It focuses on what I conceive to be the great hidden problem in American education, and I hope that it reveals this problem so compellingly that anyone who is concerned about American education will be persuaded by [my] argument and act upon it.

The standard of literacy required by modern society has been rising throughout the developed world, but American literacy rates have not risen to meet this standard. What seemed an acceptable level in the 1950s is no longer acceptable in the late 1980s, when only highly literate societies can prosper economically. Much of Japan's industrial efficiency has been credited to its almost universally high level of literacy. But in the United States, only two thirds of our citizens are literate, and even among those the average level is too low and should be raised. The remaining third of our citizens need to be brought as close to true literacy as possible. Ultimately our aim should be to attain universal literacy at a very high level, to achieve not only greater economic prosperity but also greater social justice and more effective democracy. We Americans have long accepted literacy as a paramount aim of schooling, but only recently have some of us who have done research in the field begun to realize that literacy is far more than a skill and that it requires large amounts of specific information....

Professor Chall is one of several reading specialists who have observed that "world knowledge" is essential to the development of reading and writing skills. What she calls world knowledge I call cultural literacy, namely, the network of information that all competent readers possess. It is the background information, stored in their minds, that enables them to take up a newspaper and read it with an adequate level of comprehension, getting the point, grasping the implications, relating what they read to the unstated context which alone gives meaning to what they read. In describing the contents of this neglected domain of background information, I try to direct attention to a new opening that can help our schools make the significant improvement in education that has so far eluded us. The achievement of high universal literacy is the key to all other fundamental improvements in American education.

Why is literacy so important in the modern world? Some of the reasons, like the need to fill out forms or get a good job, are so obvious that they needn't be discussed. But the chief reason is broader. The complex undertakings of modern life depend on the cooperation of many people with different specialties in different places. Where communications fail, so do the undertakings. (That is the moral of the story of the Tower of Babel.) The function of national literacy is to foster effective nationwide communications. Our chief instrument of communication over time and space is the standard national language, which is sustained by national literacy. Mature literacy alone enables the tower to be built, the business to be well managed, and the airplane to fly without crashing. All nationwide communications, whether by telephone, radio, TV, or writing are fundamentally dependent upon literacy, for the essence of literacy is not simply reading and writing but also the effective use of the standard literate language. In Spain and most of Latin America the literate language is standard written Spanish. In Japan it is standard written Japanese. In our country it is standard written English.

Linguists have used the term "standard written English" to describe both our written and spoken language, because they want to remind us that standard spoken English is based upon forms that have been fixed in dictionaries and grammars and are adhered to in books, magazines, and newspapers. Although standard written English has no intrinsic superiority to other languages and dialects, its stable written forms have now standardized the oral forms of the language spoken by educated Americans. The chief function of literacy is to make us masters of this standard instrument of knowledge and communication, thereby enabling us to give and receive complex information orally and in writing over time and space. Advancing technology, with its constant need for fast and complex communications, has made literacy ever more essential to commerce and domestic life. The literate language is more, not less, central in our society now than it was in the days before television and the silicon chip.

The recently rediscovered insight that literacy is more than a skill is based upon knowledge that all of us unconsciously have about language. We know instinctively that to understand what somebody is saying, we must understand more than the surface meanings of words; we have to understand the context as well. The need for background information applies all the more to reading and writing. To grasp the words on a page we have to know a lot of information that isn't set down on the page. . . .

In the mid 1980s American business leaders have become alarmed by the lack of communication skills in the young people they employ. Recently, top executives of some large U.S. companies, including CBS and Exxon, met to discuss the fact that their younger middle-level executives could no longer communicate their ideas effectively in speech or writing. This group of companies has made a grant to the American Academy of Arts and Sciences to analyze the causes of this growing problem. They want to know why, despite breathtaking advances in the technology of communication, the effectiveness of business communication has been slipping, to the detriment of our competitiveness in the world. The figures from NAEP [National Assessment of Educational Progress] surveys and the scores on the verbal SAT [Scholastic Aptitude Test] are solid evidence that literacy has been declining in this country just when our need for effective literacy has been sharply rising.

. . . [One] day my son asked his Latin class if they knew the name of an epic poem by Homer. One pupil shot up his hand and eagerly said, "The Alamo!" Was it just a slip for *The Iliad?* No, he didn't know what the Alamo was, either. To judge from other stories about information gaps in the young, many American schoolchildren are less well informed than this pupil. The following, by Benjamin J. Stein, is an excerpt from one of the most evocative recent accounts of youthful ignorance.

I spend a lot of time with teen agers. Besides employing three of them part-time, I frequently conduct focus groups at Los Angeles area high schools to learn about

16

*Chapter 1
The
Conservative
Tradition in
Educational
Thought*

teen agers' attitudes towards movies or television shows or nuclear arms or politicians. . . .

I have not yet found one single student in Los Angeles, in either college or high school, who could tell me the years when World War II was fought. Nor have I found one who could tell me the years when World War I was fought. Nor have I found one who knew when the American Civil War was fought. . . .

A few have known how many U.S. senators California has, but none has known how many Nevada or Oregon has. ("Really? Even though they're so small?") . . . Only two could tell me where Chicago is, even in the vaguest terms. (My particular favorite geography lesson was the junior at the University of California at Los Angeles who thought that Toronto must be in Italy. My second-favorite geography lesson is the junior at USC, a pre-law student, who thought that Washington, D.C. was in Washington State.) . . .

Only two could even approximately identify Thomas Jefferson. Only one could place the date of the Declaration of Independence. None could name even one of the first ten amendments to the Constitution or connect them with the Bill of Rights. . . .

On and on it went. On and on it goes. I have mixed up episodes of ignorance of facts with ignorance of concepts because it seems to me that there is a connection. . . . The kids I saw (and there may be lots of others who are different) are not mentally prepared to continue the society because they basically do not understand the society well enough to value it.

My son assures me that his pupils are not ignorant. They know a great deal. Like every other human group they share a tremendous amount of knowledge among themselves, much of it learned in school. The trouble is that, from the standpoint of their literacy and their ability to communicate with others in our culture, what they know is ephemeral and narrowly confined to their own generation. Many young people strikingly lack the information that writers of American books and newspapers have traditionally taken for granted among their readers from all generations. . . . [O]ur children's lack of intergenerational information is a serious problem for the nation. The decline of literacy and the decline of shared knowledge are closely related, interdependent facts. . . .

THE NATURE AND USE OF CULTURAL LITERACY

The documented decline in shared knowledge carries implications that go far beyond the shortcomings of executives and extend to larger questions of educational policy and social justice in our country. Mina Shaughnessy was a great English teacher who devoted her professional life to helping disadvantaged students become literate. At the 1980 conference dedicated to her memory, one of the speakers who followed me to the podium was the Harvard historian and sociologist Orlando Patterson. To my delight he departed from his prepared talk to mention mine. He seconded my argument that shared information is a necessary background to true literacy. Then he extended and deepened the ideas I had presented. Here is what Professor Patterson said, as recorded in the *Proceedings* of the conference.

> Industrialized civilization [imposes] a growing cultural and structural complexity which requires persons to have a broad grasp of what Professor Hirsch has called cultural literacy: a deep understanding of mainstream culture, which no longer has much to do with white Anglo-Saxon Protestants, but with the imperatives of industrial civilization. It is the need for cultural literacy, a profound conception of the whole civilization, which is often neglected in talk about literacy.

Patterson continued by drawing a connection between background information and the ability to hold positions of responsibility and power. He was particularly concerned with the importance for blacks and other minorities of possessing this information, which is essential for improving their social and economic status.

> The people who run society at the macro-level must be literate in this culture. For this reason, it is dangerous to overemphasize the problems of basic literacy or the relevancy of literacy to specific tasks, and more constructive to emphasize that blacks will be condemned in perpetuity to oversimplified, low-level tasks and will never gain their rightful place in controlling the levers of power unless they also acquire literacy in this wider cultural sense.

Although Patterson focused his remarks on the importance of cultural literacy for minorities, his observations hold for every culturally illiterate person in our nation. Indeed, as he observed, cultural literacy is not the property of any group or class.

> To assume that this wider culture is static is an error; in fact it is not. It's not a WASP culture; it doesn't belong to any group. It is essentially and constantly changing, and it is open. What is needed is recognition that the accurate metaphor or model for this wider literacy is not domination, but dialectic; each group participates and contributes, transforms and is transformed, as much as any other group.... The English language no longer belongs to any single group or nation. The same goes for any other area of the wider culture.

As Professor Patterson suggested, being taught to decode elementary reading materials and specific, job-related texts cannot constitute true literacy. Such basic training does not make a person literate with respect to newspapers or other writings addressed to a general public. Moreover, a directly practical drawback of such narrow training is that it does not prepare anyone for technological change. Narrow vocational training in one state of a technology will not enable a person to read manuals that explain new developments in the same technology. In modern life we need general knowledge that enables

18

*Chapter 1
The
Conservative
Tradition in
Educational
Thought*

us to deal with new ideas, events, and challenges. In today's world, general cultural literacy is more useful than what Professor Patterson terms "literacy to a specific task," because general literate information is the basis for many changing tasks.

Cultural literacy is even more important in the social sphere. The aim of universal literacy has never been a socially neutral mission in our country. Our traditional social goals were unforgettably renewed for us by Martin Luther King, Jr., in his "I Have a Dream" speech. King envisioned a country where the children of former slaves sit down at the table of equality with the children of former slave owners, where men and women deal with each other as equals and judge each other on their characters and achievements rather than their origins. Like Thomas Jefferson, he had a dream of a society founded not on race or class but on personal merit.

In the present day, that dream depends on mature literacy. No modern society can hope to become a just society without a high level of universal literacy. Putting aside for the moment the practical arguments about the economic uses of literacy, we can contemplate the even more basic principle that underlies our national system of education in the first place—that people in a democracy can be entrusted to decide all important matters for themselves because they can deliberate and communicate with one another. Universal literacy is inseparable from democracy and is the canvas for Martin Luther King's picture as well as for Thomas Jefferson's.

Both of these leaders understood that just having the right to vote is meaningless if a citizen is disenfranchised by illiteracy or semiliteracy. Illiterate and semiliterate Americans are condemned not only to poverty, but also to the powerlessness of incomprehension. Knowing that they do not understand the issues, and feeling prey to manipulative oversimplifications, they do not trust the system of which they are supposed to be the masters. They do not feel themselves to be active participants in our republic, and they often do not turn out to vote. The civic importance of cultural literacy lies in the fact that true enfranchisement depends upon knowledge, knowledge upon literacy, and literacy upon cultural literacy. . . .

Although nationalism may be regrettable in some of its worldwide political effects, a mastery of national culture is essential to mastery of the standard language in every modern nation. This point is important for educational policy, because educators often stress the virtues of multicultural education. Such study is indeed valuable in itself; it inculcates tolerance and provides a perspective on our own traditions and values. But however laudable it is, it should not be the primary focus of national education. It should not be allowed to supplant or interfere with our schools' responsibility to ensure our children's mastery of American literate culture. The acculturative responsibility of the schools is primary and fundamental. To teach the ways of one's own community has always been and still remains the essence of the education of our children, who enter neither a narrow tribal culture nor a transcendent world culture but a national literate culture. For profound historical reasons, this is the way of the modern world. It will not change soon, and it will certainly not be changed by educational policy alone.

Why have our schools failed to fulfill their fundamental acculturative responsibility? In view of the immense importance of cultural literacy for speaking, listening, reading, and writing, why has the need for a definite, shared body of information been so rarely mentioned in discussions of education? In the educational writings of the past decade, I find almost nothing on this topic, which is not arcane. People who are introduced to the subject quickly understand why oral or written communication requires a lot of shared background knowledge. It's not the difficulty or novelty of the idea that has caused it to receive so little attention.

Let me hazard a guess about one reason for our neglect of the subject. We have ignored cultural literacy in thinking about education—certainly I as a researcher also ignored it until recently—precisely because it was something we have been able to take for granted. We ignore the air we breathe until it is thin or foul. Cultural literacy is the oxygen of social intercourse. Only when we run into cultural illiteracy are we shocked into recognizing the importance of the information that we had unconsciously assumed.

To be sure, a minimal level of information is possessed by any normal person who lives in the United States and speaks elementary English. Almost everybody knows what is meant by *dollar* and that cars must travel on the right-hand side of the road. But this elementary level of information is not sufficient for a modern democracy. It isn't sufficient to read newspapers (a sin against Jeffersonian democracy), and it isn't sufficient to achieve economic fairness and high productivity. Cultural literacy lies *above* the everyday levels of knowledge that everyone possesses and *below* the expert level known only to specialists. It is that middle ground of cultural knowledge possessed by the "common reader." It includes information that we have traditionally expected our children to receive in school, but which they no longer do.

During recent decades Americans have hesitated to make a decision about the specific knowledge that children need to learn in school. Our elementary schools are not only dominated by the content-neutral ideas of Rousseau and Dewey, they are also governed by approximately sixteen thousand independent school districts. We have viewed this dispersion of educational authority as an insurmountable obstacle to altering the fragmentation of the school curriculum even when we have questioned that fragmentation. We have permitted school policies that have shrunk the body of information that Americans share, and these policies have caused our national literacy to decline.

At the same time we have searched with some eagerness for causes such as television that lie outside the schools. But we should direct our attention undeviatingly toward what the schools teach rather than toward family structure, social class, or TV programming. No doubt, reforms outside the schools are important, but they are harder to accomplish. Moreover, we have accumulated a great deal of evidence that faulty policy in the schools is the chief cause of deficient literacy. Researchers who have studied the factors influencing educational outcomes have found that the school curriculum is the most important control-

20

*Chapter 1
The
Conservative
Tradition in
Educational
Thought*

lable influence on what our children know and don't know about our literate culture.

It will not do to blame television for the state of our literacy. Television watching does reduce reading and often encroaches on homework. Much of it is admittedly the intellectual equivalent of junk food. But in some respects, such as its use of standard written English, television watching is acculturative. Moreover, as Herbert Walberg points out, the schools themselves must be held partly responsible for excessive television watching, because they have not firmly insisted that students complete significant amounts of homework, an obvious way to increase time spent on reading and writing. Nor should our schools be excused by an appeal to the effects of the decline of the family or the vicious circle of poverty, important as these factors are. Schools have, or should have, children for six or seven hours a day, five days a week, nine months a year, for thirteen years or more. To assert that they are powerless to make a significant impact on what their students learn would be to make a claim about American education that few parents, teachers, or students would find it easy to accept.

Just how fragmented the American public school curriculum has become is described in *The Shopping Mall High School*, a report on five years of first-hand study inside public and private secondary schools. The authors report that our high schools offer courses of so many kinds that "the word 'curriculum' does not do justice to this astonishing variety." The offerings include not only academic courses of great diversity, but also courses in sports and hobbies and a "services curriculum" addressing emotional or social problems. All these courses are deemed "educationally valid" and carry course credit. Moreover, among academic offerings are numerous versions of each subject, corresponding to different levels of student interest and ability. Needless to say, the material covered in these "content area" courses is highly varied.

Cafeteria-style education, combined with the unwillingness of our schools to place demands on students, has resulted in a steady diminishment of commonly shared information between generations and between young people themselves. Those who graduate from the same school have often studied different subjects, and those who graduate from different schools have often studied different material even when their courses have carried the same titles. The inevitable consequence of the shopping mall high school is a lack of shared knowledge across and within schools. It would be hard to invent a more effective recipe for cultural fragmentation.

The formalistic educational theory behind the shopping mall school (the theory that any suitable content will inculcate reading, writing, and thinking skills) has had certain political advantages for school administrators. It has allowed them to stay scrupulously neutral with regard to content. Educational formalism enables them to regard the indiscriminate variety of school offerings as a positive virtue, on the grounds that such variety can accommodate the different interests and abilities of different students. Educational formalism has also conveniently allowed school administrators to meet objections to the traditional literate materials that used to be taught in the schools. Objectors have said that traditional materials are class-bound, white, Anglo-Saxon, and Protestant, not to mention racist, sexist, and excessively Western. Our schools have tried to offer enough diversity to meet these objections from liberals and enough Shakespeare to satisfy conservatives. Caught between ideological parties, the schools have been attracted irresistibly to a quantitative and formal approach to curriculum making rather than one based on sound judgments about what should be taught.

Some have objected that teaching the traditional literate culture means teaching conservative material. Orlando Patterson answered that objection when he pointed out that mainstream culture is not the province of any single social group and is constantly changing by assimilating new elements and expelling old ones. Although mainstream culture is tied to the written word and may therefore seem more formal and elitist than other elements of culture, that is an illusion. Literate culture is the most democratic culture in our land: it excludes nobody; it cuts across generations and social groups and classes; it is not usually one's first culture, but it should be everyone's second, existing as it does beyond the narrow spheres of family, neighborhood, and region.

As the universal second culture, literate culture has become the common currency for social and economic exchange in our democracy, and the only available ticket to full citizenship. Getting one's membership card is not tied to class or race. Membership is automatic if one learns the background information and the linguistic conventions that are needed to read, write, and speak effectively. Although everyone is literate in some local, regional, or ethnic culture, the connection between mainstream culture and the national written language justifies calling mainstream culture *the* basic culture of the nation.

The claim that universal cultural literacy would have the effect of preserving the political and social status quo is paradoxical because in fact the traditional forms of literate culture are precisely the most effective instruments for political and social change. All political discourse at the national level must use the stable forms of the national language and its associated culture. Take the example of *The Black Panther*, a radical and revolutionary newspaper if ever this country had one. Yet the *Panther* was highly conservative in its language and cultural assumptions, as it had to be in order to communicate effectively. What could be more radical in sentiment but more conservative in language and assumed knowledge than the following passages from that paper?

> The present period reveals the criminal growth of bourgeois democracy since the betrayal of those who died that this nation might live "free and indivisible." It exposes through the trial of the Chicago Seven, and its law and order edicts, its desperate turn toward the establishment of a police state. (January 17, 1970)

> In this land of "milk and honey," the "almighty dollar" rules supreme and is being upheld by the faithful troops who move without question in the name of "law and order." Only in this garden of hypocrisy and inequality can a murderer not be considered a murderer—only here can innocent people be charged with a crime and be taken to court with the confessed criminal testifying against them. Incredible? (March 28, 1970)

> In the United States, the world's most technologically advanced country, one million youths from 11 to 17 years of age are illiterate—unable to read as well as the average fourth grader, says a new government report. Why so much illit-

22

*Chapter 1
The
Conservative
Tradition in
Educational
Thought*

eracy in a land of so much knowledge? The answer is because there is racism. Blacks and other Nonwhites receive the worst education. (May 18, 1974)

The last item of the Black Panther Party platform, issued March 29, 1972, begins

10. WE WANT LAND, BREAD, HOUSING, EDUCATION, CLOTHING, JUS-
TICE, PEACE AND PEOPLE'S CONTROL OF MODERN TECHNOLOGY.
    When in the course of human events it becomes necessary for one people
to dissolve the political bands which have connected them with another, and to
assume among the powers of the earth the separate and equal station to which
the laws of nature and nature's God entitle them, a decent respect to the opinions
of mankind requires that they should declare the causes which impel them to the
separation.

And so on for the first five hundred of Jefferson's words without the least hint, or need of one, that this is a verbatim repetition of an earlier revolutionary declaration. The writers for *The Black Panther* had clearly received a rigorous traditional education in American history, in the Declaration of Independence, the Pledge of Allegiance to the Flag, the Gettysburg Address, and the Bible, to mention only some of the direct quotations and allusions in these passages. They also received rigorous traditional instruction in reading, writing, and spelling. I have not found a single misspelled word in the many pages of radical sentiment I have examined in that newspaper. Radicalism in politics, but conservatism in literate knowledge and spelling: to be a conservative in the *means* of communication is the road to effectiveness in modern life, in whatever direction one wishes to be effective.

To withhold traditional culture from the school curriculum, and therefore from students, in the name of progressive ideas is in fact an unprogressive action that helps preserve the political and economic status quo. Middle-class children acquire mainstream literate culture by daily encounters with other literate persons. But less privileged children are denied consistent interchanges with literate persons and fail to receive this information in school. The most straightforward antidote to their deprivation is to make the essential information more readily available inside the schools.

Providing our children with traditional information by no means indoctrinates them in a conservative point of view. Conservatives who wish to preserve traditional values will find that these are not necessarily inculcated by a traditional education, which can in fact be subversive of the status quo. As a child of eleven, I turned against the conservative views of my family and the Southern community in which I grew up, precisely because I had been given a traditional education and was therefore literate enough to read Gunnar Myrdal's *An American Dilemma,* an epoch-making book in my life.

Although teaching children national mainstream culture doesn't mean forcing them to accept its values uncritically, it does enable them to understand those values in order to predict the typical attitudes of other Americans. The writers for *The Black Panther* clearly understood this when they quoted the Declaration of Independence. George Washington, for instance, is a name in our received culture that we associate with the truthfulness of the hero of the story of the cherry tree. Americans should be taught that value association, whether or not they believe the story. Far from accepting the cherry-tree tale or its implications, Oscar Wilde in "The Decay of Lying" used it ironically, in a way that is probably funnier to Americans than to the British audience he was addressing.

> [Truth telling is] vulgarizing mankind. The crude commercialism of America, its materializing spirit, its indifference to the poetical side of things, and its lack of imagination and of high unattainable ideals, are entirely due to that country having adopted for its national hero a man who, according to his own confession, was incapable of telling a lie, and it is not too much to say that the story of George Washington and the cherry tree has done more harm, and in a shorter space of time, than any other moral tale in the whole of literature.... And the amusing part of the whole thing is that the story of the cherry tree is an absolute myth.

For us no less than for Wilde, the values affirmed in traditional literate culture can serve a whole spectrum of value attitudes. Unquestionably, decisions about techniques of conveying traditions to our children are among the most sensitive and important decisions of a pluralistic nation. But the complex problem of how to teach values in American schools mustn't distract attention from our fundamental duty to teach shared content.

The failure of our schools to create a literate society is sometimes excused on the grounds that the schools have been asked to do too much. They are asked, for example, to pay due regard to the demands of both local and national acculturation. They are asked to teach not only American history but also state and city history, driving, cardiopulmonary resuscitation, consumerism, carpentry, cooking, and other special subjects. They are given the task of teaching information that is sometimes too rudimentary and sometimes too specialized. If the schools did not undertake this instruction, much of the information so provided would no doubt go unlearned. In some of our national moods we would like the schools to teach everything, but they cannot. There is a pressing need for clarity about our educational priorities.

From 1945 to 1980

Diane Ravitch is a historian of American education. In her book *The Troubled Crusade: American Education, 1945–1980* (Basic Books, 1983), she describes the educational situation in the United States in 1945 (at the end of World War II) and then records the transformation of American education through the ensuing 35 years, up to 1980. During these years efforts were made to end racial segregation in American schools in order to create greater educational opportunity for American youth and to obtain federal government aid for schooling in the states. Ravitch argues that the politics of schooling in America changed in these years. She documents the new social pressures on American school systems and universities in the decades immediately following the Second World War and describes the enormous demographic changes in the population and in the student body of the nation's schools. She also describes the crusade against ignorance in American society between 1945 and 1980 and portrays an American faith that education will provide the basis for social improvement.

The following selection is from the epilogue to *The Troubled Crusade.* In it, Ravitch synthesizes her major findings regarding the great cultural changes that affected schooling in America from 1945 to 1980.

Ravitch has been an important commentator on education and society since 1974, when she published *The Great School Wars: New York City, 1805–1973* (Basic Books, 1974). She has been a senior research fellow with the Brookings Institution and a senior research professor at New York University. Ravitch has contributed many important essays to scholarly journals, including *The American Scholar,* and she has written or edited several important books, including *Against Mediocrity: The Humanities in America's High Schools* (Holmes & Meier, 1984), edited with Chester E. Finn, Jr., and Robert T. Fancher. She is also the editor of *The American Reader: Words That Moved a Nation* (HarperCollins, 1990) and *Debating the Future of American Education: Do We Need National Standards and Assessments?* (Brookings Institution, 1995). And she coauthored, with Chester E. Finn, Jr., *What Do Our 17-Year-Olds Know? A Report on the First National Assessment of History and Literature* (Harper & Row, 1987).

Key Concept: the crusade against ignorance

When hearings on federal aid to education were held in 1945 and teachers came from around the nation to tell the Congress about the needs of their schools, the problems of American education seemed nearly insoluble. It was no accident that the teachers who testified came from rural districts, because it was there that the schools were in the direst financial straits. Urban districts were conspicuous by their absence from these hearings, because they were considered relatively privileged, well staffed, and well financed. Rural schools, however, suffered from low funding, poor facilities, obsolete teaching materials, and a critical teacher shortage.

Inequitable funding was only the most immediate problem, however. Whether urban or rural, privileged or poor, American schools reflected the racial bias that was common in the larger society. In many states, this bias was institutionalized in racially separate schools where black students received fewer months of schooling and had teachers who had less training and lower pay than their white peers. So deeply imbedded was the practice of racial segregation that there seemed little reason to believe, at war's end, that any political change might be seismic enough to destroy the power of state-enforced racial segregation. Furthermore, access to higher education—though by no means narrow when compared to other nations—was available to fewer than one of every six college-age youths. For black youths, the opportunity for higher education was far less, since they suffered the double burden of an inadequate preparation and exclusion from many "white" colleges and universities. The schools were part of a vicious circle, because exclusion from educational opportunity guaranteed exclusion from economic opportunity.

In the thirty-five years after the Second World War, American education was transformed, though not always in ways that were predictable or intended. Through the course of the fight for federal aid to education and the struggle to abolish racial segregation, the politics of American education changed substantially. In 1949, when Senator Taft's proposal for federal aid came close to passing, everyone agreed—Republican and Democrat, Catholic, Protestant, and Jew, black and white, representatives of labor and business—that there should be no federal control of education. Taft's bill stipulated that "nothing contained in this Act shall be construed to authorize any department, agency, officer, or employee of the United States to exercise any direction, supervision, or control over, or to prescribe any requirements with respect to any school, or any State educational institution or agency" which received federal funds. In 1965, when Congress was concerned above all about racial injustice, the issue of federal control was seen as a "red herring" thrown up by recalcitrant southern congressmen. Regardless of declarations, once federal dollars were involved, there was no quarantining the activities of school districts from the watchful eye of the courts, the Congress, and the federal civil rights agencies.

Over these thirty-five years, educational decision making expanded beyond the traditional state-local district connection. What a given school decided to do regarding its curriculum, its personnel policy, its disciplinary procedures, and its allocation of resources was no longer a local matter. Not every wrong would be righted, but a serious misstep invited the attention of federal officials, state officials, the national press, civil rights organizations, powerful teachers' unions, and professional associations. The rhetoric changed: in the new situation, it seemed archaic to speak about keeping the schools "out of politics." Of course, the schools had always been "in politics," in the sense that they had

26

*Chapter 1
The
Conservative
Tradition in
Educational
Thought*

to compete with other public agencies for funds, they awarded contracts for services, they selected teachers and administrators, and they made their peace with the mores of the surrounding community.

But the new politics of the schools rotated about a state-federal axis rather than a local-state axis. The good superintendent or principal in 1945 maintained good relations with the mayor, the city council, and the school board. By 1980, the alert school administrator had to stay informed about the activities of Congress, the Department of Education, federal regulatory agencies, the courts, and the state legislature in order to see whether some new program had been developed that might provide new funds or whether some current activity had been proscribed or curtailed. School politics became more like American politics in general, in which different interest groups lobbied for funds, sought special relationships with congressional committees, and fought off rival claimants.

Relations between the lay public and the teaching profession also changed in significant ways. In the 1940s, few teachers belonged to a union; strikes were uncommon; administrators were powerful within their school building or their district in hiring, promoting, and assigning teachers. Though their pay was low, teachers had more education than did the parents of their students and commanded the respect that went with the authority they wielded. Teaching attracted a number of gifted women, for whom other career opportunities were limited. In some communities, there were substantial restrictions placed on teachers' behavior; as models for the community's youth, teachers were expected not to smoke or drink or otherwise set a bad example.

The growth of higher education, and especially of community colleges, drew away from the high schools those teachers who preferred the higher status and higher pay associated with being a professor and the chance to teach without discipline problems. The growth of new opportunities for women in law, medicine, and business drew away many of the bright female college graduates who would have previously entered elementary and secondary teaching. The increased educational attainment of the population as a whole meant that teachers were no longer more educated than were parents and could not automatically count on the respect of parents; nor, after the rise of the youth culture in the 1960s, with its antiauthority attitudes, could teachers count on the respect of their adolescent students. These were part of the background conditions within which teacher unionism spread, giving teacher organizations more political power than any of the school boards they negotiated with and making teachers nearly invulnerable to the discontents of the lay public which previously had both admired and disciplined them.

So customary was it to criticize the public schools, whether in the 1940s, the 1950s, the 1960s, or the 1970s, that it was easy to forget the ways in which the schools had been amazingly successful. Americans had long ago decided, without too much discussion of the matter, that education would be the best vehicle through which to change society. The attack against racial segregation, characteristically, was fought out in the schools, and the dismantling of the racial caste system began in the schools and spread to other areas of American life. More than any other institution in American society, the schools became the means through which the goal of equity was pursued. The battle took place around the schools because they provided the setting in which children learned to get along with others beyond their immediate families and in which children and young people developed (or failed to develop) the skills, knowledge, and intelligence to realize their aspirations.

The goal of access to higher education was realized far beyond the most optimistic predictions of President Truman's Commission on Higher Education. The commission's hope that the state might establish extensive community college systems was fully realized by 1980. Its wish that 4.6 million students might attend college by 1960 was derided by many in higher education as both impossible because of the limited number of able students and undesirable because of the certainty that it would degrade the standards of higher education. But fantastic as its prediction sounded in 1947, by 1980 more than 12 million students were enrolled in institutions of higher education. And so fully engaged were colleges and universities in the life of the American people, that fully 38 percent of all their students in 1980 were over the age of twenty-five, returning to improve their minds, their skills, their credentials, or their hobbies. After 1972, college-going was substantially subsidized by a massive federal program of grants and loans, which amounted to more than $5 billion annually by 1980.

Higher levels of participation in the colleges and universities reflected the rising level of educational attainment for the population as a whole. At the end of the war, about 40 of every 100 young people remained in high school long enough to graduate, and about 16 then entered college. By 1980, 75 of every 100 youths graduated from high school, and about 45 then entered college. The gap in educational attainment between whites and blacks was narrowed substantially in the 1960s and 1970s. In 1960, about 40 percent of black youngsters finished high school, compared to some 67 percent of whites; by 1980, 70 percent of blacks did so, compared to 82.5 percent of whites. The gap remained, but the progress in reducing it was remarkable.

The democratization of access to higher education did not, as the critics feared, destroy it. Although some public institutions (like the City College of New York) were transformed from elite liberal arts colleges to open-admissions institutions, in response to egalitarian pressures, the occurrence was atypical. American higher education responded to the onrushing tide of students by adopting what one observer has called a "division of labor between and within institutions." Some colleges and universities remained elite in their admissions standards and in their commitment to teaching and research; some other institutions were or became "service institutions," dedicated to preparing young men and women for technical, vocational, and semiprofessional careers. And many big state universities combined both functions within the same institution, providing both high-quality academic departments for those who sought a liberal education and service programs for the career-oriented. This adaptation enabled higher education both to expand to meet the new demand for higher education and to protect the pre-eminence of its research and scholarship functions.

Other seemingly intractable problems were alleviated or dissipated as American society became more educated and more homogeneous. The bitter religious tensions that had long blocked federal aid to education had eased by 1980; Catholics, Protestants, and Jews had become accustomed to working together in an ecumenical spirit on common problems. Although covert anti-

28

*Chapter 1
The
Conservative
Tradition in
Educational
Thought*

Catholicism and anti-Semitism lingered, they had lost their respectability. In the rapid advance of urbanization and modernization, American society had become so secularized that the religious groups most likely to encounter bigotry were Fundamentalists, particularly Protestant and Jewish denominations that clung to biblical commands.

The rising levels of educational attainment resulted from and contributed to a fast-rising standard of living. State and federal governments supported the expansion of educational opportunity because they believed that education was an appropriate way to develop human resources and that it made sense to invest public funds in raising the population's literacy and skills. Broad participation in educational opportunities throughout the nation was both a cause and an effect of the nation's scientific and technological progress.

Yet all was not well. Absolute social progress was accompanied by a rising sense of relative deprivation. In the midst of an affluent society, the persistence of poverty was a reproach to national ideals, even if the actual condition of the poor had improved over time. The shifting demography of the postwar era created new problems. The desire for increased opportunity and the decline of agricultural employment propelled large numbers of poor blacks and Hispanics to the urban centers in the 1950s and 1960s, and the cities developed vast slum areas, where the poor concentrated, dependent on impersonal public institutions, bereft of the sense of family and community that had sustained their counterparts in rural areas. By 1980, most large cities had a black and Hispanic majority in their public schools, reflecting the flight of whites to the suburbs and private schools. Many of these big-city school systems, having staggered through conflict after conflict, over such issues as desegregation, community control, and fiscal crises, suffered from severe demoralization. For decades they had thought of themselves as the nation's pace-setting school districts, but by the 1960s their middle-class student population was leaving, achievement scores were sinking, disciplinary problems soared, vandalism became common, and the teaching staff became defensive and insulated. More and more children were staying in school longer than ever, but it was not clear to the students, the teachers, or the parents that the quality of education was as good as it had been in less complicated times.

Concern about educational quality was not limited to big-city schools. Once it had become certain that universal access to education at all levels had been largely secured, educators began to turn their attention to the state of learning, which was far from secure. The debate about standards that had been initiated as a result of the decline in SAT scores produced evidence that other standardized test scores had been dropping, beginning in about the fifth grade; that enrollments in advanced courses in mathematics and science in high school had fallen steadily since the mid-1960s; that widely-used textbooks had reduced their reading levels in order to adjust to falling verbal abilities; that homework assignments had been sharply curtailed and that grade inflation was common; that large numbers of easy or nonverbal electives had been added to the schools' curricula as substitute for demanding courses; that writing skills had declined, at least in part because writing was not systematically emphasized as a part of learning and thinking, and because short-answer quizzes and standardized tests had gained a place alongside of, or in place of, the essay.

The pervasive influence of television, that highly entertaining but passivity-inducing medium of communication, was an important element in the new situation. But also part of the heightened criticism was a question about the fate of humane culture. The issue, which echoed complaints about the permissive aspects of progressive education and open education, was whether a democratic education system best served its students by letting them choose what they wanted to study, if they wanted to study; or whether it served them best by seeing that each and every one of them received a liberal education—including literature and language, science and mathematics, history and the arts. The debate reiterated the old arguments: one side claimed that a democratic school system had to proceed through the willing consent of the governed; the other insisted that a democratic school system had to assure everyone a sound education or suffer the creation of differential elites and of intolerable popular ignorance.

Beyond the obvious gains and losses that had been registered in the course of thirty-five years was a change in climate so basic and yet so elusive that it was difficult to measure or even describe. Although some few big-city high schools were vast educational factories in 1945, most schools, colleges, and even universities were small compared to what was to come. In some communities, teachers "boarded" with families, not because of choice but because of low pay; not a situation they might have chosen, but one that assured intimate familiarity with the community and the children. Even where teachers led independent lives, they were expected to spend after-school hours as supervisors of extracurricular activities and to know their students; they, in turn, could count on parents to support and reinforce the demands made by the school. Colleges and universities never questioned their role *in loco parentis:* they were responsible for the young men and women in their care, as if the institution itself were their parents. Alcohol was seldom permitted on campus, drugs were unheard of, and even the social lives of the students were regulated; infractions of the rules of behavior might be punished by suspension or expulsion.

Much had changed by 1980. The drive to consolidate small schools and small school districts had largely succeeded, helped along by the vast expansion of enrollments in the 1950s and 1960s. Big schools became the rule, not the exception. In a society where bigger was considered better, small districts and small schools were described as backward and inefficient. The number of school districts shrank dramatically, from one hundred thousand at war's end to sixteen thousand in 1980. While total enrollment in elementary and secondary schools nearly doubled during the thirty-five-year span (from 23 million to 40 million), the number of schools dropped from one hundred and eighty-five thousand to eighty-six thousand. More and more students went to larger schools. In higher education, institutions enrolling more than twenty thousand students increased from ten in 1948 to one hundred and fifteen by 1980. Growth had many benefits: efficiency of scale, diversity of curriculum, differentiation of types of students and teachers. Enlargement meant exposure to a more varied setting and interaction with a broader variety of ideas and people than was possible in a small school or college.

The trade-off, of course, was that bigness meant impersonality, bureaucratization, diminished contact between faculty and students, formalization of

30

Chapter 1
The
Conservative
Tradition in
Educational
Thought

relationships among colleagues, a weakening of the bonds of community. Colleges and universities withdrew from the *in loco parentis* role that they had previously exercised. No longer part of a community of values shared with students and parents, teachers and administrators found it difficult to administer discipline or even to establish rules that everyone found acceptable. Teachers and professors defended themselves against the new anonymity by joining unions. Students, complaining that no one knew their names, wrote them vividly in the bathrooms and hallways of their schools. The invasion of drugs, first in college in the 1960s, then in high schools and even junior high schools in the 1970s, dulled students' senses and insulated a portion of the student body from adult standards. The lingering influence of the counterculture, that remnant of the 1960s youth rebellion, left many adults wondering whether there were any standards of learning or effort or behavior worth defending.

American education had succeeded in so many ways that were real, tangible, and important—in providing modern buildings, larger enrollment, better materials, better trained teachers, more courses, more departments, and more graduates—that it sometimes seemed difficult for educators to remember what they had accomplished or why they had struggled so hard, or not to wonder whether they had gone wrong somewhere or why so many people criticized the nation's schools, colleges, and universities.

The following vignette, not necessarily representative, is nonetheless true. In 1945, at the beginning of this account, Mrs. Florence Christmas traveled to Washington, D.C., to tell the Senate Committee on Education about the Antioch School, where she was principal. She told them that there were three teachers for 190 children; that she was not only the principal but taught all subjects in four grades. It was a moving story, not just because of the difference between the salaries of the white and black teachers or between the number of months of schooling for white and black students, but because her dedication shone through her testimony. Even more than that, what was apparent was the evident commitment of the parents to the survival of the school and the education of their children, no matter how meager their present chances. Mrs. Christmas died in 1957, not living to see the Antioch School consolidated two years later, along with other small black schools into the Hazlehurst, Mississippi, city school district. The new, all-black, elementary school was much larger; Mrs. Christmas' sister became its principal, and there were six teachers in the first grade alone.

In the late 1960s, under pressure from the federal government, the Hazlehurst district offered its black and white students "free choice" to go to whichever school they wanted. A few black students went to the white school, but most students stayed with their friends. Rowan Torrey, a nephew of Mrs. Christmas, was one of those who chose to stay in the black school; he thought it was better. He liked the school spirit; he liked the way several busloads of kids followed the football team to their matches and cheered them on, and he was proud of the seventy-member band and the school choir. Torrey graduated in 1969 and went to Millsaps College, a small, previously all-white liberal arts college in Jackson. The next year the federal government lowered the boom on Hazlehurst and required the integration of the white and black schools.

The town whites promptly opened Copiah Academy, a private school, and abandoned the public schools.

When Rowan Torrey moved back to Hazlehurst in 1980 after serving in the Marines, he went to work for the federal Job Corps, helping young people acquire basic skills and vocational training. Most of his enrollees, including some with high school diplomas, were barely literate. He began to take a close look at the schools. What he saw was a small system that was more than 90 percent black, an integrated staff with white administrators who had suffered "culture shock" after integration and who were "afraid to discipline black kids." Graduation requirements had dropped precipitously during the decade after desegregation, the college preparatory courses had been substantially reduced, students were choosing their own courses, and discipline was lax. But that was not all: the buildings needed repairs, the band instruments had largely disappeared, the choir was a sometime thing, and the football team had a season of 0 and 10.

Born and bred in Mississippi, but college educated and toughened in the Marines, Rowan Torrey decided to fight. As a lay citizen, he took up the family tradition of commitment to public education and agitated for better schools. A new superintendent (a white, third-generation Mississippian who enrolled his daughter in the elementary school) was hired, a strict disciplinarian. Graduation requirements went up, and the district began eliminating options and telling students which academic courses they would have to take. Class size in the district averaged about twenty, though it was smaller in advanced science classes. Even as it tried to right itself, the district weathered a fiscal crisis; only the steady flow of federal funds enabled it to maintain kindergartens, teachers' aides, and special reading and math programs in the early grades.

In Hazlehurst, where there is a black public school system and a white private academy, the schools are not building a new social order but they are making their contribution. In the past decade, new employment opportunities have opened up for educated blacks, as tellers and accountants in local banks, as operators of nationally franchised businesses, as administrators in public agencies. "We had a tremendous opportunity to unite our community, black and white," Rowan Torrey laments, "and we wasted it." It was not the blacks who wasted it, but the whites who fled.

Yet if one had the courage of those who served on the President's Committee on Civil Rights in 1947 and the vision of those who projected the growth of American higher education in the same year, it would be possible to counsel against despair. In the crusade against ignorance, there have been no easy victories, but no lasting defeats. Those who have labored on behalf of American education have seen so many barriers scaled, so much hatred dispelled, so many possibilities remaining to provide the basis for future reconciliation. To believe in education is to believe in the future, to believe in what may be accomplished through the disciplined use of intelligence, allied with cooperation and good will. If it seems naïvely American to put so much stock in schools, colleges, universities, and the endless prospect of self-improvement and social improvement, it is an admirable, and perhaps even a noble, flaw.

The Paideia Proposal: Rediscovering the Essence of Education

Mortimer Adler (b. 1902) is an advocate of freedom and individual responsibility who champions classical humanist educational ideals. An American philosopher and educator, Adler developed the "great books" seminars and curricula with Robert M. Hutchins. Rooted in the belief that education should be universal, the great books curricula were based on more than 400 works of major Western authors (classical and modern). Adler and Hutchins identified many of these great works in a 54-volume set of books entitled *Great Books of the Western World Between 1945 and 1952.*

Adler has many other publications to his credit, including *The American Testament* (Praeger, 1975); *Aristotle for Everybody* (Macmillan, 1978); *The Conditions of Philosophy* (Atheneum, 1965); and *The Great Ideas: A Lexicon of Western Thought* (Maxwell Macmillan International, 1992).

In the selection that follows, which is from "The Paideia Proposal: Rediscovering the Essence of Education," *The American School Board Journal* (July 1982), Adler sets down what he believes are the basic aims of education. He argues that there should be a common school curriculum for everyone to follow at some level. Adler then explores some of the basic essential characteristics upon which a common curriculum would focus.

Key Concept: the Paideia Proposal

*I*n the first 80 years of this century, we have met the obligation imposed on us by the principle of equal educational opportunity, but only in a quantitative sense. Now, as we approach the end of the century, we must achieve equality in qualitative terms.

This means a completely one-track system of schooling. It means, at the basic level, giving all the young the same kind of schooling, whether or not they are college bound.

We are aware that children, although equal in their common humanity and fundamental human rights, are unequal as individuals, differing in their capacity to learn. In addition, the homes and environments from which they come to school are unequal—either predisposing the child for schooling or doing the opposite.

Consequently, the Paideia Proposal, faithful to the principle of equal educational opportunity, includes the suggestion that inequalities due to environmental factors must be overcome by some form of preschool preparation—at least one year for all and two or even three for some. We know that to make such preschool tutelage compulsory at the public expense would be tantamount to increasing the duration of compulsory schooling from 12 years to 13, 14, or 15 years. Nevertheless, we think that this preschool adjunct to the 12 years of compulsory basic schooling is so important that some way must be found to make it available for all and to see that all use it to advantage.

THE ESSENTIALS OF BASIC SCHOOLING

The objectives of basic schooling should be the same for the whole school population. In our current two-track or multitrack system, the learning objectives are not the same for all. And even when the objectives aimed at those on the upper track are correct, the course of study now provided does not adequately realize these correct objectives. On all tracks in our current system, we fail to cultivate proficiency in the common tasks of learning, and we especially fail to develop sufficiently the indispensable skills of learning.

The uniform objectives of basic schooling should be threefold. They should correspond to three aspects of the common future to which all the children are destined: (1) Our society provides all children ample opportunity for personal development. Given such opportunity, each individual is under a moral obligation to make the most of himself and his life. Basic schooling must facilitate this accomplishment. (2) All the children will become, when of age, full-fledged citizens with suffrage and other political responsibilities. Basic schooling must do everything it can to make them good citizens, able to perform the duties of citizenship with all the trained intelligence that each is able to achieve. (3) When they are grown, all (or certainly most) of the children will engage in some form of work to earn a living. Basic schooling must prepare them for earning a living, but not by training them for this or that specific job while they are still in school.

To achieve these three objectives, the character of basic schooling must be general and liberal. It should have a single, required, 12-year course of study for all, with no electives except one—an elective choice with regard to a second language, to be selected from such modern languages as French, German, Italian, Spanish, Russian, and Chinese. The elimination of all electives, with this one exception, excludes what *should* be excluded—all forms of specialization, including particularized job training.

In its final form, the Paideia Proposal will detail this required course of study, but I will summarize the curriculum here in its bare outline. It consists

34

*Chapter 1
The
Conservative
Tradition in
Educational
Thought*

of three main columns of teaching and learning, running through the 12 years and progressing, of course, from the simple to the more complex, from the less difficult to the more difficult, as the students grow older. Understand: The three columns represent three distinct modes of teaching and learning. They do not represent a series of courses. A specific course or class may employ more than one mode of teaching and learning, but all three modes are essential to the overall course of study.

The first column is devoted to acquiring knowledge in three subject areas: (A) language, literature, and the fine arts; (B) mathematics and natural science; (C) history, geography, and social studies.

The second column is devoted to developing the intellectual skills of learning. These include all the language skills necessary for thought and communication—the skills of reading, writing, speaking, listening. They also include mathematical and scientific skills; the skills of observing, measuring, estimating, and calculating; and skills in the use of the computer and of other scientific instruments. Together, these skills make it possible to think clearly and critically. They once were called the liberal arts—the intellectual skills indispensable to being competent as a learner.

The third column is devoted to enlarging the understanding of ideas and values. The materials of the third column are books (*not* textbooks), and other products of human artistry. These materials include books of every variety—historical, scientific, and philosophical as well as poems, stories, and essays—and also individual pieces of music, visual art, dramatic productions, dance productions, film or television productions. Music and works of visual art can be used in seminars in which ideas are discussed; but as with poetry and fiction, they also are to be experienced aesthetically, to be enjoyed and admired for their excellence. In this connection, exercises in the composition of poetry, music, and visual works and in the production of dramatic works should be used to develop the appreciation of excellence.

The three columns represent three different kinds of learning on the part of the student and three different kinds of instruction on the part of teachers.

In the first column, the students are engaged in acquiring information and organized knowledge about nature, man, and human society. The method of instruction here, using textbooks and manuals, is didactic. The teacher lectures, invites responses from the students, monitors the acquisition of knowledge, and tests that acquisition in various ways.

In the second column, the students are engaged in developing habits of performance, which is all that is involved in the development of an art of skill. Art, skill, or technique is nothing more than a cultivated, habitual ability to do a certain kind of thing well, whether that is swimming and dancing or reading and writing. Here, students are acquiring linguistic, mathematical, scientific, and historical *know-how* in contrast to what they acquire in the first column, which is *know-that* with respect to language, literature, and the fine arts, mathematics and science, history, geography, and social studies. Here, the method of instruction cannot be didactic or monitorial; it cannot be dependent on textbooks. It must be coaching, the same kind used in the gym to develop bodily skills; only here it is used by a different kind of coach in the classroom to develop intellectual skills.

In the third column, students are engaged in a process of enlightenment, the process whereby they develop their understanding of the basic and controlling ideas in all fields of subject matter and come to appreciate better all the human values embodied in works of art. Here, students move progressively from understanding less to understanding more—understanding better what they already know and appreciating more what they already have experienced. Here, the method of instruction cannot be either didactic or coaching. It must be the Socratic, or maieutic, method of questioning and discussing. It should not occur in an ordinary classroom with the students sitting in rows and the teacher in front of the class, but in a seminar room, with the students sitting around a table and the teacher sitting with them as an equal, even though a little older and wiser.

Of these three main elements in the required curriculum, the third column is completely innovative. Nothing like this is done in our schools, and because it is completely absent from the ordinary curriculum of basic schooling, the students never have the experience of having their minds addressed in a challenging way or of being asked to think about important ideas, to express their thoughts, to defend their opinions in a reasonable fashion.

The only thing that is innovative about the second column is the insistence that the method of instruction here must be coaching carried on either with one student at a time or with very small groups of students. Nothing else can be effective in the development of a skill, be it bodily or intellectual. The absence of such individualized coaching in our schools explains why most of the students cannot read well, write well, speak well, listen well, or perform well any of the other basic intellectual operations.

The three columns are closely interconnected and integrated, but the middle column—the one concerned with linguistic, mathematical, and scientific skills—is central. It both supports and is supported by the other two columns. All the intellectual skills with which it is concerned must be exercised in the study of the three basic subject-matters and in acquiring knowledge about them, and these intellectual skills must be exercised in the seminars devoted to the discussion of books and other things.

In addition to the three main columns in the curriculum, ascending through the 12 years of basic schooling, there are three adjuncts: One is 12 years of physical training, accompanied by instruction in bodily care and hygiene. The second, running through something less than 12 years, is the development of basic manual skills, such as cooking, sewing, carpentry, and the operation of all kinds of machines. The third, reserved for the last year or two, is an introduction to the whole world of work—the range of occupations in which human beings earn their livings. This is not particularized job training. It is the very opposite. It aims at a broad understanding of what is involved in working for a living and of the various ways in which that can be done. If, at the end of 12 years, students wish training for specific jobs, they should get that in two-year community or junior colleges, or on the job itself, or in technical institutes of one sort or another.

Everything that has not been specifically mentioned as occupying the time of the school day should be reserved for after-hours and have the status of extracurricular activities.

36

*Chapter 1
The
Conservative
Tradition in
Educational
Thought*

Please, note: The required course of study just described is as important for what it *displaces* as for what it introduces. It displaces a multitude of elective courses, especially those offered in our secondary schools, most of which make little or no contribution to general, liberal education. It eliminates all narrowly specialized job training, which now abounds in our schools. It throws out of the curriculum and into the category of optional extracurricular activities a variety of things that have little or no educational value.

If it did not call for all these displacements, there would not be enough time in the school day or year to accomplish everything that is essential to the general, liberal learning that must be the content of basic schooling.

THE QUINTESSENTIAL ELEMENT

So far, I have set forth the bare essentials of the Paideia Proposal with regard to basic schooling. I have not yet mentioned the quintessential element—the *sine qua non*—without which nothing else can possibly come to fruition, no matter how sound it might be in principle. The heart of the matter is the quality of learning and the quality of teaching that occupies the school day, not to mention the quality of the homework after school.

First, the learning must be active. It must use the whole mind, not just the memory. It must be learning by discovery, in which the student, never the teacher, is the primary agent. Learning by discovery, which is the only genuine learning, may be either unaided or aided. It is unaided only for geniuses. For most students, discovery must be aided.

Here is where teachers come in—as aids in the process of learning by discovery, not as knowers who attempt to put the knowledge they have into the minds of their students. The quality of the teaching, in short, depends crucially upon how the teacher conceives his role in the process of learning, and that must be as an aid to the student's process of discovery.

I am prepared for the questions that must be agitating you by now: How and where will we get the teachers who can perform as teachers should? How will we be able to staff the program with teachers so trained that they will be competent to provide the quality of instruction required for the quality of learning desired?

The first part of our answer to these questions is negative: We *cannot* get the teachers we need for the Paideia program from schools of education *as they are now constituted*. As teachers are now trained for teaching, they simply will not do. The ideal—an impracticable ideal—would be to ask for teachers who are, themselves, truly educated human beings. But truly educated human beings are too rare. Even if we could draft all who are now alive, there still would be far too few to staff our schools.

Well, then, what can we look for? Look for teachers who are actively engaged in the process of *becoming* educated human beings, who are themselves deeply motivated to develop their own minds. Assuming this is not too much to ask for the present, how should teachers be schooled and trained in the future? First, they should have the same kind of basic schooling that is recommended in the Paideia Proposal. Second, they should have additional schooling, at the college and even the university level, in which the same kind of general, liberal learning is carried on at advanced levels—more deeply, broadly, and intensively than it can be done in the first 12 years of schooling. Third, they must be given something analogous to the clinical experience in the training of physicians. They must engage in practice-teaching under supervision, which is another way of saying that they must be *coached* in the arts of teaching, not just given didactic instruction in educational psychology and in pedagogy. Finally, and most important of all, they must learn how to teach well by being exposed to the performances of those who are masters of the arts involved in teaching.

It is by watching a good teacher at work that they will be able to perceive what is involved in the process of assisting others to learn by discovery. Perceiving it, they must then try to emulate what they observe, and through this process, they slowly will become good teachers themselves.

The Paideia Proposal recognizes the need for three different kinds of institutions at the collegiate level: The two-year community or junior college should offer a wide choice of electives that give students some training in one or another specialized field, mainly those fields of study that have something to do with earning a living. The four-year college also should offer a wide variety of electives, to be chosen by students who aim at the various professional or technical occupations that require advanced study. Those elective majors chosen by students should be accompanied, for all students, by one required minor, in which the kind of general and liberal learning that was begun at the level of basic schooling is continued at a higher level in the four years of college. And we should have still a third type of collegiate institution—a four-year college in which general, liberal learning at a higher level constitutes a required course of study that is to be taken by all students. *It is this third type of college, by the way, that should be attended by all who plan to become teachers in our basic schools.*

At the university level, there should be a continuation of general, liberal learning at a still higher level to accompany intensive specialization in this or that field of science or scholarship, this or that learned profession. Our insistence on the continuation of general, liberal learning at all the higher levels of schooling stems from our concern with the worst cultural disease that is rampant in our society—*the barbarism of specialization.*

There is no question that our technologically advanced industrial society needs specialists of all sorts. There is no question that the advancement of knowledge in all fields of science and scholarship, and in all the learned professions, needs intense specialization. But for the sake of preserving and enhancing our cultural traditions, as well as for the health of science and scholarship, we need specialists who also are generalists—generally cultivated human beings, not just good plumbers. We need truly educated human beings who can perform their special tasks better precisely because they have general cultivation as well as intensely specialized training.

Changes indeed are needed in higher education, but those improvements cannot reasonably be expected unless improvement in basic schooling makes that possible.

THE FUTURE OF OUR FREE INSTITUTIONS

I already have declared as emphatically as I know how that the quality of human life in our society depends on the quality of the schooling we give our young people, both basic and advanced. But a marked elevation in the quality of human life is not the only reason improving the quality of schooling is so necessary—not the only reason we must move heaven and earth to stop the deterioration of our schools and turn them in the opposite direction. The other reason is to safeguard the future of our free institutions.

They cannot prosper, they may not even survive, unless we do something to rescue our schools from their current deplorable deterioration. Democracy, in the full sense of that term, came into existence only in this century and only in a few countries on earth, among which the United States is an outstanding example. But democracy came into existence in this century only in its initial conditions, all of which hold out promises for the future that remain to be fulfilled. Unless we do something about improving the quality of basic schooling for all and the quality of advanced schooling for some, there is little chance that those promises ever will be fulfilled. And if they are not, our free institutions are doomed to decay and wither away.

We face many insistently urgent problems. Our prosperity and even our survival depend on the solution of those problems—the threat of nuclear war, the exhaustion of essential resources and of supplies of energy, the pollution or spoilage of the environment, the spiraling of inflation accompanied by the spread of unemployment.

To solve these problems, we need resourceful and innovative leadership. For that to arise and be effective, an educated populace is needed. Trained intelligence—not only on the part of leaders, but also on the part of followers—holds the key to the solution of the problems our society faces. Achieving peace, prosperity, and plenty could put us on the threshold of an early paradise. But a much better educational system than now exists also is needed, for that alone can carry us across the threshold. Without it, a poorly schooled population will not be able to put to good use the opportunities afforded by the achievement of the general welfare. Those who are not schooled to enjoy society can only despoil its institutions and corrupt themselves.

CHAPTER 2 Student Experience Centered— Progressive Education

2.1 JOHN DEWEY

Democracy and Education: An Introduction to the Philosophy of Education

In 1916 John Dewey published what was to become one of the most influential and debated works on the philosophy of education. *Democracy and Education: An Introduction to the Philosophy of Education* (Macmillan, 1916), from which the following selection has been excerpted, is a comprehensive textbook on the philosophy of education and a sharp, progressive-liberal pedagogical response to the rhetoric of classical humanist scholars. The book became a major focus of controversy because there was a spirited classical humanist opposition to Dewey's pragmatic-progressive theory of education.

At the time that *Democracy and Education* was published, Dewey (1859–1952) was in his 12th year as a professor of philosophy at Columbia University and his 32d year as a university professor. Dewey taught a total of 33 years at Columbia before retiring from teaching in 1937. He then became

40

*Chapter 2
Student
Experience
Centered—
Progressive
Education*

a world traveler and a highly acclaimed commentator on the challenges facing democratic societies in the 1930s. He continued to write and publish right up to his death at almost 93 years of age. In addition to *Democracy and Education*, Dewey is also the author of *Essays in Experimental Logic* and *Reconstruction in Philosophy,* both of which were published in 1916.

Key Concept: education as a reconstruction or reorganization of experience

Education as Reconstruction

In its contrast with the ideas both of unfolding of latent powers from within, and of formation from without, whether by physical nature or by the cultural products of the past, the ideal of growth results in the conception that education is a constant reorganizing or reconstructing of experience. It has all the time an immediate end, and so far as activity is educative, it reaches that end —the direct transformation of the quality of experience. Infancy, youth, adult life—all stand on the same educative level in the sense that what is really *learned* at any and every stage of experience constitutes the value of that experience, and in the sense that it is the chief business of life at every point to make living thus contribute to an enrichment of its own perceptible meaning.

We thus reach a technical definition of education: It is that reconstruction or reorganization of experience which adds to the meaning of experience, and which increases ability to direct the course of subsequent experience. (1) The increment of meaning corresponds to the increased perception of the connections and continuities of the activities in which we are engaged. The activity begins in an impulsive form; that is, it is blind. It does not know what it is about; that is to say, what are its interactions with other activities. An activity which brings education or instruction with it makes one aware of some of the connections which had been imperceptible.... [A] child who reaches for a bright light gets burned. Henceforth he *knows* that a certain act of touching in connection with a certain act of vision (and *vice-versa*) means heat and pain; or, a certain light means a source of heat. The acts by which a scientific man in his laboratory learns more about flame differ no whit in principle. By doing certain things, he makes perceptible certain connections of heat with other things, which had been previously ignored. Thus his acts in relation to these things get more meaning; he knows better what he is doing or 'is about' when he has to do with them; he can *intend* consequences instead of just letting them happen —all synonymous ways of saying the same thing. At the same stroke, the flame has gained in meaning; all that is known about combustion, oxidation, about light and temperature, may become an intrinsic part of its intellectual content.

(2) The other side of an educative experience is an added power of subsequent direction or control. To say that one knows what he is about, or can intend certain consequences, is to say, of course, that he can better anticipate what is going to happen; that he can, therefore, get ready or prepare in advance so as to secure beneficial consequences and avert undesirable ones. A genuinely educative experience, then, one in which instruction is conveyed and ability increased, is contradistinguished from a routine activity on one hand, and a

capricious activity on the other. (*a*) In the latter one 'does not care what happens'; one just lets himself go and avoids connecting the consequences of one's act (the evidences of its connections with other things) with the act. It is customary to frown upon such aimless random activity, treating it as willful mischief or carelessness or lawlessness. But there is a tendency to seek the cause of such aimless activities in the youth's own disposition, isolated from everything else. But in fact such activity is explosive, and due to maladjustment with surroundings. Individuals act capriciously whenever they act under external dictation, or from being told, without having a purpose of their own or perceiving the bearing of the deed upon other acts. One may learn by doing something which he does not understand; even in the most intelligent action, we do much which we do not mean, because the largest portion of the connections of the act we consciously intend are not perceived or anticipated. But we learn only because after the act is performed we note results which we had not noted before. But much work in school consists in setting up rules by which pupils are to act of such a sort that even after pupils have acted, they are not led to see the connection between the result—say the answer—and the method pursued. So far as they are concerned, the whole thing is a trick and a kind of miracle. Such action is essentially capricious, and leads to capricious habits. (*b*) Routine, action, action which is automatic, may increase skill to do a *particular* thing. In so far, it might be said to have an educative effect. But it does not lead to new perceptions of bearings and connections; it limits rather than widens the meaning-horizon. And since the environment changes and our way of acting has to be modified in order successfully to keep a balanced connection with things, an isolated uniform way of acting becomes disastrous at some critical moment. The vaunted 'skill' turns out gross ineptitude.

The essential contrast of the idea of education as continuous reconstruction with ... other one-sided conceptions ... is that it identifies the end (the result) and the process. This is verbally self-contradictory, but only verbally. It means that experience as an active process occupies time and that its later period completes its earlier portion; it brings to light connections involved, but hitherto unperceived. The later outcome thus reveals the meaning of the earlier, while the experience as a whole establishes a bent or disposition toward the things possessing this meaning. Every such continuous experience or activity is educative, and all education resides in having such experiences.

It remains only to point out (what will receive more ample attention later) that the reconstruction of experience may be social as well as personal. For purposes of simplification we have spoken ... somewhat as if the education of the immature which fills them with the spirit of the social group to which they belong, were a sort of catching up of the child with the aptitudes and resources of the adult group. In static societies, societies which make the maintenance of established custom their measure of value, this conception applies in the main. But not in progressive communities. They endeavor to shape the experiences of the young so that instead of reproducing current habits, better habits shall be formed, and thus the future adult society be an improvement on their own. Men have long had some intimation of the extent to which education may be consciously used to eliminate obvious social evils through starting the young on paths which shall not produce these ills, and some idea of the extent in which

42

*Chapter 2
Student
Experience
Centered—
Progressive
Education*

education may be made an instrument of realizing the better hopes of men. But we are doubtless far from realizing the potential efficacy of education as a constructive agency of improving society, from realizing that it represents not only a development of children and youth but also of the future society of which they will be the constituents. . . .

THE DEMOCRATIC CONCEPTION IN EDUCATION

For the most part, save incidentally, we have hitherto been concerned with education as it may exist in any social group. We have now to make explicit the differences in the spirit, material, and method of education as it operates in different types of community life. To say that education is a social function, securing direction and development in the immature through their participation in the life of the group to which they belong, is to say in effect that education will vary with the quality of life which prevails in a group. Particularly is it true that a society which not only changes but which has the ideal of such change as will improve it, will have different standards and methods of education from one which aims simply at the perpetuation of its own customs. To make the general ideas set forth applicable to our own educational practice, it is, therefore, necessary to come to closer quarters with the nature of present social life.

The Implications of Human Association

Society is one word, but many things. Men associate together in all kinds of ways and for all kinds of purposes. One man is concerned in a multitude of diverse groups, in which his associates may be quite different. It often seems as if they had nothing in common except that they are modes of associated life. Within every larger social organization there are numerous minor groups: not only political subdivisions, but industrial, scientific, religious, associations. There are political parties with differing aims, social sets, cliques, gangs, corporations, partnerships, groups bound closely together by ties of blood, and so in endless variety. In many modern states, and in some ancient, there is great diversity of populations, of varying languages, religions, moral codes, and traditions. From this standpoint, many a minor political unit, one of our large cities, for example, is a congeries of loosely associated societies, rather than an inclusive and permeating community of action and thought.

The terms society, community, are thus ambiguous. They have both a eulogistic or normative sense, and a descriptive sense; a meaning *de jure* and a meaning *de facto*. In social philosophy, the former connotation is almost always uppermost. Society is conceived as one by its very nature. The qualities which accompany this unity, praiseworthy community of purpose and welfare, loyalty to public ends, mutuality of sympathy, are emphasized. But when we look at the facts which the term *denotes* instead of confining our attention to its intrinsic *connotation*, we find not unity, but a plurality of societies, good and bad.

Men banded together in a criminal conspiracy, business aggregations that prey upon the public while serving it, political machines held together by the interest of plunder, are included. If it is said that such organizations are not societies because they do not meet the ideal requirements of the notion of society, the answer, in part, is that the conception of society is then made so "ideal" as to be of no use, having no reference to facts; and in part, that each of these organizations, no matter how opposed to the interests of other groups, has something of the praiseworthy qualities of "Society" which hold it together. There is honor among thieves, and a band of robbers has a common interest as respects its members. Gangs are marked by fraternal feeling, and narrow cliques by intense loyalty to their own codes. Family life may be marked by exclusiveness, suspicion, and jealousy as to those without, and yet be a model of amity and mutual aid within. Any education given by a group tends to socialize its members, but the quality and value of the socialization depends upon the habits and aims of the group.

Hence, once more, the need of a measure for the worth of any given mode of social life. In seeking this measure, we have to avoid two extremes. We cannot set up, out of our heads, something we regard as an ideal society. We must base our conception upon societies which actually exist, in order to have any assurance that our ideal is a practicable one. But, as we have just seen, the ideal cannot simply repeat the traits which are actually found. The problem is to extract the desirable traits of forms of community life which actually exist, and employ them to criticize undesirable features and suggest improvement. Now in any social group whatever, even in a gang of thieves, we find some interest held in common, and we find a certain amount of interaction and coöperative intercourse with other groups. From these two traits we derive our standard. How numerous and varied are the interests which are consciously shared? How full and free is the interplay with other forms of association? If we apply these considerations to, say, a criminal band, we find that the ties which consciously hold the members together are few in number, reducible almost to a common interest in plunder; and that they are of such a nature as to isolate the group from other groups with respect to give and take of the values of life. Hence, the education such a society gives is partial and distorted. If we take, on the other hand, the kind of family life which illustrates the standard, we find that there are material, intellectual, aesthetic interests in which all participate and that the progress of one member has worth for the experience of other members—it is readily communicable—and that the family is not an isolated whole, but enters intimately into relationships with business groups, with schools, with all the agencies of culture, as well as with other similar groups, and that it plays a due part in the political organization and in return receives support from it. In short, there are many interests consciously communicated and shared; and there are varied and free points of contact with other modes of association.

... The two elements in our criterion both point to democracy. The first signifies not only more numerous and more varied points of shared common interest, but greater reliance upon the recognition of mutual interests as a factor in social control. The second means not only freer interaction between social groups (once isolated so far as intention could keep up a separation) but change in social habit—its continuous readjustment through meeting the new situa-

44

*Chapter 2
Student
Experience
Centered—
Progressive
Education*

tions produced by varied intercourse. And these two traits are precisely what characterize the democratically constituted society.

Upon the educational side, we note first that the realization of a form of social life in which interests are mutually interpenetrating, and where progress, or readjustment, is an important consideration, makes a democratic community more interested than other communities have cause to be in deliberate and systematic education. The devotion of democracy to education is a familiar fact. The superficial explanation is that a government resting upon popular suffrage cannot be successful unless those who elect and who obey their governors are educated. Since a democratic society repudiates the principle of external authority, it must find a substitute in voluntary disposition and interest; these can be created only by education. But there is a deeper explanation. A democracy is more than a form of government; it is primarily a mode of associated living, of conjoint communicated experience. The extension in space of the number of individuals who participate in an interest so that each has to refer his own action to that of others, and to consider the action of others to give point and direction to his own, is equivalent to the breaking down of those barriers of class, race, and national territory which kept men from perceiving the full import of their activity. These more numerous and more varied points of contact denote a greater diversity of stimuli to which an individual has to respond; they consequently put a premium on variation in his action. They secure a liberation of powers which remain suppressed as long as the incitations to action are partial, as they must be in a group which in its exclusiveness shuts out many interests.

The widening of the area of shared concerns, and the liberation of a greater diversity of personal capacities which characterize a democracy, are not of course the product of deliberation and conscious effort. On the contrary, they were caused by the development of modes of manufacture and commerce, travel, migration, and intercommunication which flowed from the command of science over natural energy. But after greater individualization on one hand, and a broader community of interest on the other have come into existence, it is a matter of deliberate effort to sustain and extend them. Obviously a society to which stratification into separate classes would be fatal, must see to it that intellectual opportunities are accessible to all on equable and easy terms. A society marked off into classes need be specially attentive only to the education of its ruling elements. A society which is mobile, which is full of channels for the distribution of a change occurring anywhere, must see to it that its members are educated to personal initiative and adaptability. Otherwise, they will be overwhelmed by the changes in which they are caught and whose significance or connections they do not perceive. The result will be a confusion in which a few will appropriate to themselves the results of the blind and externally directed activities of others.

2.2 WILLIAM HEARD KILPATRICK

The Project Method

William Heard Kilpatrick (1871–1965) is regarded as one of the principal founders of progressive, experience-based education. He attended Mercer University in Macon, Georgia, and did his graduate studies at Johns Hopkins University in Baltimore, Maryland. He was a teacher in the Mercer public schools and at Mercer University, and he was appointed to the faculty of Teachers College, Columbia University, as a professor of the philosophy of education in 1909. This appointment allowed Kilpatrick to develop a close working relationship with fellow progressive educator John Dewey, a faculty member in the Department of Philosophy at Columbia. Kilpatrick became one of the leading exponents of child-centered, experience-based schooling in the early decades of the twentieth century, and his long, active career at Teachers College continued until 1938. Kilpatrick was a major interpreter of the early writings of John Dewey, and he had many works published, including *Education for a Changing Civilization* (1926). The following selection is from "The Project Method," which was published in Columbia University's *Teachers College Record* in September 1918. In it, Kilpatrick describes his "project method" of teaching, emphasizing the use of purposeful activity as the basis of education.

Key Concept: the project method

My whole philosophic outlook had made me suspicious of so-called 'fundamental principles'. Was there yet another way of attaining unity? I do not mean to say that I asked these questions, either in these words or in this order. Rather is this a retrospective ordering of the more important outcomes. As the desired unification lay specifically in the field of method, might not some typical unit of concrete procedure supply the need—some unit of conduct that should be, as it were, a sample of life, a fair sample of the worthy life and consequently of education? As these questionings rose more definitely to mind, there came increasingly a belief—corroborated on many sides—that the unifying idea I sought was to be found in the conception of wholehearted purposeful activity proceeding in a social environment, or more briefly, in the unit element of such activity, the hearty purposeful act.

It is to this purposeful act with the emphasis on the word purpose that I myself apply the term 'project'. I did not invent the term nor did I start it on its educational career. Indeed, I do not know how long it had already been in use. I

46

*Chapter 2
Student
Experience
Centered—
Progressive
Education*

did, however, consciously appropriate the word to designate to myself and for my classes the typical unit of the worthy life described above. Others who were using the term seemed to me either to use it in a mechanical and partial sense or to be intending in a general way what I tried to define more exactly. The purpose of this article is to attempt to clarify the concept underlying the term as much as it is to defend the claim of the concept to a place in our educational thinking. The actual terminology with which to designate the concept is, as was said before, to my mind a matter of relatively small moment. If, however, we think of a project as a pro-ject, something pro-jected, the reason for adopting the term may better appear.

Postponing yet a little further the more systematic presentation of the matter, let us from some typical instances see more concretely what is contemplated under the term project or hearty purposeful act. Suppose a girl has made a dress. If she did in hearty fashion purpose to make the dress, if she planned it, if she made it herself, then I should say the instance is that of a typical project. We have in it a wholehearted purposeful act carried on amid social surroundings. That the dressmaking was purposeful is clear; and the purpose once formed dominated each succeeding step in the process and gave unity to the whole. That the girl was wholehearted in the work was assured in the illustration. That the activity proceeded in a social environment is clear; other girls at least are to see the dress. As another instance, suppose a boy undertakes to get out a school newspaper. If he is in earnest about it, we again have an effective purpose as the essence of a project. So we may instance a pupil writing a letter (if the hearty purpose is present), a child listening absorbedly to a story, Newton explaining the motion of the moon on the principles of terrestrial dynamics, Demosthenes trying to arouse the Greeks against Philip, Da Vinci painting the *Last Supper*, my writing this article, a boy solving with felt purpose an 'original' in geometry. All of the foregoing have been acts of individual purposing, but there are just as truly group projects: a class presents a play, a group of boys organize a baseball nine, three pupils prepare to read a story to their comrades. It is clear then that projects may present every variety that purposes present in life. It is also clear that a mere description of outwardly observable facts might not disclose the essential factor, namely the presence of a dominating purpose. It is equally true that there can be every degree of approximation to full projects according as the animating purpose varies in clearness and strength. If we conceive activities as ranging on a scale from those performed under dire compulsion up to those into which one puts his 'whole heart', the argument herein made restricts the term 'project' or purposeful act to the upper portions of the scale. An exact dividing line is hard to draw, and yields indeed in importance to the notion that psychological value increases with the degree of approximation to 'wholeheartedness'. As to the social environment element, some may feel that, however important this is to the fullest educative experience, it is still not essential to the conception of the purposeful act as here presented. These might, therefore, wish to leave this element out of the defining discussion. To this I should not object if it were clearly understood that the resulting concept—now essentially psychological in character—demands, generally speaking, the social situation both for its practical working and for the comparative valuation of proffered projects.

*William Heard
Kilpatrick*

With this general introduction, we may, in the first place, say that the purposeful act is the typical unit of the worthy life. Not that all purposes are good, but that the worthy life consists of purposive activity and not mere drifting. We scorn the man who passively accepts what 'fate' or mere chance brings to him. We admire the man who is master of his fate, who with deliberate regard for a total situation forms clear and far-reaching purposes, who plans and executes with nice care the purposes so formed. A man who habitually so regulates his life with reference to worthy social aims meets at once the demands for practical efficiency and of moral responsibility. Such a one presents the ideal of democratic citizenship. It is equally true that the purposeful act is not the unit of life for the serf or the slave. . . .

As the purposeful act is thus the typical unit of the worthy life in a democratic society, so also should it be made the typical unit of school procedure. We of America have for years increasingly desired that education be considered as life itself and not as a mere preparation for later living. The conception before us promises a definite step toward the attainment of this end. If the purposeful act be in reality the typical unit of the worthy life, then it follows that to base education on purposeful acts is exactly to identify the process of education with worthy living itself. The two become then the same. All the arguments for placing education on a life basis seem, to me at any rate, to concur in support of this thesis. On this basis education has become life. And if the purposeful act thus makes of education life itself, could we reasoning in advance expect to find a better preparation for later life than practice in living now? We have heard of old that "we learn to do by doing," and much wisdom resides in the saying. If the worthy life of the coming day is to consist of well-chosen purposeful acts, what preparation for that time could promise more than practice now, under discriminating guidance, in forming and executing worthy purposes? To this end must the child have within rather large limits the opportunity to purpose. For the issues of his act he must—in like limits—be held accountable. That the child may properly progress, the total situation—all the factors of life, including comrades—speaking, if need be through the teacher, must make clear its selective judgment upon what is done, approving the better, rejecting the worse. In a true sense the whole remaining discussion is but to support the contention here argued in advance that education based on the purposeful act prepares best for life while at the same time it constitutes the present worthy life itself. . . .

How then does the purposeful act utilize the laws of learning? A boy is intent upon making a kite that will fly. Hitherto he has not succeeded. His purpose is clear. This purpose is but the 'set' consciously and volitionally bent on its end. As set the purpose is the inner urge that carries the boy on in the face of hindrance and difficulty. It brings 'readiness' to pertinent inner resources of knowledge and thought. Eye and hand are made alert. The purpose acting as aim guides the boy's thinking, directs his examination of plan and material, elicits from within appropriate suggestions, and tests these several suggestions by their pertinency to the end in view. The purpose in that it contemplates a specific end defines success: the kite must fly or he has failed. The progressive attaining of success with reference to subordinate aims brings satisfaction at the successive stages of completion. . . . The purpose thus supplies the motive power, makes available inner resources, guides the process to its preconceived

48

*Chapter 2
Student
Experience
Centered—
Progressive
Education*

end, and by this satisfying success fixes in the boy's mind and character the successful steps as part and parcel of one whole. The purposeful act does utilize the laws of learning.

But this account does not yet exhaust the influence of the purpose on the resulting learning. Suppose as extreme cases two boys making kites, the one with wholeheartedness of purpose, as we have just described, the other under direct compulsion as a most unwelcome task. For simplicity's sake suppose the latter under enforced directions makes a kite identical with the other. The steps that in either case actually produced the kite let us call the *primary* responses for that case. Evidently these will, in the two cases, in part agree, and in part differ. The respects in which they agree furnish the kind of responses that we can and customarily do assign as tasks—the external irreducible minimum for the matter at hand. Upon such we can feasibly insist, even to the point of punishment if we do so decide. Additional to the primary responses which produced the respective kites, there will be yet other responses that accompany the kitemaking, not so much by way of outward doing as of inward thought and feeling. These additional responses may be divided into *associate* and *concomitant* responses. By associate responses we refer to those thoughts which are suggested in rather close connection with the primary responses and with the materials used and the ends sought.[1] By the term concomitant reference is made to certain responses yet a little further off from the immediate operation of kitemaking, which result ultimately in attitudes and generalizations. It is in this way that such attitudes are produced as self-respect or the contrary, and such relatively abstract ideals as accuracy or neatness. These words, primary, associate, and concomitant, will be used as well of the resulting learning as of the responses that bring the learning. The terminology is not entirely happy, and exact lines of division are not easy to draw; but the distinctions may perhaps help us to see a further function of purpose.

... The factor of 'set' conditions the learning process. A strong set acting through the satisfaction which attends success fixes quickly and strongly the bonds which brought success. In the case of coercion, however, a different state of affairs holds. There are in effect two sets operating: one set, kept in existence solely through coercion, is concerned to make a kite that will pass muster; the other set has a different end and would pursue a different course were the coercion removed. Each set in so far as it actually exists means a possible satisfaction and in that degree a possible learning. But the two sets, being opposed, mean at times a confusion as to the object of success; and in every case each set destroys a part of the other's satisfaction and so hampers the primary learning. Moreover, for the wholehearted act the several steps of the primary responses are welded together, as it were, at the forge of conscious purpose, and so have not only a stronger connection of part with part but greater flexibility of the whole to thought. So far then as concerns even the barest mechanics of kitemaking, the boy of wholehearted purpose will emerge with a higher degree of skill and knowledge and his learning will longer abide with him.

In the case of the associate responses, the difference is equally noticeable. The unified set of wholeheartedness will render available all the pertinent connected inner resources. A wealth of marginal responses will be ready to come forward at every opportunity. Thoughts will be turned over and over, and each step will be connected in many ways with other experiences. Alluring leads in various allied directions will open before the boy, which only the dominant present purpose could suffice to postpone. The element of satisfaction will attend connections seen, so that the complex of allied thinking will the longer remain as a mental possession. All of this is exactly not so with the other boy. The forbidden 'set', so long as it persists, will pretty effectually quench the glow of thought. Unreadiness will rather characterize his attitude. Responses accessory to the work at hand will be few in number, and the few that come will lack the element of satisfaction to fix them. Where the one boy has a wealth of associated ideas, the other has poverty. What abides with the one, is fleeting with the other. Even more pronounced is the difference in the by-products or concomitants from these contrasted activities. The one boy looks upon his school activity with joy and confidence and plans yet other projects; the other counts his school a bore and begins to look elsewhere for the expression there denied. To the one the teacher is a friend and comrade; to the other, a taskmaster and enemy. The one easily feels himself on the side of the school and other social agencies, the other with equal ease considers them all instruments of suppression. Furthermore, under the allied readiness which follows purpose, attention is more easily led to helpful generalizations of method and to such ideals as exactness or fairness. Desirable concomitants are more likely with the hearty purposeful act.

The contrasts here made are consciously of extremes. Most children live between the two. The question is whether we shall not consciously put before us as an ideal the one type of activity and approximate it as closely as we can rather than supinely rest content to live as close to the other type as do the general run of our American schools. Does not the ordinary school among us put its almost exclusive attention on the primary responses and the learning of these in the second fashion here described? Do we not too often reduce the subject matter of instruction to the level of this type alone? Does not our examination system —even our scientific tests at times—tend to carry us in the same direction? How many children at the close of a course decisively shut the book and say, "Thank gracious, I am through with that!" How many people 'get an education' and yet hate books and hate to think?

The thought suggested at the close of the preceding paragraph may be generalized into a criterion more widely applicable. The richness of life is seen upon reflection to depend, in large measure at least, upon the tendency of what one does to suggest and prepare for succeeding activities. Any activity —beyond the barest physical want—which does not thus 'lead on' becomes in time stale and flat. Such 'leading on' means that the individual has been modified so that he sees what before he did not see or does what before he could not do. But this is exactly to say that the activity has had an educative effect. Not to elaborate the argument, we may assert that the richness of life depends exactly on its tendency to lead one on to other like fruitful activity; that the degree of this tendency consists exactly in the educative effect of the activity involved; and that we may therefore take as the criterion of the value of any activity— whether intentionally educative or not—its tendency directly or indirectly to lead the individual and others whom he touches on to other like fruitful activity. If we apply this criterion to the common run of American schools we find

50

*Chapter 2
Student
Experience
Centered—
Progressive
Education*

exactly the discouraging results indicated above. It is the thesis of this paper that these evil results must inevitably follow the effort to found our educational procedure on an unending round of set tasks in conscious disregard of the element of dominant purpose in those who perform the tasks. This again is not to say that every purpose is good nor that the child is a suitable judge as between purposes nor that he is never to be forced to act against a purpose which he entertains. We contemplate no scheme of subordination of teacher or school to childish whim; but we do mean that any plan of educational procedure which does not aim consciously and insistently at securing and utilizing vigorous purposing on the part of the pupils is founded essentially on an ineffective and unfruitful basis. Nor is the quest for desirable purposes hopeless. There is no necessary conflict in kind between the social demands and the child's interests. . . . It is the special duty and opportunity of the teacher to guide the pupil through his present interests and achievement into the wider interests and achievement demanded by the wider social life of the older world.

The question of moral education was implicitly raised in the preceding paragraph. What is the effect on morals of the plan herein advocated? A full discussion is unfortunately impossible. Speaking for myself, however, I consider the possibilities for building moral character in a régime of purposeful activity one of the strongest points in its favor; and contrariwise the tendency toward a selfish individualism one of the strongest counts against our customary set-task sit-alone-at-your-own-desk procedure. Moral character is primarily an affair of shared social relationships, the disposition to determine one's conduct and attitudes with reference to the welfare of the group. This means, psychologically, building stimulus-response bonds such that when certain ideas are present as stimuli certain approved responses will follow. We are then concerned that children get a goodly stock of ideas to serve as stimuli for conduct, that they develop good judgment for selecting the idea appropriate in a given case, and that they have firmly built such response bonds as will bring—as inevitably as possible—the appropriate conduct once the proper idea has been chosen. In terms of this (necessarily simplified) analysis we wish such school procedure as will most probably result in the requisite body of ideas, in the needed skill in judging a moral situation, and in unfailing appropriate response bonds. To get these three can we conceive of a better way than by living in a social *milieu* which provides, under competent supervision, for shared coping with a variety of social situations? In the school procedure here advocated children are living together in the pursuit of a rich variety of purposes, some individually sought, many conjointly. As must happen in social commingling, occasions of moral stress will arise, but here—fortunately—under conditions that exclude extreme and especially harmful cases. Under the eye of the skillful teacher the children as an embryonic society will make increasingly finer discriminations as to what is right and proper. Ideas and judgment come thus. Motive and occasion arise together; the teacher has but to steer the process of evaluating the situation. The teacher's success—if we believe in democracy—will consist in gradually eliminating himself or herself from the success of the procedure. . . .

The question of the growth or building of interests is important in the theory of the plan here discussed. Many points still prove difficult, but some things can be said. Most obvious is the fact of 'maturing' (itself a difficult topic).

At first an infant responds automatically to his environment. Only later, after many experiences have been organized, can he, properly speaking, entertain purposes; and in this there are many gradations. Similarly, the earliest steps involved in working out a 'set' are those that have been instinctively joined with the process. Later on, steps may be taken by 'suggestion' (the relatively automatic working of acquired associations). Only comparatively late do we find true adaptation of means to end, the conscious choice of steps to the attainment of deliberately formed purposes. These considerations must qualify any statements made regarding child purposes. One result of the growth here discussed is the 'leading on' it affords. A skill acquired as end can be applied as means to new purposes. Skill or idea arising first in connection with means may be singled out for special consideration and so form new ends. This last is one of the most fruitful sources of new interests, particularly of the intellectual kind.

In connection with this 'maturing' goes a general increase in the 'interest span', the length of time during which a set will remain active, the time within which a child will—if allowed—work at any given project. What part of this increase is due to nature and physical maturing, what part to nurture, why the span is long for some activities and short for others, how we can increase the span in any given cases, are questions of the greatest moment for the educator. It is a matter of common knowledge that within limits 'interests' may be built up, the correlative interest spans appreciably increased....

It may be well to come closer to the customary subject matter of the school. Let us consider the classification of the different types of projects: Type 1, where the purpose is to embody some idea or plan in external form, as building a boat, writing a letter, presenting a play; type 2, where the purpose is to enjoy some (esthetic) experience, as listening to a story, hearing a symphony, appreciating a picture; type 3, where the purpose is to straighten out some intellectual difficulty, to solve some problem, as to find out whether or not dew falls, to ascertain how New York outgrew Philadelphia; type 4, where the purpose is to obtain some item or degree of skill or knowledge, as learning to write grade 14 on the Thorndike Scale, learning the irregular verbs in French. It is at once evident that these groupings more or less overlap and that one type may be used as means to another as end. It may be of interest to note that with these definitions the project method logically includes the problem method as a special case. The value of such a classification as that here given seems to me to lie in the light it should throw on the kind of projects teachers may expect and on the procedure that normally prevails in the several types. For type 1 the following steps have been suggested: purposing, planning, executing, and judging. It is in accord with the general theory here advocated that the child as far as possible take each step himself. Total failure, however, may hurt more than assistance. The opposed dangers seem to be on the one hand that the child may not come out master of the process, on the other, that he may waste time. The teacher must steer the child through these narrows, taking care meanwhile to avoid the other dangers previously discussed. The function of the purpose and the place of thinking in the process need but be mentioned. Attention may be called to the fourth step, that the child as he grows older may increasingly judge the result in terms of the aim and with increasing care and success draw from the process its lessons for the future.

52

*Chapter 2
Student
Experience
Centered—
Progressive
Education*

Type 2, enjoying an esthetic experience, may seem to some hardly to belong in the list of projects. But the factor of purpose undoubtedly guides the process and—I must think—influences the growth of appreciation. I have, however, as yet no definite procedure steps to point out.

Type 3, that of the problem, is of all the best known, owing to the work of Professors Dewey and McMurry. The steps that have been used are those of the Dewey analysis of thought.[2] The type lends itself, next to type 4, best of all to our ordinary schoolroom work. For this reason I have myself feared its over-emphasis. Our schools—at least in my judgment—do emphatically need a great increase in the social activity possible in type 1. Type 4, where the purpose has to do with specific items of knowledge or skill, would seem to call for the same steps as type 1—purposing, planning, executing, and judging. Only here, the planning had perhaps best come from the psychologist. In this type also there is danger of over-emphasis. Some teachers indeed may not closely discriminate between drill as a project and a drill as a set task, although the results will be markedly different. . . .

In conclusion, then, we may say that the child is naturally active, especially along social lines. Heretofore a régime of coercion has only too often reduced our schools to aimless dawdling and our pupils to selfish individualists. Some in reaction have resorted to foolish humoring of childish whims. The contention of this paper is that wholehearted purposeful activity in a social situation as the typical unit of school procedure is the best guarantee of the utilization of the child's native capacities now too frequently wasted. Under proper guidance purpose means efficiency, not only in reaching the projected end of the activity immediately at hand, but even more in securing from the activity the learning which it potentially contains. Learning of all kinds and in its all desirable ramifications best proceeds in proportion as wholeheartedness of purpose is present. With the child naturally social and with the skillful teacher to stimulate and guide his purposing, we can especially expect that kind of learning we call character building. The necessary reconstruction consequent upon these considerations offers a most alluring 'project' to the teacher who but dares to purpose.

NOTES

1. The term accessory was used in the original article where the word associate is now used with a slight difference of meaning, however.
2. Dewey, *How We Think,* Chap. VI.

2.3 MARIA MONTESSORI

Discipline

The following selection is taken from *The Montessori Method*, Maria Montessori's 1912 treatise on her theory of instruction. Specifically, it is from her chapter on "discipline" as the practice of liberty (freedom). In it, she describes how teachers can teach children to become self-disciplined persons. She discusses the concept of "active discipline," whereby teachers learn to observe student-initiated behaviors and to discern when to permit student-initiated action to proceed uninhibited. Montessori argues that teachers should interfere with antisocial or harmful student-initiated behaviors but that constructive student-initiated behavior should be encouraged. She provides examples of constructive student-initiated behaviors, defined as those that serve socially useful purposes in the classroom.

Montessori stresses that the child should not confuse "good" simply with "immobility," or "passivity," nor "evil" with "activity." The goal of school discipline should be the development of *self-disciplined*, free persons; this goal, Montessori argues, cannot be achieved simply by teaching children to be silent and obedient.

Montessori (1870–1952) earned her M.D. in 1896, making her the first woman in Italy to become a physician. She opened her first school, which she called a "Children's House," in 1905. By 1914 she was a world renowned figure in the field of education, and the "Montessori schools" that she developed featured kindergarten through eighth grade curricula. Her ideas had great influence in the development of the open primary and elementary schools in the United Kingdom in the 1930s and 1940s. Among her many important writings are *The Child in the Family*; *The Formation of Man*; *From Childhood to Adolescence*; *The Discovery of the Child*; *Dr. Montessori's Own Handbook*; *Education and Peace*; *Education for a New World*; and *To Educate the Human Potential*.

Key Concept: discipline through the use of liberty

*T*he pedagogical method of *observation* has for its base the *liberty* of the child; and *liberty is activity*.

Discipline must come through liberty. Here is a great principle which is difficult for followers of common-school methods to understand. How shall one obtain *discipline* in a class of free children? Certainly in our system, we have

54

*Chapter 2
Student
Experience
Centered—
Progressive
Education*

a concept of discipline very different from that commonly accepted. If discipline is founded upon liberty, the discipline itself must necessarily be *active*. We do not consider an individual disciplined only when he has been rendered as artificially silent as a mute and as immovable as a paralytic. He is an individual *annihilated*, not *disciplined*.

We call an individual disciplined when he is master of himself, and can, therefore, regulate his own conduct when it shall be necessary to follow some rule of life. Such a concept of *active discipline* is not easy either to comprehend or to apply. But certainly it contains a great *educational* principle, very different from the old-time absolute and undiscussed coercion to immobility.

A special technique is necessary to the teacher who is to lead the child along such a path of discipline, if she is to make it possible for him to continue in this way all his life, advancing indefinitely toward perfect self mastery. Since the child now learns to *move* rather than to *sit still*, he prepares himself not for the school, but for life; for he becomes able, through habit and through practice, to perform easily and correctly the simple acts of social or community life. The discipline to which the child habituates himself here is, in its character, not limited to the school environment but extends to society.

The liberty of the child should have as its *limit* the collective interest; as its *form*, what we universally consider good breeding. We must, therefore, check in the child whatever offends or annoys others, or whatever tends toward rough or ill-bred acts. But all the rest,—every manifestation having a useful scope,— whatever it be, and under whatever form it expresses itself, must not only be permitted, but must be *observed* by the teacher. Here lies the essential point; from her scientific preparation, the teacher must bring not only the capacity, but the desire, to observe natural phenomena. In our system, she must become a passive, much more than an active, influence, and her passivity shall be composed of anxious scientific curiosity, and of absolute *respect* for the phenomenon which she wishes to observe. The teacher must understand and *feel* her position of *observer:* the *activity* must lie in the *phenomenon*.

Such principles assuredly have a place in schools for little children who are exhibiting the first psychic manifestations of their lives. We cannot know the consequences of suffocating a *spontaneous action* at the time when the child is just beginning to be active: perhaps we suffocate *life itself*. Humanity shows itself in all its intellectual splendour during this tender age as the sun shows itself at the dawn, and the flower in the first unfolding of the petals; and we must *respect* religiously, reverently, these first indications of individuality. If any educational act is to be efficacious, it will be only that which tends to *help* toward the complete unfolding of this life. To be thus helpful it is necessary rigorously to avoid the *arrest* of *spontaneous movements and the imposition of arbitrary tasks*. It is of course understood, that here we do not speak of useless or dangerous acts, for these must be *suppressed, destroyed*.

Actual training and practice are necessary to fit for this method teachers who have not been prepared for scientific observation, and such training is especially necessary to those who have been accustomed to the old domineering methods of the common school. My experiences in training teachers for the work in my schools did much to convince me of the great distance between these methods and those. Even an intelligent teacher, who understands the principle, finds much difficulty in putting it into practice. She can not understand that her new task is apparently *passive,* like that of the astronomer who sits immovable before the telescope while the worlds whirl through space. This idea, that *life acts of itself,* and that in order to study it, to divine its secrets or to direct its activity, it is necessary to observe it and to understand it without intervening—this idea, I say, is very difficult for anyone to *assimilate* and to *put into practice.*

The teacher has too thoroughly learned to be the one free activity of the school; it has for too long been virtually her duty to suffocate the activity of her pupils. When in the first days in one of the "Children's Houses" she does not obtain order and silence, she looks about her embarrassed as if asking the public to excuse her, and calling upon those present to testify to her innocence. In vain do we repeat to her that the disorder of the first moment is necessary. And finally, when we oblige her to do nothing but *watch,* she asks if she had not better resign, since she is no longer a teacher.

But when she begins to find it her duty to discern which are the acts to hinder and which are those to observe, the teacher of the old school feels a great void within herself and begins to ask if she will not be inferior to her new task. In fact, she who is not prepared finds herself for a long time abashed and impotent; whereas the broader the teacher's scientific culture and practice in experimental psychology, the sooner will come for her the marvel of unfolding life, and her interest in it.

Notari, in his novel, "My Millionaire Uncle," which is a criticism of modern customs, gives with that quality of vividness which is peculiar to him, a most eloquent example of the old-time methods of discipline. The "uncle" when a child was guilty of such a number of disorderly acts that he practically upset the whole town, and in desperation he was confined in a school. Here "Fufu," as he was called, experiences his first wish to be kind, and feels the first moving of his soul when he is near to the pretty little Fufetta, and learns that she is hungry and has no luncheon.

"He glanced around, looked at Fufetta, rose, took his little lunch basket, and without saying a word placed it in her lap.

"Then he ran away from her, and, without knowing why he did so, hung his head and burst into tears.

"My uncle did not know how to explain to himself the reason for this sudden outburst.

"He had seen for the first time two kind eyes full of sad tears, and he had felt moved within himself, and at the same time a great shame had rushed over him; the shame of eating near to one who had nothing to eat.

"Not knowing how to express the impulse of his heart, nor what to say in asking her to accept the offer of his little basket, nor how to invent an excuse to justify his offering it to her, he remained the victim of this first deep movement of his little soul.

"Fufetta, all confused, ran to him quickly. With great gentleness she drew away the arm in which he had hidden his face.

" 'Do not cry, Fufu,' she said to him softly, almost as if pleading with him. She might have been speaking to her beloved rag doll, so motherly and intent was her little face, and so full of gentle authority, her manner.

56

*Chapter 2
Student
Experience
Centered—
Progressive
Education*

"Then the little girl kissed him, and my uncle yielding to the influence which had filled his heart, put his arms around her neck, and, still silent and sobbing, kissed her in return. At last, sighing deeply, he wiped from his face and eyes the damp traces of his emotion, and smiled again.

"A strident voice called out from the other end of the courtyard:

"'Here, here, you two down there—be quick with you; inside, both of you!'

"It was the teacher, the guardian. She crushed that first gentle stirring in the soul of a rebel with the same blind brutality that she would have used toward two children engaged in a fight.

"It was the time for all to go back into the school—and everybody had to obey the rule."

Thus I saw my teachers act in the first days of my practice school in the "Children's Houses." They almost involuntarily recalled the children to immobility without *observing* and *distinguishing* the nature of the movements they repressed. There was, for example, a little girl who gathered her companions about her and then, in the midst of them, began to talk and gesticulate. The teacher at once ran to her, took hold of her arms, and told her to be still; but I, observing the child, saw that she was playing at being teacher or mother to the others, and teaching them the morning prayer, the invocation to the saints, and the sign of the cross: she already showed herself as a *director*. Another child, who continually made disorganised and misdirected movements, and who was considered abnormal, one day, with an expression of intense attention, set about moving the tables. Instantly they were upon him to make him stand still because he made too much noise. Yet this was one of the *first manifestations*, in this child, of *movements* that were *coordinated* and *directed toward a useful end*, and it was therefore an action that should have been respected. In fact, after this the child began to be quiet and happy like the others whenever he had any small objects to move about and to arrange upon his desk.

It often happened that while the directress replaced in the boxes various materials that had been used, a child would draw near, picking up the objects, with the evident desire of imitating the teacher. The first impulse was to send the child back to her place with the remark, "Let it alone; go to your seat." Yet the child expressed by this act a desire to be useful; the time, with her, was ripe for a lesson in order.

One day, the children had gathered themselves, laughing and talking, into a circle about a basin of water containing some floating toys. We had in the school a little boy barely two and a half years old. He had been left outside the circle, alone, and it was easy to see that he was filled with intense curiosity. I watched him from a distance with great interest; he first drew near to the other children and tried to force his way among them, but he was not strong enough to do this, and he then stood looking about him. The expression of thought on his little face was intensely interesting. I wish that I had had a camera so that I might have photographed him. His eye lighted upon a little chair, and evidently he made up his mind to place it behind the group of children and then to climb up on it. He began to move toward the chair, his face illuminated with hope, but at that moment the teacher seized him brutally (or, perhaps, she would have said, gently) in her arms, and lifting him up above the heads of the other children showed him the basin of water, saying, "Come, poor little one, you shall see too!"

Undoubtedly the child, seeing the floating toys, did not experience the joy that he was about to feel through conquering the obstacle with his own force. The sight of those objects could be of no advantage to him, while his intelligent efforts would have developed his inner powers. The teacher *hindered* the child, in this case, from educating himself, without giving him any compensating good in return. The little fellow had been about to feel himself a conqueror, and he found himself held within two imprisoning arms, impotent. The expression of joy, anxiety, and hope, which had interested me so much faded from his face and left on it the stupid expression of the child who knows that others will act for him.

When the teachers were weary of my observations, they began to allow the children to do whatever they pleased. I saw children with their feet on the tables, or with their fingers in their noses, and no intervention was made to correct them. I saw others push their companions, and I saw dawn in the faces of these an expression of violence; and not the slightest attention on the part of the teacher. Then I had to intervene to show with what absolute rigour it is necessary to hinder, and little by little suppress, all those things which we must not do, so that the child may come to discern clearly between good and evil.

If discipline is to be lasting, its foundations must be laid in this way and these first days are the most difficult for the directress. The first idea that the child must acquire, in order to be actively disciplined, is that of the difference between *good* and *evil*; and the task of the educator lies in seeing that the child does not confound *good* with *immobility*, and *evil* with *activity*, as often happens in the case of the old-time discipline. And all this because our aim is to discipline *for activity, for work, for good*; not for *immobility*, not for *passivity*, not for *obedience*.

A room in which all the children move about usefully, intelligently, and voluntarily, without committing any rough or rude act, would seem to me a classroom very well disciplined indeed.

To seat the children in rows, as in the common schools, to assign to each little one a place, and to propose that they shall sit thus quietly observant of the order of the whole class as an assemblage—this can be attained later, as *the starting place* of *collective education*. For also, in life, it sometimes happens that we must all remain seated and quiet; when, for example, we attend a concert or a lecture. And we know that even to us, as grown people, this costs no little sacrifice.

If we can, when we have established individual discipline, arrange the children, sending each one to *his own place, in order,* trying to make them understand the ideal that thus placed they look well, and that it is a *good thing* to be thus placed in order, that it is a *good and pleasing arrangement in the room,* this ordered and tranquil adjustment of theirs—then their remaining in their places, *quiet* and *silent*, is the result of a species of *lesson*, not an *imposition*. To make them understand the idea, without calling their attention too forcibly to the practice, to have them *assimilate a principle of collective order*—that is the important thing.

If, after they have understood this idea, they rise, speak, change to another place, they no longer do this without knowing and without thinking, but they

58

*Chapter 2
Student
Experience
Centered—
Progressive
Education*

do it because they *wish* to rise, to speak, etc.; that is, from that *state of repose and order,* well understood, they depart in order to undertake *some voluntary action;* and knowing that there are actions which are prohibited, this will give them a new impulse to remember to discriminate between good and evil.

The movements of the children from the state of order become always more co-ordinated and perfect with the passing of the days; in fact, they learn to reflect upon their own acts. Now (with the idea of order understood by the children) the observation of the way in which the children pass from the first disordered movements to those which are spontaneous and ordered—this is the book of the teacher; this is the book which must inspire her actions; it is the only one in which she must read and study if she is to become a real educator.

For the child with such exercises makes, to a certain extent, a selection of his own *tendencies,* which were at first confused in the unconscious disorder of his movements. It is remarkable how clearly *individual differences* show themselves, if we proceed in this way; the child, conscious and free, *reveals himself.*

There are those who remain quietly in their seats, apathetic, or drowsy; others who leave their places to quarrel, to fight, or to overturn the various blocks and toys, and then there are those others who set out to fulfill a definite and determined act—moving a chair to some particular spot and sitting down in it, moving one of the unused tables and arranging upon it the game they wish to play.

Our idea of liberty for the child cannot be the simple concept of liberty we use in the observation of plants, insects, etc.

The child, because of the peculiar characteristics of held lessness with which he is born, and because of his qualities as a social individual is circumscribed by *bonds* which *limit* his activity.

An educational method that shall have *liberty* as its basis must intervene to help the child to a conquest of these various obstacles. In other words, his training must be such as shall help him to diminish, in a rational manner, the *social bonds, which limit* his activity.

Little by little, as the child grows in such an atmosphere, his spontaneous manifestations will become more *clear, with the clearness of truth,* revealing his nature. For all these reasons, the first form of educational intervention must tend to lead the child toward independence.

INDEPENDENCE

No one can be free unless he is independent: therefore, the first, active manifestations of the child's individual liberty must be so guided that through this activity he may arrive at independence. Little children, from the moment in which they are weaned, are making their ways toward independence.

What is a weaned child? In reality it is a child that has become independent of the mother's breast. Instead of this one source of nourishment he will find various kinds of food; for him the means of existence are multiplied, and he can to some extent make a selection of his food, whereas he was at first limited absolutely to one form of nourishment.

Nevertheless, he is still dependent, since he is not yet able to walk, and cannot wash and dress himself, and since he is not yet able to *ask* for things in a language which is clear and easily understood. He is still in this period to a great extent the *slave* of everyone. By the age of three, however, the child should have been able to render himself to a great extent *independent* and free.

That we have not yet thoroughly assimilated the highest concept of the term *independence,* is due to the fact that the social form in which we live is still *servile*. In an age of civilisation where servants exist, the concept of that *form of life* which is *independence* cannot take root or develop freely. Even so in the time of slavery, the concept of liberty was distorted and darkened.

Our servants are not our dependents, rather it is we who are dependent upon them.

It is not possible to accept universally as a part of our social structure such a deep human error without feeling the general effects of it in the form of moral inferiority. We often believe ourselves to be independent simply because no one commands us, and because we command others; but the nobleman who needs to call a servant to his aid is really a dependent through his own inferiority. The paralytic who cannot take off his boots because of a pathological fact, and the prince who dare not take them off because of a social fact, are in reality reduced to the same condition.

Any nation that accepts the idea of servitude and believes that it is an advantage for man to be served by man, admits servility as an instinct, and indeed we all too easily lend ourselves to *obsequious service,* giving to it such complimentary names as *courtesy, politeness, charity.*

In reality, *he who is served is limited* in his independence. This concept will be the foundation of the dignity of the man of the future; "I do not wish to be served, *because* I am not an impotent." And this idea must be gained before men can feel themselves to be really free.

Any pedagogical action, if it is to be efficacious in the training of little children, must tend to *help* the children to advance upon this road of independence. We must help them to learn to walk without assistance, to run, to go up and down stairs, to lift up fallen objects, to dress and undress themselves, to bathe themselves, to speak distinctly, and to express their own needs clearly. We must give such help as shall make it possible for children to achieve the satisfaction of their own individual aims and desires. All this is a part of education for independence.

We habitually *serve* children; and this is not only an act of servility toward them, but it is dangerous, since it tends to suffocate their useful, spontaneous activity. We are inclined to believe that children are like puppets, and we wash them and feed them as if they were dolls. We do not stop to think that the child *who does not do, does not know how to do*. He must, nevertheless, do these things, and nature has furnished him with the physical means for carrying on these various activities, and with the intellectual means for learning how to do them. And our duty toward him is, in every case, that of *helping him* to make a conquest of such useful acts as nature intended he should perform for himself. The mother who feeds her child without making the least effort to teach him to

60

*Chapter 2
Student
Experience
Centered—
Progressive
Education*

hold the spoon for himself and to try to find his mouth with it, and who does not at least eat herself, inviting the child to look and see how she does it, is not a good mother. She offends the fundamental human dignity of her son,—she treats him as if he were a doll, when he is, instead, a man confided by nature to her care.

Who does not know that to *teach* a child to feed himself, to wash and dress himself, is a much more tedious and difficult work, calling for infinitely greater patience, than feeding, washing and dressing the child one's self? But the former is the work of an educator, the latter is the easy and inferior work of a servant. Not only is it easier for the mother, but it is very dangerous for the child, since it closes the way and puts obstacles in the path of the life which is developing.

The ultimate consequences of such an attitude on the part of the parent may be very serious indeed. The grand gentleman who has too many servants not only grows constantly more and more dependent upon them, until he is, finally, actually their slave, but his muscles grow weak through inactivity and finally lose their natural capacity for action. The mind of one who does not work for that which he needs, but commands it from others, grows heavy and sluggish. If such a man should some day awaken to the fact of his inferior position and should wish to regain once more his own independence, he would find that he had no longer the force to do so. These dangers should be presented to the parents of the privileged social classes, if their children are to use independently and for right the special power which is theirs. Needless help is an actual hindrance to the development of natural forces.

Oriental women wear trousers, it is true, and European women, petticoats; but the former, even more than the latter, are taught as a part of their education the art of *not moving*. Such an attitude toward woman leads to the fact that man works not only for himself, but for woman. And the woman wastes her natural strength and activity and languishes in slavery. She is not only maintained and served, she is, besides, diminished, belittled, in that individuality which is hers by right of her existence as a human being. As an individual member of society, she is a cypher. She is rendered deficient in all those powers and resources which tend to the preservation of life. Let me illustrate this:

A carriage containing a father, mother, and child, is going along a country road. An armed brigand stops the carriage with the well-known phrase, "Your money or your life." Placed in this situation, the three persons in the carriage act in very different ways. The man, who is a trained marksman, and who is armed with a revolver, promptly draws, and confronts the assassin. The boy, armed only with the freedom and lightness of his own legs, cries out and betakes himself to flight. The woman, who is not armed in any way whatever, neither artificially nor naturally (since her limbs, not trained for activity, are hampered by her skirts), gives a frightened gasp, and sinks down unconscious.

These three diverse reactions are in close relation to the state of liberty and independence of each of the three individuals. The swooning woman is she whose cloak is carried for her by attentive cavaliers, who are quick to pick up any fallen object that she may be spared all exertion.

The peril of servilism and dependence lies not only in that "useless consuming of life," which leads to helplessness, but in the development of individual traits which indicate all too plainly a regrettable perversion and degeneration of the normal man. I refer to the domineering and tyrannical behaviour with examples of which we are all only too familiar. The domineering habit develops side by side with helplessness. It is the outward sign of the state of feeling of him who conquers through the work of others. Thus it often happens that the master is a tyrant toward his servant. It is the spirit of the task-master toward the slave.

Let us picture to ourselves a clever and proficient workman, capable, not only of producing much and perfect work, but of giving advice in his workshop, because of his ability to control and direct the general activity of the environment in which he works. The man who is thus master of his environment will be able to smile before the anger of others, showing that great mastery of himself which comes from consciousness of his ability to do things. We should not, however, be in the least surprised to know that in his home this capable workman scolded his wife if the soup was not to his taste, or not ready at the appointed time. In his home, he is no longer the capable workman; the skilled workman here is the wife, who serves him and prepares his food for him. He is a serene and pleasant man where he is powerful through being efficient, but is domineering where he is served. Perhaps if he should learn how to prepare his soup he might become a perfect man! The man who, through his own efforts, is able to perform all the actions necessary for his comfort and development in life, conquers himself, and in doing so multiplies his abilities and perfects himself as an individual.

We must make of the future generation, *powerful men*, and by that we mean men who are independent and free.

The Self-Actualizing Person

The following selection represents a synthesis of what humanistic psychologists of the 1940s, 1950s, and 1960s referred to as the "self-actualizing person." C. H. Patterson builds his work on that of Abraham Maslow, the great definer and synthesizing intellect of the concepts of "growth motivation" and "self-actualization," as well as the work of Carl Rogers and other major humanistic psychologists of that time, such as Arthur W. Combs and Donald Snygg, who contributed to the development of these concepts. In the following selection, Patterson identifies 14 defining characteristics of persons who are in the process of self-actualization. The author also summarizes the advantages of having self-actualizing persons in society. It is important for educators to know this concept well because it can be very helpful in planning or evaluating instruction; it can have substantive and procedural relevance to the classroom instruction as well as to management of life in classrooms. The idea of self-actualization is relevant in teaching persons of all ages, from early childhood to adulthood. The humanistic psychologists, such as Patterson, are opposed by the behaviorist school in psychology because the behaviorists believe that there is insufficient empirical data to support the humanistic psychologists' generalizations with regard to self-actualizing persons. Cognitivist psychologists frequently agree with the behaviorist critique of humanistic psychological theory as well as with its methods of studying phenomena, which are rooted in the Gestaltist and phenomenological schools of psychological thought (e.g., the work of Carl Jung).

Patterson was a professor at the University of Illinois at the time of the publication of the book from which the following selection was taken. *Humanistic Education* (Prentice-Hall Publishers, 1972) was widely used as a text in American colleges and universities and represents a good consensus of what the humanistic psychology movement of the 1950s, 1960s, and early 1970s had to offer to educators.

Key Concept: self-actualization

A major criticism of a broad, general goal such as self-actualization is that it is too general and vague to be useful. The behaviorists ask for a specific, objective or operational definition. It is necessary then, to give some consideration to defining or describing self-actualization so that, as an objective of education, criteria can be developed by which we can judge whether the objective is being achieved. While it is not possible at present to provide simple objective criteria, and accurate measures of them, the measurement of self-actualization is in principle possible, and some progress has already been made. A review of some of the discussions of self-actualization will help us to understand its nature and to arrive at a definition, or a description, of self-actualizing persons.

In the first edition of their book in 1949 [Donald] Snygg and [Arthur W.] Combs put forth the concept that human beings are motivated by one basic striving, the maintenance and enhancement of the self. Man seeks to develop an *adequate* self.[1] The adequate person perceives himself in positive ways: he has a positive self-concept, he accepts himself. The adequate person also accepts others: "we are so entirely dependent upon the good will and cooperation of others in our society that it would be impossible to achieve feelings of adequacy without some effective relationship with them. The adequate personality must be capable of living effectively and efficiently with his fellows."[2] In addition, the adequate person is able to accept into awareness all his perceptions, without distortion, or rejection. From a behavioral point of view, the adequate person is characterized by more efficient behavior, since he is not handicapped by defensiveness and is more open to experience. He is also spontaneous and creative since, being secure, he can take chances, experiment, and explore. Since the adequate person is secure and accepting of himself he is capable of functioning independently, that is, he finds that this own feelings, beliefs and attitudes are adequate guides to behavior. Finally, the adequate person, according to Combs and Snygg, is compassionate. Being less defensive, he can relate closely with others with concern rather than hostility or fear.

Carl Rogers proposes that the organism has "one basic tendency and striving—to actualize, maintain, and enhance the experiencing organism."[3] This tendency leads to or is manifested by growth and maturation, differentiation, independence and autonomy, and self-responsibility. His extensive experience in psychotherapy led him to the conviction that each individual, even though seriously disturbed, manifests this forward-moving tendency.

Rogers later developed the concept of the fully functioning person to describe the results of this striving in the optimal person, whether emerging from completely successful education or psychotherapy. He describes three major characteristics of such a fully functioning person: (1) Such a person is open to his experience, to all the external and internal stimuli; he has no need for defensiveness or distortion. He is keenly aware of himself and his environment; he experiences both positive and negative feelings. (2) The fully functioning person lives existentially. Each moment is new. Life is fluid, not rigid. The person is changing, in process, flexible and adaptable. (3) "This person would find his organism a trustworthy means of arriving at the most satisfying behavior in each existential situation."[4] His behavior is determined from within; the locus of control is internal. Being open to his experience, he would have available all relevant data on which to base his behavior. Behavior would not always be perfect, since some relevant data may be missing, but the resulting unsatisfying behavior would be corrected on the basis of feedback. Such a person would

64

*Chapter 2
Student
Experience
Centered—
Progressive
Education*

be a creative and self-actualizing person.... [S]uch a person is realistically so-cialized. "We do not need to ask who will control his aggressive impulses, for when he is open to all of his impulses, his need to be liked by others and his tendency to give affection are as strong as his impulses to strike out or to seize for himself. He will be aggressive in situations in which aggression is realistically appropriate, but there will be no runaway need for aggression."[5]

Earl Kelley describes the fully functioning person in terms similar to those of Combs and Rogers. Such a person thinks well of himself, feeling able or competent, though being aware of his limitations. He also thinks well of others, and sees their importance to him as opportunities for self-development. He sees himself as changing and developing. The fully functioning person develops and holds human values; he lives by these values rather than by external demands. Kelley also sees the fully functioning person as creative. In addition to these characteristics which are similar to those included by Combs and Rogers, Kelley says that the fully functioning person recognizes the value of mistakes, since in the process of changing and growing he cannot be right all the time. He sees mistakes as a source of learning and profits from them.[6]

Abraham Maslow has perhaps studied the nature of self-actualization to a greater extent than any one else. His description of the self-actualizing person draws together the characteristics considered above, with others resulting from his work, into a comprehensive picture of the highly self-actualizing person.

Maslow adopted an accepted and sound method in his attempt to study the nature of self-actualization. He selected a criterion group of persons (living and dead) on the basis of a professional judgment that they were outstanding as self-actualizing persons, using as a general definition "the full use and exploitation of talents, capacities, potentialities, etc. Such people seem to be fulfilling themselves and to be doing the best that they are capable of doing. They are people who have developed or are developing the full stature of which they are capable."[7]

These subjects were studied intensively, to determine both what characteristics they had in common, and which differentiated them from ordinary or average people. Fourteen characteristics emerged:

More efficient perception of reality and more comfortable relations with it. This includes the detection of the phony and dishonest person, and the accurate perception of what exists rather than the distortion of perception by one's needs. *Self-actualizing people are more aware of their environment,* both human and nonhuman. They are not afraid of the unknown, and can tolerate the doubt, uncertainty, and tentativeness accompanying the perception of the new and unfamiliar.

Acceptance of self, others and nature. Self-actualizing persons are not ashamed or guilty about their human nature, with its shortcomings, imperfections, frailties and weaknesses. Nor are they critical of these characteristics in others. *They respect and esteem themselves and others.* Moreover, *they are open, genuine, without pose or facade.* They are not, however, self-satisfied, but are concerned about discrepancies between what is and what might or should be in themselves, others, and society.

Spontaneity. Self-actualizing persons are not hampered by convention, but they do not flout it. *They are not conformists,* but neither are they anti-conformist for the sake of being so. They are not externally motivated, or even goal di-rected—rather their motivation is the internal one of growth and development, the actualization of their selves and potentialities.

Problem-centering. Self-actualizing persons are not ego-centered, but focus on problems outside themselves. They are *mission oriented,* often on the basis of a *sense of responsibility, duty, or obligation* rather than of personal choice.

The quality of detachment; the need for privacy. *The self-actualizing person enjoys solitude and privacy.* It is possible for him to remain unruffled and undis-turbed by much which upsets others. He may even appear to others to be asocial.

Autonomy, independence of culture and environment. Self-actualizing per-sons, though dependent on others for the satisfaction of the basic needs of love, safety, respect, and belongingness, "are not dependent for their main satisfac-tions on the real world, or other people or culture or means-to-ends, or in gen-eral, on extrinsic satisfactions. *Rather they are dependent for their own development and continued growth upon their own potentialities and latent resources."*[8]

Continued freshness of appreciation. *Self-actualizing persons repeatedly* (though not continuously) *experience awe, pleasure, and wonder in their everyday world.*

The "mystic experience," the "oceanic feeling." In varying degrees and with varying frequencies, *self-actualizing persons have experiences of ecstasy, awe, and wonder,* with feelings of limitless horizons opening up, followed by the convic-tion that the experience was important and valuable and had a carry over into daily life.

Gemeinschaftsgefühl. *Self-actualizing persons have a deep feeling of empathy, sym-pathy or compassion for human beings in general.* This feeling is in a sense uncon-ditional, in that it exists along with the recognition of the existence of negative qualities in others which provoke occasional anger, impatience and disgust.

Interpersonal relations. *Self-actualizing people have deep interpersonal relations with others.* They are selective, however, and the circle of friends is small, usu-ally consisting mainly of other self-actualizing persons. They attract others to them as admirers or disciples.

The democratic character structure. *The self-actualizing person does not discrimi-nate* on the basis of class, education, race or color. He is humble in his recog-nition of what he knows in comparison with what could be known, and is ready to learn from anyone. *He respects everyone* as potential contributors to his knowledge, but also just because they are human beings.

Means and ends. Self-actualizing persons are highly ethical. *They clearly distin-guish between means and ends, and subordinate means to ends.*

Philosophical, unhostile sense of humor. Although all the self-actualizing sub-jects studied by Maslow had a sense of humor, it was not of the ordinary type. Their sense of humor was the spontaneous, thoughtful type, intrinsic to the situation. Their humor did not involve hostility, superiority, or sarcasm.

Creativeness. All Maslow's subjects were judged to be creative, each in his own way. The creativity involved here is not the special-talent creativeness.

66

*Chapter 2
Student
Experience
Centered—
Progressive
Education*

It is a creativeness potentially inherent in everyone, but usually suffocated by acculturation. *It is a fresh, naive, direct way of looking at things.*

These characteristics give a description of the kind of person who would not only be desirable in our society, but who would be functioning at a high level, using his potentials and experiencing personal satisfaction. In fact, it could be said that unless there are enough individuals possessing a minimal degree of the characteristics of the self-actualizing person society cannot survive. Historically, such men have been contributors to the development of civilization, and where societies have not included some such persons, they have disintegrated and disappeared.

From the standpoint of the individual, perhaps a question could be raised as to whether individuals who are open and honest, and accepting and trusting of others, could exist in a society such as ours. Henry suggests that "in a society where competition for the basic cultural goods is a pivot of action, people cannot be taught to love one another, for those who do cannot compete with one another, except in play."[9] It is questionable, though, that such persons would be at so great a disadvantage. But more important is the question as to how our situation, our society, can be changed. Since society is composed of individuals and consists of interpersonal relations, to change society, one must change both. This is the only place we can start. The outlook is not necessarily grim. One can reason that, since these characteristics are necessary for the survival of society, and societies have survived as long as they have, there must have been, and be, a sufficient number of persons with these characteristics in contemporary society. Moreover, it could be argued that such characteristics being of survival value, persons with these characteristics have to some extent been selected in the evolutionary process. Anthropologists (e.g., Ashley Montagu) have pointed out that cooperation, rather than competition, among men has been the basis for the survival of groups and societies. Thus there is perhaps potential in human beings for the development of these characteristics in greater measure. There is evidence, from the education and training of counselors and psychotherapists, that these characteristics, at least some of them, can be increased by education and training. Finally, there is evidence that the qualities or characteristics of self-actualizing persons are stimulated or brought out in others with whom the possessors have contact, by what is known as the principle of reciprocal effect.

NOTES

1. Arthur W. Combs & Donald Snygg, *Individual Behavior* (New York: Harper & Row, 1959), p. 45.

2. Combs and Snygg, p. 246. See also Arthur W. Combs, "A Perceptual View of the Adequate Personality," in Arthur W. Combs, ed. *Perceiving, Behaving, Becoming* (Washington, D. C.: National Education Association, 1962), pp. 50–64.

3. Carl R. Rogers, *Client-Centered Therapy, Its Current Practice, Implications, and Theory* (Boston: Houghton Mifflin, 1951), p. 487.

4. Carl R. Rogers, *Freedom to Learn* (Columbus, Ohio: C. E. Merrill, 1969), p. 286. See also C. R. Rogers, "Toward Becoming a Fully Functioning Person," in Arthur W. Combs, ed., *Perceiving, Behaving, Becoming,* pp. 21–33.

5. *Ibid.*, p. 291.

6. Earl C. Kelley, "The Fully Functioning Self," in Combs, ed., *Perceiving, Behaving, Becoming,* pp. 9–20.

7. Abraham H. Maslow, "Self-Actualizing People: A Study of Psychological Health," in Clark E. Moustakas, ed., *The Self: Explorations in Personal Growth* (New York: Harper & Row, 1956), pp. 161–162.

8. *Ibid.*, p. 176.

9. Jules Henry, "In Suburban Classrooms," in Beatrice & Ronald Gross, eds. *Radical School Reform* (New York: Simon & Schuster, 1969), p. 83.

CHAPTER 3

Some
Alternative Perspectives
in Educational Thought

3.1 JOEL SPRING

The Great Civil Rights Movement and the New Culture Wars

Joel Spring is a distinguished professor of the history of American education who has published several important books, including *Sorting Machine:
National Educational Policy Since 1945* (McKay, 1976).

In the following selection from *Deculturalization and the Struggle for
Equality: A Brief History of the Education of Dominated Cultures in the
United States,* 2d ed. (McGraw-Hill, 1997), Spring describes the deculturalization of minority populations in the United States as the process generated
by the great civil rights movement that swept the United States in the 1950s
and 1960s, leading to a major shift in the direction of American social
thought in the 1960s and 1970s. Spring reflects on the struggle for equality
of educational opportunity in the United States.

In this selection, Spring provides a brief summary of the historical
background of the civil rights movement in the United States, and he briefly

traces the role of the federal courts in the struggle to desegregate U.S. public schools. He examines the roles of important civil rights organizations in the cause of civil rights, such as the National Association for the Advancement of Colored People (NAACP), the Congress of Racial Equality (CORE), and the Southern Christian Leadership Conference (SCLC). Spring discusses the philosophical bases for the thought and strategies of Dr. Martin Luther King, Jr., as well as the points of view on social action of other leaders in the American struggle for civil rights. He describes the origins and use of the philosophy of nonviolent confrontation used in the civil rights movement. Spring notes the importance of the Civil Rights Act of 1964 and the Elementary and Secondary Education Act of 1965 in enforcing the implementation of federal school desegregation policy.

Spring describes how acts of Congress reinforced the efforts of the federal courts. He refers to the "culture wars" as cultural minority populations struggling for equality of educational opportunity. Spring provides the background to the origins of the movement for multicultural education. He notes that the debates concerning multicultural education helped to address concerns over how to empower oppressed populations and how to include the culture heritages of minority populations in the curricula of schools.

Key Concept: the civil rights movement and the "culture wars"

*E*xtending from the 1940s into the 1990s, the great civil rights movement was a continuation of the culture wars initiated by English colonists when they invaded Native American lands in North America. From the time of the invasion to the 1990s, many citizens tried to assure that Protestant Anglo-American culture would be the dominant culture of the United States. For instance, in the 1990s, historian Arthur Schlesinger, who opposed multicultural education in public schools and advocated the teaching of Protestant Anglo-American culture, wrote, "For better or worse, the white Anglo-Saxon Protestant tradition was for two centuries—and in crucial respects still is—the dominant influence on American culture and society."[1]

In the nineteenth and twentieth centuries, those believing the United States should be united by a Protestant Anglo-American culture advocated the "civilization" and deculturalization of Native Americans, Mexican Americans, Puerto Ricans, and Jewish and Catholic immigrants from southern and eastern Europe. Some citizens believed in the racial superiority of whites that resulted in the segregation of African Americans, Native Americans, Mexican Americans, and Asian Americans. In the early twentieth century, believers in the racial superiority of whites, particularly whites from England and Germany, used standardized testing to provide validity to their views.

The great civil rights movement was composed of dominated groups who protested the domination of Protestant Anglo-American culture. Activists among Native Americans, African Americans, Mexican Americans, Asian Americans, and Puerto Ricans demanded restoration and recognition of their cultures. Many of these activists rejected the idea of a single dominating culture for the idea of a pluralistic society with many cultures given recognition in the public schools. Besides demands for cultural pluralism, activists demanded the end of school segregation and racism in educational practices.

Leading the way in the great civil rights movement were members of the National Association for the Advancement of Colored People (NAACP), who fought the continuation of segregation in schools and public facilities, and the lack of opportunity to participate in the American economic system. In addition, they demanded recognition for African-American culture in the public schools. The actions of African Americans contributed to the militancy of other groups in demanding equality of educational opportunity and recognition of their cultures in public schools.

Native Americans campaigned for self-determination and cultural recognition. Mexican Americans continued their struggles against segregation and they sought preservation of Mexican culture and the Spanish language in the schools. By the 1960s, Puerto Ricans joined Mexican Americans in supporting bilingual education.

Also, the great civil rights movement opened the door to demands that the public schools reflect minority cultures. African Americans, Native Americans, Mexican Americans, Asian Americans, and Puerto Ricans demanded that their unique cultures be recognized and be given a place in the school curriculum. These demands gave impetus to the movement for multicultural education in the 1980s and 1990s.

SCHOOL DESEGREGATION

The desegregation of American schools was the result of over a half century of struggle by the black community. Since its founding in the early part of the twentieth century, the NAACP had struggled to end discriminatory practices against minority groups. The school desegregation issue was finally decided by the U.S. Supreme Court in 1954 in *Brown v. Board of Education of Topeka*. The decision did not bring immediate results, because resistance to court-ordered desegregation arose. The frustration caused by the slow pace of school integration and the continuation of other forms of discrimination contributed to the growth of a massive civil rights movement in the late 1950s and early 1960s. The response of national political leaders to the civil rights movement was the enactment of strong civil rights legislation.

It is important to remember that school desegregation and civil rights legislation were not the products of a benign government but were the result of tremendous struggle and public demonstrations. Politically, African Americans were forced by their lack of power at local and state levels to seek redress for their grievances from the federal government. National leaders tried to avoid dealing with civil rights issues but were finally forced by public demonstrations to take action. With regard to schooling, federal action resulted in greater federal control of local schools and a feeling among school board members that local control of education was rapidly disappearing.

The key legal issue in the struggle for desegregation was the interpretation of the Fourteenth Amendment to the Constitution. This constitutional amendment was ratified in 1868, shortly after the close of the Civil War. One of its purposes was to extend the basic guarantees of the Bill of Rights into the areas under state and local government control. The most important and controversial section of the Fourteenth Amendment states, "No State shall make or enforce any law which shall abridge the privileges or immunities of citizens . . . nor . . . deprive any person of life, liberty, or property, without due process of law; nor deny to any person within its jurisdiction the equal protection of the laws."

A major test of the meaning of the Fourteenth Amendment with regard to segregation occurred in 1895 in a Supreme Court case involving Homer Plessy, who was one-eighth black and seven-eighths white and had been arrested for refusing to ride in the "colored" coach of a train, as required by Louisiana law. The Supreme Court ruled that segregation did not create a badge of inferiority if segregated facilities were equal and the law was reasonable. In establishing the "separate but equal doctrine," the Supreme Court failed to clearly define what constitutes equal facilities and what is reasonable.

The overturning of the separate but equal doctrine and a broader application of the Fourteenth Amendment came in 1954 in the historic and controversial Supreme Court decision *Brown* v. *Board of Education of Topeka*. In 1953, *Brown* was one of the five school segregation suits to reach the Supreme Court. It became the first case simply because the five cases were heard in alphabetical order. The Brown case began in 1951, when Oliver Brown and twelve other parents represented by NAACP lawyers brought suit to void a Kansas law that permitted but did not require local segregation of the schools. In this particular case, Oliver Brown's daughter was denied the right to attend a white elementary school within five blocks of her home and forced to cross railroad tracks and travel twenty-one blocks to attend an all-black school. The federal district court in Kansas ruled against Oliver Brown, using the argument that the segregated schools named in the suit were substantially equal and thus fell within the separate but equal doctrine.

In preparing its brief for the Supreme Court, the NAACP defined two important objectives: (1) to show that the climate of the times required an end to segregation laws and (2) to show that the separate but equal doctrine contained a contradiction in terms—that is, that separate facilities were inherently unequal. Evidence from recent findings in the social sciences presented by the NAACP to prove that separate facilities were inherently unequal provided the basis for overturning the separate but equal doctrine. It also caused a storm of protest alleging that the Supreme Court was basing decisions on nonlegal arguments. Throughout the South, it was widely believed that the Court was being persuaded by communist-oriented social scientists. Billboards appeared on highways demanding the impeachment of Chief Justice Earl Warren for his role in subverting the Constitution.

The Supreme Court argued in the Brown decision, "In the field of public education the doctrine of 'separate but equal' has no place. Separate educational facilities are inherently unequal." To support this argument, the Supreme Court wrote one of the most controversial single sentences ever to appear in a

Court decision: "Whatever may have been the extent of psychological knowledge at the time of *Plessy* v. *Ferguson* this finding is amply supported by modern authority."[2]

In 1955 the Supreme Court issued its enforcement decree for the desegregation of schools. One problem facing the Court was the lack of machinery for supervising and ensuring the desegregation of vast numbers of segregated school districts. The Court resolved this problem by relying on federal district courts to determine the equitable principles for desegregation. Federal judges were often part of the social fabric of their local communities and resisted attempts at speedy desegregation. Consequently, integration occurred at a slow pace until additional civil rights legislation was passed in the 1960s and the mounting frustrations in the black community fed the flames of a militant civil rights movement.[3]

The evolution of the mass media in the 1950s was an important factor in the civil rights movement because it became possible to turn local problems into national issues. Thus, even though presidents had traditionally shown a great deal of deference to the important white southern political structure, the emergence of the mass media as a powerful force allowed both the federal government and civil rights groups to put unprecedented pressure on southern political leaders, forcing them to comply with national civil rights legislation. In fact, enforcement of the Supreme Court school desegregation ruling depended in large part on civil rights groups making effective use of television. In one sense, the struggle that took place was a struggle between public images. Concern over America's international image grew as pictures of racial injustice flashed around the world, and the president's public image was often threatened when examples of racial injustice were shown to millions of television viewers and the question was asked, What is our president doing about this situation?

The most dramatic technique used by civil rights groups was nonviolent confrontation. The massive nonviolent response of black people in the South confronted with an array of cattle prods, clubs, and fire hoses wielded by cursing southern law enforcement units provided dramatic and shocking television viewing for the nation. The Congress of Racial Equality (CORE), the Student Nonviolent Coordinating Committee (SNCC), and the Southern Christian Leadership Conference (SCLC), led by the Reverend Martin Luther King, Jr., provided the national drama and the final push for national civil rights legislation.

The introduction of nonviolent confrontation into the civil rights movement came from the Christian student movement of the 1930s, which, under the leadership of the Fellowship for Reconciliation, was committed to use of the Gandhian technique of *satyagraha* (nonviolent direct action) in solving racial and industrial problems in the United States. CORE, a major organization in the civil rights movement, was organized at the University of Chicago in 1942. The two basic doctrines of the early CORE movement were commitment to racial integration and the use of Christian nonviolent techniques.

CORE did not rise to national prominence until the late 1950s, when another Christian leader, Dr. Martin Luther King, Jr., made nonviolent confrontation the central drama of the civil rights movement. King was born in 1929 in

Atlanta, Georgia, into a family of Baptist ministers. His maternal grandfather founded the Ebenezer Baptist Church, and his father made the church into one of the largest and most prestigious Baptist churches in Atlanta. In 1944, King entered Atlanta's Morehouse College, where he claimed to have been influenced by his reading of Henry David Thoreau's *Essay on Civil Disobedience*. He later wrote about the essay, "Fascinated by the idea of refusing to cooperate with an evil system, I was so deeply moved that I reread the work several times. This was my first intellectual contact with the theory of non-violent resistance."[4]

In 1948, King entered the Crozier Theological Seminary in Chester, Pennsylvania, where for the first time he became acquainted with pacifism through a lecture by A. J. Muste. King wrote that at the time he considered Muste's pacifist doctrine impractical in a world confronted by the armies of totalitarian nations. Of more importance to King's intellectual development was his exposure to the social gospel philosophy of Walter Rauschenbusch, which actively involved the church in social reform as a means of creating a kingdom of God on earth. Although he rejected the optimistic elements in the social gospel, King argued that any concern with the souls of humans required a concern with social and economic conditions.

King also studied the lectures and works of Mohandas K. Gandhi. The Indian leader's work convinced King that the Christian doctrine of love could be a force for social change. King wrote, "Gandhi was probably the first person in history to lift the love ethic of Jesus above mere interaction between individuals to a powerful and effective social force on a large scale." Like the early members of CORE, King became convinced that nonviolent resistance "was the only morally and practically sound method open to oppressed people in their struggle for freedom."[5]

The incident that launched Martin Luther King's civil rights activities and provided scope for his Gandhian form of the social gospel occurred on December 1, 1955. On that date, Rosa Parks, who had worked a regular day as a seamstress in one of the leading department stores in Montgomery, Alabama, boarded a bus and took the first seat behind the section reserved for whites. Later during the journey home, several white passengers boarded the bus. The driver ordered Rosa Parks and three other black passengers to stand so that the white passengers could have seats. Rosa Parks refused and was arrested. The black ministers in the community quickly organized in response to this incident, and on December 5 the Montgomery bus boycott began.

The bus boycott lasted for over a year and finally ended on December 21, 1956, when, after a Supreme Court decision against segregation on buses, the Montgomery transit system was officially integrated. King emerged from the struggle a national hero among dominated groups. In 1957 he organized the Southern Christian Leadership Conference (SCLC), which became the central organization in the civil rights struggle.

After SCLC was formed, boycotts and nonviolent demonstrations began to occur throughout the South. On May 17, 1957, Martin Luther King gave his first national address in Washington, D.C. He told his audience, "Give us the ballot and we will quietly, lawfully, and nonviolently, without rancor or bitterness, implement the May 17, 1954, decision of the Supreme Court." For King, meaningful school desegregation depended on the power of the black voter.

As civil rights demonstrations increased in intensity, national leaders began to work for federal legislation. In 1957 and 1960, two ineffective forms of civil rights legislation were passed by Congress. The most important civil rights legislation was not enacted until 1964, when violence in Birmingham, Alabama, and a mass march on Washington forced a response from the federal government. The civil rights movement made Birmingham and its director of safety, Eugene "Bull" Connor, symbols of the oppression of black people in the United States. President John F. Kennedy was quoted as saying, "Our judgment of Bull Connor should not be too harsh. After all, in his way, he has done a good deal for civil rights legislation this year."[6] The March on Washington symbolized to Congress and the American people the growing strength of the civil rights movement and provided the stage for television coverage of speeches by civil rights leaders.

The result of these activities was the Civil Rights Act of 1964. Under eleven different titles, the power of federal regulations was extended in the areas of voting rights, public accommodations, education, and employment. Titles IV and VI of the legislation were intended to end school segregation and provide authority for implementing the Brown decision.

Title VI, the most important section, establishes the precedent for using disbursement of government money as a means of controlling educational policies. Originally, President Kennedy merely proposed a requirement that institutions receiving federal funds must end discriminatory practices. In its final form, Title VI required mandatory withholding of federal funds to institutions that did not comply with its mandates. It states that no person, on the basis of race, color, or national origin, can be excluded from or denied the benefits of any program receiving federal financial assistance, and it requires all federal agencies to establish guidelines to implement this policy. Refusal by institutions or projects to follow these guidelines will result in the "termination of or refusal to grant or to continue assistance under such program or activity."

The power of Title VI rests in its ability to withhold federal money from financially pressed school systems. This became a more crucial issue after the passage in 1965 of the Elementary and Secondary Education Act. The rate of desegregation was more rapid after the 1964 Civil Rights Act than before, but abundant evidence by the end of the 1960s showed that segregated education continued in the South. One political scientist argued that school desegregation in the South by 1968 looked massive compared to the level in the early 1960s, but compared to an ideal of total integration, the actual results could be labeled as token. By defining a desegregated school as one that blacks attended and where more than 20 percent of the school population was white, a sample of 894 counties in the South found that 5 percent or less of the black pupils were attending integrated schools in 25 percent of the counties and 10 percent or less in 40 percent of the counties. At a level approaching genuine integration, in 20 percent of the counties 90 percent or more of the black pupils were reported to be attending integrated schools. For all southern counties, the median attending integrated schools was 15.6 percent.[7]

School desegregation moved at an even slower pace in the North. Originally it was believed that the Brown decision would affect only those states whose laws required segregated education. However, by the late 1960s, the courts began to rule that the Brown decision applied to all schools in the country, if it could be proved that segregation was the result of intentional actions by school boards or school administrators. ...

75

Joel Spring

MULTICULTURAL EDUCATION, IMMIGRATION, AND THE CULTURE WARS

The reform atmosphere of the great civil rights movement contributed to the passage of the 1965 Immigration Act that did away with the restrictive immigration quota system of the 1924 Immigration Act. The new wave of immigration to the United States occurred at the same time that Native Americans, Mexican Americans, Puerto Ricans, and African Americans were demanding a place for their cultures in the public school curriculum. As a result of these demands and the problems posed in educating a new wave of immigrants, some educators began to advocate the teaching about a variety of cultures—multiculturalism—in the public schools.

The multiculturalism movement renewed the culture wars. Opponents of multiculturalism argued that the public schools should emphasize a single culture—traditional Anglo-American culture. In contrast to the late nineteenth and early twentieth centuries, when immigrants from southern and eastern Europe were greeted with Americanization programs designed for deculturalization and the implanting of Anglo-American values, the new immigrants were swept up into the debate over multiculturalism initiated by the civil rights movement.

Influenced by the great civil rights movement, the 1965 Immigration Act eliminated the blatantly racist and ethnocentric aspects of the 1924 Immigration Act. The results of the Army Alpha and Beta examinations administered during World War I contributed to the belief in the superior intelligence of northern Europeans. Wanting to protect the existing racial composition of the United States, the 1924 Immigration Act established an annual quota for immigration from individual countries based on the percentage that national group comprised of the total U.S. population in 1920. The openly stated purpose of the legislation was to limit immigration of nonwhite populations. Immigration to the United States sharply declined after 1924. After passage of the 1965 Immigration Act, immigration rapidly increased and by 1980 the top five sources of immigration were Mexico, Vietnam, the Philippines, Korea, and China-Taiwan.[8]

By the 1990s, as a result of the civil rights movement and the new immigration, the debate about multicultural education ranged from concerns with empowering oppressed people to creating national unity by teaching common cultural values. Originally, leaders of the multicultural movement in the 1960s and 1980s, such as James Banks, Christine Sleeter, and Carl Grant, were concerned with empowering oppressed people by integrating the history and culture of dominated groups into public school curricula and textbooks. In general, they wanted to reduce prejudice, eliminate sexism, and equalize educational opportunities.[9]

It was argued that the integration of different histories and culture into the curriculum would empower members of dominated and oppressed immigrant cultures by providing an understanding of the methods of cultural domination and by helping to build self esteem. For instance, the study of African-American, Native American, Puerto Rican, and Mexican-American history would serve the dual purpose of building self esteem and empowerment. In addition, empowerment of women and people with disabilities would involve, in part, the inclusion of their histories and stories in textbooks and in the curriculum. . . .

The culture wars of the late twentieth century reflect the centuries-old effort to make English and Anglo-American Protestant culture the unifying language and culture of the United States. Originating in the sense of cultural superiority brought to North America by English colonists and emerging during cultural wars throughout U.S. history, the attempt to make Anglo-American culture the dominant culture of the United States was seriously challenged by the great civil rights movement and the new immigration.

NOTES

1. Arthur M. Schlesinger Jr., *The Disuniting of America* (Knoxville, TN: Whittle Direct Books, 1991), p. 8.

2. *Brown et al. v. Board of Education of Topeka et al.* (1954), reprinted in Albert P. Blaustein and Clarence C. Ferguson, Jr., *Desegregation and the Law* (New Brunswick, NJ: Rutgers University Press, 1957), pp. 273–282.

3. "The Effects of Segregation and the Consequences of Desegregation: A Social Science Statement," appendix to Appellants' Brief filed in the *School Segregation Cases* in the Supreme Court of the United States, October term, 1952, in John Bracey, August Meier, and Elliott Rudwick, eds., *The Afro-Americans: Selected Documents* (Boston: Allyn & Bacon, 1972), pp. 661–671.

4. Ibid.

5. Gunnar Myrdal, *An American Dilemma: The Negro Problem and Modern Democracy* (New York: Harper & Row, 1944), pp. lxxii–lxxiii.

6. Martin Luther King, Jr., *Stride Toward Freedom: The Montgomery Story* (New York: Harper & Row, 1958), p. 91.

7. Ibid., pp. 94–97.

8. David Reimers, *Still the Golden Door: The Third World Comes to America* (New York: Columbia University Press, 1985).

9. See James Banks, "Multicultural Education: Historical Development, Dimensions, and Practice," *Review of Research in Education 19,* edited by Linda Darling-Hammond (Washington, D.C.: American Educational Research Association, 1993), pp. 3–50; and Sonia Nieto, *Affirming Diversity: The Sociopolitical Context of Multicultural Education* (White Plains, NY: Longman Inc., 1992).

3.2 HENRY A. GIROUX

Culture, Power and Transformation in the Work of Paulo Freire

Henry A. Giroux, a scholar in critical theory of education, is considered one of the most important writers on critical pedagogy. Formerly a professor at Miami University in Oxford, Ohio, he presently holds an endowed professorial chair at Pennsylvania State University in University Park, Pennsylvania. His many publications, including *Theory and Resistance: A Pedagogy for the Opposition* (Bergin & Garvey, 1983), have been widely read and cited. Among his most recent books are *Border Crossings* (Routledge, 1992) and *Living Dangerously* (Peter Lang, 1993). He is also coeditor, with Paulo Freire, of the Critical Studies in Education series (Bergin & Garvey).

In the selection that follows, which is from *Teachers as Intellectuals: Toward a Critical Pedagogy of Learning* (Bergin & Garvey, 1988), Professor Giroux discusses the ideas of culture, power, and transformation in the work of educator Paulo Freire. He points out that Freire sees education as an empowering force for people, that education necessarily addresses a kind of cultural politics. Giroux agrees with Freire that cultural politics is a broader concept than any particular political doctrine. Giroux concludes that the liberation of persons through education must necessarily involve critical engagement with and evaluation of the dominant cultural and political forces in any society.

Key Concept: education and cultural politics

Paulo Freire's work continues to represent a theoretically refreshing and politically viable alternative to the current impasse in educational theory and practice in North America. Freire has appropriated the unclaimed heritage of emancipatory ideas in those versions of secular and religious philosophy located within the corpus of bourgeois thought. He has also critically integrated into his work a heritage of radical thought without assimilating many of the problems that have plagued it historically. In effect, Freire combines what I have called the "language of critique" with the "language of possibility."

Utilizing the language of critique, Freire has fashioned a theory of education that takes seriously the relationship between radical critical theory and the imperatives of radical commitment and struggle. Drawing upon his experiences in Latin America, Africa, and North America, he has generated a discourse that deepens our understanding of the dynamics and complexity of domination. In this instance, Freire rightly argues that domination cannot be reduced exclusively to a form of class domination. With the notion of difference as a guiding theoretical thread, Freire rejects the idea that there is a universalized form of oppression. Instead, he acknowledges and locates within different social fields forms of suffering that speak to particular modes of domination and, consequently, diverse forms of collective struggle and resistance. By recognizing that certain forms of oppression are not reducible to class oppression, Freire steps outside standard Marxist Analyses; he argues that society contains a multiplicity of contradictory social relations, over which social groups can struggle and organize themselves. This is manifest in those social relations in which the ideological and material conditions of gender, racial, and age discrimination are at work.

Equally important is the insight that domination is more than the simple imposition of arbitrary power by one group over another. Instead, for Freire, the logic of domination represents a combination of historical and contemporary ideological and material practices that are never completely successful, always embody contradictions, and are constantly being fought over within asymmetrical relations of power. Underlying Freire's language of critique, in this case, is the insight that history is never foreclosed. Just as the actions of men and women are limited by the specific constraints in which they find themselves, they also make those constraints and the possibilities that may follow from challenging them.

Within this theoretical juncture Freire introduces a new dimension to radical educational theory and practice. I say new because he links the process of struggle to the particularities of people's lives while simultaneously arguing for a faith in the power of the oppressed to struggle in the interests of their own liberation. This is a notion of education fashioned in more than critique and Orwellian pessimism; it is a discourse that creates a new starting point by trying to make hope realizable and despair unconvincing.

Education in Freire's view becomes both an ideal and a referent for change in the service of a new kind of society. As an ideal, education "speaks" to a form of cultural politics that transcends the theoretical boundaries of any one specific political doctrine, while simultaneously linking social theory and practice to the deepest aspects of emancipation. Thus, as an expression of radical social theory, Freire's cultural politics is broader and more fundamental than any one specific political discourse such as classical Marxist theory, a point that often confuses his critics. In fact, his represents a theoretical discourse whose underlying interests are fashioned around a struggle against all forms of subjective and objective domination as well as a struggle for forms of knowledge, skills, and social relations that provide the conditions for social and, hence, self-emancipation.

As a referent for change, education represents both a site and a particular type of engagement with the dominant society. For Freire, education includes and moves beyond the notion of schooling. Schools are only one important site where education takes place, where men and women both produce and are the product of specific social and pedagogical relations. Education represents, in Freire's view, both a struggle for meaning and a struggle over power relations. Its dynamic springs from the dialectical relation between individuals and groups who live out their lives within specific historical conditions and structural constraints, on the one hand, and those cultural forms and ideologies that give rise to the contradictions and struggles that define the lived realities of various societies on the other. Education is that terrain where power and politics are given a fundamental expression, where the production of meaning, desire, language, and values engage and respond to the deeper beliefs about what it means to be human, to dream, and to name and struggle for a particular future and form of social life. Education becomes a form of action that joins the languages of critique and possibility. It represents, finally, the need for a passionate commitment by educators to make the political more pedagogical, that is, to make critical reflection and action fundamental parts of a social project that not only engages forms of oppression but develops a deep and abiding faith in the struggle to humanize life itself. It is the particular nature of this social project that gives Freire's work its theoretical distinctiveness.

The theoretical distinctiveness of Freire's work can best be understood by examining briefly how his discourse stands between two radical traditions. On the one hand, the language of critique as it is expressed in Freire's work embodies many of the analyses that characterize what has been called the new sociology of education. On the other hand, Freire's philosophy of hope and struggle is rooted in a language of possibility that draws extensively from the tradition of liberation theology. It is from the merging of these two traditions that Freire has produced a discourse that not only gives meaning and theoretical coherence to his work, but also provides the basis for a more comprehensive and critical theory of pedagogical struggle.

THE NEW SOCIOLOGY OF EDUCATION AND THE LANGUAGE OF CRITIQUE

The new sociology of education emerged in full strength in England and the United States over a decade ago as a critical response to what can be loosely termed the discourse of traditional educational theory and practice. The central question, against which it developed its criticism of traditional schooling as well as its own theoretical discourse, is typically Freirean: How does one make education meaningful so as to make it critical and, one hopes, emancipatory.

Radical critics, for the most part, agree that educational traditionalists generally ignore the question. They elude the issue through the paradoxical depoliticizing [of] the language of schooling while reproducing and legitimating capitalist ideologies. The most obvious expression of this approach can be seen in the positivist discourse used by traditional educational theorists. A positivist discourse, in this case, takes as its most important concerns the mastery of pedagogical techniques and the transmission of knowledge instrumental to the existing society. In the traditional world view, schools are merely instructional sites.

Critical educational theorists argue that traditional educational theory suppresses important questions regarding knowledge, power, and domination. Furthermore, schools do not provide opportunities in the broad western humanist tradition for self- and social empowerment in the society at large. In contrast, critical educators provide theoretical arguments and enormous amounts of empirical evidence to suggest that schools are in fact, agencies of social, economic and cultural reproduction. At best, public schooling offers limited individual mobility to members of the working class and other oppressed groups, but, in the final analysis, public schools are powerful instruments for the reproduction of capitalist relations of production and the legitimating ideologies of everyday life.

For the new sociology of education, schools are analyzed primarily within the language of critique and domination. Yet, since schools are viewed primarily as reproductive in nature, left critics fail to provide a programmatic discourse through which the opportunity for counterhegemonic practices could be established. The agony of the left in this case is that its language of critique offered no hope for teachers, parents, or students to wage a political struggle within the schools themselves. Consequently, the language of critique is subsumed within the discourse of despair.

Freire's earlier work shares a remarkable similarity with some of the major theoretical tenets found in the new sociology of education. By redefining and politicizing the notion of literacy, Freire develops a similar type of critical analysis in which he claims that traditional forms of education function primarily to objectify and alienate oppressed groups. Moreover, Freire explores in great depth the reproductive nature of dominant culture and systematically analyzed how it functions through specific social practices and texts to produce and maintain a "culture of silence" among the Brazilian peasants with whom he worked. Though Freire does not use the term "hidden curriculum" as part of his discourse, he demonstrates pedagogical approaches through which groups of learners can decode ideological and material practices whose form, content, and selective omissions contain the logic of domination and oppression. In addition, Freire links the selection, discussion, and evaluation of knowledge to the pedagogical processes that provide a context for such activity. In his view, it is impossible to separate one from the other, and any viable pedagogical practice has to link radical forms of knowledge with corresponding radical social practices.

The major difference between Freire's work and the new sociology of education is that the latter appears to start and end with the logic of political, economic, and cultural reproduction, whereas Freire's analysis begins with the process of production, that is, the various ways human beings construct their own voices and validate their contradictory experiences within specific historical settings and constraints. The reproduction of capitalist rationality and other forms of oppression is only one political and theoretical moment in the process of domination, rather than an all-encompassing aspect of human existence. It is something to be decoded, challenged, and transformed but only within the on-going discourse, experiences, and histories of the oppressed themselves. It is in this shift from the discourse of reproduction and critique to the language of possibility and engagement that Freire draws from other traditions and fashions a more comprehensive and radical pedagogy.

LIBERATION THEOLOGY AND THE LANGUAGE OF POSSIBILITY

Central to Freire's politics and pedagogy is a philosophical vision of a liberated humanity. The nature of this vision is rooted in a respect for life. The hope and vision of the future that it inspires are not meant to provide consolation for the oppressed as much as to promote ongoing forms of critique and a struggle against objective forces of oppression. By combining the dynamics of critique and collective struggle with a philosophy of hope, Freire has created a language of possibility, what he calls a permanent prophetic vision. Underlying this prophetic vision is a faith, which Dorothée Soelle argues in *Choosing Life*, "makes life present to us and so makes it possible.... It is a great 'Yes' to life ... [one that] presupposes our power to struggle."

Freire's opposition to all forms of oppression, his call to link ideology critique with collective action, and the prophetic vision central to his politics are heavily indebted to the spirit and ideological dynamics that have both informed and characterized the Liberation Theology Movement that has emerged primarily out of Latin America in the last decade. In truly dialectical fashion, Freire has both criticized and rescued the radical underside of revolutionary Christianity. As the reader will discover, Freire is a harsh critic of the reactionary church. At the same time, he situates his faith and sense of hope in the God of history and the oppressed whose teachings make it impossible, in Freire's words, to "reconcile Christian love with the exploitation of human beings."

Within the discourse of liberation theology, Freire fashions a powerful antidote to the cynicism and despair of many left radical critics. Though utopian, his analysis is concrete in its nature and appeal, taking as its starting point collective actors in their various historical settings and the particularity of their problems and forms of oppression. It is utopian only in its refusal to surrender to the risks and dangers that face all challenges to dominant power structures. It is prophetic in that it views the Kingdom of God as something to be created on earth but only through a faith in both other human beings and the necessity of permanent struggle. The notion of faith that emerges in Freire's work is informed by the memory of the oppressed, the suffering that must not be allowed to continue, and the need never to forget that the prophetic vision is an ongoing process, a vital aspect of the very nature of human life. By combining the discourses of critique and possibility Freire joins history and theology so as to provide the theoretical basis for a radical pedagogy that expresses hope, critical reflection, and collective struggle.

It is at this juncture that the work of Paulo Freire becomes crucial to the development of a radical pedagogy. For in Freire we find the dialectician of contradictions and emancipation. His discourse bridges the relationship between agency and structure, situates human action in constraints forged in historical and contemporary practices, while simultaneously pointing to the spaces, contradictions, and forms of resistance that raise the possibility for social struggle. I will conclude by turning briefly to those theoretical elements in Freire's work that seem vital to developing a new language and theoretical foundation for a radical theory of pedagogy, particularly in a North American context.

Two qualifications must be made before I begin. First, Freire's mode of analysis cannot be dismissed as irrelevant to a North American context. Although critics have argued that his experiences with Brazilian peasants do not translate adequately for educators in the advanced industrial countries of the West, Freire makes it clear through the force of his examples and the variety of pedagogical experiences he provides that the context for his work is international in scope. Not only does he capitalize on his experiences in Brazil, he also draws on his work in Chile, Africa, and the United States. Furthermore, he not only takes as the object of his criticism adult education, but also the pedagogical practices of the Catholic Church, social workers, and public education. As he has pointed out repeatedly, the object of his analysis and the language he uses is for the oppressed everywhere; his concept of the Third World is ideological and political rather than merely geographic.

This leads to the second qualification. In order to be true to the spirit of Freire's most profound pedagogical beliefs, it must be stated that he would never argue that his work is meant to be adopted unproblematically to any site or pedagogical context. What Freire does provide is a metalanguage that generates a set of categories and social practices. Freire's work is not meant to offer radical recipes for instant forms of critical pedagogy; it is a series of theoretical signposts that need to be decoded and critically appropriated within the specific contexts in which they might be useful.

THE DISCOURSE OF POWER

Power, for Freire, [is] both a negative and a positive force, its character is dialectical, and its mode of operation is always more than simply repressive. Power works on and through people. Domination is never so complete that power is experienced exclusively as a negative force, yet power is at the basis of all forms of behavior in which people resist, struggle, and fight for a better world. In a general sense, Freire's theory of power and his demonstration of its dialectical character serve the important function of broadening the spheres and terrains on which power operates. Power, in this instance, is not exhausted in those public and private spheres by governments, ruling classes, and other dominant groups. It is more ubiquitous and is expressed in a range of oppositional public spaces and spheres that traditionally have been characterized by the *absence* of power and thus any form of resistance.

Freire's view of power suggests not only an alternative perspective to those radical theorists trapped in the straitjacket of despair and cynicism, it also stresses that there are always cracks, tensions, and contradictions in various social spheres such as schools where power can be exercised as a positive force in the name of resistance. Furthermore, Freire understands that power—domination—is not simply imposed by the state through agencies such as the police, the army, and the courts. Domination is also expressed in the way in which power, technology, and ideology come together to produce knowledge, social relations, and other concrete cultural forms that indirectly silence people. It is also found in the way in which the oppressed internalize and thus participate in their own oppression. This is an important point in Freire's work and directs us to the ways in which domination is subjectively experienced through its internalization and sedimentation in the very needs of the personality. What is at work here is an important attempt to examine the psychically repressive aspects of domination and the internal obstacles to self-knowledge and, thus, to forms of social and self emancipation.

Freire broadens the notion of learning to include how the body learns tacitly, how habit translates into sedimented history, and, most importantly, how knowledge itself may block the development of certain subjectivities and ways of experiencing the world. Ironically, emancipatory forms of knowledge may be refused by those who could most benefit from such knowledge. In this case, accommodation to the logic domination by the oppressed may take the form of actively resisting forms of knowledge that pose a challenge to their world view. Rather than a passive acceptance of domination, knowledge becomes instead an active dynamic of negation, an active refusal to listen, to hear, or to affirm one's own possibilities. The pedagogical questions that emerge from this view of domination are: How do radical educators assess and address the elements of repression and forgetting at the heart of this domination? What accounts for the conditions that sustain an active refusal to know or to learn in the face of knowledge that may challenge the nature of domination itself?

The message that emerges from Freire's pedagogy is relatively clear. If radical educators are to understand the meaning of liberation, they must first be aware of the form that domination takes, the nature of its location, and the problems it poses to those who experience it as both a subjective and objective force. But such a project would be impossible unless one took the historical and cultural particularities, the forms of social life, of subordinate and oppressed groups as a starting point for such an analysis. It is to this issue in Freire's work that I now turn.

FREIRE'S PHILOSOPHY OF EXPERIENCE AND CULTURAL PRODUCTION

One of the most important theoretical elements for a radical pedagogy that Freire provides is his view of experience and cultural production. Freire's notion of culture is at odds with both conservative and progressive positions. In the first instance, he rejects the notion that culture can be divided easily into high, popular, and low forms, with high culture representing the most advanced heritage of a nation. Culture, in this view, hides the ideologies that legitimate and distribute specific forms of culture as if they were unrelated to ruling class interests and existing configurations of power. In the second instance, he rejects the notion that the moment of cultural creation rests solely with ruling groups and that dominant cultural forms harbor merely the seeds of domination. Related to this position, and also rejected by Freire, is the assumption that oppressed groups possess by their very location in the apparatus of domination a progressive and revolutionary culture waiting only to be released from the fetters of ruling class domination.

For Freire, culture is the representation of lived experiences, material artifacts, and practices forged within the unequal and dialectical relations that different groups establish in a given society at a particular historical point. Culture is a form of production whose processes are intimately connected with the structuring of different social formations, particularly those that are gender, age, racial, and class related. It is also a form of production that helps human agents, through their use of language and other material resources, to transform society. In this case, culture is closely related to the dynamics of power and produces asymmetries in the ability of individuals and groups to define and achieve their goals. Furthermore, culture is also an arena of struggle and contradiction, and there is no one culture in the homogeneous sense. On the contrary, there are dominant and subordinate cultures that express different interests and operate from different and unequal terrains of power.

Freire argues for a notion of cultural power that takes as its starting point the social and historical particularities that constitute the problems, sufferings, visions, and acts of resistance that comprise the cultural forms of subordinate groups. Cultural power then has a dual focus as part of his strategy to make the political more pedagogical. First, educators will have to work with the experiences that students bring to schools and other educational sites. This means making these experiences, public and private, the object of debate and confirmation; it means legitimating such experiences in order to give those who live and move within them a sense of affirmation and to provide the conditions for students and others to display an active voice and presence. The pedagogical experience here becomes an invitation to make visible the languages, dreams, values, and encounters that constitute the lives of those whose histories are often actively silenced. But Freire does more than argue for the legitimation of the culture of the oppressed. He also recognizes that such experiences are contradictory in nature and harbor not only radical potentialities but also the sedimentations of domination. Cultural power takes a twist in this instance and refers to the need to *work on* the experiences that make up the lives of the oppressed. Such experiences in their varied cultural forms have to be recovered critically so as to reveal both their strengths and weaknesses. Moreover, self-critique is complimented in the name of a radical pedagogy designed to unearth and critically appropriate those unclaimed emancipatory moments in bourgeois knowledge and experience that further provide the skills the oppressed will need to exercise leadership in the dominant society.

What is striking in this presentation is that Freire has fashioned a theory of cultural power and production that begins with popular education. Instead of offering abstract generalities about human nature, he rightly argues for pedagogical principles that arise from the concrete practices—the terrains on which people live out their everyday experiences. All of this suggests taking seriously the cultural capital of the oppressed, developing critical and analytical tools to interrogate it, and staying in touch with dominant definitions of knowledge so we can analyze them for their usefulness and for the ways in which they bear the logic of domination.

FREIRE, TRANSFORMATIVE INTELLECTUALS, AND THE THEORY-PRACTICE RELATIONSHIP

Radical social theory has been plagued historically by the development of the relationship between intellectuals and the masses, on the one hand, and the relationship between theory and practice. Under the call for the unity of theory and practice, the possibility for emancipatory practice has often been negated through forms of vanguardism in which intellectuals effectively removed from the popular forces the ability to define for themselves the limits of their aims and practice. By assuming a virtual monopoly in the exercise of theoretical leadership, intellectuals unknowingly reproduced the division of mental and manual labor that was at the core of most forms of domination. Instead of developing theories of practice, which were rooted in the concrete experience of listening and learning with the oppressed, Marxist intellectuals developed theories for practice or technical instruments for change that ignored the necessity for a dialectical reflection on the everyday dynamics and problems of the oppressed within the context of radical social transformation.

Freire refutes this approach to the theory-practice relationship and redefines the very idea of the intellectual. Like the Italian social theorist, Antonio Gramsci, Freire redefines the category of intellectual and argues that all men and women are intellectuals. That is, regardless of social and economic function all human beings perform as intellectuals by constantly interpreting and giving meaning to the world and by participating in a particular conception of the world. Moreover, the oppressed need to develop their own organic and transformative intellectuals who can learn with such groups while simultaneously helping to foster modes of self-education and struggle against various forms of oppression. In this case, intellectuals are organic in that they are *not* outsiders bringing theory to the masses. On the contrary, they are theorists fused organically with the culture and practical activities of the oppressed. Rather than casually dispense knowledge to the grateful masses, intellectuals fuse with the oppressed in order to make and remake the conditions necessary for a radical social project.

This position is crucial in highlighting the political function and importance of intellectuals. Equally significant is the way it redefines the notion of political struggle by emphasizing its pedagogical nature and the centrality of the popular and democratic nature of such a struggle. This raises the important question of how Freire defines the relation between theory and practice.

For Freire, "there is no theoretic context if it is not in a dialectical unity with the concrete context." Rather than call for the collapse of theory into practice, Freire argues for a certain distance between theory and practice. He views theory as anticipatory in its nature and posits that it must take the concepts of understanding and possibility as its central moments. Theory is informed by an oppositional discourse that preserves its critical distance from the "facts" and experiences of the given society. The tension, indeed, the conflict with practice belongs to the essence of theory and is grounded in its very structure. Theory does not dictate practice; rather, it serves to hold practice at arm's length so as to mediate and critically comprehend the type of praxis needed within a specific setting at a particular time. There is no appeal to universal laws or historical necessity here; theory emerges within specific contexts and forms of experience in order to examine such contexts critically and then to intervene on the basis of an informed praxis.

But Freire's contribution to the nature of theory and practice and the role of the intellectual in the process of social transformation contains another important dimension. Theory must be seen as the production of forms of discourse that arise from various specific social sites. Such a discourse may arise from the universities, from peasant communities, from workers' councils, or from within various social movements. The issue here is that radical educators recognize that these different sites give rise to various forms of theoretical production and practice. Each of these sites provides diverse and critical insights into the nature of domination and the possibilities for social and self-emancipation, and they do so from the historical and social particularities that give them meaning. What brings them together is a mutual respect forged in criticism and the need to struggle against all forms of domination.

3.3 PAULO FREIRE

Pedagogy of the Oppressed

Paulo Freire's philosophy of education was based on his belief in human liberation through the use of critical consciousness and dialogical methods of interaction between persons. He rejected traditional authoritarian "banking" conceptions of teaching, in which teachers "deposit" official knowledge in students' minds. He favored instead a "problem-posing" approach to teaching, in which teachers and students enter into a genuine dialogue devoted to developing their own visions of the world through the free exercise of their own voices. For Freire, education is "the practice of freedom." In the following selection, which is from the revised, twentieth-anniversary edition of *Pedagogy of the Oppressed* (Continuum, 1993), Freire critiques the "banking" method of teaching and promotes "problem-posing" approaches to the educational process.

Freire (1921–1997) was an educator of worldwide stature. In 1964, when *Pedagogy of the Oppressed* was first published in Brazil, the military government "invited" him to leave the nation. He first went to Chile and then to the United States, where he spent several years. The first English translation of *Pedagogy* appeared in 1970. Since that time it has become a modern classic. When a democratic government was elected in Brazil, Freire returned to his homeland. There he served as minister of education of the state of São Paulo, after which he moved back to the United States to work as a professor in the Harvard Graduate School of Education. He returned to teaching in Brazil, where he remained until his death.

Freire's many publications include *Letters to Cristina: Reflections on My Life and Work* (Routledge, 1996); *Pedagogy in Process: The Letters to Guinea-Bissau* (Seabury Press, 1978); *Cultural Action for Freedom* (Harvard Education Review Monograph No. 1, 1975 and 1983); *Education for Critical Consciousness* (Seabury Press, 1973); *Literacy: Reading the Word and the World*, coauthored with Donaldo Macedo (Bergin & Garvey, 1987); *Pedagogy of Hope: Reliving Pedagogy of the Oppressed* (Continuum, 1994); *A Pedagogy for Liberation: Dialogues on Transforming Education*, coauthored with Ira Shor (Bergin & Garvey, 1987); and *The Politics of Education: Culture, Power, and Liberation* (Bergin & Garvey, 1985).

Key Concept: education as the practice of freedom

A careful analysis of the teacher-student relationship at any level, inside or outside the school, reveals its fundamentally *narrative* character. This relationship involves a narrating Subject (the teacher) and patient, listening objects (the students). The contents, whether values or empirical dimensions of reality, tend in the process of being narrated to become lifeless and petrified. Education is suffering from narration sickness.

The teacher talks about reality as if it were motionless, static, compartmentalized, and predictable. Or else he expounds on a topic completely alien to the existential experience of the students. His task is to "fill" the students with the contents of his narration—contents which are detached from reality, disconnected from the totality that engendered them and could give them significance. Words are emptied of their concreteness and become a hollow, alienated, and alienating verbosity.

The outstanding characteristic of this narrative education, then, is the sonority of words, not their transforming power. "Four times four is sixteen; the capital of Pará is Belém." The student records, memorizes, and repeats these phrases without perceiving what four times four really means, or realizing the true significance of "capital" in the affirmation "the capital of Pará is Belém," that is, what Belém means for Pará and what Pará means for Brazil.

Narration (with the teacher as narrator) leads the students to memorize mechanically the narrated content. Worse yet, it turns them into "containers," into "receptacles" to be "filled" by the teacher. The more completely she fills the receptacles, the better a teacher she is. The more meekly the receptacles permit themselves to be filled, the better students they are.

Education thus becomes an act of depositing, in which the students are the depositories and the teacher is the depositor. Instead of communicating, the teacher issues communiqués and makes deposits which the students patiently receive, memorize, and repeat. This is the "banking" concept of education, in which the scope of action allowed to the students extends only as far as receiving, filing, and storing the deposits. They do, it is true, have the opportunity to become collectors or cataloguers of the things they store. But in the last analysis, it is the people themselves who are filed away through the lack of creativity, transformation, and knowledge in this (at best) misguided system. For apart from inquiry, apart from the praxis, individuals cannot be truly human. Knowledge emerges only through invention and re-invention, through the restless, impatient, continuing, hopeful inquiry human beings pursue in the world, with the world, and with each other.

In the banking concept of education, knowledge is a gift bestowed by those who consider themselves knowledgeable upon those whom they consider to know nothing. Projecting an absolute ignorance onto others, a characteristic of the ideology of oppression, negates education and knowledge as processes of inquiry. The teacher presents himself to his students as their necessary opposite; by considering their ignorance absolute, he justifies his own existence. The students, alienated like the slave in the Hegelian dialectic, accept their ignorance as justifying the teacher's existence—but, unlike the slave, they never discover that they educate the teacher.

The *raison d'être* of libertarian education, on the other hand, lies in its drive towards reconciliation. Education must begin with the solution of the teacher-student contradiction, by reconciling the poles of the contradiction so that both are simultaneously teachers *and* students.

This solution is not (nor can it be) found in the banking concept. On the contrary, banking education maintains and even stimulates the contradiction through the following attitudes and practices, which mirror oppressive society as a whole:

1. the teacher teaches and the students are taught;
2. the teacher knows everything and the students know nothing;
3. the teacher thinks and the students are thought about;
4. the teacher talks and the students listen—meekly;
5. the teacher disciplines and the students are disciplined;
6. the teacher chooses and enforces his choice, and the students comply;
7. the teacher acts and the students have the illusion of acting through the action of the teacher;
8. the teacher chooses the program content, and the students (who were not consulted) adapt to it;
9. the teacher confuses the authority of knowledge with his or her own professional authority, which she and he sets in opposition to the freedom of the students;
10. the teacher is the Subject of the learning process, while the pupils are mere objects.

It is not surprising that the banking concept of education regards men as adaptable, manageable beings. The more students work at storing the deposits entrusted to them, the less they develop the critical consciousness which would result from their intervention in the world as transformers of that world. The more completely they accept the passive role imposed on them, the more they tend simply to adapt to the world as it is and to the fragmented view of reality deposited in them.

The capability of banking education to minimize or annul the students' creative power and to stimulate their credulity serves the interests of the oppressors, who care neither to have the world revealed nor to see it transformed. The oppressors use their "humanitarianism" to preserve a profitable situation. Thus they react almost instinctively against any experiment in education which stimulates the critical faculties and is not content with a partial view of reality but always seeks out the ties which link one point to another and one problem to another.

Indeed, the interests of the oppressors lie in "changing the consciousness of the oppressed, not the situation which oppresses them";[1] for the more the oppressed can be led to adapt to that situation, the more easily they can be dominated. To achieve this end, the oppressors use the banking concept of education in conjunction with a paternalistic social action apparatus, within which the oppressed receive the euphemistic title of "welfare recipients." They are treated as individual cases, as marginal persons who deviate from the general configuration of a "good, organized, and just" society. The oppressed are regarded as the pathology of the healthy society, which must therefore adjust these "incompetent and lazy" folk to its own patterns by changing their mentality. These marginals need to be "integrated," "incorporated" into the healthy society that they have "forsaken."

The truth is, however, that the oppressed are not "marginals," are not people living "outside" society. They have always been "inside"—inside the structure which made them "beings for others." The solution is not to "integrate" them into the structure of oppression, but to transform that structure so that they can become "beings for themselves." Such transformation, of course, would undermine the oppressors' purposes; hence their utilization of the banking concept of education to avoid the threat of student *conscientização*.

The banking approach to adult education, for example, will never propose to students that they critically consider reality. It will deal instead with such vital questions as whether Roger gave green grass to the goat, and insist upon the importance of learning that, on the contrary, Roger gave green grass to the *rabbit*. The "humanism" of the banking approach masks the effort to turn women and men into automatons—the very negation of their ontological vocation to be more fully human.

Those who use the banking approach, knowingly or unknowingly (for there are innumerable well-intentioned bank-clerk teachers who do not realize that they are serving only to dehumanize), fail to perceive that the deposits themselves contain contradictions about reality. But, sooner or later, these contradictions may lead formerly passive students to turn against their domestication and the attempt to domesticate reality. They may discover through existential experience that their present way of life is irreconcilable with their vocation to become fully human. They may perceive through their relations with reality that reality is really a *process*, undergoing constant transformation. If men and women are searchers and their ontological vocation is humanization, sooner or later they may perceive the contradiction in which banking education seeks to maintain them, and then engage themselves in the struggle for their liberation.

But the humanist, revolutionary educator cannot wait for this possibility to materialize. From the outset, her efforts must coincide with those of the students to engage in critical thinking and the quest for mutual humanization. His efforts must be imbued with a profound trust in people and their creative power. To achieve this, they must be partners of the students in their relations with them.

The banking concept does not admit to such partnership—and necessarily so. To resolve the teacher-student contradiction, to exchange the role of depositor, prescriber, domesticator, for the role of student among students would be to undermine the power of oppression and serve the cause of liberation.

Implicit in the banking concept is the assumption of a dichotomy between human beings and the world: a person is merely *in* the world, not *with* the world or with others; the individual is spectator, not re-creator. In this view, the person is not a conscious being *(corpo consciente);* he or she is rather the possessor of *a* consciousness: an empty "mind" passively open to the reception of deposits of reality from the world outside. For example, my desk, my books, my coffee cup, all the objects before me—as bits of the world which surround me—would be "inside" me, exactly as I am inside my study right now. This view makes no distinction between being accessible to consciousness and entering consciousness. The distinction, however, is essential: the objects which surround me are simply accessible to my consciousness, not located within it. I am aware of them, but they are not inside me.

It follows logically from the banking notion of consciousness that the educator's role is to regulate the way the world "enters into" the students. The teacher's task is to organize a process which already occurs spontaneously, to "fill" the students by making deposits of information which he or she considers to constitute true knowledge.[2] And since people "receive" the world as passive entities, education should make them more passive still, and adapt them to the world. The educated individual is the adapted person, because she or he is better "fit" for the world. Translated into practice, this concept is well suited to the purposes of the oppressors, whose tranquility rests on how well people fit the world the oppressors have created, and how little they question it.

The more completely the majority adapt to the purposes which the dominant minority prescribe for them (thereby depriving them of the right to their own purposes), the more easily the minority can continue to prescribe. The theory and practice of banking education serve this end quite efficiently. Verbalistic lessons, reading requirements,[3] the methods for evaluating "knowledge," the distance between the teacher and the taught, the criteria for promotion: everything in this ready-to-wear approach serves to obviate thinking.

The bank-clerk educator does not realize that there is no true security in his hypertrophied role, that one must seek to live *with* others in solidarity. One cannot impose oneself, nor even merely co-exist with one's students. Solidarity requires true communication, and the concept by which such an educator is guided fears and proscribes communication.

Yet only through communication can human life hold meaning. The teacher's thinking is authenticated only by the authenticity of the students' thinking. The teacher cannot think for her students, nor can she impose her thought on them. Authentic thinking, thinking that is concerned about *reality*, does not take place in ivory tower isolation, but only in communication. If it is true that thought has meaning only when generated by action upon the world, the subordination of students to teachers becomes impossible.

Because banking education begins with a false understanding of men and women as objects, it cannot promote the development of what Fromm calls "biophily," but instead produces its opposite: "necrophily."

> While life is characterized by growth in a structured, functional manner, the necrophilous person loves all that does not grow, all that is mechanical. The necrophilous person is driven by the desire to transform the organic into the inorganic, to approach life mechanically, as if all living persons were things.... Memory, rather than experience; having, rather than being, is what counts. The necrophilous person can relate to an object—a flower or a person—only if he possesses it; hence a threat to his possession is a threat to himself; if he loses possession he loses contact with the world.... He loves control, and in the act of controlling he kills life.[4]

Oppression—overwhelming control—is necrophilic; it is nourished by love of death, not life. The banking concept of education, which serves the interests of oppression, is also necrophilic. Based on a mechanistic, static, naturalistic, spatialized view of consciousness, it transforms students into receiving objects. It attempts to control thinking and action, leads women and men to adjust to the world, and inhibits their creative power.

When their efforts to act responsibly are frustrated, when they find themselves unable to use their faculties, people suffer. "This suffering due to impotence is rooted in the very fact that the human equilibrium has been disturbed."[5] But the inability to act which causes people's anguish also causes them to reject their impotence, by attempting

> ... to restore [their] capacity to act. But can [they], and how? One way is to submit to and identify with a person or group having power. By this symbolic partici-pation in another person's life, [men have] the illusion of acting, when in reality [they] only submit to and become a part of those who act.[6]

Populist manifestations perhaps best exemplify this type of behavior by the oppressed, who, by identifying with charismatic leaders, come to feel that they themselves are active and effective. The rebellion they express as they emerge in the historical process is motivated by that desire to act effectively. The dominant elites consider the remedy to be more domination and repres-sion, carried out in the name of freedom, order, and social peace (that is, the peace of the elites). Thus they can condemn—logically, from their point of view —"the violence of a strike by workers and [can] call upon the state in the same breath to use violence in putting down the strike."[7]

Education as the exercise of domination stimulates the credulity of stu-dents, with the ideological intent (often not perceived by educators) of indoctri-nating them to adapt to the world of oppression. This accusation is not made in the naïve hope that the dominant elites will thereby simply abandon the prac-tice. Its objective is to call the attention of true humanists to the fact that they cannot use banking educational methods in the pursuit of liberation, for they would only negate that very pursuit. Nor may a revolutionary society inherit these methods from an oppressor society. The revolutionary society which prac-tices banking education is either misguided or mistrusting of people. In either event, it is threatened by the specter of reaction.

Unfortunately, those who espouse the cause of liberation are themselves surrounded and influenced by the climate which generates the banking con-cept, and often do not perceive its true significance or its dehumanizing power. Paradoxically, then, they utilize this same instrument of alienation in what they consider an effort to liberate. Indeed, some "revolutionaries" brand as "inno-cents," "dreamers," or even "reactionaries" those who would challenge this educational practice. But one does not liberate people by alienating them. Au-thentic liberation—the process of humanization—is not another deposit to be made in men. Liberation is a praxis: the action and reflection of men and women upon their world in order to transform it. Those truly committed to the cause of liberation can accept neither the mechanistic concept of consciousness as an empty vessel to be filled, nor the use of banking methods of domination (propaganda, slogans—deposits) in the name of liberation.

Those truly committed to liberation must reject the banking concept in its entirety, adopting instead a concept of women and men as conscious beings, and consciousness as consciousness intent upon the world. They must abandon the educational goal of deposit-making and replace it with the posing of the problems of human beings in their relations with the world. "Problem-posing" education, responding to the essence of consciousness—*intentionality*—rejects communiqués and embodies communication. It epitomizes the special characteristic of consciousness: being *conscious of*, not only as intent on objects but as turned in upon itself in a Jasperian "split"—consciousness as consciousness *of* consciousness.

Liberating education consists in acts of cognition, not transferrals of information. It is a learning situation in which the cognizable object (far from being the end of the cognitive act) intermediates the cognitive actors—teacher on the one hand and students on the other. Accordingly, the practice of problem-posing education entails at the outset that the teacher-student contradiction be resolved. Dialogical relations—indispensable to the capacity of cognitive actors to cooperate in perceiving the same cognizable object—are otherwise impossible.

Indeed, problem-posing education, which breaks with the vertical patterns characteristic of banking education, can fulfill its function as the practice of freedom only if it can overcome the above contradiction. Through dialogue, the teacher-of-the-students and the students-of-the-teacher cease to exist and a new term emerges: teacher-student with students-teachers. The teacher is no longer merely the-one-who-teaches, but one who is himself taught in dialogue with the students, who in turn while being taught also teach. They become jointly responsible for a process in which all grow. In this process, arguments based on "authority" are no longer valid; in order to function, authority must be *on the side of* freedom, not *against* it. Here, no one teaches another, nor is anyone self-taught. People teach each other, mediated by the world, by the cognizable objects which in banking education are "owned" by the teacher.

The banking concept (with its tendency to dichotomize everything) distinguishes two stages in the action of the educator. During the first, he cognizes a cognizable object while he prepares his lessons in his study or his laboratory; during the second, he expounds to his students about that object. The students are not called upon to know, but to memorize the contents narrated by the teacher. Nor do the students practice any act of cognition, since the object towards which that act should be directed is the property of the teacher rather than a medium evoking the critical reflection of both teacher and students. Hence in the name of the "preservation of culture and knowledge" we have a system which achieves neither true knowledge nor true culture.

The problem-posing method does not dichotomize the activity of the teacher-student: she is not "cognitive" at one point and "narrative" at another. She is always "cognitive," whether preparing a project or engaging in dialogue with the students. He does not regard cognizable objects as his private property, but as the object of reflection by himself and the students. In this way, the problem-posing educator constantly re-forms his reflections in the reflection of the students. The students—no longer docile listeners—are now critical co-investigators in dialogue with the teacher. The teacher presents the material to the students for their consideration, and re-considers her earlier considerations as the students express their own. The role of the problem-posing educator is to create, together with the students, the conditions under which knowledge at the level of the *doxa* is superseded by true knowledge, at the level of the *logos*.

Whereas banking education anesthetizes and inhibits creative power, problem-posing education involves a constant unveiling of reality. The former attempts to maintain the *submersion* of consciousness; the latter strives for the *emergence* of consciousness and *critical intervention* in reality.

Students, as they are increasingly posed with problems relating to themselves in the world and with the world, will feel increasingly challenged and obliged to respond to that challenge. Because they apprehend the challenge as interrelated to other problems within a total context, not as a theoretical question, the resulting comprehension tends to be increasingly critical and thus constantly less alienated. Their response to the challenge evokes new challenges, followed by new understandings; and gradually the students come to regard themselves as committed.

Education as the practice of freedom—as opposed to education as the practice of domination—denies that man is abstract, isolated, independent, and unattached to the world; it also denies that the world exists as a reality apart from people. Authentic reflection considers neither abstract man nor the world without people, but people in their relations with the world. In these relations consciousness and world are simultaneous: consciousness neither precedes the world nor follows it.

NOTES

1. Simone de Beauvoir, *La Pensée de Droite, Aujord'hui* (Paris); ST, *El Pensamiento político de la Derecha* (Buenos Aires, 1963), p. 34.

2. This concept corresponds to what Sartre calls the "digestive" or "nutritive" concept of education, in which knowledge is "fed" by the teacher to the students to "fill them out." See Jean-Paul Sartre, "Une idée fundamentale de la phénomenologie de Husserl: L'intentionalité," *Situations I* (Paris, 1947).

3. For example, some professors specify in their reading lists that a book should be read from pages 10 to 15—and do this to "help" their students!

4. Fromm, *op. cit.,* p. 41.

5. *Ibid.,* p. 31.

6. *Ibid.*

7. Reinhold Niebuhr, *Moral Man and Immoral Society* (New York, 1960), p. 130.

Deschooling Society

Ivan Illich believes that schools as we know them are a destructive force in the lives of the youth who are exposed to them. He feels that the hidden assumptions in school curricula encourage the young to accept indoctrination into the values of the hegemonic forces that are in control of society.

In the following selection, which is from *Deschooling Society* (Harper & Row, 1971), Illich portrays childhood as a social construct designed to encourage children to accept the authority of teachers and to allow those teachers to mold them to fit into socially acceptable roles. These roles, Illich argues, are predetermined by teachers, and they deny the young control over their own destinies. Illich critiques the Western cultural concept of childhood, saying that "childhood" is a burden to many of those few who are allowed it. He takes the position that if society were to abandon the concept of "childhood" and to permit the young to learn naturally in the world, rather than in schools under the direction of teachers, all children would be better off. Illich further argues that we have all learned most of what we know outside of the schools.

The following selection shows how Illich conceives of the phenomenology of schooling and the Western cultural conceptualization of childhood. Other publications that illustrate Illich's beliefs are *Celebration of Awareness: A Call for Institutional Revolution* (Doubleday, 1970); *H₂0 and the Waters of Forgetfulness: Reflections on the Historicity of "Stuff"* (Dallas Institute of Humanities and Culture, 1985); and *In the Mirror of the Past: Lectures and Addresses, 1978–1990* (Marion Boyars, 1992). Illich's lectures and addresses have also been widely circulated.

Key Concept: the phenomenology of school and childhood

WHY WE MUST DISESTABLISH SCHOOL

The escalation of the schools is as destructive as the escalation of weapons but less visibly so. Everywhere in the world school costs have risen faster than enrollments and faster than the GNP [gross national product]; everywhere expenditures on school fall even further behind the expectations of parents, teachers, and pupils. Everywhere this situation discourages both the motivation and the financing for large-scale planning for nonschooled learning. The United States is proving to the world that no country can be rich enough to afford a school system that meets the demands this same system creates simply by existing, because a successful school system schools parents and pupils to the supreme value of a larger school system, the cost of which increases disproportionately as higher grades are in demand and become scarce.

Rather than calling equal schooling temporarily unfeasible, we must recognize that it is, in principle, economically absurd, and that to attempt it is intellectually emasculating, socially polarizing, and destructive of the credibility of the political system which promotes it. The ideology of obligatory schooling admits of no logical limits. The White House recently provided a good example. Dr. Hutschnecker, the "psychiatrist" who treated Mr. Nixon before he was qualified as a candidate, recommended to the President that all children between six and eight be professionally examined to ferret out those who have destructive tendencies, and that obligatory treatment be provided for them. If necessary, their re-education in special institutions should be required. This memorandum from his doctor the President sent for evaluation to HEW [Department of Health, Education, and Welfare]. Indeed, preventive concentration camps for predelinquents would be a logical improvement over the school system.

Equal educational opportunity is, indeed, both a desirable and a feasible goal, but to equate this with obligatory schooling is to confuse salvation with the Church. School has become the world religion of a modernized proletariat, and makes futile promises of salvation to the poor of the technological age. The nation-state has adopted it, drafting all citizens into a graded curriculum leading to sequential diplomas not unlike the initiation rituals and hieratic promotions of former times. The modern state has assumed the duty of enforcing the judgment of its educators through well-meant truant officers and job requirements, much as did the Spanish kings who enforced the judgments of their theologians through the conquistadors and the Inquisition.

Two centuries ago the United States led the world in a movement to disestablish the monopoly of a single church. Now we need the constitutional disestablishment of the monopoly of the school, and thereby of a system which legally combines prejudice with discrimination. The first article of a bill of rights for a modern, humanist society would correspond to the First Amendment to the U.S. Constitution: "The State shall make no law with respect to the establishment of education." There shall be no ritual obligatory for all.

To make this disestablishment effective, we need a law forbidding discrimination in hiring, voting, or admission to centers of learning based on previous attendance at some curriculum. This guarantee would not exclude performance tests of competence for a function or role, but would remove the present absurd discrimination in favor of the person who learns a given skill with the largest expenditure of public funds or—what is equally likely —has been able to obtain a diploma which has no relation to any useful skill or job. Only by protecting the citizen from being disqualified by anything in his career in school can a constitutional disestablishment of school become psychologically effective.

Neither learning nor justice is promoted by schooling because educators insist on packaging instruction with certification. Learning and the assignment of social roles are melted into schooling. Yet to learn means to acquire a new skill or insight, while promotion depends on an opinion which others have formed.

Learning frequently is the result of instruction, but selection for a role or category in the job market increasingly depends on mere length of attendance.

Instruction is the choice of circumstances which facilitate learning. Roles are assigned by setting a curriculum of conditions which the candidate must meet if he is to make the grade. School links instruction—but not learning—to these roles. This is neither reasonable nor liberating. It is not reasonable because it does not link relevant qualities or competences to roles, but rather the process by which such qualities are supposed to be acquired. It is not liberating or educational because school reserves instruction to those whose every step in learning fits previously approved measures of social control.

Curriculum has always been used to assign social rank. At times it could be prenatal: karma ascribes you to a caste and lineage to the aristocracy. Curriculum could take the form of a ritual, of sequential sacred ordinations, or it could consist of a succession of feats in war or hunting, or further advancement could be made to depend on a series of previous princely favors. Universal schooling was meant to detach role assignment from personal life history: it was meant to give everybody an equal chance to any office. Even now many people wrongly believe that school ensures the dependence of public trust on relevant learning achievements. However, instead of equalizing chances, the school system has monopolized their distribution.

To detach competence from curriculum, inquiries into a man's learning history must be made taboo, like inquiries into his political affiliation, church attendance, lineage, sex habits, or racial background. Laws forbidding discrimination on the basis of prior schooling must be enacted. Laws, of course, cannot stop prejudice against the unschooled—nor are they meant to force anyone to intermarry with an autodidact—but they can discourage unjustified discrimination.

A second major illusion on which the school system rests is that most learning is the result of teaching. Teaching, it is true, may contribute to certain kinds of learning under certain circumstances. But most people acquire most of their knowledge outside school, and in school only insofar as school, in a few rich countries, has become their place of confinement during an increasing part of their lives. . . .

PHENOMENOLOGY OF SCHOOL

Some words become so flexible that they cease to be useful. "School" and "teaching" are such terms. Like an amoeba they fit into almost any interstice of the language. ABM will teach the Russians, IBM will teach Negro children, and the army can become the school of a nation.

The search for alternatives in education must therefore start with an agreement on what it is we mean by "school." This might be done in several ways. We could begin by listing the latent functions performed by modern school systems, such as custodial care, selection, indoctrination, and learning. We could make a client analysis and verify which of these latent functions render a service or a disservice to teachers, employers, children, parents, or the professions. We could survey the history of Western culture and the information gathered by anthropology in order to find institutions which played a role like that now performed by schooling. We could, finally, recall the many normative statements which have been made since the time of Comenius, or even since Quintilian, and discover which of these the modern school system most closely approaches. But any of these approaches would oblige us to start with certain assumptions about a relationship between school and education. To develop a language in which we can speak about school without such constant recourse to education, I have chosen to begin with something that might be called a phenomenology of public school. For this purpose I shall define "school" as the age-specific, teacher-related process requiring full-time attendance at an obligatory curriculum.

Age.   School groups people according to age. This grouping rests on three unquestioned premises. Children belong in school. Children learn in school. Children can be taught only in school. I think these unexamined premises deserve serious questioning.

We have grown accustomed to children. We have decided that they should go to school, do as they are told, and have neither income nor families of their own. We expect them to know their place and behave like children. We remember, whether nostalgically or bitterly, a time when we were children, too. We are expected to tolerate the childish behavior of children. Mankind, for us, is a species both afflicted and blessed with the task of caring for children. We forget, however, that our present concept of "childhood" developed only recently in Western Europe and more recently still in the Americas.[1]

Childhood as distinct from infancy, adolescence, or youth was unknown to most historical periods. Some Christian centuries did not even have an eye for its bodily proportions. Artists depicted the infant as a miniature adult seated on his mother's arm. Children appeared in Europe along with the pocket watch and the Christian moneylenders of the Renaissance. Before our century neither the poor nor the rich knew of children's dress, children's games, or the child's immunity from the law. Childhood belonged to the bourgeoisie. The worker's child, the peasant's child, and the nobleman's child all dressed the way their fathers dressed, played the way their fathers played, and were hanged by the neck as were their fathers. After the discovery of "childhood" by the bourgeoisie all this changed. Only some churches continued to respect for some time the dignity and maturity of the young. Until the Second Vatican Council, each child was instructed that a Christian reaches moral discernment and freedom at the age of seven, and from then on is capable of committing sins for which he may be punished by an eternity in Hell. Toward the middle of this century, middle-class parents began to try to spare their children the impact of this doctrine, and their thinking about children now prevails in the practice of the Church.

Until the last century, "children" of middle-class parents were made at home with the help of preceptors and private schools. Only with the advent of industrial society did the mass production of "childhood" become feasible and come within the reach of the masses. The school system is a modern phenomenon, as is the childhood it produces.

Since most people today live outside industrial cities, most people today do not experience childhood. In the Andes you till the soil once you have become "useful." Before that, you watch the sheep. If you are well nourished, you should be useful by eleven, and otherwise by twelve. Recently, I was talking to my night watchman, Marcos, about his eleven-year-old son who works in a barbershop. I noted in Spanish that his son was still a *"niño."* Marcos, surprised, answered with a guileless smile: "Don Ivan, I guess you're right." Realizing that until my remark the father had thought of Marcos primarily as his "son," I felt guilty for having drawn the curtain of childhood between two sensible persons. Of course if I were to tell the New York slum-dweller that his working son is still a "child," he would show no surprise. He knows quite well that his eleven-year-old son should be allowed childhood, and resents the fact that he is not. The son of Marcos has yet to be afflicted with the yearning for childhood; the New Yorker's son feels deprived.

Most people around the world, then, either do not want or cannot get modern childhood for their offspring. But it also seems that childhood is a burden to a good number of those few who are allowed it. Many of them are simply forced to go through it and are not at all happy playing the child's role. Growing up through childhood means being condemned to a process of inhuman conflict between self-awareness and the role imposed by a society going through its own school age. Neither Stephen Daedalus nor Alexander Portnoy enjoyed childhood, and neither, I suspect, did many of us like to be treated as children.

If there were no age-specific and obligatory learning institution, "childhood" would go out of production. The youth of rich nations would be liberated from its destructiveness, and poor nations would cease attempting to rival the childishness of the rich. If society were to outgrow its age of childhood, it would have to become livable for the young. The present disjunction between an adult society which pretends to be humane and a school environment which mocks reality could no longer be maintained.

The disestablishment of schools could also end the present discrimination against infants, adults, and the old in favor of children throughout their adolescence and youth. The social decision to allocate educational resources preferably to those citizens who have outgrown the extraordinary learning capacity of their first four years and have not arrived at the height of their self-motivated learning will, in retrospect, probably appear as bizarre.

Institutional wisdom tells us that children need school. Institutional wisdom tells us that children learn in school. But this institutional wisdom is itself the product of schools because sound common sense tells us that only children can be taught in school. Only by segregating human beings in the category of childhood could we ever get them to submit to the authority of a schoolteacher.

Teachers and pupils.   By definition, children are pupils. The demand for the milieu of childhood creates an unlimited market for accredited teachers. School is an institution built on the axiom that learning is the result of teaching. And institutional wisdom continues to accept this axiom, despite overwhelming evidence to the contrary.

We have all learned most of what we know outside school. Pupils do most of their learning without, and often despite, their teachers. Most tragically, the majority of men are taught their lesson by schools, even though they never go *to* school.

Everyone learns how to live outside school. We learn to speak, to think, to love, to feel, to play, to curse, to politick, and to work without interference from a teacher. Even children who are under a teacher's care day and night are no exception to the rule. Orphans, idiots, and schoolteachers' sons learn most of what they learn outside the "educational" process planned for them. Teachers have made a poor showing in their attempts at increasing learning among the poor. Poor parents who want their children to go to school are less concerned about what they will learn than about the certificate and money they will earn. And middle-class parents commit their children to a teacher's care to keep them from learning what the poor learn on the streets. Increasingly educational research demonstrates that children learn most of what teachers pretend to teach them from peer groups, from comics, from chance observations, and above all from mere participation in the ritual of school. Teachers, more often than not, obstruct such learning of subject matters as goes on in school.

Half of the people in our world never set foot in school. They have no contact with teachers, and they are deprived of the privilege of becoming dropouts. Yet they learn quite effectively the message which school teaches: that they should have school, and more and more of it. School instructs them in their own inferiority through the tax collector who makes them pay for it, or through the demagogue who raises their expectations of it, or through their children once the latter are hooked on it. So the poor are robbed of their self-respect by subscribing to a creed that grants salvation only through the school. At least the Church gave them a chance to repent at the hour of death. School leaves them with the expectation (a counterfeit hope) that their grandchildren will make it. That expectation is of course still more learning which comes from school but not from teachers.

Pupils have never credited teachers for most of their learning. Bright and dull alike have always relied on rote, reading, and wit to pass their exams, motivated by the stick or by the carrot of a desired career.

Adults tend to romanticize their schooling. In retrospect, they attribute their learning to the teacher whose patience they learned to admire. But the same adults would worry about the mental health of a child who rushed home to tell them what he learned from his every teacher.

Schools create jobs for schoolteachers, no matter what their pupils learn from them.

Full-time attendance.   Every month I see another list of proposals made by some U.S. industry to AID [Agency for International Development], suggesting the replacement of Latin-American "classroom practitioners" either by disciplined systems administrators or just by TV. In the United States teaching as a team enterprise of educational researchers, designers, and technicians is gaining acceptance. But, no matter whether the teacher is a schoolmarm or a team of men in white coats, and no matter whether they succeed in teaching the subject matter listed in the catalogue or whether they fail, the professional teacher creates a sacred milieu.

Uncertainty about the future of professional teaching puts the classroom into jeopardy. Were educational professionals to specialize in promoting learning, they would have to abandon a system which calls for between 750 and 1,000 gatherings a year. But of course teachers do a lot more. The institutional wisdom of schools tells parents, pupils, and educators that the teacher, if he is to teach, must exercise his authority in a sacred precinct. This is true even for teachers whose pupils spend most of their school time in a classroom without walls.

School, by its very nature, tends to make a total claim on the time and energies of its participants. This, in turn, makes the teacher into custodian, preacher, and therapist.

In each of these three roles the teacher bases his authority on a different claim. The *teacher-as-custodian* acts as a master of ceremonies, who guides his pupils through a drawn-out labyrinthine ritual. He arbitrates the observance of rules and administers the intricate rubrics of initiation to life. At his best, he sets the stage for the acquisition of some skill as schoolmasters always have. Without illusions of producing any profound learning, he drills his pupils in some basic routines.

The *teacher-as-moralist* substitutes for parents, God, or the state. He indoctrinates the pupil about what is right or wrong, not only in school but also in society at large. He stands *in loco parentis* for each one and thus ensures that all feel themselves children of the same state.

The *teacher-as-therapist* feels authorized to delve into the personal life of his pupil in order to help him grow as a person. When this function is exercised by a custodian and preacher, it usually means that he persuades the pupil to submit to a domestication of his vision of truth and his sense of what is right.

The claim that a liberal society can be founded on the modern school is paradoxical. The safeguards of individual freedom are all canceled in the dealings of a teacher with his pupil. When the schoolteacher fuses in his person the functions of judge, ideologue, and doctor, the fundamental style of society is perverted by the very process which should prepare for life. A teacher who combines these three powers contributes to the warping of the child much more than the laws which establish his legal or economic minority, or restrict his right to free assembly or abode.

Teachers are by no means the only professionals who offer therapy. Psychiatrists, guidance counselors, and job counselors, even lawyers, help their clients to decide, to develop their personalities, and to learn. Yet common sense tells the client that such professionals should abstain from imposing their opinion of what is right or wrong, or from forcing anyone to follow their advice. Schoolteachers and ministers are the only professionals who feel entitled to pry into the private affairs of their clients at the same time as they preach to a captive audience.

Children are protected by neither the First nor the Fifth Amendment when they stand before that secular priest, the teacher. The child must confront a man who wears an invisible triple crown, like the papal tiara, the symbol of triple authority combined in one person. For the child, the teacher pontificates as pastor, prophet, and priest—he is at once guide, teacher, and administrator of a sacred ritual. He combines the claims of medieval popes in a society constituted under the guarantee that these claims shall never be exercised together by one established and obligatory institution—church or state.

Defining children as full-time pupils permits the teacher to exercise a kind of power over their persons which is much less limited by constitutional and consuetudinal restrictions than the power wielded by the guardians of other social enclaves. Their chronological age disqualifies children from safeguards which are routine for adults in a modern asylum—madhouse, monastery, or jail.

Under the authoritative eye of the teacher, several orders of value collapse into one. The distinctions between morality, legality, and personal worth are blurred and eventually eliminated. Each transgression is made to be felt as a multiple offense. The offender is expected to feel that he has broken a rule, that he has behaved immorally, and that he has let himself down. A pupil who adroitly obtains assistance on an exam is told that he is an outlaw, morally corrupt, and personally worthless.

Classroom attendance removes children from the everyday world of Western culture and plunges them into an environment far more primitive, magical, and deadly serious. School could not create such an enclave within which the rules of ordinary reality are suspended, unless it physically incarcerated the young during many successive years on sacred territory. The attendance rule makes it possible for the schoolroom to serve as a magic womb, from which the child is delivered periodically at the schoolday's and school year's completion until he is finally expelled into adult life. Neither universal extended childhood nor the smothering atmosphere of the classroom could exist without schools. Yet schools, as compulsory channels for learning, could exist without either and be more repressive and destructive than anything we have come to know. To understand what it means to deschool society, and not just to reform the educational establishment, we must now focus on the hidden curriculum of schooling. We are not concerned here, directly, with the hidden curriculum of the ghetto streets which brands the poor or with the hidden curriculum of the drawing room which benefits the rich. We are rather concerned to call attention to the fact that the ceremonial or ritual of schooling itself constitutes such a hidden curriculum. Even the best of teachers cannot entirely protect his pupils from it. Inevitably, this hidden curriculum of schooling adds prejudice and guilt to the discrimination which a society practices against some of its members and compounds the privilege of others with a new title to condescend to the majority. Just as inevitably, this hidden curriculum serves as a ritual of initiation into a growth-oriented consumer society for rich and poor alike.

NOTES

1. For parallel histories of modern capitalism and modern childhood see Philippe Aries, *Centuries of Childhood*, Knopf, 1962.

PART TWO

Curriculum and Instruction

On the Internet . . .

Sites appropriate to Part Two

This Web site provides resources on curriculum theory, including a list of curriculum definitions, a bibliography, and a list of links to other sites.

```
http://jan.ucc.nau.edu/~jwb2/research/
    CurriculumTheory/CurriculumTheory.html
```

The Center for Dewey Studies at Southern Illinois University at Carbondale was established in 1961 as the "Dewey Project." In the course of collecting and editing Dewey's works, the Center amassed a wealth of source materials for the study of philosopher-educator John Dewey. Links to information about these works can be found at this site.

```
http://www.siu.edu/~deweyctr/index.html
```

In *Fairness and Core Knowledge,* sponsored by the Core Knowledge Foundation, E. D. Hirsch, Jr., argues for the adoption of a Core Knowledge Sequence in order to overcome educational injustice.

```
http://www.coreknowledge.org/CKproto2/
    about/articles/fair.htm
```

4.1 HERBERT R. KOHL

Ten Minutes a Day

Herbert R. Kohl has been a leading author on teaching and learning in the United States for many years. Some of his most famous books are *36 Children* (New American Library, 1967), *On Teaching* (Schocken Books, 1976), and *The Open Classroom: A Practical Guide to a New Way of Teaching* (New York Review, 1969), from which the following selection has been taken. In the selection that follows, Kohl argues for nonauthoritarian forms of teaching, which relate what is taught in the schools to the experience of the learners. In doing so, his ideas remind us somewhat of the ideas about the conduct of teaching expressed by John Dewey and other early-twentieth-century progressive educators.

Kohl provides a critique of authoritarian approaches to teaching. He relates his concept of a nonauthoritarian approach to teaching to his own experience as a teacher, and he relates his problems as he learned to believe in the idea of nonauthoritarian teaching. Kohl says that changing the way life is conducted in classrooms is almost as difficult as changing ourselves. He believes that the beginning of change in how a teacher teaches begins with a sense of discontent with how one is teaching; one must believe in the necessity and the desirability of changing how one interacts with one's students. Kohl's own memories of how boring authoritarian approaches to teaching were in school encouraged him to change how he taught. He urges readers to reflect on their own learning experiences in school.

Kohl says that one way to begin to change one's methods of teaching is to try a different approach for a short period of time each day (10 minutes) and then expand that period of time possibly until one spends the whole day teaching differently. He offers suggestions from his own teaching experience on how to do this. Kohl's insights are practical for classroom teachers and for those who are planning to teach. He further encourages bringing in adult nonteachers from the community to visit with the students and to share ideas with them. Kohl believes in taking the students into the communities where they live and relating their experiences to their communities.

Key Concept: nonauthoritarian ways of teaching

*P*eople who have been students in authoritarian classrooms cannot expect themselves to develop their own open classrooms easily. I started out as an authoritarian teacher. It was the only way I knew to teach; the way I had been taught. It took several years before I was able to function in a freer environment. Indeed, the students were much more ready for freedom than their teacher was. Perhaps it was better to start tentatively than to pretend that a change had come over me suddenly, and to try to turn everything upside down in the classroom. My beliefs in a free, nonauthoritarian classroom always ran ahead of my personal ability to teach in one.

There are several ways to experiment in the classroom. It depends upon who the teacher is. One ought not to try something basically incompatible with one's personality. It is likely to cause frustration and hostility, and to make further experimentation seem more dangerous than it really is. A crucial thing to realize is that changing the nature of life in the classroom is no less difficult than changing one's own personality, and every bit as dangerous and time-consuming. It is also as rewarding.

The starting point of change is discontent. If you are perfectly content with an authoritarian style of teaching and pleased with your pupil's lives in the classroom there, an attempt to change will be pointless. Some of the best authoritarian teachers, often charming and brilliant people who succeed in persuading young people to perform what the school demands and to like it at the same time, may find change irrelevant.

If, on the other hand, the authoritarian mode is distressing—if being an unquestioned authority is too difficult and unpleasant a role to sustain, if the boredom of your pupils or the irrelevance of what they are learning distresses you, then perhaps other approaches should be tried. Before doing so you should try to think as honestly as you can about your teaching experience and try to articulate to yourself or a friend what it is that makes you want to change. It also may be of use to remember yourself as a pupil in school—to think back to your early experiences of frustration, joy, anxiety, learning, boredom in the classroom. I found that my memories of school helped me to avoid doing hateful things to my pupils that my teachers had done to me. This isn't to say that you will be able to make a list of all that's troubling you. But it is a good way to begin perceiving the classroom as a place where strong and interesting experiences take place, rather than one where the objective performances of students are measured.

One way to begin a change is to devote ten minutes a day to doing something different. There is never any problem of finding ten minutes to play with, since what the pupils "must cover" is usually padded in order to fill up time. During that ten minutes present the class with a number of things they can choose to do. Present them with options you feel may interest them. Allow them the option of sitting and doing nothing if they choose. Moreover, make it clear that nothing done during that period will be graded, and nothing need be shown or explained to the teacher. That ten minutes is to be their time and is to be respected as such. Step out of the way and observe the things your pupils choose to do.

Step out of the way, but don't disappear. Make it clear that you won't tell people what to do or how to do it, but that you will be available to help in any way you can, or just to talk. For ten minutes cease to be a teacher and be an adult with young people, a resource available if needed, and possibly a friend, but not a director, a judge, or an executioner. Also try to make it possible for the ten minutes to grow to fifteen, twenty, so long as it makes sense to you and your pupils. It is not unlikely that those ten minutes may become the most important part of the day, and after a while may even become the school day.

Some specific hints on the use of the ten minutes:

- in English class it is possible to read, write (set three or four themes and leave it open for students to develop other ones), talk, act.
- in mathematics the students can set problems, solve problems, build computers, compute, design buildings (or other structures or things), talk about money, set problems for each other and the teacher.
- in social studies it is possible to talk about history; about newspapers, events, people; write about them; compose or listen to poems, play songs about them; talk or invite people in to talk about what's happening.
- in all classes students can do nothing, gossip, write, start a newspaper, a newsletter, listen to music, dance, talk about or play games, bring in things that may interest the teacher or other students and talk about them, write about them....

Think about what is happening during those ten minutes and learn to be led by the students. If certain things are particularly interesting to one group, find out about those things, learn as much as you can, and, seeing their interest, present them with ways of getting more deeply into what they care about. If, for example, a group of students is interested in animals and their relationship to people, you can refer them to fables, to Konrad Lorenz, to experimental psychology, to whatever you can discover yourself. And if you don't know about such matters find someone who does, and invite him to class to meet your pupils.[1] Then—and this is crucial—step out of the way again. Do not insist that because you have uncovered all these new options for your students that they *must* pursue them. Maintain your own freedom from the authoritarian mode and help your students maintain their freedom, however modest it may be. Learn, though it is difficult, to allow your students to say, "No," to what you want them to learn no matter how much stake you have in it. This means that one must understand one's own stake in making young people learn what one wants them to learn and not take it overseriously. Teachers must develop a sense of what they look like to young people and understand how pointless and even funny it can seem to young people to see adults losing their cool over someone's refusal to take the division of fractions or the imagery in Act I of Macbeth seriously.

OPENING OUT

In public schools learning is supposed to take place within the classroom. Occasionally a class takes a supervised trip to a museum, a library, or a ball game. These experiences, however, are considered secondary to "real" learning, which consists of reading books, looking at educational material (films, models of machines, etc.), and listening to the teacher. I remember taking my sixth grade class out of school two days a week. We walked around the community, visited factories, the university, artists' studios, chemical laboratories, film studios, people's houses, supermarkets, furniture stores, etc. Many other teachers at the school felt that our trips were not educational, and that we were leaving school so that I could avoid doing "real" teaching and the students could avoid submitting to "real" learning.

But the trips were a vital part of our experience together. We saw some of the world, talked to people, got a sense of the environments in which different types of work are done, and in a few places made friends and set up after-school programs for the students. The kids got a sense of what adults do with their time and a feel for possible careers for themselves.

Not everything we saw was pleasant. We went to court, the welfare department, the police department, the children's shelter. We hung around and watched and recorded the ways that our society deals with people. And when we returned to class we had things to talk about and study in depth. We compared, for example, our impressions of factory work with the one presented in the school's vocational guidance manual. We talked of justice as we saw it work against poor and black people in the courts and as the civics textbook explained it.

Visits are valuable, but they are limited. First impressions are often misleading. I feel that it would be a very good thing if young people could spend time as apprentices to artists, technicians, businessmen, etc. They could also be participant observers in places of work, and plan some of their program in the classroom around their experiences away from the school. This year some of my students will spend time at a TV studio, a design workshop, a boutique, a highway construction job, a laboratory, and at several departments of the University of California.

Schools are afraid to let their students go into the world away from the critical eye of the teacher. It won't be easy to leave the school several times a week with the class, much less develop apprenticeships for individual students away from the school building. However, you can move slowly, and should get as much help from the kids' parents as possible. Visit where they work, get to know the neighborhood you teach in. Ask the kids to tell you what's happening and to take you places. If there are places they feel you shouldn't know about, don't press.

The whole community ought to be the school, and the classroom a home base for the teachers and kids, a place where they can talk and rest and learn together, but not the sole place of learning. The classroom ought to be a communal center, a comfortable environment in which plans can be made and experiences assessed. However, one can open up the classroom as much by moving out of it as by changing the life within it.

Note: Increasingly, people are abandoning the public schools as hopeless. They have been setting up schools in storefronts, parks, homes, and factories. These schools use the community much more than do the public schools. There are many people around who care about the young and are delighted to give their time and energy. They are not "professional" teachers and therefore would have a difficult time finding places in public schools. They do things like make films, or paint or write poems, or build houses and highways, design and manufacture machines, deal with human relations or with marketing products. Often they will be delighted to come into the classroom and will invite kids to visit them at their work.

It is important for teachers to seek out people who do things and bring them into the classroom. It's not so hard—often all that is necessary is to go to a place, announce that one is a teacher, and invite people to come to class and meet the kids. There are, however, school administrators who will resist visitors they can't completely control. In these cases it may make sense to invite people anyway and not tell anybody. The more adults the kids get to know, the more easily they can move in a world which is still, after all, largely controlled by adults.

NOTES

1. It is always a good idea to bring as many non-teachers into your classroom as possible. Painters, writers, businessmen, journalists all have valuable experience to offer young people that teachers don't have. So do people who have no specific vocations to talk about.

4.2 KATHERINE CAMP MAYHEW AND ANNA CAMP EDWARDS

The Dewey School

Katherine Camp Mayhew and Anna Camp Edwards were teachers in the Laboratory School of the University of Chicago, which was founded by John Dewey in 1896. This school was an educational laboratory for exploring the ideas on curriculum and instruction being developed by Dewey. The school, which later became the School of Education, was created to involve parents, teachers, and professors in dialogue regarding the 10 ideas about experience-based pedagogy being developed by Dewey and other progressive educators. Mayhew and Edwards published a now-classic book on the early years of this experimental school entitled *The Dewey School: The Laboratory School of the University of Chicago, 1896–1903* (D. Appleton-Century, 1936). The selection that follows is from that book.

The students of the Dewey school were broken into groups by relative age. Each group was designated by a Roman numeral. To give the reader a flavor of how the school was conducted, this selection includes the authors' descriptions of the experiments in specialized activities by "Group XI" (ages 14 to 15) for the 1901–1902 school year. Also included are brief comments by Mayhew and Edwards regarding the school's philosophy of student growth.

Key Concept: the Dewey school

EXPERIMENTS IN SPECIALIZED ACTIVITIES

Group XI (Age Fourteen to Fifteen)

In a developing experiment such as that of the school, the work of the oldest children is of necessity highly exploratory and tentative in character. Because of the school's early demise also, many of the courses for this age were repeated but once, or at the most twice. An account of them is, therefore, only suggestive of a way in which the interests and activities of the elementary stage may be guided into the deviating paths of the more specialized interests and subject-matter of the secondary period.

Careful study of the school's brief and very condensed records during the year 1901–1902 seems to indicate that in this year the two older groups were united into one. This was true for at least certain of their studies. The oldest

110

*Katherine Camp
Mayhew and
Anna Camp
Edwards*

members of this united group (who normally would have been classified as Group XII) were given special tutoring and review courses in preparation for their college board examinations, which were complicating the program. Had the group consisted solely of those who had followed the consecutively developing program of the school, and had it not been hampered by the demands of college entrance examinations, the various courses for the oldest children doubtless would have followed a far different and more logical plan, hints of which appear in the records. Roman history would have been studied from the point of view of the political state; the history of industry and of social groupings would have been developed; and more of the specialized sciences gradually would have found their places in the curriculum. As it was, the theoretical plan for the oldest children was greatly altered by circumstances. There was also lack of space and of proper laboratories and equipment for older children. Many of these difficulties were swept away in the following year when the Laboratory School, for one year, became a part of the School of Education, and moved into its beautiful new building. Records of the work of that year (1902–1903), however, were not available; hence the history of the school ends with the records of Group XI.

The Work of the Fall Quarter

For two years the course in general science for these children had been separated into its physiographical and biological aspects. The year before the children had continued the study of the various forms of energy with special emphasis on light. This course had included a fundamental consideration of various theories of energy and had been in the nature of an introduction to the technical study of physics, which would soon enter the program of those preparing for college entrance examinations. The science course planned for Group XI was a continued and more detailed consideration of their earlier study of existing types of animal life. This was constantly related to the evolutionary processes touched upon in the geological study of North America the preceding year. It was characterized by more laboratory work and outdoor excursions than usually mark a study of biology in the secondary period. The aim was to preserve the spirit of individual investigation and rediscovery that had characterized the children's scientific work from the beginning.

The study of mathematics also became more highly specialized. The work in algebra included involution, evolution, the theory of exponents, and operations involving radical quantities. In geometry, each member of the group worked out, for the most part independently, from twenty to thirty propositions and exercises and wrote up his demonstrations with a varying degree of care. In addition to that of clarifying the children's fundamental mathematical ideas, three ulterior purposes were kept in view by the teacher of this course: to train each individual into the highest degree of independence and perseverance in attacking new and difficult work, to aid him in developing a clear concept of what constitutes a geometrical demonstration, to attain clear, definite, and concise expression.

In the second quarter the pupils used Will's *Essentials of Geometry* as the basis of their work and were able to work more rapidly than when they had had to make constructions as well as work out demonstrations from dictated exercises. The propositions of Book I and many other related exercises were covered —in all about one hundred. In order to have time to finish the desired work in algebra, geometry was discontinued in May without reviewing the work done. The remainder of the quarter was spent in the study of radical equations, quadratic equations, the theory of quadratics, and problems involving quadratics. Although all the work usually prescribed for college entrance was taken up, only a few of the group completed the course in a satisfactory way. Some of them were hampered by lack of a ready command of fundamental principles and processes. Others did not put sufficient time on study to acquire familiarity with and ready application of the principles. The work of three was highly satisfactory, but even these needed a month of review before taking college examinations. It was felt that other members of the group would require at least another quarter's work on the important and more technical parts of the subject.

The work in history was also more specialized than in previous years. Six years' study of social living the world over, as well as that of their own present, had more or less adequately prepared these children to appreciate a study of certain thoroughly differentiated and, so to speak, peculiar types of social life. It was hoped that on the basis of their rather thorough knowledge of both the principles and facts of social life they would be able to discover for themselves the special significance of each civilization and the particular contribution it had made to the world's history. The plan, therefore, was to change from the psychological approach to a study of history to the chronological, to begin with the ancient world around the Mediterranean and come down again through the European story to the peculiar and differentiating factors of American history. The plan, however, was tried for two years only, and the records of the work of the last year are too meagre for inferences of any value to be drawn as to its ultimate success. In history, much time was also given to making up the lacks in the consecutive study of history required by college entrance examinations.

The shop-work of this group for the quarter was not up to the standard of that of Groups VIII or IX. The pupils chose their own work, and the results were unsatisfactory. Some showed a lack of ambition to undertake any worthy object; some were ambitious beyond their skill; and some lacked decision and perseverance. When careful work was required, most of the group worked very slowly. The boys took some time to complete the tool drawers in their benches, did some repair work about the school and finished a tripod for a camera and a bread board. The girls completed tool boxes, a mail box, two or three book racks, a window seat, an oak table, an oak music rack, and other smaller articles. The whole-hearted effort and genuine interest of other years seems to have been lacking. The cooking as a course had been discontinued with Group IX, but on occasions when distinguished guests were present at luncheon, the older groups were called in to plan, prepare, and serve the meal.

The work in languages, French, Latin, and English, took on a specialized character. In Latin, before beginning Caesar's Commentaries, the class read

Katherine Camp
Mayhew and
Anna Camp
Edwards

his biography from *Viri Romae*. In translation, emphasis was laid on syntax. In composition, the aim was to help the children to gain a free use of Latin idioms in their translation of English into Latin and in their condensed historical reports. Sight reading was also part of the program, and in connection with work on the Gallic wars a detailed study of the life of Caesar's times was made, of its outstanding men and the social, intellectual, and political events of the period. In this year the children also started their first formal study of the English language, and English was chosen as the subject for special emphasis during the year. Some intensive work was done on Latin derivatives. The points emphasized were: (1) consonant and vowel changes; (2) suffixes and prefixes, their value and changes; (3) growth and change in the meaning of derivatives. Coöperation with the French teacher was necessary as the Latin element in the English language, while partly derived directly from Latin, has, in the main, come through French, and has been largely modified in the process.

The first piece of work in composition was a theme relating to summer experience. The children's style was clear and fluent, but inclined to be loose and inaccurate in sentence structure. Careful criticism brought out some difficult grammatical points which were analyzed and discussed; considerable logical power was evidenced in attacking these grammatical problems. After this preliminary work, the reading of one of Shakespeare's plays was undertaken. As these children had not the habit of reading aloud, they were very awkward. They had never read a play, with the exception of two pupils. They knew nothing of Shakespeare, nor of dramatic history, so a brief sketch of Shakespeare's life and the prominent social features of his time was made from books which the children read themselves. They had no way of expressing their ideas of meter and in the beginning found it difficult to tell when they omitted a syllable or inserted one which did not belong in the phrase. As their attention had to be continually interrupted to discover errors in reading, the work went very slowly at first. They had had Roman History so that they understood the story of the play. They committed to memory some couplets and short passages, and as soon as the study of the first act was completed, they prepared an abstract. By this time they had enough command of method to understand the character of work expected of them, and their interest in the story and the dramatic setting was thoroughly aroused. The play was completed by Christmas time; abstracts of each act were written; and an outline of the entire play given by every pupil in the class. In a general way they understood the difference between the Shakespearean drama and preceding English drama. They were familiar with the versification so far as its use went, although no technical terms were given to them. The class showed particular interest in the character study. Two members carried on a two-day debate over the comparative virtues of Brutus and Cassius. Each member of the class had weighed all the main characters and could give an opinion on their virtues or vices and the relative importance of the part each had in the drama.

This study cleared the way for a return to a study of the village life and history of Shakespeare's time. Notes were made of the many incidental allusions to the commercial changes which were taking place in England. To explain these allusions a study of the Tudor family's position and importance in history was made in the winter quarter. The religious attitude of France, Spain, Italy, and the Netherlands was also discussed. Since the pupils had no idea of the reasons why this period was called the Renaissance of Learning, biographies of the great discoverers in science were read. The discovery of the New World and its commercial importance they already understood. They studied the lives of Copernicus, of Sir Thomas More, Martin Luther, the inventors of printing, and the story of the rise of Protestantism and the settlement of Ireland. Working back in history from Shakespeare and Queen Elizabeth to the Wars of the Roses, they studied Shakespeare's *King Richard III*, following the same method used in *Julius Caesar*. About five or six weeks were spent on the play. The class was much shocked by the evil portrayed, and interest was somewhat depressed by the shock to their feelings. The outlines and abstracts of the acts were prepared, and a very good idea of the historical setting was gained. The class was somewhat critical of the play and inclined to compare it with *Julius Caesar*, which they considered much superior. However, in the end they were all impressed by the intellect of King Richard, as well as horrified by his wickedness.

The Work of the Spring Quarter

In the spring quarter work followed quite different lines. It consisted of a critical analysis of the class papers prepared in science. The subjects of these papers were volcanoes, glaciers, and other physiographical features. The first task was to prepare an outline of what they themselves were to write. They had no idea how to attack this and in the first attempt were quite as likely to put descriptions into their outlines as to separate the headings or main topics. However, as the subject-matter had been given them in logical order in the science class, they soon grasped the idea that the order of composition was simply the logic of thought or subject-matter, and rapidly gained power to prepare clear and accurate outlines. The only details taken up were those of grammar and sentence structure. The differentiation between English and Latin caused them some difficulty. In the former, they had to learn to depend upon their own analysis to determine the relation of a word to the sentence. They were inclined at first to define such terms as subject and object in too restricted a way. They came to see that where no endings existed to place the word, the difficulty of defining its use was increased. The main points in sentence analysis, they soon grasped. Certain forms of diagramming sentences were given, but these were not used for more than two days, although the class showed an inclination to come back to them. As time went on, they improved greatly in definiteness of statement and in ability to criticize their own forms of expression. Considerable time was spent throughout the entire year in studying the derivations of words and the historical development of their meanings. At the beginning of the year the whole class was satisfied with a very loose explanation of the meaning of a word, but after the year's study not one was satisfied until he had looked it up in the Century Dictionary. They often followed a word to its roots in other languages.

Group XI also carried on the printing of a daily newspaper for a short time, as did other groups. This did much to interest the children in language expression. On account of the pressure of time, inconvenient quarters, and type of press, the work was more limited than it might have been under more flexible conditions. At one time the press was of great service in printing the reading lessons for the younger children. Developments in later progressive schools have shown that carried out in the same way in which other occupations in the school were pursued, printing might have been an absorbing interest and of great educational value.

*Katherine Camp
Mayhew and
Anna Camp
Edwards*

The group was active in school clubs and in the club-house project. The Educational Club was under the special guidance of these children. It started out with fine spirit the last year of the school. The constitution of the club allowed any member of the school to become a member, and several new names were voted on. A committee was appointed to attend to the finances of the club-house and to confer with an adviser to consider the best method of raising the money for it. A new president, secretary, and treasurer were elected. The club then voted to take charge of the Friday afternoon exercises of the school. A committee of three members was appointed for this purpose. The children voted to have a general adviser, and a teacher was appointed. At a special meeting the Monday before Thanksgiving, the club decided to raise the dues of club members to twenty-five cents a month until the house was paid for. They also formed an athletic department, and the president appointed a committee of three to decide definitely on the work of this department.

Development of Expression Through the Weekly Assembly

The weekly general assembly of the older children on Friday afternoon of each week was always a social occasion and was usually directed by the older groups. In the beginning, one of the girls read a story of her own composition. The children were then asked to bring in suggestions for programs. One offered to have a friend come and play the piano. A girl offered the play that she had been writing, volunteering to select the actors and actresses and drill them in it. They all voted to ask Professor Judson of the University to come to talk about the trouble in China, requesting that they be allowed to ask all the questions they wished. Extracts from the records of some of these assemblies follow:

At the general exercises held on the Wednesday afternoon before Thanksgiving, the children sang their songs of last year. Professor MacClintock read a Thanksgiving story—Whittier's *The Pumpkin*. On another occasion, papers written by the children of the various groups on their class work were read. One read a long account of the conquest of Peru, another, an account of a series of experiments carried on in science during the fall.

One week Mr. F— gave a very informal talk to the children about his experiences in Cuba during the late war. The children were so much interested that they stayed half an hour afterwards asking questions. In February Mr. Jenkin Lloyd Jones was invited to talk on the subject of Lincoln. He accepted the invitation and entertained them for half an hour with stories illustrating Lincoln's characteristics.

At the next meeting the children celebrated Washington's birthday, Group IX prepared the program, in which each child had a part. One played the boyhood of Washington; another, his school-days; another, his part in the French and Indian War; Washington in the Revolution; Washington as president; and Washington at home. One girl said that she knew several stories of Washington which did not come under any of these heads, so she wrote and read a paper on "Incidents in the life of Washington." On this occasion they worked together as a class better than ever before. Another afternoon Miss Harmer talked to the children on the Horace Mann School, and they asked many questions and seemed interested in the subject. At the next assembly Dr. Coulter gave a description of his trip to the Yellowstone Park in 1870 when he went out with an expedition appointed by the government to explore the Wyoming geysers. On one occasion when a speaker failed to come, the children had an old-fashioned spelling contest, Groups IX and X doing themselves credit. On another, to which friends were invited, the program consisted of a German play, the composition of which had formed the basis of Group VIII-*b's* work for the winter quarter; in addition there were songs and English and French recitations.

In the later years of the school the debating society became very active and frequently took charge of the assembly program. It was noticeable that a child speaking to children always got rapt attention, and judgment of points in a debate grew to be very discerning. All these weekly assemblies were productive of good results, but a great handicap was the lack of an auditorium and any stage facilities.

The boys and girls of Group XI were divided for their music periods. The latter sang well and with much enthusiasm. Sight singing was emphasized, and they learned Schumann's "The Wanderer," Schubert's "Haiden Roslein" (in German) by note and spent a large portion of their time in writing a long two-part song which they notated on the board and copied. The boys of the group, having completed the work on key and time signatures, were told that unless they wished to sing, there was nothing further to do, for them, in music. They responded to this by suggesting that they write a song and chose as a topic "La Journée" such as they had seen described in their recent study of *Ivanhoe* in a literature course. The words finished, they were at a loss for the music, and finally decided that the teacher had better write it. Accordingly, she put a phrase of music on the board which they proceeded to change by telling on what line or space each note should be placed. They then listened to and criticized the result. In this manner the song was completed. The three older groups were allowed to learn it. They were then to invite the composers to chorus practice and sing it for them. The latter, however, were not pleased with the result, saying the voices were too high to do justice to the song, and finally decided to learn to sing it themselves. This they did and, finding they could, continued to sing for the rest of the quarter.

The work in the art studio centered around the furnishing and decorating of the now completed club-house. All the groups of the school had been drawn into interested participation in the final touches on the cherished project, but the older groups designed and made most of the furniture, hangings, and rugs. At various times the center of activity shifted from the studio to the science laboratory for experimentation on vegetable dyes (aniline dyes were viewed with scorn) or for the right mixture of stain for the woodwork; again the carpentry shop was sought out for some necessary construction of wood or metal; or it was back to the textile studio for sewing and embroidery of the curtains,

*Katherine Camp
Mayhew and
Anna Camp
Edwards*

or weaving the rugs already planned and designed. Through all these activities ran the artistic motive—a genuine longing that the house and all that was to be put therein should be beautiful and appropriate. Interest and effort harnessed as a team, driven by genuine desire that sprang from genuine need, accomplished results of real quality. Although skilled guidance was at hand and irremediable errors were not permitted, the children had great freedom in directing their project. Naturally many mistakes were made, some of which took much time and hard labor to correct, but which taught much otherwise never learned. The groups primarily responsible for the project had organized themselves into various executive committees. The committee on house decoration decided in favor of a dark stain (then in vogue) for the woodwork of the house and, in spite of the advice of those guiding the work, carried their idea through. They were much criticized by the rest for the gloomy effect of their choice, a criticism some of them recall to this day.

Summary

The little house when finished represented the best thought and genuine interest as well as labor of many children, and it grew out of genuine need. Its construction and decoration had been guided by skilled persons, interested in helping the children to conceive and achieve their ideals, and in the process to learn to judge and critically evaluate their own results. With these older children, as with all the groups in the school, the motives for art expressions sprang out of other activities and thus held vital relations for the children. The ideal of the school was that skill in the technique of artistic expression should keep pace with the children's intellectual concepts of the way they wished to refine, adorn, or represent in line, color, or clay the thing they were making. This was an ideal difficult to attain and more often than not failed of achievement. That it was achieved, in a measure, in art, in music, and to a still more limited degree in drama was a real achievement for those in charge. These were pioneer days, and previous attempts to cultivate artistic quality of expression from the kindergarten to the studio were quite unknown. Since these early days great progress has been made in the teaching of the musical and those representative activities usually called the fine arts. There is great value in this type of activity for securing freedom of expression and joyous creative effort. For the child this is what might be called consummatory experience.

In justice it should be said that at all times the experiment was much hampered by its limited quarters and equipment. Because of the lack of library and laboratory facilities especially, many of the things done with the three older groups were second choices as to subject-matter. The very nature of the school also made it necessary for the children to concentrate under difficult conditions of noise and interruption. This was not conducive to the development of the habit of consecutive study necessary to the best expression of individual thought in language or in any other medium. Lack of a library, lack of quiet, lack of beauty, lack of adequate space for club meetings, all made it impossible to carry out many individual and group plans. As was stated at the time, "It was never practically possible to act adequately upon the best ideas obtained, because of administrative difficulties, due to lack of funds, difficulties centering in the lack of a proper building and appliances and in inability to pay the amounts necessary to secure the complete time of teachers in some important lines. Indeed, with the growth of the school in numbers and in the age and maturity of the pupils, it was always a grave question how long it was fair to the experiment to carry it on without more adequate facilities."

Although the school had a number of children who were finishing the third stage of growth of the elementary period, it was not in existence long enough so that many typical inferences as to results for this period could be safely drawn. There did seem reason to hope, however, that with the consciousness of difficulties, needs, and resources gained in the experience of five years, children can be brought to and through this period not only without sacrifice of thoroughness, mental discipline, and command of the technical tools of learning, but also with a positive enlargement of life, and a wider, freer, and more open outlook upon it.

At least it can be said that at fourteen these children had the background of an unusually wide first-hand experience upon which to base their more technical study, not only of artistic forms and appreciations, but of all forms of knowledge, whether scientific or practical, that had come within the range of their activities. Where these experiences had taken root in the good soil of native aptitudes, tendrils of intellectual and spiritual appreciations of beauty of color, line, and form, of harmony and rhythm, of ethical, social, and moral values and responsibilities were reaching out, searching for the light of broader opportunities. They represented permanently rooted motives and vocational interests which, given a chance, would grow into continuing purposes and well-planned social action. This was by no means true of all the children who had come through the processes of the school. It possibly was true only of a very few, but it is not too much to hold that what was accomplished gave those who had eyes to see and ears to hear faith to believe that here lay the way of an education that was also the way of developing life.

PRINCIPLES OF GROWTH GUIDING SELECTION OF ACTIVITIES

In the school, education was recognized as a maturing process, in which the young child grows in body and mind and in ability to handle himself in his physical environment and in his social relationships. The conditions for healthy bodily growth had long been recognized, but the idea that power to think depends upon the healthy growth and proper functioning of the mechanism of thought and its expression was, at that time, quite new. The bearing upon education of psychological science as a study of this mechanism, and of the conditions that minister to and promote its normal development in mental power and intelligent action was still for the most part unrecognized.

Two psychological assumptions of the school's hypothesis, basic to its theory and controlling its practices, were radically different from those that underlay the prevalent educational theory and practice. The first of these recognized a psychological and biological distinction between the child and the adult, as a result of which it is neither physiologically nor mentally possible to describe children as "little men and women." The adult is a person with a calling and position in life. These place upon him specific responsibilities which he must meet. They call into play formed habits. The child's primary calling is growth. He is forming habits as well as using those already formed. He is, therefore, absorbed in making contacts with persons and things and in getting that range of acquaintance with the physical and ideal factors of life which should be the background and afford the material for the specialized activities of later life. Recognition of this difference, therefore, conditioned the selection and arrangement of all school materials and methods in order to facilitate full normal growth. It also required faith in the results of growth to provide the power and ability for later specialization.

The second assumption was that the conditions which make for mental and moral progress are the same for the child as for the adult. For one, as for the other, power and control are obtained through realizing personal ends and problems, through personal choosing of suitable ways and means, and through adapting, applying and thereby testing what is selected in experimental and socially acceptable action.

Katherine Camp Mayhew and Anna Camp Edwards

CHAPTER 5 Curriculum Theory and Practice

Current Conceptions of the Function of the School

Hilda Taba (1902–1967) was a major influence on curriculum theory and practice during her career in teacher education. Strongly grounded in educational theory and philosophy, Taba committed herself to working in schools and observing relations among students and teachers. She conducted pioneering longitudinal research studies on human relations in school settings, and she wrote books and guides on improving intergroup understanding in schools. Her work laid a solid foundation in curriculum theory and development for what would later be called multicultural education.

The selection that follows is from Taba's *Curriculum Development: Theory and Practice* (Harcourt, Brace & World, 1962), which was heavily cited by the United States Commission on Civil Rights in its 1975 report *A Better Chance to Learn*. Taba believed that it is important to understand the social context of education and the cultural forces that impact those who create school curricula. Here she provides a synthesis of the leading theories of her time on the roles that schools play in human cultures.

Key Concept: schools and society

Society's concept of the function of the public school determines to a great extent what kind of curriculum schools will have. Yet, in a complex culture with a pluralistic value system, it is difficult to establish a single central function for any agency. In a democratic society these formulations are further complicated by the fact that different layers of society participate in the process of determining what education in general and public schools specifically should be and do. It is, therefore, more difficult to determine the central function of schools in a democracy than in a totalitarian society where a small power group decides both what society should be and what role schools shall play in it.

Our society today has by no means agreed about what the central function of the school should be. One could even say that "the great debate about schools and their function" is in effect a debate about many of the issues our society faces: the balance between freedom and control and between change and tradition, whether the elite should be of power or of intellect, who should participate in shaping the public policy, and many others. It is generally agreed that the main outlines of the "crisis in education" are shaped and complicated by the convergence of two phenomena: the transformative effects of science and technology on society and the emergence of Communist totalitarianism as an expanding imperialist power. In the light of this setting the examination of the functions of the public school is highly pertinent, but extremely difficult, because the issues tend to be confused and the viewpoints somewhat less than objective.

Whatever the specific viewpoints regarding the functions of the public schools, there seems to be little disagreement about the importance of the role of education. American society has always expected a great deal of education and, in Walter Lippmann's phrase, has expressed great faith in it as the "life-giving principle of national power." Historically the American people have assumed that education has the power to reduce poverty and distress, to prevent child delinquency and crime, and to promote the well-being of the individual, the intelligent use of suffrage, and the welfare and stability of the state. Indeed, even today education, if not the public school, is considered an antidote against evils in the minds of men and an ally in achieving all good causes. The very attacks on the schools express the faith of the American public that the schools matter because of their influence not only on individuals, but on society as well. Some critics, for example, seem to reason that the strength of our current enemies is the *result* of *their* education and, correspondingly, that the weakness in our position is the *fault* of *our* education.

These high expectations and the naive faith in the power of education are at once a curse and a blessing. No doubt they have given American education a certain vigor by insisting that it respond to social ideologies and needs. They have also made it more subject to passing hysterias and changing moods of the public than may have been good for a healthy development. Anyone tracing the various "trends" in curriculum development in the United States will note a zigzag movement in which one "trend" swallows and annihilates the preceding one with an almost unbelievable discontinuity in theoretical thought. When education is overly sensitive to public opinion, changes are bound to be made thoughtlessly. Continuity in capitalizing on past achievements is jeopardized in the heat of hastily formulated reforms and changes. It is no wonder, then, that in periods of crisis the question of the central function of schools in society becomes a subject of heated controversy, with the nature of the relationships of education to society at the very core of that controversy. It is no wonder also that there are many variations in the conceptions of what the essential function of the public school is.

There is relatively little disagreement also about the idea that schools function on behalf of the culture in which they exist. The school is created by a society for the purpose of reproducing in the learner the knowledge, attitudes, values, and techniques that have cultural relevancy or currency. There is generally also no quarrel with the idea that of the many educative agencies of society, the school is the one which specializes in inducting youth into the culture and is thus responsible for the continuity of that culture.

However, opinion is divided about the precise nature of this function. The differences range from conceptions which assume a strong cultural determination of everything schools do and should do to postulations about ideals of individual development which are quite independent of cultural norms. This division of opinion extends also to views on the extent to which the program of the school is or should be subject to the values and norms of the culture, and in what measure the materials it uses and the ideologies that control its shaping should be drawn from the life of the culture. While in all concepts it is accepted that schools must transmit culture, there are sharp differences about what should be transmitted and the manner in which it is to be done. Some conceptions emphasize education as an agent of change, while others stress its preserving functions.

Sometimes, especially in theoretical discussions, these divisions of views appear as rather stark and even unrealistic alternatives. Speaking of the function of general education, Conant states one such alternative neatly:

> Roughly speaking, the basic argument about general education turns on the degree to which the literary and philosophical traditions of the western world, as interpreted by scholars and connoisseurs before World War I, should be the basis of the education of *all* American youth. The watershed between two fundamentally opposed positions can be located by raising the question: For what purpose do we have a system of public education? If the answer is to develop effective citizens of a free democratic country, then we seem to be facing in one direction. If the answer is to develop the student's rational powers and immerse him in the stream of our cultural heritage, then we appear to be facing in the opposite direction. By and large, the first position represents the modern approach to education; the latter the more conventional view. Those who look down one valley regard conventional "book learning" as only one element in the landscape; those who look down the other believe that developing the "life of the mind" is the primary aim of civilization and this can be accomplished only by steeping youth in our literary and philosophical heritage.

All the same, the overlappings in these conceptions are too great to make possible a refined classification of concepts of the function of education....

EDUCATION AS PRESERVER AND TRANSMITTER OF THE CULTURAL HERITAGE

One group of theorists stresses the preserving function of education: the preserving of the cultural heritage, especially that of the Western culture. This group argues that since all cultural traditions have roots, cultural continuity is possible only if education preserves this heritage by passing on the truths worked out in the past to the new generation, thus developing a common cultural background and loyalties. The specific ideas regarding what this heritage consists of are not always clear. In the main the transmission of the accumulated wisdom of the race and of basic truths and values is emphasized.

The Harvard Report on General Education is one example of an emphasis on the importance of preserving tradition and maintaining roots from the past. This report argues that education can develop a unifying purpose and idea only as it develops this sense of heritage, which in turn requires a common ground in training and outlook. This heritage is basic to education because it uses the past to clarify or even to determine what is important in the present. The report points out that it is the function of education to pass on the *inherited* (italics mine) view of man and society, and that its main task is to perpetuate such ideas as the dignity of man and common beliefs in what is good. "Classical antiquity handed on a working system of truths which relied on both reason and experience and was designed to provide a norm for civilized life." It is the business of education to instill a commitment to these truths.

This assertion of the necessity for imparting the common heritage is, however, modified by a certain recognition of the role of new experience and change. The report attempts to reconcile the necessity for common belief with the equally obvious necessity for new and independent insight by pointing out that a certain tough-mindedness in reaching conclusions by scientific methods of thought, a curiosity, and a readiness for change are also necessary; that education cannot be wholly devoted to the commitment to tradition or to the view that means are valuable apart from ideals; that it upholds at the same time the tradition and the experiment, the ideal and the means, and, like our culture itself, change within the commitment. While the report makes a bow to experiment and change, it seems to say that the basic ideals of what constitutes a good man in our society come from tradition. In other words, since the modern society is only an extension of the traditional one, changes will come from applying the ancient truths to the modern scene. Because the common heritage is a way of building unity in culture, and since the classical tradition has handed down a norm for civilized life, the task of education is to "shape the student" to "receive" this ideal.

This preserving or conserving function of education is still more strongly accentuated by a group of theorists philosophically classified as rational humanists and classicists. Their conception of the function of education is intimately bound up with and derived from their conception of human nature, which has as its major premise that the essence of human nature is its rational character. Rationality is a common characteristic of all men, apart and independent of the culture in which they exist. The world can be understood by the exercise of this faculty of rationality. Therefore, the chief function of education is to develop this rationality, and the understanding of the eternal truths revealed by these rational faculties. "Education, if it is rightly understood, is the cultivation of the intellect. Only this is what belongs to man as man, and his individuality is only his caprice, self-will, and unique propensities."

Being preoccupied with the essence of things, this viewpoint also insists that learning should be concerned with *essentials*, that is, the first principles articulated in the great books and the classical tradition. Since rationality is essential, the subjects of greatest rational content should also have priority in the curriculum. These subjects are the liberal arts and, among the liberal arts, the humanities.

This viewpoint does not deny that societies differ, that education must train citizens for its own society, or that problems of societies vary. However, it insists that these differences are ephemeral and idiosyncratic and that these problems must be understood and interpreted in the light of the universal eternal truths embodied in the classical literature of great books. Such truths are our main cultural heritage, which education must transmit. They constitute the liberalizing education. Further, liberalizing education is the same everywhere, because "truth" is the same everywhere. Thus is set the case not only for the preserving function of education, but also for the requirements for "essentials" and for the uniformity of curriculum.

A rejection of technical subjects and of vocational education of any sort as a narrowing influence is the logical consequence of this viewpoint. That type of "education" is considered to be not education, but training. It is an uncalled-for "encroachment" on the essential task of liberal education.

While this view of the function of education was originally put forth in reference to college education, recently the same orientation has been applied to criticism of and proposals for the public-school curriculum by a group organized around the concept of basic education. This group insists also that the transmission of cultural heritage is the chief function of public schools. This heritage is defined by stress on three points, each of which has consequences on what may be proposed for the curriculum.

First, a strong case is made for intellectual development as the distinctive function of public schools. As defined by Bestor this intellectual development must stress the understanding of principles and the ability to handle and to apply complex ideas, to make use of a wide range of accurate knowledge, and to command the means of effective communication. No one would quarrel with this definition. But there is reason to quarrel with another assumption Bestor makes—namely, that because education has been extended to classes and groups which have hitherto been deprived of it, any "weakness" in intellectual training creates a void into which steps anti-intellectualism. In order to prevent this from happening, the case for this intellectual purpose of the school must be made so clear that the anti-intellectual masses cannot distort it.

Second, this type of intellectual training is possible only by centering the educational effort on basic skills and disciplines: reading, writing, and arithmetic on the lower level, and logic, history, philosophy, mathematics, science, art, and philosophy on the higher levels. These lead the hierarchy of subjects, or the "basics" of education. The assumption that there is a hierarchy of subjects according to "their power to enhance intellectual development" and that the traditional liberal arts subjects are at the top of that hierarchy runs through most of the writings of the basic educators.

This belief that certain subjects are superior to others as means for intellectual training is made perfectly clear by Clifton Fadiman, who argues that since the cultural tradition includes many more things than can be handled in schools "without running into chaos," men in the past have imposed on cultural tradition a form and a hierarchy which is constituted into the disciplines of liberal arts, as encompassed in a New York City public school he attended. . . .

The third characteristic of "basic education" is a complete rejection of certain current functions of the schools, among them education for democratic citizenship, for moral values, and for ability to deal with social problems, and the concern for the "whole child" or any form of "life adjustment," including education for vocations. These functions put basic educators in an especially aggressive and combative mood. According to Bestor, modern education suffers from an enormous extension of functions which schools have no business in assuming: In this extension there is peril to basic education and to the development of intelligence. This extension also unnecessarily pre-empts the functions of other agencies. Thus, job training is the problem of industry. Training in cultural traits, mores, and the ethical systems belongs to the family and the church. Neither should the school be concerned about "social conditioning," partly because it works against tremendous odds and therefore is ineffectual, partly because the socialization of the individual is the very means of squelching the creativity and independence of the intellect. A thoughtless transfer of functions from one agency to another only creates problems; this transfer should be resisted, even though pressures exist for it.

In other words, basic education is a case against any goals for schools beyond those for intellectual development, for a return to the pure form of disciplines as defined by classical tradition, and for limiting general education to those who show a certain level of intellectual promise.

There are, of course, many criticisms of and questions about this definition of the function of the public school. One criticism pertains to the validity of the assumption that, since men are rational and truth is everywhere the same, education everywhere must be uniformly addressed to these truths and to the exclusive task of developing the rational powers. The recent explosion of knowledge seems to have disestablished many truths that were considered perennial. Rational powers seems to be interlocked with cultural conditions and personal factors in a way that forces reinterpretation of ancient truths. "Ancient truths" are not always applicable to the realities and the needs of modern society except in a sense so general as to be unachievable short of a lifetime of study. Further, modern social analysis seems to indicate a greater break with tradition than any of the basic educators are willing to admit, and therefore the transmission of outdated wisdom might even be dangerous. It seems more likely that society today needs to create its own image of the true, the beautiful, and the just.

It is questionable also whether intellectual development can take place effectively in such a grand isolation from the cultural milieu as the advocates of this viewpoint seem to assume. This assumption contradicts the tenor of many studies which point to the relationship between the development of an individual and his cultural milieu. Further, while there is a general agreement about the central importance of intellectual development, the weight of recent knowledge about learning points to the fact that intellectuality cannot be neatly separated from other aspects of personality development without the danger of cultivating an academic intellectuality instead of a functioning intelligence.

Finally, the argument for the purified liberal arts disciplines as a sole way to wisdom is strongly contradicted by the very developments in these disciplines. Often so-called practical application of what is known becomes the very mainspring of theory, or "pure" thought.

EDUCATION AS AN INSTRUMENT FOR TRANSFORMING CULTURE

An opposing view is held by many educators and social analysts who maintain, in effect, that education can and does play a creative role in modifying and even reshaping the culture in which it functions, that education and public policy are intimately related, and that progress in one is limited without progress in the other. They maintain that education must deal with the needs of current culture and even help to shape the future.

The idea that education has a constructive role to play in shaping the society has deep roots in American tradition. It is implicitly expressed in the general public faith in the power of education to deal with problems of culture. It is also articulated in much of educational writing over a long period of time. Horace Mann underscored the integral relationship between popular education and social problems, such as freedom and the republican government. This theme resounds through his twelve reports: "A nation cannot long remain ignorant and free. No political structure, however artfully devised, can inherently guarantee the rights and liberties of citizens, for freedom can be secure only as knowledge is widely distributed among the populace." Facing the social reality of the times, the public discord of a nation not yet unified, and "Fearing the destructive possibilities of religious, political and class discord," he sought a common value system which might undergird American republicanism and within which a healthy diversity might thrive. His quest was for *public philosophy,* a sense of community which might be shared by Americans of every variety and persuasion. His effort was to use education to fashion a new American character out of a maze of conflicting cultural traditions. And his tool was the *Common School.* The common school for him was the instrument for his limitless faith in the perfectibility of human life and institutions. In this sense, then, Horace Mann regarded education as an arm of public policy and an instrument for dealing with the problems facing the nation at that time.

A flowering of the idea that education is a social process, the primary and most effective instrument of social reconstruction, came with the work and writings of Dewey and his followers. The main thesis of this group was that the school is not merely a residual institution to maintain things as they are: education has a creative function to play in the shaping of individuals and through them in the shaping of the culture. Dewey consistently saw the function of the school in both psychological and social terms. As early as 1897 he wrote:

> I believe that: all education proceeds by the participation of the individuals in the social consciousness of the race. This process... is continually shaping the individual's powers, saturating his consciousness, forming his habits, training his ideas, and arousing his feelings and emotions.... The most formal and technical education in the world cannot safely depart from this general process.... This educational process has two sides—one psychological, and one sociological and... neither can be subordinated to the other, or neglected, without evil consequences... knowledge of social conditions of the present state of civilization is necessary in order to properly interpret the child's powers... and that the school is primarily a social institution.

In subsequent development one fork of this dual orientation of Dewey on the function of education matured into an elaboration of the social responsibilities of the school, while the other centered more emphatically on individual development.

Dewey's concept of democracy was that of an intentionally progressive society, committed to change, organized as intelligently and as scientifically as possible. The role of education in such a society is to inculcate the habits that would make it possible for individuals to control their surroundings rather than merely to submit to them. A progressive society would "endeavor to shape the experience of the young so that instead of reproducing current habits, better habits shall be formed, and thus the future adult society be an improvement on their own.... We are doubtless far from realizing the potential efficacy of education as a constructive agency of improving society, from realizing that it represents not only a development of children and youth but also of the future society of which they will be the constituents."

This viewpoint dictated priorities for curriculum. Dewey was concerned that essentials be placed first and refinements second, but he defined as essentials the things which are most fundamental socially, which have to do with experience shared by the widest groups. He was also deeply critical of the dualism between culture and vocation and concerned with the effects on democracy of a scheme of education in which there is a narrow utilitarian education for one class of people and a broad liberal education for another. In addition to insisting on the cultivation of the "method of intelligence" and of scientific inquiry as the first tasks of the curriculum, he also stressed the necessity of introducing vocational subjects not merely to build utilitarian skills but as "points of departure" for increasingly intellectualized ventures into the life and meaning of industrial society.

The subsequent elaborations of the social function of the school took on several different shadings, which ranged from emphasis on changing society by changing individuals to stress on planned reconstruction of the social system.

Some of the elaborations stress primarily the responsibility of the school to meet current social needs. The deeper interpretation of this responsibility involves shaping the school program according to a long-term perspective on the realities of the changing society, and an adequate study of a whole range of social needs. A shallower interpretation makes demands on the school on behalf of immediate difficulties and problems. The current insistence on redoubled study of mathematics and physical science, growing in part out of the "somewhat adolescent feeling of national humiliation" at Soviet advances in missile technology and in part out of temporary anxieties regarding manpower needs in these fields, illustrates the shallow perspective.

Others see the social function of education as one of promoting a critical orientation toward the current scene. This interpretation has led to an emphasis on problem solving in the social sciences and to the introduction of problem courses. An emphasis on an understanding of the social forces that generate cultural lag and dislocation is part of this orientation. Some educators interpret the social function of education chiefly as an instrument for social change, either through gradual reform by reshaping the outlook of the oncoming generation or through planned effort at reconstruction.

But whatever the variations in concepts of the social functions of education, certain fundamental ideas tend to run through all. One is the understanding that education must, and usually does, work in the cultural setting of a given society, at a given time, in a given place, shaping the individual in some measure to participate in that society. All decisions about education, including those about curriculum, are made within the context of a society. The values and forces of that society determine not only what manner of man exists but also to some extent what manner of man is needed. The decision-makers themselves are immersed in the culture and therefore subject to the culturally conditioned conceptions of how education is to serve that society. As Childs puts it, the schools are doubly social in nature. They are the arm instituted by society for the education of the young. But the very materials which constitute the program of the school are also drawn from the life of that society.

This concept means that not only is intellectual training to be directed to understanding the forces of the culture and to mastering the intellectual tools necessary for that understanding, but also that there is a fundamental responsibility for training in the culture's essential values and loyalties. In this view, then, social cohesion depends not so much on transmission of the common knowledge as the sharing of common values and concerns.

A second important element in these concepts is the profound appreciation of the fact of change in modern culture and of the meaning of social change. If the society and the culture are changing, then it is the task of schools to play a constructive role in that change. Education must adjust its aims and program to changing conditions, and, if possible, foreshadow them, especially under the conditions of rapid change introduced by modern technology. Without a continual reorientation to changing conditions, education becomes unreal and in a sense useless because it does not prepare youth for life's problems and responsibilities. To meet changing conditions means, of course, that both the aims of education and the programs devised to implement these aims, including the orientation brought to bear on materials used, must be changed also. It is of central importance to use critical intelligence (not intellectuality as described in the preceding section) and scientific attitudes in understanding and solving human and social problems. These qualities of mind can be cultivated to the extent that the "subject matter" of education is significant to the ongoing experience and concerns of the culture, and that experience is used as the key for giving meaning to knowledge and for translating subject matter into behavior and action.

The third important element of this concept is the idea that education is a moral undertaking. It begins and ends with value decisions. Educational decisions, whether regarding aims or curricular selections, always involve value judgments. For this reason education always will involve an element of prescription. Although scientific inquiry will determine what is, it will not prescribe what should be. Education is a moral enterprise also in that it selects which parts of the culture, what wisdom, which values, what ideals to transmit. No school in any society can be completely neutral; the difference lies in whether the basis for selection is made clear and whether the selection is made with some degree of rational method and scientific inquiry.

The concept of education as a reconstruction of society goes further than any of the above. The proponents of this view speak of education as management and control of social change and as social engineering, and of educators as statesmen. The idea that education should not only foster changes in society but should change the very social order was first expressed by Counts. It was later reiterated in *The Educational Frontier*, the thesis of which was that the task of education is "to prepare individuals to take part intelligently in the management of conditions under which they live, to bring them to an understanding of the forces which are moving, to equip them with the intellectual tools by which they can themselves enter into the direction of these forces." To implement such an education it would be necessary to launch a massive adult program that would build political and educational support for a radically different school curriculum, to develop a public which is education conscious and wise in the realities of industrial civilization, to reorient professional education, and to alert teachers to the pressing social issues of the day.

More recently a group of educators who call themselves the "reconstructionists" have argued in a similar vein and with the same sense of urgency about the social mission of education. In analyzing the orientation needed for developing a curriculum theory, B. Othanel Smith concludes by observing: "It is clear that the time for building a comprehensive social perspective is here. We are now living in a time when we can no longer depend upon custom and unconscious control to regulate our social existence. There is no longer any substitute for human management of the vast social machine. As a people we have much knowledge of and techniques for social engineering. The question is: can we learn to use it rapidly enough to control the social machine before it either enslaves us or destroys us?"

The main theses of the reconstructionist position are somewhat as follows: the transformation of society by technological and scientific revolution is so radical as to require a new moral and intellectual consensus capable of molding and directing this transformation. It is the task of educators to analyze the social trends, to discern the problems society is facing, to speculate on the consequences of the current social dynamics, and to project the values and the goals which need to be sought to maintain a democratic way of life. Because social changes today are rapid and radical, and because there are blind consequences to the technological revolution which seem to endanger the democratic way of life, tradition is a poor guide. A continuous critical reexamination of the meaning of the democratic way of life under the altered social conditions is needed. Critical examination and reconstruction of the cultural heritage—or social ideas, beliefs, and institutions—in the light of current problems and conditions, rather than inculcation of traditional ideas, must constitute the core of the educational program of today. In addition, educators must be statesmen, and in cooperation with other agencies must study and discuss the implication of the new "intellectual and moral order" for the "institutional structure of society."

In this scheme a rather exalted role is allotted to education and the schools. Educators must take close account of social forces, of the social institutions, and of their educative effects. They must translate this knowledge of culture and society into "educational policy," that is, a curriculum which will aid students in understanding these forces and in developing the techniques and attitudes necessary for participation in democratic reconstruction. The total educative impact of the school must encompass and coordinate changes in beliefs, personality structures, and social arrangements. Educators must carry the rest of the community to an agreement with their proposals. Curriculum planning needs to focus on building "social goals" and a "common social orientation." Individual goals and diverse group goals must be integrated into a system of social ends. Curriculum development in this sense becomes a way of making public policy.

The capacity of education in general and of public schools in particular to assume a leading role in changing the society and particularly the social structure has been seriously questioned. To sociologists concerned with the relationship of school and society it seems altogether unrealistic for schools to be animated by goals which differ radically from those of the culture in which they work. They point out that usually the aims of education are conservative —that is, they are consonant with the conceptions of the ideal adult which society wishes to produce—and educational institutions can pursue only those aims that society considers desirable. Historically, the aims of education have shifted, but these shifts have followed, not preceded, the changes in society's ideals of a desirable adult. It is therefore somewhat utopian to think of education as a means for a radical reconstruction of society, such as a new social order.

Other critics suggest, in addition, that it is easy to exaggerate both the actual and the potential ability of any formal institution, including the schools, to contribute to consensus in society, whether the means to achieve this consensus be the formation of basic personality or inculcation of a common set of values. This is especially so in industrial societies with their mass patterns of educational service, in which instruction looms larger than education, and in school settings in which it is impossible except under extreme conditions either to isolate or to exclude from its personnel those groups who do not share the dominant goals of the institution. It is possible, of course, that the sociologists and other critics may because of their own limited insight into the dynamics of the educational process underestimate what schools can do. The conditions under which creative educational aims can be conceived and implemented might well form the subject of further serious study and research.

5.2 HENRY T. TRUEBA

Integration of Minorities and Minority School Achievement

Henry T. Trueba is a distinguished scholar on issues relating to linguistic acquisition and on the rights of linguistic minority students in the United States. He has studied the curricular issues relating to bilingual educational programs in the schools, and his publications are highly regarded by many people in the field of education. The selection that follows is from his book *Raising Silent Voices: Educating the Linguistic Minorities for the Twenty-First Century* (Newbury House, 1989). In it, he identifies the linguistic minority populations in the United States and provides a summary of their demographic population numbers. He addresses issues related to Limited English Proficient (LEP) students in the book as a whole; in this selection, he gives specific demographic data as of 1989 with regard to these populations as well as the 1989 population projections for the year 2000.

Trueba discusses the reasons for academic failure or success of linguistic minority student populations in American schools. He relates this to the research that European scholars have done on linguistic minority student populations in European nations. Trueba notes that one of the most serious problems in doing such research is that of defining what we mean by "success" and "failure." Of Hispanic heritage himself, he perceives the importance of cultural heritage in helping linguistic minority students to recapture and to preserve their cultural voices in their lives.

Trueba discusses social interaction and learning from the perspective of the famous Russian psychologist Lev Vygotsky and examines how a Vygotskian approach to this topic might inform us. He believes that "the content and substance of much of the academic endeavors in elementary education assume cultural knowledge and life experiences that many minority children do not have."

Key Concept: linguistic minority children and stress

WHO ARE THE LINGUISTIC MINORITIES?

According to the 1980 U.S. Bureau of the Census data (as cited in the 5th Annual Report of the National Advisory Council for Bilingual Education, 1980–1981, and published by the Bureau of the Census 1983, and 1984; see Table 1) the language minority population (that is, people whose mother tongue is other than English, regardless of their proficiency in English) in the United States was about 30 million (projected to reach about 40 million by the year 2000) with a school-age population of 3.5 million children. The population of limited English proficient (LEP) students, which was 2.4 million in 1980, is conservatively projected to reach about 3.5 million by the year 2000, not counting the children of undocumented workers.

TABLE 1

Linguistic Minority Student Population With Limited English Proficiency, Aged 5–14 (in Thousands)

| | Projections | | | | | |
| | 1980 | | 1990 | | 2000 | |
Language	N	%	N	%	N	%
Spanish	1727.6	72.2	2092.7	74.8	2630.0	77.4
Italian	94.9	4.0	100.1	3.6	109.6	3.2
French	89.0	3.7	93.9	3.4	102.9	3.0
German	88.8	3.7	93.7	3.4	102.6	3.0
Filipino	33.2	1.4	35.0	1.2	38.3	1.1
Chinese	31.3	1.3	33.0	1.2	36.2	1.0
Greek	26.5	1.1	27.9	1.0	30.6	0.9
Vietnamese	24.9	1.0	26.2	0.9	28.7	0.8
Navajo	24.3	1.0	25.6	0.9	28.1	0.8
Polish	24.0	1.0	25.3	0.9	27.5	0.8
Portuguese	23.8	1.0	25.1	0.9	27.5	0.8
Yiddish	22.5	0.9	23.7	0.8	26.0	0.7
Japanese	13.3	0.6	14.0	0.5	15.3	0.4
Korean	12.2	0.5	12.8	0.4	14.1	0.4
Not accounted for and other	158.5	6.6	167.5	6.0	192.9	5.4
Total	2394.2		2795.9		3400.0	

Source: Adapted from National Advisory Council for Bilingual Education, 1980–81.

The Spanish-speaking LEP student population, which is now about 80 percent of the total LEP student population, has unique characteristics, is concentrated in the southwest and northeast part of the country, and deserves special discussion. According to the 1980 U.S. Census (Walker, 1987), there were

13.2 million Spanish-speaking persons in this country, not counting undocumented workers. As the National Center for Education Statistics indicates:

> In 1976 there were 3 million Hispanic children enrolled in elementary and secondary school programs, 6 percent of the total school-age population. Of this group, 63 percent (approximately two-thirds) are Mexican–American, 15 percent are Puerto Rican, 5 percent are Cuban, and 16 percent are of other Hispanic background (Walker, 1987:18).

Population trends indicate a rapid increase in the Hispanic population relative to other minorities and to overall population growth within the country. We know that Hispanics coming from monolingual Spanish-speaking homes form a substantial group of recent immigrants but there are as yet no reliable data on their exact numbers (O'Malley, 1981; Ulibarri, 1982; Duran, 1983; Walker, 1987). What is clear is the overall underachievement of Hispanics in schools, as documented by many recent scholars (Duran, 1983; Walker, 1987). The latter authors indicate that Hispanics in the early 1980s have fewer median years of schooling (10.3) than non-Hispanic whites (12.5) or blacks (11.9), and that the dropout rate for Hispanics aged 14–25, including those who have already left school by their fourteenth birthday, is 40 percent. . . .

At times, immigrants in the United States have faced drastic changes and gone through adjustment crises over a period of several generations. Sometimes second and third generations have lost their language and culture, but still have not been integrated into mainstream American society. Their continued marginal status must be explained. In many respects, alienated second- and third-generation immigrants have more in common with the low-income mainstream disenfranchised poor than with their ethnic counterparts in the host country or mother country. Both the loss of the home language and culture and the social isolation in this country seem to be rooted in similar causes. One of these may be the collective inability of these groups to respond to the social and cultural discontinuities (and rejection) presented by the dominant culture. Both types of groups have in common very low social status, low educational levels, poverty, isolation, and helplessness in the face of rejection. On the other hand, some minority groups seem better suited to adjusting to their new lives in the United States. DeVos (1983) has discussed the success of Japanese Americans. Likewise, Roosens (1987:8) has pointed out in discussing the Japanese that " . . . the internal logic of large parts of the pre-industrial culture can be harmonized with the modern model much more easily and much more quickly than is the case with others."

Regardless of their country of origin, linguistic minority families assimilate at different rates into the dominant social and cultural life of modern industrial societies. Their speed of assimilation seems to be connected with their relative familiarity with complex industrial societies and the functions of various institutions such as banks, schools, hospitals, and government. The less acquainted a family is with a pluralist, complex, literate, technologically sophisticated society, the greater the time needed for assimilation. Thus, while families coming from the same country may share overall characteristics of language and culture, they may differ in value orientation as well as in their understanding of how the host society and its institutions operate.

REASONS FOR ACADEMIC SUCCESS OR FAILURE

Academic achievement is only part of the "success" or "failure" of the overall process of minority integration into industrial societies. The problem of assimilating varied ethnic groups is not unique to the United States and Canada. Indeed, there are waves of migration all over the world. Turkish, Spanish, Moroccan, Italian, and other workers take their families to Germany, Belgium, Switzerland, or France in search of better jobs and educational opportunities. The successful adaptation of immigrant children has been, for the last two decades, the concern of research organizations affiliated with various American, Latin American, and European universities. Since the 1960s the Center for Social and Cultural Anthropology of the Katholieke Universiteit Leuven in Belgium, along with the Indigenist Institute in Mexico, has been conducting migration and assimilation studies. More recently, the Linguistic Minority Research Project at the University of California has created interdisciplinary teams to conduct basic and applied research on linguistic minorities in their homes and at school.

One of the most serious difficulties in such research is defining "success" and "failure," not only from the standpoint of the host society but also in terms of the ethnic groups under study. Another difficulty is creating adequate theoretical approaches that are compatible across disciplines. Social scientists have attempted to explain minority success and failure (academic, social, and economic) using a number of approaches and hypotheses that are not universally recognized as valid. Many of these theoretical approaches are still in their infancy and lack empirical evidence. A brief summary of some of the most important approaches is presented below.

In the last 10 years, sociologists, cultural anthropologists, psychologists, and linguists have been searching for a better understanding of immigrant and minority cultures. Accurate descriptions are seen as a fundamental first step toward understanding the social integration and academic success of minorities. Experts have adopted the use of what is known as an "emic" description, one that presents the perspective of the members of a given linguistic and cultural group (Pike, 1954), in contrast with an "etic" description, which presents an "analytical standpoint ... [from] outside of a particular culture" (Pike, 1954:10) and is adopted for the purpose of making cross-cultural comparisons.

The same social scientists have also made special efforts to study success or failure from the vantage point of their various disciplines. Their descriptions of how culture has an impact on learning are truly "grounded," meaning they are based on the data collected. In order to understand and explain to others the relationship between culture and learning, they have carefully examined the use of language, assuming along with earlier anthropologists that people "construe their world of experience from the way they talk about it" (Frake, 1964:132).

The emphasis on culture is particularly welcome after years of controversy regarding the relative significance of linguistic factors in determining the academic achievement of minority students. The narrow focus on linguistic differences and the overpoliticization of linguistic models did not lead to a better understanding of the success or failure of linguistic minorities. While excellent research was produced on first- and second-language use in the 1970s and early 1980s, the actual cognitive ability of minority children was not directly addressed until the more recent work of Cummins (1976, 1978, 1981a,b, 1983, 1986), Duran (1983, 1985), Heath (1983), Krashen (1980), Wong-Fillmore (1976, 1982), and other scholars. Language and culture are so intimately related during the process of early socialization that one cannot be studied without the other. Examining language isolated from cultural factors leads to a serious misunderstanding of the minority person's process of resocialization and consequently of integration, knowledge acquisition, and successful participation in the various institutions of the host society.

Leading European social scientists, such as Roosens in Belgium (1971, 1981, 1987) and Zeroulou (1985) and Camilleri (1985) in France, have joined American and Japanese (see Wagatsuma & DeVos, 1984; Ogbu, 1974, 1978, 1981; Suarez-Orozco, 1986, 1987, in press) researchers in seeking explanations for the differential scholastic achievement of minorities and immigrants. Their approaches attempt to combine psychological and sociological factors of achievement across cultures. Their overall concern is with the general process of minority integration into modern technological societies, and specifically with cultural adaptation to the host country. . . .

SOCIAL INTERACTION AND LEARNING: A VYGOTSKIAN APPROACH

Roosens's hypotheses deal with the general process of cultural integration and the resulting academic outcomes. They do not address the specifics of academic success or failure in terms of the particular achievement levels, knowledge, motivation, skills, endurance, and other requirements for success. In other words, the specific context of academic success or failure is not discussed. Nevertheless, the perspectives of Roosens and Ogbu have made a significant contribution to anthropology and education by calling our attention to the broad cultural and sociological factors affecting the overall mainstreaming of minorities.

These broad factors differentially affect minority groups as well as individuals within a single minority group. A complementary perspective, logically following that of Roosens and Ogbu, is proposed by scholars in the United States who, recognizing the significance of the broader theoretical perspectives (social, economic, and others) suggest that a "context-specific" approach, which views the psychological reality of knowledge acquisition in its immediate social and cultural context, would bring about a further understanding of the varied achievement among minorities (Diaz et al., 1986). This approach, based on the studies of Vygotsky and other Soviet scholars, can be summarized as follows:

"If all children exhibit similar linguistic and cognitive capabilities required for literacy and school achievement in the home environment, why do they exhibit vast differences in ability and academic performance in school?" (Trueba, 1986:256).

As previously mentioned, central to the discussion of minority student achievement is the body of literature developed by Vygotsky, a Jewish Russian sociohistorical psychologist who died in 1934, and those inspired by him. Having experienced prejudice and social injustice, and having closely studied children with learning difficulties, Vygotsky proposed a new way to assess children's potential.

Contrary to the thinking of western psychologists, Vygotsky postulated a notion of cognitive development rooted in social interaction and inseparable from social development. Thus, he opposed the use of standardized tests to measure intellectual ability and presented an alternative assessment of differential learning potentials through the notion of a personal "zone of proximal development" (ZPD). This is the sum of experiences, background knowledge, and conceptual synthesis with which the individual approaches the task of inferring meaning from social interactions. He defined it as " . . . the distance between the actual development level as determined by independent problem-solving and the level of potential development as determined through problem-solving under adult guidance or in collaboration with more capable peers" (Vygotsky, 1978:86).

In this approach, social scientists view success or failure as related to the communicative process, which is central to the process of socialization and acculturation. Context-specific approaches are based on the "ethnography of communication" (Gumperz & Hymes, 1964, 1972), as well as on the concept of "education as cultural transmission" (G. Spindler, 1955, 1982, 1987; Spindler & Spindler, 1987a,b). These scholars ask: Why do some individuals seem to acquire and accept sociocultural knowledge readily, while others have problems in doing so? More specifically, what are the educational problems and needs of linguistic minorities in this country? What should educators do in order to make the instructional system more responsive to these minorities' needs?

Particularly relevant to the context-specific approach is the theoretical perspective of Vygotsky (1978) and scholars whose work is based on Vygotsky's theories. Their efforts are focused on the development of higher psychological functions (Scribner & Cole, 1981; Griffin et al., 1981; Cole & D'Andrade, 1982; Cole & Griffin, 1983; Wertsch, 1985). One of the common assumptions is that language and communicative competence are critical for the development of higher psychological abilities. Another assumption is that this development is possible only if children participate in culturally meaningful activities. It is also assumed that development consists of an increased ability to manipulate symbols and use them in inter- and intrapsychological operations (Wertsch, 1985). Symbolic systems, especially language, are presumed to mediate between the mind and outside reality. Consequently, the role of teachers in helping children to understand symbolic systems is of crucial importance. Recent studies (Rueda & Mehan, 1986; Trueba et al., 1984; G. Spindler, 1987; Spindler & Spindler, 1987a; Trueba, 1987a,b, in press) combine current anthropological, sociological, psychological, and linguistic methods with Vygotsky's theoretical framework.

Vygotsky's sociohistorical school of psychology departs significantly from traditional western thought in that it requires the child to take an active role in determining his or her level of activity and to engage in a mental or social activity congruent with his or her ZPD. Activity is understood as an intellectual and social task composed of action and operations, which can be interpsychological (carried out in interaction with others) or intrapsychological (carried out inside the mind). For children to play an active role and work effectively within their ZPD, they must move continuously between the interpsychological and intrapsychological realms. In effect, every developmental step is mediated in social situations by inter- and intrapsychological activities (Griffin et al., 1981).

If we assume, within this theoretical perspective, that all children normally succeed in learning if given the opportunity to interact socially within their ZPD, it follows that failure in learning is "systemic." It is not an individual failure, but a failure of the social system to provide the child with an opportunity for social intercourse. This "systemic failure" is a social phenomenon understandable only in its own historical, economic, and political context. It is not the failure of a single social institution, such as the school, or the result of faulty instruction alone. In fact, the failure may exist in the classroom, home, workplace, community, and/or society at large. Consequently, in order to overcome systemic failure one needs to change the system by means of planned (social) instructional interventions in the various learning contexts (Cole & Griffin, 1983; DeVos, 1980, 1983).

The Nature of Learning Problems Revisited

Within the theoretical framework of Vygotsky, children's inability to handle oral language, text, and other symbolic systems is rooted in the failure of society to provide them with opportunities to engage in the social and cognitive activities necessary for learning within their ZPD. The socialization process of these children is flawed by prejudice or neglect. To prevent this, one must begin by adequately socializing minority individuals for success in the most important learning environments, the home and the school (G. Spindler, 1987). The formation of academic concepts is based on formal schooling and requires mastery of the use of taxonomic systems (systems that classify objects according to certain properties). Thus, in jobs requiring the grasp of taxonomic systems and an ability to process knowledge, schooled populations outperform cognitively nonschooled populations (Cole & D'Andrade, 1982). Ultimately, however, cognitive development is manifested in higher-order mental functions that are rooted in social interaction. This theoretical position is called by Vygotskians "culturally- or socially-based notion of cognitive development," and it has important implications for the study of linguistic minority children's adjustment to the culture of their schools.

Researchers guided by the context-specific approach and by a neo-Vygotskian perspective are not satisfied with information resulting from making general inquiries. What teams of researchers and practitioners (especially teachers) seek is a sequence of specific interactional contexts in which children demonstrate their handling of school work. Researchers need information leading to more specific analytical inferences and pragmatic instructional suggestions. The following four points based on limited study (Trueba, 1983; Trueba et al., 1984; Mehan et al., 1986; Rueda & Mehan, 1986; Trueba, 1987b; Jacobs, 1987; Kirton, 1985; Rueda, 1987, among others) are representative of the findings obtained through the context-specific approach.

1. Children's abstract categories of objects do not seem to correspond to those used by school personnel.
2. Children cannot articulate linguistically the concepts and their interrelationships apparently grasped during instruction.
3. Children's ability to remember curriculum content appears erratic and unpredictable.
4. Domain-specific skills in math, reading, or writing develop at different rates and correspond to children's English language proficiency.

While individual differences in learning ability and style may be evident, it is also important to identify characteristics shared by all children. These include lack of exposure to experiences relevant to school work, including the language used in classroom activities, and/or the opportunity and willingness to "absorb" American cultural information through school at a pace that permits them to understand such experiences. Empirical evidence supportive of the above generalizations will allow researchers to develop theories that attempt to explain the learning problems of minority students.

For educators to engage successfully in the reorganization of instructional activities, they must first explore different hypotheses concerning the success or failure of minority groups. If, for example, one advances the hypothesis that some minority groups cannot handle psychological stress in the host society and cannot function well in school because of that stress, one could generate further studies suggesting educational practices congruent with the main hypothesis, for example, that stress reduction will enhance learning. One question might be how we can examine the effects of time fragmentation on the development of high stress levels during early attempts by linguistic minority children to enter their ZPD and adjust to a new linguistic and cultural environment.

THE ZONE OF PROXIMAL DEVELOPMENT IN "DISABLED" MINORITIES

One could try to relate stress and children's inability to learn to a fundamental barrier to entering the ZPD (in Vygotsky's terms): that is, the difficulty in relating previous knowledge and experiences, acquired through the mother language and culture, to the new knowledge and experiences of the school. For example, the researcher could explore the possibility that fragmentation of time during initial experiences in an American school may result in the negative response to social and cultural discontinuities alluded to by Roosens. Within this context-specific approach, one could still pursue specific areas of inquiry that would eventually lead researchers and practitioners toward better instructional design. Such areas of inquiry are reflected in the following questions:

1. Do minority children have the opportunity to understand the nature of different classroom activities, and the transition from one behavioral context to another?
2. Do they experience trauma associated with continual changes of activities without fully understanding the conceptual content or expected behavior?
3. Can English be acquired under high levels of stress resulting from continual fragmentation and trauma?

Teams of researchers and practitioners ultimately need to find more useful theories and possible explanations that permit them to improve instructional design. For example, the team may discover that the child becomes confused because he or she never quite understands either the content of the instructional activity or the expected behavior during such an activity. The function of researchers is to identify the role that culture plays in the acquisition of knowledge and in the overall emotional and intellectual development of students.

... [T]he content and substance of much of the academic endeavors in elementary education assume cultural knowledge and life experiences that many minority children do not have. Reflecting on the ideas and hypotheses presented above, what can we do to maximize minority children's learning potential? What are our best strategies for classroom instruction? What should teachers do to become more effective in the classroom?

CONCLUDING THOUGHTS

Academic achievement appears to be linked to successful integration into the host society, which is, in turn, a complex and difficult process taking place at different levels: at the larger macrosocial level, as part of a group of immigrants that has low social and economic status and is viewed with certain prejudices; and at the school level, where there are rigid norms of behavior and instructional principles tailored to fit middle-class, mainstream populations. Competitive performance is extremely important in school, and testing is the most common mechanism used to assess children's performance, classify them accordingly, and declare them academic successes or failures.

In the efforts by social scientists to understand academic success or failure, two main complementary approaches have emerged as the most useful. The first is the broad psychosociological approach outlining social, economic, and educational factors that are part of the infrastructure of American society and determine the social status of minorities along with their relative access to resources. The second approach, which recognizes the importance of the broad psychosociological factors, focuses on the context-specific learning setting, that is, on the mechanisms that allow an individual to obtain the necessary social and cultural knowledge as well as the cognitive skills to learn. One of the most crucial steps in the initial acquisition of skills required for learning is gaining the ability to establish dyadic and peer learning relationships.

If we take the perspective of the linguistic minority child, we realize that, without having any say in the matter, he or she is uprooted from a familiar environment, placed in a strange and often radically different learning environment, and asked to learn a new language, acquire new values, and perform in competition with natives who already have significant advantages (particularly in the form of linguistic, social, and cultural knowledge). As the linguistic minority child attempts to adjust, he or she finds it extremely stressful to communicate as well as to meet the expectations of adults and peers.

Linguistic minority children need to cope with stress and they face serious social and psychological challenges (including a redefinition of self during the transition from home culture to school culture) in establishing these learning relationships. Communicative ability (requiring linguistic, social, cultural, and cognitive skills) is critical in the process of self-redefinition and adjustment. Curriculum content and level of performance are secondary during the initial phases of adjustment; consequently, priority should be given to increasing students' participation in communicative activities.

CHAPTER 6 Curriculum Development and the Language of Educational Debate

6.1 CHRISTOPHER LASCH

The Common Schools

In the selection that follows from *The Revolt of the Elites and the Betrayal of Democracy* (W. W. Norton, 1995), American historian Christopher Lasch provides an insightful look at the history of public schooling in the United States. He focuses on the 12 annual reports of Horace Mann, secretary to the board of education of Massachusetts in the mid-nineteenth century (1838–1848) when public schooling began to become a forceful social tool for achieving national unity among a multicultural national population. Lasch provides an important critique of Mann's point of view and educational efforts. He compares Mann's point of view with the points of view of Adam Smith and Orestes Brownson and then discusses various late-twentieth-century studies of Mann's work and various interpretations of it.

Lasch argues that Mann's views were weakened by "the assumption that education takes place only in schools." He examines how Mann's focus on social realism actually contributed to an assault on helping students to become imaginative and creative citizens. This is an interesting assessment of Mann's thought and effort in the field of education. Lasch questions why Mann wanted to keep politics out of the schools, and he offers a cogent and

142

Chapter 6
Curriculum
Development
and the
Language of
Educational
Debate

plausible analysis as to Mann's political and moral thought. Mann's attempt to keep social controversy and religious debate out of the public schools is criticized for preventing the development of creativity in students and is said to have led to some of the major problems that exist in the schools today. The schools cannot save society, argues Lasch; instead, we must prepare citizens to face controversy, to be inspired by learning about such things as honor and character as well as by learning the skills of debating moral issues. Thus, concludes Lasch, Mann's drive for social consensus and the elimination of controversial issues in the schools had the effect of stifling imagination.

Key Concept: social purposes of public schools

*I*f we cast a cold eye over the wreckage of the school system in America, we may find it hard to avoid the impression that something went radically wrong at some point, and it is not surprising, therefore, that so many critics of the system have turned to the past in the hope of explaining just when things went wrong and how they might be set to rights.[1] The critics of the fifties traced the trouble to progressive ideologies, which allegedly made things too easy for the child and drained the curriculum of its intellectual rigor. In the sixties a wave of revisionist historians insisted that the school system had come to serve as a "sorting machine," in Joel Spring's phrase, a device for allocating social privileges that reinforced class divisions while ostensibly promoting equality. Some of these revisionists went so far as to argue that the common school system was distorted from the outset by the requirements of the emerging industrial order, which made it almost inevitable that the schools would be used not to train an alert, politically active body of citizens but to inculcate habits of punctuality and obedience.

There is a good deal to be learned from the debates that took place in the formative period of the school system, the 1830s and 1840s, but an analysis of those debates will not support any such one-dimensional interpretation of the school's function as an agency of "social control." I do not see how anyone who reads the writings of Horace Mann, which did so much to justify a system of common schools and to persuade Americans to pay for it, can miss the moral fervor and democratic idealism that informed Mann's program. It is true that Mann resorted to a variety of arguments in favor of common schools, including the argument that they would teach steady habits of work. But he insisted that steady habits would benefit workers as well as employers, citing in favor of this contention the higher wages earned by those who enjoyed the advantages of a good education. He was careful to point out, moreover, that a positive assessment of the effects of schooling on men's "worldly fortunes or estates" was far from the "highest" argument in favor of education. Indeed, it might "justly be regarded as the lowest" (V:81). More important arguments for education, in Mann's view, were the "diffusion of useful knowledge," the promotion of tolerance, the equalization of opportunity, the "augmentation of national resources," the eradication of poverty, the overcoming of "mental imbecility and torpor," the encouragement of light and learning in place of "superstition and ignorance," and the substitution of peaceful methods of governance for coercion and warfare (IV:10; V:68, 81, 101, 109; VII:187). If Mann pretty clearly preferred the high ground of moral principle to the lower ground of industrial expediency, he could still appeal to prudential motives with a good conscience, since he did not perceive a contradiction between them. Comforts and conveniences were good things in themselves, even if there were loftier goods to aim at. His vision of "improvement" was broad enough to embrace material as well as moral progress; it was precisely their compatibility, indeed their inseparability, that distinguished Mann's version of the idea of progress from those that merely celebrated the wonders of modern science and technology.

As a child of the Enlightenment, Mann yielded to no one in his admiration for science and technology, but he was also a product of New England Puritanism, even though he came to reject Puritan theology. He was too keenly aware of the moral burden Americans inherited from their seventeenth-century ancestors to see a higher standard of living as an end in itself or to join those who equated the promise of American life with the opportunity to get rich quick. He did not look kindly on the project of getting enormously rich even in the long run. He deplored extremes of wealth and poverty—the "European theory" of social organization, as he called it—and upheld the "Massachusetts theory," which stressed "equality of condition" and "human welfare" (XII:55). It was to escape "extremes of high and low," Mann believed, that Americans had "fled" Europe in the first place, and the reemergence of those extremes, in nineteenth-century New England, should have been a source of deepest shame to his countrymen (VII:188, 191). When Mann dwelled on the accomplishments of his ancestors, it was with the intention of holding Americans to a higher standard of civic obligation than the standard prevailing in other countries. His frequent appeals to the "heroic period of our country's history" did not issue from a "boastful or vain-glorious spirit," he said. An appreciation of America's mission brought "more humiliation than pride" (VII:195). America should have "stood as a shining mark and exemplar before the world," instead of which it was lapsing into materialism and moral indifference (VII:196).

It is quite pointless to ask whether reformers like Horace Mann were more interested in humanitarianism than in work discipline and "social control." A good deal of fruitless debate among historians has been devoted to this question. Mann was not a radical, and he was undeniably interested in social order, but that does not make him any less a humanitarian. He was genuinely moved by the spectacle of poverty and suffering, though he also feared that poverty and suffering would breed "agrarianism," as he and his contemporaries called it—the "revenge of poverty against wealth" (XII:60). When he preached the duty to "bring forward those unfortunate classes of the people, who, in the march of civilization, have been left in the rear," there is no reason to think that he was concerned only with the danger of social revolution (XII:135). He defended property rights, to be sure, but he denied that property rights were "absolute and unqualified" (X:115). The earth was given to mankind "for the subsistence and benefit of the whole race," and the "rights of successive owners" were "limited by the rights of those who are entitled to the subsequent possession and use" (X:114–15). Every generation had an obligation to improve its inheritance and to pass it on to the next. "The successive generations of men, taken collectively, constitute one great commonwealth" (X:127). The doctrine of

144

*Chapter 6
Curriculum
Development
and the
Language of
Educational
Debate*

absolute property rights, which denied the solidarity of mankind, was a morality for "hermits" (X:120). In Mann's view, the "successive holders" of property were "trustees, bound to the faithful execution of their trust, by the most sacred obligations" (X:127). If they defaulted on those obligations, they could expect "terrible retributions" in the form of "poverty and destitution," "violence and misrule," "licentiousness and debauchery," "political profligacy and legalized perfidy" (X:126). Here Mann was truly prophetic, in the strict sense of the term. He called his people to account, pointing out that they had inherited a demanding set of obligations to live up to and foretelling the "certain vengeance of Heaven" if they failed (X:126). He was a prophet in the vulgar sense as well: His predictions have come true—his predictions, that is, of the specific evils that would follow from a failure to provide a system of education assuring "knowledge and virtue," the necessary foundations of a republican form of government (XII:142). Who can look at America today without recognizing the accuracy of Mann's cautionary rhetoric, right down to the "legalized perfidy" of our political leaders? The only thing Mann failed to foresee was the drug epidemic, though that could be included, I suppose, under the heading of "licentiousness and debauchery."

Yet Mann's efforts on behalf of the common schools bore spectacular success, if we consider the long-term goals (and even the immediate goals) he was attempting to promote. His countrymen heeded his exhortations after all. They built a system of common schools attended by all classes of society. They rejected the European model, which provided a liberal education for the children of privilege and vocational training for the masses. They abolished child labor and made school attendance compulsory, as Mann had urged. They enforced a strict separation between church and state, protecting the schools from sectarian influences. They recognized the need for professional training of teachers, and they set up a system of normal schools to bring about this result. They followed Mann's advice to provide instruction not only in academic subjects but in the "laws of health," vocal music, and other character-forming disciplines (VI:61, 66). They even followed his advice to staff the schools largely with women, sharing his belief that women were more likely than men to govern their pupils by the gentle art of persuasion. They honored Mann himself, even during his lifetime, as the founding father of their schools. If Mann was a prophet in some respects, he was hardly a prophet without honor in his own country. He succeeded beyond the wildest dreams of most reformers, yet the result was the same as if he had failed.

Here is our puzzle, then: Why did the success of Mann's program leave us with the social and political disasters he predicted, with uncanny accuracy, in the event of his failure? To put the question this way suggests that there was something inherently deficient in Mann's educational vision, that his program contained some fatal flaw in its very conception. The flaw did not lie in Mann's enthusiasm for "social control" or his halfhearted humanitarianism. The history of reform—with its high sense of mission, its devotion to progress and improvement, its enthusiasm for economic growth and equal opportunity, its humanitarianism, its love of peace and its hatred of war, its confidence in the welfare state, and, above all, its zeal for education—is the history of liberalism, not conservatism, and if the reform movement gave us a society that bears little resemblance to what was promised, we have to ask not whether the reform movement was insufficiently liberal and humanitarian but whether liberal humanitarianism provides the best recipe for a democratic society.

We get a little insight into Mann's limitations by considering his powerful aversion to war—superficially one of the more attractive elements of his outlook. Deeply committed to the proposition that a renunciation of war and warlike habits provided an infallible index of social progress, of the victory of civilization over barbarism, Mann complained that school and town libraries were full of history books glorifying war.

> How little do these books contain, which is suitable for children!... Descriptions of battles, sackings of cities, and the captivity of nations, follow each other with the quickest movement, and in an endless succession. Almost the only glimpses, which we catch of the education of youth, present them, as engaged in martial sports, and the mimic feats of arms, preparatory to the grand tragedies of battle;—exercises and exhibitions, which, both in the performer and the spectator, cultivate all the dissocial emotions, and turn the whole current of the mental forces into the channel of destructiveness [III:58].

Mann called himself a republican (in order to signify his opposition to monarchy), but he had no appreciation of the connection between martial virtue and citizenship, which had received so much attention in the republican tradition. Even Adam Smith, whose liberal economics dealt that tradition a crippling blow, regretted the loss of armed civic virtue. "A man, incapable either of defending or of revenging himself, evidently wants one of the most essential parts of the character of a man." It was a matter for regret, in Smith's view, that the "general security and happiness which prevail in ages of civility and politeness" gave so "little exercise to the contempt of danger, to patience in enduring labor, hunger, and pain." Given the growth of commerce, things could not be otherwise, according to Smith, but the disappearance of qualities so essential to manhood and therefore to citizenship was nevertheless a disturbing development. Politics and war, not commerce, served as the "great school of self-command." If commerce was now displacing "war and faction" as the chief business of mankind (to the point where the very term "business" soon became a synonym for commerce), the educational system would have to take up the slack, sustaining values that could no longer be acquired through participation in public events.

Horace Mann, like Smith, believed that formal education could take the place of other character-forming experiences, but he had a very different conception of the kind of character he wanted to form. He shared none of Smith's enthusiasm for war and none of his reservations about a society composed of peace-loving men and women going about their business and largely indifferent to public affairs. As we shall see, Mann's opinion of politics was no higher than his opinion of war. His educational program did not attempt to supply the courage, patience, and fortitude formerly supplied by "war and faction." It therefore did not occur to him that historical narratives, with their stirring accounts of exploits carried out in the line of military or political duty, might fire the imagination of the young and help to frame their own aspirations. Perhaps it would be more accurate to say that he distrusted *any* sort of appeal to the

146

*Chapter 6
Curriculum
Development
and the
Language of
Educational
Debate*

imagination. His educational philosophy was hostile to imagination as such. He preferred fact to fiction, science to mythology. He complained that young people were given a "mass of fictions," when they needed "true stories" and "real examples of real men" (III:90–91). But his conception of the truths that could safely be entrusted to children turned out to be very limited indeed. History, he thought, "should be rewritten" so as to enable children to compare "the right with the wrong" and to give them "some option of admiring and emulating the former" (III:59–60). Mann's objections to the kind of history children were conventionally exposed to was not only that it acclaimed military exploits but that right and wrong were confusingly mixed up together—as they are always mixed up, of course, in the real world. It was just this element of moral ambiguity that Mann wanted to eliminate. "As much of History now stands, the examples of right and wrong ... are ... brought and shuffled together" (III:60). Educators had a duty to sort them out and to make it unambiguously clear to children which was which.

Mann's plea for historical realism betrayed not only an impoverished conception of reality but a distrust of pedagogically unmediated experience—attitudes that have continued to characterize educational thinking ever since. Like many other educators, Mann wanted children to receive their impressions of the world from those who were professionally qualified to decide what it was proper for them to know, instead of picking up impressions haphazardly from narratives (both written and oral) not expressly designed for children. Anyone who has spent much time with children knows that they acquire much of their understanding of the adult world by listening to what adults do not necessarily want them to hear—by eavesdropping, in effect, and just by keeping their eyes and ears open. Information acquired in this way is more vivid and compelling than any other since it enables children to put themselves imaginatively in the place of adults instead of being treated simply as objects of adult solicitude and didacticism. It was precisely this imaginative experience of the adult world, however—this unsupervised play of young imaginations—that Mann hoped to replace with formal instruction. Thus he objected to "novels and all that class of books," which offered "mere *amusement*, as contradistinguished from instruction in the practical concerns of life." His objection, to be sure, was directed mainly against "light reading," which allegedly distracted people from "reflection upon the great realities of experience"; but he did not specifically exempt more serious works of fiction, nor is there any indication, in the vast body of his educational writings, that he recognized the possibility that the "great realities of existence" are treated more fully in fiction and poetry than in any other kind of writing (III:60).

The great weakness in Mann's educational philosophy was the assumption that education takes place only in schools. Perhaps it is unfair to say that Mann bequeathed this fatal assumption to subsequent generations of educators, as part of his intellectual legacy. An inability to see beyond the school after all —a tendency to speak as if schooling and education were synonymous terms— should probably be regarded as an occupational hazard of professional educators, a form of blindness that is built into the job. Still, Mann was one of the first to give it official sanction. His thinking on this point was more striking in what it omitted than in what it said in so many words. It simply did not occur to him that activities like politics, war, and love—the staple themes of the books he deplored—were educative in their own right. He believed that partisan politics, in particular, was the bane of American life. In his Twelfth Report he described the excitement surrounding the presidential election of 1848 in language that unmistakably conveyed the importance of politics as a form of popular education, only to condemn the campaign (in which he himself had won election to the House of Representatives) as a distraction from his more important work as an educator.

> Agitation pervaded the country. There was no stagnant mind; there was no stagnant atmosphere.... Wit, argument, eloquence, were in such demand, that they were sent for at the distance of a thousand miles—from one side of the Union to the other. The excitement reached the humblest walks of life. The mechanic in his shop made his hammer chime to the music of political rhymes; and the farmer, as he gathered in his harvest, watched the aspects of the political, more vigilantly than of the natural, sky. Meetings were every where held.... The press showered its sheets over the land, thick as snowflakes in a wintry storm. Public and private histories were ransacked, to find proofs of honor or proofs of dishonor; political economy was invoked; the sacred names of patriotism, philanthropy, duty to God, and duty to man, were on every tongue.

The campaign of 1848, as Mann described it, elicited an intensity of popular response that would be the envy of our own times, yet Mann could find in all this only "violence" and "din"—a "Saturnalia of license, evil speaking, and falsehood." He wished that the energy devoted to politics could be devoted instead to "getting children into the schools" (XII:25–26). Elsewhere in the same report he likened politics to a conflagration, a fire raging out of control, or again to a plague, an "infection" or "poison" (XII:87).

Reading these passages, one begins to see that Mann wanted to keep politics out of the school not only because he was afraid that his system would be torn apart by those who wished to use it for partisan purposes but because he distrusted political activity as such. It produced an "inflammation of the passions" (XII:26). It generated controversy—a necessary part of education, it might be argued, but in Mann's eyes, a waste of time and energy. It divided men instead of bringing them together. For these reasons Mann sought not only to insulate the school from political pressures but to keep political history out of the curriculum. The subject could not be ignored entirely; otherwise children would gain only "such knowledge as they may pick up from angry political discussions, or from party newspapers." But instruction in the "nature of a republican government" was to be conducted so as to emphasize only "those articles in the creed of republicanism, which are accepted by all, believed in by all, and which form the common basis of our political faith." Anything controversial was to be passed over in silence or, at best, with the admonition that "the schoolroom is neither the tribunal to adjudicate, nor the forum to discuss it" (XII:89).

Although it is somewhat tangential to my main point, it is worth pausing to see what Mann considered to be the common articles in the republican creed, the "elementary ideas" on which everyone could agree (XII:89). The most

148

*Chapter 6
Curriculum
Development
and the
Language of
Educational
Debate*

important of these points, it appears, were the duty of citizens to appeal to the courts, if wronged, instead of taking the law into their own hands, and the duty to change the laws "by an appeal to the ballot, and not by rebellion" (XII:85). Mann did not see that these "elementary ideas" were highly controversial in themselves or that others might quarrel with his underlying assumption that the main purpose of government was to keep order. But the substance of his political views is less germane to my purpose than his attempt to palm them off as universal principles. It is bad enough that he disguised the principles of the Whig party as principles common to all Americans and thus protected them from reasonable criticism. What is even worse is the way in which his bland tutelage deprived children of anything that might have appealed to the imagination or—to use his own term—the "passions." Political history, taught along the lines recommended by Mann, would be drained of controversy, sanitized, bowdlerized, and therefore drained of excitement. It would become mild, innocuous, and profoundly boring, trivialized by a suffocating didacticism. Mann's idea of political education was of a piece with his idea of moral education, on which he laid such heavy-handed emphasis in his opposition to merely intellectual training. Moral education, as he conceived it, consisted of inoculation against "social vices and crimes": "gaming, intemperance, dissoluteness, falsehood, dishonesty, violence, and their kindred offenses" (XII:97). In the republican tradition—compared with which Mann's republicanism was no more than a distant echo—the concept of virtue referred to honor, ardor, superabundant energy, and the fullest use of one's powers. For Mann, virtue was only the pallid opposite of "vice." Virtue was "sobriety, frugality, probity"—qualities not likely to seize the imagination of the young (XII:97).

The subject of morality brings us by a short step to religion, where we see Mann's limitations in their clearest form. Here again I want to call into question the very aspects of Mann's thought that have usually been singled out for the highest praise. Even his detractors—those who see his philanthropy as a cover for social control—congratulate Mann on his foresight in protecting the schools from sectarian pressures. He was quite firm on the need to banish religious instruction based on the tenets of any particular denomination. In his lifetime he was unfairly accused of banishing religious instruction altogether and thus undermining public morals. To these "grave charges" he replied, plausibly enough, that sectarianism could not be tolerated in schools that everyone was expected to attend—compelled to attend, if he were to have his way (XII:103). But he also made it clear that a "rival system of 'Parochial' or 'Sectarian' schools" was not to be tolerated either (XII:104). His program envisioned the public school system as a monopoly, in practice, if not in law. It implied the marginalization, if not the outright elimination, of institutions that might compete with the common schools.

His opposition to religious sectarianism did not stop with its exclusion from the public sector of education. He was against sectarianism as such, for the same reasons that made him take such a dim view of politics. Sectarianism, in his view, breathed the spirit of fanaticism and persecution. It gave rise to religious controversy, which was no more acceptable to Mann than political controversy. He spoke of both in images of fire. If the theological "heats and animosities engendered in families, and among neighbors, burst forth in a devouring fire" into school meetings, the "inflammable materials" would grow so intense that no one could "quench the flames," until the "zealots" themselves were "consumed in the conflagration they have kindled" (XII:129). It was not enough to keep the churches out of the public schools; it was necessary to keep them out of public life altogether, lest the "discordant" sounds of religious debate drown out the "one, indivisible, all-glorious system of Christianity" and bring about the "return of Babel" (XII:130). The perfect world, as it existed in Mann's head, was a world in which everyone agreed, a heavenly city where the angels sang in unison. He sadly admitted that "we can hardly conceive of a state of society upon earth so perfect as to exclude all differences of opinion," but at least it was possible to relegate disagreements "about rights" and other important matters to the sidelines of social life, to bar them from the schools and, by implication, from the public sphere as a whole (XII:96).

None of this meant that the schools should not teach religion; it meant only that they should teach the religion that was common to all, or at least to all Christians. The Bible should be read in school, on the assumption that it could "speak for itself," without commentaries that might give rise to disagreement (XII:117). Here again Mann's program invites a type of criticism that misses the point. His nondenominational instruction is open to the objection that it still excluded Jews, Muhammadans, Buddhists, and atheists. Ostensibly tolerant, it was actually repressive in equating religion narrowly with Christianity. This is a trivial objection. At the time Mann was writing, it still made sense to speak of the United States as a Christian nation, but the reasoning on which he justified a nondenominational form of Christianity could easily be extended to include other religions as well. The real objection is that the resulting mixture is so bland that it puts children to sleep instead of awakening feelings of awe and wonder. Orestes Brownson, the most perceptive of Mann's contemporary critics, pointed out in 1839 that Mann's system, by suppressing everything divisive in religion, would leave only an innocuous residue. "A faith, which embraces generalities only, is little better than no faith at all." Children brought up in a mild and nondenominational "Christianity ending in nothingness," in schools where "much will be taught in general, but nothing in particular," would be deprived of their birthright, as Brownson saw it. They would be taught "to respect and preserve what is"; they would be cautioned against the "licentiousness of the people, the turbulence and brutality of the mob," but they would never learn a "love of liberty" under such a system.

Although Brownson did not share Mann's horror of dissension, he too deplored the widening gap between wealth and poverty and saw popular education as a means of overcoming these divisions. Unlike Mann, however, he understood that the real work of education did not take place in the schools at all. Anticipating John Dewey, Brownson pointed out that

> our children are educated in the streets, by the influence of their associates, in the fields and on the hill sides, by the influences of surrounding scenery and overshadowing skies, in the bosom of the family, by the love and gentleness, or wrath and fretfulness of parents, by the passions or affections they see manifested, the

150

*Chapter 6
Curriculum
Development
and the
Language of
Educational
Debate*

conversations to which they listen, and above all by the general pursuits, habits, and moral tone of the community.

These considerations, together with Brownson's extensive discussion of the press and the lyceum, seemed to point to the conclusion that people were most likely to develop a love of liberty through exposure to wide-ranging public controversy, the "free action of mind on mind."

Wide-ranging public controversy, as we have seen, was just what Mann wanted to avoid. Nothing of educational value, in his view, could issue from the clash of opinions, the noise and heat of political and religious debate. Education could take place only in institutions deliberately contrived for that purpose, in which children were exposed exclusively to knowledge professional educators considered appropriate. Some such assumption, I think, has been the guiding principle of American education ever since. Mann's reputation as the founding father of the public school is well deserved. His energy, his missionary enthusiasm, his powers of persuasion, and the strategic position he enjoyed as secretary of the Massachusetts Board of Education made it possible for him to leave a lasting mark on the educational enterprise. One might go so far as to say that the enterprise has never recovered from the mistakes and misconceptions built into it at the very outset.

Not that Horace Mann would be pleased with our educational system as it exists today. On the contrary, he would be horrified. Nevertheless, the horrors are at least indirectly a consequence of his own ideas, unleavened by the moral idealism with which they were once associated. We have incorporated into our schools the worst of Mann and somehow managed to lose sight of the best. We have professionalized teaching by setting up elaborate requirements for certification, but we have not succeeded in institutionalizing Mann's appreciation of teaching as an honorable calling. We have set up a far-ranging educational bureaucracy without raising academic standards or improving the quality of teaching. The bureaucratization of education has the opposite effect, undermining the teacher's autonomy, substituting the judgment of administrators for that of the teacher, and incidentally discouraging people with a gift for teaching from entering the profession at all. We have followed Mann's advice to de-emphasize purely academic subjects, but the resulting loss of intellectual rigor has not been balanced by an improvement in the school's capacity to nourish the character traits Mann considered so important: self-reliance, courteousness, and the capacity for deferred gratification. The periodic rediscovery that intellectual training has been sacrificed to "social skills" has led to a misplaced emphasis on the purely cognitive dimension of education, which lacks even Mann's redeeming awareness of its moral dimension. We share Mann's distrust of the imagination and his narrow conception of truth, insisting that the schools should stay away from myths and stories and legends and stick to sober facts, but the range of permissible facts is even more pathetically limited today than it was in Mann's day.

History has given way to an infantilized version of sociology, in obedience to the misconceived principle that the quickest way to engage children's attention is to dwell on what is closest to home: their families; their neighborhoods;

the local industries; the technologies on which they depend. A more sensible assumption would be that children need to learn about faraway places and olden times before they can make sense of their immediate surroundings. Since most children have no opportunity for extended travel, and since travel in our world is not very broadening anyway, the school can provide a substitute—but not if it clings to the notion that the only way to "motivate" them is to expose them to nothing not already familiar, nothing not immediately applicable to themselves.

Like Mann, we believe that schooling is a cure-all for everything that ails us. Mann and his contemporaries held that good schools could eradicate crime and juvenile delinquency, do away with poverty, make useful citizens out of "abandoned and outcast children," and serve as the "great equalizer" between rich and poor (XII:42, 59). They would have done better to start out with a more modest set of expectations. If there is one lesson we might have been expected to learn in the 150 years since Horace Mann took charge of the schools of Massachusetts, it is that the schools can't save society. Crime and poverty are still with us, and the gap between rich and poor continues to widen. Meanwhile, our children, even as young adults, don't know how to read and write. Maybe the time has come—if it hasn't already passed—to start all over again.

NOTES

1. All the quotations in this [selection], except the ones from Adam Smith and Orestes Brownson, come from the long reports [Horace] Mann submitted to the Massachusetts legislature as secretary of the Board of Education. The page references cited in the text are from the *Annual Report of the Board of Education, together with the Annual Report of the Secretary of the Board* (Boston: Dutton and Wentworth, 1838–1848), in twelve volumes. Smith's reflections on the demoralizing effects of commerce appear in *The Wealth of Nations*, Book V, chapter 1 ("incapable either of defending or of revenging himself"), and *The Theory of Moral Sentiments*, ed. D. D. Raphael and A. L. Macfie (Oxford: Clarendon Press, 1976), pp. 146 ("great school of self-command"), 152–53 ("war and faction"), 205 ("general security and happiness"). Brownson's attack on Mann appeared in the *Boston Quarterly Review* 2 (1839): 394 ("educated in the streets"), 404 ("a faith, which embraces generalities only"; "much in general, nothing in particular"), 411 ("respect and preserve what is"; "licentiousness of the people"; "love of liberty"), 434 ("free action of mind on mind").

    Jonathan Messerli, *Horace Mann* (New York: Alfred A. Knopf, 1972) is the standard biography. Discussions of Mann's educational ideas and program appear in Merle Curti, *The Social Ideas of American Educators* (New York: Scribner's, 1935); Rush Welter, *Popular Education and Democratic Thought in America* (New York: Columbia University Press, 1962); David Tyack and Elizabeth Hansot, *Managers of Virtue: Public School Leadership in America, 1820–1980* (New York: Basic Books, 1982); Maxine Green, *The Public School and the Private Vision* (New York: Random House, 1965); Carl F. Kaestle, *Pillars of the Republic: Common Schools and American Society, 1780–1860* (New York: Hill and Wang, 1983); R. Freeman Butts, *Public Education in the United States* (New York: Holt, Rinehart, and Winston, 1978); and many other books on American education.

Multiculturalism and the Postmodern Critique

Peter McLaren is an associate professor of administration, curriculum, and teaching studies. He earned his Ph.D. in curriculum and educational theory in 1983 from the Ontario Institute for Studies in Education at the University of Toronto, Canada. His current research interests include postcolonial and postmodern theories as applied to curriculum development and instruction. He has published many books, including *Critical Pedagogy and Predatory Culture: Oppositional Politics in the Postmodern Era* (Routledge, 1995) and *Schooling as a Ritual Performance: Towards a Political Economy of Educational Symbols and Gestures,* 2d ed. (Routledge, 1993).

The selection that follows is from "Multiculturalism and the Postmodern Critique: Toward a Pedagogy of Resistance and Transformation," in Henry A. Giroux and Peter McLaren, eds., *Between Borders: Pedagogy and the Politics of Cultural Studies.* In it, McLaren offers insight into the state of injustice in present-day society and discusses how the struggle for social justice can be engaged by educators and other cultural workers. McLaren positions the discussion of "multiculturalism" in the competing social and ideological contexts of our time. He argues that a "resistance" postmodernist method of social critique can help teachers and students to clarify issues relating to "difference" and "diversity" and the importance of accepting cultural and personal differences and diversity.

McLaren argues that social and personal justice needs to be continually created—that the quest for justice in society is a constant struggle. Educators and other cultural workers can help the young to position themselves in this struggle by learning to define and locate their own voices in their own localities in critiquing local and national social practices and policies. He points out that in applying resistance postmodernist methods of social critique, individuals need to always rethink the relationship between identity and difference. A resistance postmodernist educational critique, McLaren maintains, must *not* see cultural differences as merely "other than white"; the concept of white ethnicity must itself be critiqued as part of creating accurate awareness of its hegemonic (dominating) impact.

Key Concept: multiculturalism and postmodernism

For the proletariat does not need all the thousands of little words by which the bourgeoisie masks class struggles in its own pedagogy. The "unprejudiced," "understanding," "empathetic" bourgeoisie practices, the "child-loving" teachers—these we can do without.

—Walter Benjamin, "Program for a Proletarian Children's Theater"

SOCIAL JUSTICE UNDER SIEGE

We inhabit skeptical times, historical moments spawned in a temper of distrust, disillusionment, and despair. Social relations of discomfort and diffidence have always preexisted us but the current historical juncture is particularly invidious in this regard, marked as it is by a rapture of greed, untempered and hypereroticized consumer will, racing currents of narcissism, severe economic and racial injustices, and heightened social paranoia. The objective conditions of Western capitalism now appear so completely incompatible with the realization of freedom and liberation that it is no understatement to consider them mutually antagonistic enterprises. Situated beyond the reach of ethically convincing forms of accountability, capitalism has dissolved the meaning of democracy and freedom into glossy aphorisms one finds in election campaign sound bytes or at bargain basement sales in suburban shopping malls. The American public has been proferred a vision of democracy that is a mixture of Sunday barbecue banality, American Gladiator jocksniffery, AMWAY enterprise consciousness, and the ominous rhetoric of "New World Order" jingoism.

The heroic cult of modernism which has naturalized the power and privilege of "dead white men" and accorded the pathology of domination the status of cultural reason has all but enshrined a history of decay, defeat, and moral panic. As illustrated so vividly in Oliver Stone's television mini-series, *Wild Palms,* greed, avarice, and cynicism have insinuated themselves into virtually every aspect of cultural life, and have become rationalized and aestheticized as necessary resources that must be fed into a vast technological machine known as Western civilization. It is history that has installed Willie Horton into our structural unconscious and helped make possible and desirable the legal torture and dehumanization of Rodney King and peoples of color in general. That the fortified, postmodern *noir* metropolises of this fin-de-siècle era have grown more Latinophobic, homophobic, xenophobic, sexist, racist, and bureaucratically cruel is not reflective of the self-understanding of the public at large but of the way that the public has been constructed through a politics of representation linked to the repressive moralism of the current conservative political regime and current counterattacks on cultural democracy from the Right. We should not forget, as well, the spectatorial detachment of those postmodern free-floating intellectuals who, despite their claim to be part of a collective deconstructive project, often fail to mobilize intellectual work in the interest of a liberatory praxis.

154

*Chapter 6
Curriculum
Development
and the
Language of
Educational
Debate*

The present moral apocalypse, perhaps most vividly represented by the maelstrom of anger and violence under the smoke-filled skies of Los Angeles—what Mike Davis calls the "L.A. Intifada" (Katz and Smith, 1992)—has not been brought on simply by the existence of midnight hustlers, the drug trade, skewered ambition, or gang members taking advantage of public outrage over the justice system but by shifting economic, political, and cultural relations that have worsened over the last two decades. We have been standing at the crossroads of a disintegrating culture for the last two decades where we have witnessed a steady increase in the disproportionate level of material wealth, economic dislocation, and intergenerational poverty suffered by African-Americans, Latinos, and other minorities. Such conditions have been brought about by the frenetic and, at times, savage immorality of the Reagan and Bush administrations, as evidenced in their direct attacks on the underclass, the disintegration of social programs, and the general retreat from civil rights that occurred during their tenure in office.

Other characteristics of this current juncture include: changes in the structure of the U.S. economy; the declining inner-city job market; growing national "unemployment rates; a drastic decline in the number of unskilled positions in traditional blue-collar industries in urban areas; the increasing numbers of youth competing for fewer and fewer entry-level unskilled jobs; the automation of clerical labor; the movement of the African-American middle class out of the once multiclass ghetto; the shifting of service-sector employment to the suburbs" (Kasinitz 1988); the destructive competition among nations that results from a free-trade policy fueled by the retrograde notion that other nations can achieve economic growth by unbalanced sales to the U.S. market; increased global competition provoking capitalist manufacturing firms to reduce costs by exploiting immigrant workers in U.S. cities or "out-sourcing" to Third World countries; and a post-Fordist demonopolization of economic structures and the deregulation and globalization of markets, trade, and labor as well as deregulated local markets "that [make] local capital vulnerable to the strategies of corporate raiders" (Featherstone 1990, 7).

In addition, we are faced with an increasing assault on human intelligence by the architects of mass culture, an increasing dependency on social cues manufactured by the mass media to construct meaning and build consensus on moral issues, and the strengthening of what Piccone (1988, 9) has called the "unholy symbiosis of abstract individualism and managerial bureaucracies." The white-controlled media (often backed by victim-blaming white social scientists) have ignored the economic and social conditions responsible for bringing about in African-American communities what Cornel West has called a "*walking nihilism* of pervasive drug addiction, pervasive alcoholism, pervasive homicide, and an exponential rise in suicide" (cited in Stephanson 1988, 276).

Furthermore, the white media have generated the racially pornographic term "wilding" to account for recent acts of violence in urban centers by groups of young African-Americans (Cooper 1989). Apparently the term "wilding," first reported by New York City newspapers in relation to the Central Park rapists, was relevant only to the violence of black male youth, since it was conspicuously absent in press reports of the attack of white male youths on Yusef Hawkins in Bensonhurst (Wallace 1991). Thus, the postmodern image which many white people now entertain in relation to the African-American underclass is one constructed upon violence and grotesquery—a population spawning mutant Willie Horton–type youths who, in the throes of bloodlust, roam the perimeter of the urban landscape high on angel dust, randomly hunting whites with steel pipes.... Latino youth fare no better in the public eye.

THE DILEMMA OF POSTMODERN CRITIQUE AND THE DEBATE OVER MULTICULTURALISM

I have foregrounded the social and cultural situatedness of oppression as a background for my discussion of multiculturalism since I share Michele Wallace's conviction that the debates over multiculturalism cannot afford to have their connection to wider material relations occulted by a focus on theoretical issues divorced from the lived experiences of oppressed groups. She is worth quoting on this issue:

> Many individual events on the current cultural landscape conspire to make me obsessed with contemporary debates over "multiculturalism" in both the art world and the culture at large, but my concern is grounded first and foremost in my observation of the impact of present material conditions on an increasing sector of the population. These material conditions, which include widespread homelessness, joblessness, illiteracy, crime, disease (including AIDS), hunger, poverty, drug addiction, alcoholism as well as the various habits of ill health, and the destruction of the environment are (let's face it) the myriad social effects of late multinational capitalism. (1991, 6)

A focus on the material and global relations of oppression can help us to avoid reducing the "problem" of multiculturalism to simply one of attitudes and temperament or, in the case of the academy, to a case of textual disagreement and discourse wars. It also helps to emphasize the fact that in the United States the concoction called "multiculturalism," which has resulted from a forensic search for equality and the political ladling of the long-brewing "melting pot," has produced an aversion to rather than a respect for difference. Regrettably, multiculturalism has been too often transformed into a code word in contemporary political jargon that has been fulsomely invoked in order to divert attention from the imperial legacy of racism and social injustice in this country and the ways in which new racist formations are being produced in spaces culturally dedifferentiated and demonized by neoconservative platforms that anathematize difference through attacks on the concept of heterogeneous public cultures (see Ravitch 1990, 1991; Kimball 1991; Browder 1992).

In the sections that follow, I want to discuss recent articulations of the postmodern critique in order to examine the limitations of current conservative and liberal formulations of multiculturalism. In doing so, I would like to pose

156

*Chapter 6
Curriculum
Development
and the
Language of
Educational
Debate*

an alternative analysis. I shall argue that, despite its limitations for constructing an emancipatory politics, postmodern criticism can offer educators and cultural workers a means of problematizing the issue of difference and diversity in ways that can deepen and extend existing debates over multiculturalism, pedagogy, and social transformation. Certain new strands of postmodern critique that fall under the rubric of "political" and "critical" postmodernism deserve serious attention in this regard.

More specifically, I shall redraw the discussion of multiculturalism from the perspective of new strands of postmodern critique that emphasize the construction of "a politics of difference." I will conclude by urging critical educators to reclaim the importance of relational or global critique—in particular the concept of "totality"—in their efforts to bring history and materiality back into theoretical and pedagogical discourses. . . .

MULTICULTURALISM AND THE POSTMODERN CRITIQUE

In this section I want to bring a critical or resistance postmodernist perspective to bear on the issue of multiculturalism. For me, the key issue for critical educators is to develop a multicultural curriculum and pedagogy that attends to the specificity (in terms of race, class, gender, sexual orientation, etc.) of difference (which is in keeping with ludic postmodernism) yet at the same time addresses the commonality of diverse Others under the law with respect to guiding referents of freedom and liberation (which is in keeping with resistance postmodernism).

Viewed from the perspective of resistance postmodernism, the liberal and conservative attacks on multiculturalism as separatist and ethnocentric carry with them the erroneous assumption that North American society fundamentally constitutes social relations of uninterrupted accord. This view furthermore underscores the idea that North American society is largely a forum of consensus with different minority viewpoints simply accretively added on. This constitutes a politics of pluralism which largely ignores the workings of power and privilege. More specifically, it "involves a very insidious exclusion as far as any structural politics of change is concerned: it excludes and occludes global or structural relations of power as 'ideological' and 'totalizing' " (Ebert forthcoming). In addition, it presupposes harmony and agreement —an undisturbed space in which differences can coexist. Yet such a presupposition is dangerously problematic. Chandra Mohanty (1989/90) notes that the difference cannot be formulated as negotiation among culturally diverse groups against a backdrop of presumed cultural homogeneity. Difference is the recognition that knowledges are forged in histories that are riven with differentially constituted relations of power; that is, knowledges, subjectivities, and social practices are forged within "asymmetrical and incommensurate cultural spheres" (1989/90, 181).

Peter McLaren

Too often liberal and conservative positions on diversity constitute an attempt to view culture as a soothing balm—the aftermath of historical disagreement—some mythical present where the irrationalities of historical conflict have been smoothed out. This is not only a disingenuous view of culture, it is profoundly dishonest. The liberal and conservative positions on culture also assume that justice already exists and needs only to be evenly apportioned. However, both teachers and students need to realize that justice does not already exist simply because laws exist. Justice needs to be continually created, constantly struggled for. The question that I want to pose to teachers is this: Do teachers and cultural workers have access to a language that allows them to sufficiently critique and transform existing social and cultural practices that are defended by liberals and conservatives as democratic?...

CRITICAL PEDAGOGY: TEACHING FOR A HYBRID CITIZENRY AND MULTICULTURAL SOLIDARITY

"There's room for all at the rendez-vous of victory"

—Cesaire

Resistance postmodernism has figured prominently in the development of new forms of pedagogical praxis concerned with rethinking educational politics in a multicultural society (Giroux 1992; McLaren and Leonard, forthcoming; McLaren forthcoming; Aronwitz and Giroux 1991). Of particular significance is Giroux's concept of a "border pedagogy" which enables educators to affirm and legitimate local meanings and constellations of meanings that grow out of particular discursive communities but at the same time interrogate the interests, ideologies, and social practices that such knowledges serve when viewed from the perspective of more global economies of power and privilege.

A pedagogy informed significantly by resistance postmodernism suggests that teachers and cultural workers need to take up the issue of "difference" in ways that don't replay the monocultural essentialism of the "centrisms"—Anglocentrism, Eurocentrism, phallocentrism, androcentrism, and the like. They need to create a politics of alliance building, of dreaming together, of solidarity that moves beyond the condescensions of, say, "race awareness week," which actually serves to keep forms of institutionalized racism intact. A solidarity has to be struggled for that is not centered around market imperatives but develops out of the imperatives of freedom, liberation, democracy, and critical citizenship.

The notion of the citizen has been pluralized and hybridized, as Kobena Mercer notes, by the presence of a diversity of social subjects. Mercer is instructive in pointing out that "solidarity does not mean that everyone thinks the same way, it begins when people have the confidence to disagree over issues because they 'care' about constructing a common ground" (1990, 68). Solidarity is not impermeably solid but depends to a certain degree on antagonism

158

*Chapter 6
Curriculum
Development
and the
Language of
Educational
Debate*

and uncertainty. Timothy Maliqualim Simone calls this type of multiracial solidarity "geared to maximizing points of interaction rather than harmonizing, balancing, or equilibrating the distribution of bodies, resources, and territories" (1989, 191).

While guarding against the privileging of a false universalism, a false unity that denies the internal rifts of bodily desire, both teachers and students need to open themselves to the possibility of Otherness so that the particularity of individual being can become visible in relation to larger relations of power and privilege. Students especially need to be provided with opportunities to devise different assemblages of the self by dismantling and interrogating the different kinds of discursive segmentarity that inform their subjectivities, subverting those stratified and hierarchized forms of subjectivity that code the will, and developing nomadic forms of individual and collective agency that open up new assemblages of desire and modes of being-in-the-world (Grossberg 1988).

Educators must examine the development of pedagogical discourses and practices that demonize Others who are different (through transforming them into absence or deviance). A resistance postmodernism that takes multiculturalism seriously calls attention to the dominant meaning systems readily available to students—most of which are ideologically stitched into the fabric of Western imperialism and patriarchy. It challenges meaning systems that impose attributes on the Other under the direction of sovereign signifiers and tropes. And this means not directing all our efforts at understanding ethnicity as "other than white," but interrogating the culture of whiteness itself. This is crucial because unless we do this—unless we give white students a sense of their own identity as an emergent ethnicity—we naturalize whiteness as a cultural marker against which Otherness is defined. Coco Fusco warns that "to ignore white ethnicity is to redouble its hegemony by naturalizing it. Without specifically addressing white ethnicity there can be no critical evaluation of the construction of the other" (cited in Wallace 1991, 7). White groups need to examine their ethnic histories so that they are less likely to judge their own cultural norms as neutral and universal. "Whiteness" does not exist outside of culture but constitutes the prevailing social texts in which social norms are made and remade. As part of a politics of signification that passes unobserved into the rhythms of daily life, and a "politically constructed category parasitic on 'Blackness'" (West 1990, 29), "whiteness" has become the invisible norm for how the dominant culture measures its own civility.

With this in mind, a critical pedagogy that embraces a resistance postmodernism needs to construct a politics of refusal that can provide both the conditions for interrogating the institutionalization of formal equality based on the prized imperatives of a white, Anglo male world and for creating spaces to facilitate an investigation of the way in which dominant institutions must be transformed so that they no longer serve simply as conduits for a motivated indifference to victimization for a Euroimperial aesthetics, for depredations of economic and cultural dependency, and for the production of asymmetrical relations of power and privilege....

A pedagogy that takes resistance postmodernism seriously does not make the nativist assumption that knowledge is preontologically available and that various disciplinary schools of thought may be employed in order to tease our different readings of the same "commonsense" reality in a context of impartiality. Rather, the discourses that inform the educator's problematics are understood as constitutive of the very reality that he or she is attempting to understand. Consequently, the classroom is the site of the teacher's own embodiment in theory/discourse, ethical disposition as moral and political agent, and situatedness as a cultural worker within a larger narrative identity. In recognizing the important role played by "place" in any critical pedagogy, it should be clear that we are talking not about the physical milieu where knowledge is made visible within preordained and circumscribed limits but rather the textual space that one occupies and the effective space one creates as a teacher. In other words, the discursive practice of "doing pedagogy" does not simply treat knowledge outside of the way that it is taken up by both teachers and students *as a form of dialogue.* I am referring here to the multi-voicedness of democratic discourse not in the sense of unrestrained intersubjective exchange but rather as challenging "the logic of dialogue as equal linguistic exchange." Such a challenge involves interrogating the ideological interests of the speaker, the social overdeterminations of utterances, and the social context in which utterances are both historically produced and culturally understood (Hitchcock, 1993, 7). Knowledge can never be treated as a cultural artifact or possession that serves as a pristine, prefigurative source of cultural authenticity inviting unbiased analysis.

The project of critical pedagogy means bringing the laws of cultural representation face to face with their founding assumptions, contradictions, and paradoxes. It also means encouraging teachers to participate in the affective as well as intellectual cultures of the oppressed, and to challenge in the spirit of Ernst Bloch's "militant optimism" ethical and political quietism in the face of operating homilies such as "progress is inevitable" or what might seem like historical inevitability—a perspective that leads to the cult of the mausoleum. Educators can no longer project onto the student-as-Other that part of themselves that out of fear and loathing they rejected or subtracted from their identities in their attempt to become unified subjects—that "split-off" part of themselves which prevents them from becoming whole, that disfiguring surplus that they have cast out in order to become white or live in the thrall of racelessness, that metaphysical double that guarantees their own self-regarding autonomy. From this point of view, liberation is never an encapsulated fulfillment of some prefigured end constructed in the temple of memory but a lived tension between the duration of history and the discourse of possibility. It resides in an approach to the *"Aufhebung"*—our passing *into* the "not-yet," and seeking the immanent utopia in the crisis of meaning and the social relations that inform it. It is found, too, in the proleptic consciousness of liminality—the liberating intention of the reflective will caught in the "subjunctive" moment of the "ought" and disabused of metaphysical illusion. It is formed out of an ethical intent commen-

160

*Chapter 6
Curriculum
Development
and the
Language of
Educational
Debate*

surate with the love that Paulo Freire and Che Guevara both argue constitutes the ground from which all revolutionary action should take place....

Educators need to do more than to help students redescribe or represent themselves in new ways—although the way we seek to imagine ourselves is an important step in the struggle for liberation. As Sander L. Gilman has pointed out in his study of stereotypes of sexuality, race, and madness, "we view our own images, our own mirages, our own stereotypes as embodying qualities that exist in the world. And we act upon them" (1985, 242). More specifically, a pedagogy must be made available to teachers that will enable them along with their students to outface the barrenness of postmodern culture by employing a discourse and set of social practices that will not be content with infusing their pedagogies with the postmodern élan of the ludic metropolitan intellectual, with resurrecting a nostalgic past which can never be reclaimed, or with redescribing the present by simply textualizing it, leaving in place its malignant hierarchies of power and privilege, its defining pathologies. For these latter acts only stipulate the lineage of and give sustenance to those social relations responsible for the very injustice critical educators are trying to struggle against. Educators need to stare boldly and unflinchingly into the historical present and assume a narrative space where conditions may be created where students can tell their own stories, listen closely to the stories of others, and dream the dream of liberation. Identity formation must be understood in terms of how subjectivity is contextually enacted within the tendential forces of history (Grossberg, 1992). The exploration of identity should consist of mapping one's subject position in the field of multiple relationships and should be preceded by a critique of hegemony (San Juan, Jr. 1992, 128). This suggests that educators and students need to uncouple themselves from the "disciplined mobilizations" that regulate their social lives and rearticulate the sites of their affective investments in order to create new strategies and alliances of struggle.

A critical pedagogy also demands political and cultural tactics that can fight multiple forms of oppression yet achieve a cohesiveness with divergent social groups working toward liberatory goals. To this end, Chela Sandoval (1991) suggests that cultural workers develop "tactical subjectivities" which she describes as forms of oppositional and differential consciousness and counter-hegemonic praxis (which she discusses in the context of feminism). Tactical subjectivity enables teachers as social agents to recenter their multiple subjectivities with respect to the kind of oppression that is being confronted and "permits the practitioner to choose tactical positions, that is, to self-consciously break and reform ties to ideology, activities which are imperative for the psychological and political practices that permit the achievement of coalition across differences" (Sandoval 1991, 15).

REFERENCES

Aronowitz, Stanley, and Giroux, Henry (1991). *Postmodern Education.* Minneapolis, Minn.: University of Minnesota Press.

Browder, Leslie H. (1992). "Which America 2000 Will Be Taught in Your Class, Teacher?" *International Journal of Educational Reform 1*, no. 2:111–33.

Cooper, B. M. (1989). "Cruel and the Gang: Exposing the Schomburg Posse." *Village Voice 34*, no. 19:27–36.

Ebert, Teresa (forthcoming). "Writing in the Political Resistance (Post) Modernism."

Featherstone, Mike (1990). "Global Culture: An Introduction." *Theory, Culture, and Society* nos. 2–3:1–14.

Gilman, Sander L. (1985). *Difference and Pathology*. Ithaca, New York: Cornell University Press.

Giroux, Henry (1992). *Border Crossings*. London and New York: Routledge.

Grossberg, Larry (1988). *It's a Sin*. University of Sydney, Australia: Power Publications.

Grossberg, Larry (1992). *We Gotta Get Out of This Place*. New York and London: Routledge.

Hitchcock, Peter (1993). *Dialogics of the Oppressed*. Minneapolis and London: University of Minnesota Press.

Kasinitz, P. (1988). "Facing Up to the Underclass." *Telos* 76:170–80.

Katz, Cindi and Smith, Neil (1992). "L.A. Intifada: Interview with Mike Davis." *Social Text*. 33:19–33.

Kimball, Roger (1991). "Tenured Radicals: A Postscript." *The New Criterion 9*, no. 5:4–13.

McLaren, Peter (ed.) (forthcoming). *Postmodernism, Postcolonialism and Pedagogy*. Albert Park, Australia: James Nicholas Publishers.

McLaren, Peter, and Leonard, Peter (1993). *Paulo Freire: A Critical Encounter*. London and New York: Routledge.

Mercer, Kobena (1990). "Welcome to the Jungle: Identity and Diversity in Postmodern Politics." In Jonathan Rutherford (ed.), *Identity: Community, Culture, Difference*. London: Lawrence and Wishart. 43–71.

Mohanty, Chandra (1989/90). "On Race and Voice: Challenges for Liberal Education in the 1990s." *Cultural Critique* 19:179–208.

Piccone, Paul (1988). "Roundtable on Communitarianism." *Telos* no. 76:2–32.

Ravitch, Diane (1990). "Multiculturalism: E Pluribus Plures." *The American Scholar 59*, no. 3:337–54.

Ravitch, Diane (1991). "A Culture in Common." *Educational Leadership* (December): 8–16.

Sandoval, Chela (1991). "U.S. Third World Feminism: The Theory and Method of Oppositional Consciousness in the Postmodern World." *Genders* no. 10:1–24.

San Juan, Jr., E. (1992). *Racial Formations/Critical Formations*. New Jersey and London: Humanities Press.

Simone, Timothy Maliqualim (1989). *About Face: Race in Postmodern America*. Brooklyn, NY: Autonomedia.

Stephanson, Anders (1988). "Interview with Cornel West." In Andrew Ross (ed), *Universal Abandon? The Politics of Postmodernism*. Minneapolis: University of Minnesota Press. 269–86.

Wallace, Michele (1991). "Multiculturalism and Oppositionality." *Afterimage* (October): 6–9.

West, Cornel (1990). "The New Cultural Politics of Difference." In Russell Ferguson, Martha Gever, Trinh T. Minh-ha, and Cornel West (eds.), *Out There: Marginalization and Contemporary Cultures*. Cambridge, Mass.: MIT Press and the New Museum of Contemporary Art, New York. 19–36.

PART THREE

Schools in a Multicultural Society

On the Internet . . .

Sites appropriate to Part Three

The National Center for ESL Literacy Education (NCLE), an adjunct ERIC Clearinghouse at the Center for Applied Linguistics (CAL), is the only national center focusing on literacy education, including family literacy, workplace literacy, and native language literacy for adults and out-of-school youth learning English as a second language (ESL). NCLE's mission is to provide timely information about adult ESL literacy education.

```
http://www.cal.org/ncle/
```

The W. E. B. Du Bois Virtual University is a series of pages detailing various aspects of Du Bois studies. It has been created to serve as a clearinghouse for information on Du Bois and to spur intelligent scholarship and discussion of his life, legacy, and works.

```
http://members.tripod.com/~DuBois/
   index.htm
```

This page contains links to papers on literacy and education and also includes links to several related gopher sites.

```
http://eserver.org/literacy/
```

CHAPTER 7 The Struggle for Freedom in Education

7.1 CORNEL WEST

Race Matters

Cornel West has been called a very insightful observer of intercultural relations in the United States, especially in the area of race relations. The following selection is from the introduction to one of his books, *Race Matters* (Beacon Press, 1993). In it, West discusses racial relations in the context of American historical experience, especially American cultural experience in the 1990s. The author philosophizes about the interactions of cultural groups in American life. He argues that we must see people from minority cultures as "constitutive elements of that life."

West attempts to identify the major issues that all Americans must confront and negotiate with to ensure that all American children receive just and fair opportunities to develop well in American society. He critiques Afrocentrist rhetoric because it reinforces traditional narrow discussions of the issue of race. West argues that to come to a just understanding of one another as Americans, we must acknowledge as a people "the basic humanness and Americanness of each of us." He further argues that we must, together, develop a new conceptual framework with regard to one another and our respective cultural heritages. We must have a new framework for the discussion of racial issues, which is positive and affirmative in our conceptualization of one another.

West writes of a decline in racial relations in America in the 1980s and 1990s. He believes that America is becoming more segregated. Thus,

Americans must acknowledge their national unity because they are on "a slippery slope toward economic strife, social turmoil, and cultural chaos." West calls for Americans to invoke a traditional, commonly shared American commitment to the ideas of freedom, democracy, and equality in efforts to understand one another better. Furthermore, there is "vast intelligence, imagination, humor, and courage" that all Americans can share in the effort to achieve social justice. This selection has great relevance for teachers and teachers to be, as these groups need to clarify their views on race and education.

Key Concept: race in America

What happened in Los Angeles in April of 1992 was neither a race riot nor a class rebellion. Rather, this monumental upheaval was a multiracial, trans-class, and largely male display of justified social rage. For all its ugly, xenophobic resentment, its air of adolescent carnival, and its downright barbaric behavior, it signified the sense of powerlessness in American society. Glib attempts to reduce its meaning to the pathologies of the black underclass, the criminal actions of hoodlums, or the political revolt of the oppressed urban masses miss the mark. Of those arrested, only 36 percent were black, more than a third had full-time jobs, and most claimed to shun political affiliation. What we witnessed in Los Angeles was the consequence of a lethal linkage of economic decline, cultural decay, and political lethargy in American life. Race was the visible catalyst, not the underlying cause.

The meaning of the earthshaking events in Los Angeles is difficult to grasp because most of us remain trapped in the narrow framework of the dominant liberal and conservative views of race in America, which with its worn-out vocabulary leaves us intellectually debilitated, morally disempowered, and personally depressed. The astonishing disappearance of the event from public dialogue is testimony to just how painful and distressing a serious engagement with race is. Our truncated public discussions of race suppress the best of who and what we are as a people because they fail to confront the complexity of the issue in a candid and critical manner. The predictable pitting of liberals against conservatives, Great Society Democrats against self-help Republicans, reinforces intellectual parochialism and political paralysis.

The liberal notion that more government programs can solve racial problems is simplistic—precisely because it focuses *solely* on the economic dimension. And the conservative idea that what is needed is a change in the moral behavior of poor black urban dwellers (especially poor black men, who, they say, should stay married, support their children, and stop committing so much crime) highlights immoral actions while ignoring public responsibility for the immoral circumstances that haunt our fellow citizens.

The common denominator of these views of race is that each still sees black people as a "problem people," in the words of Dorothy I. Height, president of the National Council of Negro Women, rather than as fellow

American citizens with problems. Her words echo the poignant "unasked question" of W. E. B. Du Bois, who, in *The Souls of Black Folk* (1903), wrote:

> They approach me in a half-hesitant sort of way, eye me curiously or compassionately, and then instead of saying directly, How does it feel to be a problem? they say, I know an excellent colored man in my town.... Do not these Southern outrages make your blood boil? At these I smile, or am interested, or reduce the boiling to a simmer, as the occasion may require. To the real question, How does it feel to be a problem? I answer seldom a word.

Nearly a century later, we confine discussions about race in America to the "problems" black people pose for whites rather than consider what this way of viewing black people reveals about us as a nation.

This paralyzing framework encourages liberals to relieve their guilty consciences by supporting public funds directed at "the problems"; but at the same time, reluctant to exercise principled criticism of black people, liberals deny them the freedom to err. Similarly, conservatives blame the "problems" on black people themselves—and thereby render black social misery invisible or unworthy of public attention.

Hence, for liberals, black people are to be "included" and "integrated" into "our" society and culture, while for conservatives they are to be "well behaved" and "worthy of acceptance" by "our" way of life. Both fail to see that the presence and predicaments of black people are neither additions to nor defections from American life, but rather *constitutive elements of that life.*

To engage in a serious discussion of race in America, we must begin not with the problems of black people but with the flaws of American society—flaws rooted in historic inequalities and longstanding cultural stereotypes. How we set up the terms for discussing racial issues shapes our perception and response to these issues. As long as black people are viewed as a "them," the burden falls on blacks to do all the "cultural" and "moral" work necessary for healthy race relations. The implication is that only certain Americans can define what it means to be American—and the rest must simply "fit in."

The emergence of strong black-nationalist sentiments among blacks, especially among young people, is a revolt against this sense of having to "fit in." The variety of black-nationalist ideologies, from the moderate views of Supreme Court Justice Clarence Thomas in his youth to those of Louis Farrakhan today, rest upon a fundamental truth: white America has been historically weak-willed in ensuring racial justice and has continued to resist fully accepting the humanity of blacks. As long as double standards and differential treatment abound—as long as the rap performer Ice-T is harshly condemned while former Los Angeles Police Chief Daryl F. Gates's antiblack comments are received in polite silence, as long as Dr. Leonard Jeffries's anti-Semitic statements are met with vitriolic outrage while presidential candidate Patrick J. Buchanan's anti-Semitism receives a genteel response—black nationalisms will thrive.

Afrocentrism, a contemporary species of black nationalism, is a gallant yet misguided attempt to define an African identity in a white society perceived to be hostile. It is gallant because it puts black doings and sufferings, not white anxieties and fears, at the center of discussion. It is misguided because—out of fear of cultural hybridization and through silence on the issue of class, retrograde views on black women, gay men, and lesbians, and a reluctance to link race to the common good—it reinforces the narrow discussions about race.

To establish a new framework, we need to begin with a frank acknowledgment of the basic humanness and Americanness of each of us. And we must acknowledge that as a people—*E Pluribus Unum*—we are on a slippery slope toward economic strife, social turmoil, and cultural chaos. If we go down, we go down together. The Los Angeles upheaval forced us to see not only that we are not connected in ways we would like to be but also, in a more profound sense, that this failure to connect binds us even more tightly together. The paradox of race in America is that our common destiny is more pronounced and imperiled precisely when our divisions are deeper. The Civil War and its legacy speak loudly here. And our divisions are growing deeper. Today, eighty-six percent of white suburban Americans live in neighborhoods that are less than 1 percent black, meaning that the prospects for the country depend largely on how its cities fare in the hands of a suburban electorate. There is no escape from our interracial interdependence, yet enforced racial hierarchy dooms us as a nation to collective paranoia and hysteria—the unmaking of any democratic order.

The verdict in the Rodney King case which sparked the incidents in Los Angeles was perceived to be wrong by the vast majority of Americans. But whites have often failed to acknowledge the widespread mistreatment of black people, especially black men, by law enforcement agencies, which helped ignite the spark. The verdict was merely the occasion for deep-seated rage to come to the surface. This rage is fed by the "silent" depression ravaging the country—in which real weekly wages of all American workers since 1973 have declined nearly 20 percent, while at the same time wealth has been upwardly distributed.

The exodus of stable industrial jobs from urban centers to cheaper labor markets here and abroad, housing policies that have created "chocolate cities and vanilla suburbs" (to use the popular musical artist George Clinton's memorable phrase), white fear of black crime, and the urban influx of poor Spanish-speaking and Asian immigrants—all have helped erode the tax base of American cities just as the federal government has cut its supports and programs. The result is unemployment, hunger, homelessness, and sickness for millions.

And a pervasive spiritual impoverishment grows. The collapse of meaning in life—the eclipse of hope and absence of love of self and others, the breakdown of family and neighborhood bonds—leads to the social deracination and cultural denudement of urban dwellers, especially children. We have created rootless, dangling people with little link to the supportive networks—family, friends, school—that sustain some sense of purpose in life. We have witnessed the collapse of the spiritual communities that in the past helped Americans face despair, disease, and death and that transmit through the generations dignity and decency, excellence and elegance.

The result is lives of what we might call "random nows," of fortuitous and fleeting moments preoccupied with "getting over"—with acquiring pleasure, property, and power by any means necessary. (This is not what Malcolm X meant by this famous phrase.) Post-modern culture is more and more a market culture dominated by gangster mentalities and self-destructive wantonness. This culture engulfs all of us—yet its impact on the disadvantaged is devastating, resulting in extreme violence in everyday life. Sexual violence against women and homicidal assaults by young black men on one another are only the most obvious signs of this empty quest for pleasure, property, and power.

Last, this rage is fueled by a political atmosphere in which images, not ideas, dominate, where politicians spend more time raising money than debating issues. The functions of parties have been displaced by public polls, and politicians behave less as thermostats that determine the climate of opinion than as thermometers registering the public mood. American politics has been rocked by an unleashing of greed among opportunistic public officials—who have followed the lead of their counterparts in the private sphere, where, as of 1989, 1 percent of the population owned 37 percent of the wealth and 10 percent of the population owned 86 percent of the wealth—leading to a profound cynicism and pessimism among the citizenry.

And given the way in which the Republican Party since 1968 has appealed to popular xenophobic images—playing the black, female, and homophobic cards to realign the electorate along race, sex, and sexual-orientation lines—it is no surprise that the notion that we are all part of one garment of destiny is discredited. Appeals to special interests rather than to public interests reinforce this polarization. The Los Angeles upheaval was an expression of utter fragmentation by a powerless citizenry that includes not just the poor but all of us.

What is to be done? How do we capture a new spirit and vision to meet the challenges of the post-industrial city, post-modern culture, and post-party politics?

First, we must admit that the most valuable sources for help, hope, and power consist of ourselves and our common history. As in the ages of Lincoln, Roosevelt, and King, we must look to new frameworks and languages to understand our multilayered crisis and overcome our deep malaise.

Second, we must focus our attention on the public square—the common good that undergirds our national and global destinies. The vitality of any public square ultimately depends on how much we *care* about the quality of our lives together. The neglect of our public infrastructure, for example—our water and sewage systems, bridges, tunnels, highways, subways, and streets—reflects not only our myopic economic policies, which impede productivity, but also the low priority we place on our common life.

The tragic plight of our children clearly reveals our deep disregard for public well-being. About one out of every five children in this country lives in poverty, including one out of every two black children and two out of every five Hispanic children. Most of our children—neglected by overburdened parents and bombarded by the market values of profit-hungry corporations—are ill-equipped to live lives of spiritual and culture quality. Faced with these facts, how do we expect ever to constitute a vibrant society?

One essential step is some form of large-scale public intervention to ensure access to basic social goods—housing, food, health care, education, child care, and jobs. We must invigorate the common good with a mixture of government, business, and labor that does not follow any existing blueprint. After a period in which the private sphere has been sacralized and the public square gutted, the temptation is to make a fetish of the public square. We need to resist such dogmatic swings.

Last, the major challenge is to meet the need to generate new leadership. The paucity of courageous leaders—so apparent in the response to the events in Los Angeles—requires that we look beyond the same elites and voices that recycle the older frameworks. We need leaders—neither saints nor sparkling television personalities—who can situate themselves within a larger historical narrative of this country and our world, who can grasp the complex dynamics of our peoplehood and imagine a future grounded in the best of our past, yet who are attuned to the frightening obstacles that now perplex us. Our ideals of freedom, democracy, and equality must be invoked to invigorate all of us, especially the landless, propertyless, and luckless. Only a visionary leadership that can motivate "the better angels of our nature," as Lincoln said, and activate possibilities for a freer, more efficient, and stable America—only that leadership deserves cultivation and support.

This new leadership must be grounded in grass-root organizing that highlights democratic accountability. Whoever *our* leaders will be as we approach the twenty-first century, their challenge will be to help Americans determine whether a genuine multiracial democracy can be created and sustained in an era of global economy and a moment of xenophobic frenzy.

Let us hope and pray that the vast intelligence, imagination, humor, and courage of Americans will not fail us. Either we learn a new language of empathy and compassion, or the fire this time will consume us all.

7.2   BOOKER T. WASHINGTON

The Atlanta Exposition Address, September 18, 1895

Booker T. Washington (1856–1915), who was born into slavery, founded the Tuskegee Normal and Industrial Institute in Alabama in 1881. At the Tuskegee Institute he emphasized industrial, skilled trade education rather than traditional college-level liberal arts studies. Washington pursued this policy because he believed that the majority of African Americans needed industrial and artisan skills to escape the sharecropper system of dependent agriculture in the post–Civil War South. He was able to influence many powerful conservative whites to support his program at the institute. Washington also founded the National Negro Business League in 1900. He owned several newspapers, and his ideas carried much weight among other Black-owned publishing enterprises of his day. Washington's most famous articulation of his educational philosophy was given to a business convention on September 18, 1895, in Atlanta, Georgia. This speech, called "The Atlanta Exposition Address," is reprinted in the following selection.

Washington was severely critiqued for his educational position, which focused on economic empowerment and practical skills and less so on intellectual empowerment. Black intellectual leader W. E. B. Du Bois was a notable critic of Washington's views, and he called for the development of an African American intellectual elite that would be able to argue and struggle for African American rights with the white American elite. Actually, many contemporary sociologists agree that both Washington's and Du Bois's social agendas for African American freedpersons were correct—both greater numbers of skilled Black workers *and* a Black American intelligentsia were necessary for African Americans to attain their constitutional rights in the late nineteenth and twentieth centuries.

Key Concept: practical education and "intercultural understanding" as the path to liberation

171

One-third of the population of the South is of the Negro race. No enterprise seeking the material, civil, or moral welfare of this section can disregard this element of our population and reach the highest success. I but convey to you, Mr. President and Directors, the sentiment of the masses of my race when I say that in no way have the value and manhood of the American Negro been more fittingly and generously recognized than by the managers of this magnificent Exposition at every stage of its progress. It is a recognition that will do more to cement the friendship of the two races than any occurrence since the dawn of freedom.

Not only this, but the opportunity here afforded will awaken among us a new era of industrial progress. Ignorant and inexperienced, it is not strange that in the first years of our new life we began at the top instead of at the bottom; that a seat in Congress or the State Legislature was more sought than real estate or industrial skill; that the political convention or stump speaking had more attractions than starting a dairy farm or truck garden.

A ship lost at sea for many days suddenly sighted a friendly vessel. From the mast of the unfortunate vessel was seen a signal: "Water, water, we die of thirst." The answer from the friendly vessel at once came back, "Cast down your bucket where you are." A second time the signal, "Water, water, send us water," ran up from the distressed vessel and was answered, "Cast down your bucket where you are." And a third and fourth signal for water was answered "Cast down your bucket where you are." The captain of the distressed vessel, at last heeding the injunction, cast down his bucket and it came up full of fresh, sparkling water from the mouth of the Amazon River.

To those of my race who depend on bettering their condition in a foreign land, or who underestimate the importance of cultivating friendly relations with the Southern white man who is their next-door neighbor, I would say: Cast down your bucket where you are; cast it down in making friends, in every manly way, of the people of all races by whom we are surrounded. Cast it down in agriculture, mechanics, in commerce, in domestic service, and in the professions. And in this connection it is well to bear in mind that whatever other sins the South may be called upon to bear, when it comes to business pure and simple, it is in the South that the Negro is given a man's chance in the commercial world, and in nothing is this Exposition more eloquent than in emphasizing this chance. Our greatest danger is that, in the great leap from slavery to freedom, we may overlook the fact that the masses of us are to live by the productions of our hands and fail to keep in mind that we shall prosper in the proportion as we learn to dignify and glorify common labor, and put brains and skill into the common occupations of life; shall prosper in proportion as we learn to draw the line between the superficial and the substantial, the ornamental gewgaws of life and the useful. No race can prosper till it learns that there is as much dignity in tilling a field as in writing a poem. It is at the bottom of life we must begin, and not at the top. Nor should we permit our grievances to overshadow our opportunities.

Booker T. Washington

To those of the white race who look to the incoming of those of foreign birth and strange tongue and habits for the prosperity of the South, were I permitted I would repeat what I say to my own race, "Cast down your bucket where you are." Cast it down among the 8,000,000 Negroes whose habits you know, whose fidelity and love you have tested in days when to have proved treacherous meant the ruin of your firesides. Cast down your bucket among these people who have, without strikes and labor wars, tilled your fields, cleared your forests, builded your railroads and cities, and brought forth treasures from the bowels of the earth and helped make possible this magnificent representation of the progress of the South. Casting down your bucket among my people, helping and encouraging them as you are doing on these grounds, and, with education of head, hand and heart, you will find that they will buy your surplus land, make blossom the waste places in your fields, and run your factories.

While doing this, you can be sure in the future, as in the past, that you and your families will be surrounded by the most patient, faithful, law-abiding, and unresentful people that the world has seen. As we have proved our loyalty to you in the past, in nursing your children, watching by the sickbed of your mothers and fathers, and often following them with tear-dimmed eyes to their graves, so in the future, in our humble way, we shall stand by you with a devotion that no foreigner can approach, ready to lay down our lives, if need be, in defense of yours; interlacing our industrial, commercial, civil, and religious life with yours in a way that shall make the interests of both races one. In all things that are purely social we can be as separate as the fingers, yet one as the hand in all things essential to mutual progress.

There is no defense or security for any of us except in the highest intelligence and development of all. If anywhere there are efforts tending to curtail the fullest growth of the Negro, let these efforts be turned into stimulating, encouraging and making him the most useful and intelligent citizen. Effort or means so invested will pay a thousand percent interest. These efforts will be twice blessed—"blessing him that gives and him that takes."

There is no escape, through law of man or God, from the inevitable:

> The laws of changeless justice bind
> Oppressor with oppressed,
> And close as sin and suffering joined
> We march to fate abreast.

Nearly sixteen million hands will aid you in pulling the load upward, or they will pull against you the load downward. We shall constitute one-third and more of the ignorance and crime of the South, or one-third its intelligence and progress; we shall contribute one-third to the business and industrial prosperity of the South, or we shall prove a veritable body of death, stagnating, depressing, retarding every effort to advance the body politic.

Gentlemen of the Exposition: As we present to you our humble effort at an exhibition of our progress, you must not expect overmuch. Starting thirty years ago with ownership here and there in a few quilts and pumpkins and chickens (gathered from miscellaneous sources), remember: the path that has led us from these to the invention and production of agricultural implements, buggies, steam engines, newspapers, books, statuary, carving, paintings, the management of drugstores and banks, has not been trodden without contact with thorns and thistles. While we take pride in what we exhibit as a result of our independent efforts, we do not for a moment forget that our part in this exhibition would fall far short of your expectations but for the constant help that has come to our educational life, not only from the Southern states, but especially from Northern philanthropists who have made their gifts a constant stream of blessing and encouragement.

The wisest among my race understand that the agitation of questions of social equality is the extremest folly, and that progress in the enjoyment of all the privileges that will come to us must be the result of severe and constant struggle rather than of artificial forcing. No race that has anything to contribute to the markets of the world is long in any degree ostracized. It is important and right that all privileges of the laws be ours, but it is vastly more important that we be prepared for the exercise of those privileges. The opportunity to earn a dollar in a factory just now is worth infinitely more than the opportunity to spend a dollar in an opera house.

In conclusion, may I repeat that nothing in thirty years has given us more hope and encouragement and drawn us so near to you of the white race as this opportunity offered by the Exposition; and here bending, as it were, over the altar that represents the results of the struggles of your race and mine, both starting practically empty-handed three decades ago, I pledge that, in your effort to work out the great and intricate problem which God has laid at the doors of the South, you shall have at all times the patient, sympathetic help of my race. Only let this be constantly in mind that, while from representations in these buildings of the product of field, of forest, of mine, of factory, letters and art, much good will come—yet by far above and beyond material benefits, will be that higher good, that let us pray God will come, in a blotting out of sectional differences and racial animosities and suspicions, in a determination to administer absolute justice, in a willing obedience among all classes to the mandates of law. This, coupled with material prosperity, will bring into our beloved South a new heaven and a new earth.

7.3 W. E. B. DU BOIS

Of Mr. Booker T. Washington and Others

W. E. B. (William Edward Burghardt) Du Bois (1868–1963) was one of the greatest African American intellectual leaders. In 1895 he became the first African American scholar to receive a Ph.D. from Harvard University. He cofounded the National Association for the Advancement of Colored People (NAACP) in 1909, and he was the founding editor of the NAACP magazine *Crisis*. Du Bois called the conference of African American leaders and scholars in 1905 that sparked the Niagara Movement, the civil rights movement that eventually produced the NAACP. He published many scholarly studies on the situation of African Americans. A great scholar and a valiant advocate for the civil liberties of all African Americans, Du Bois dedicated his life to the cause of human rights. He died on August 27, 1963, in Accra, Ghana, on the eve of the famous civil rights march and demonstration in Washington, D.C., to petition the U.S. Congress to pass a civil rights act to protect and enforce the constitutional rights of all persons (Congress did so in 1964).

A chronology of Du Bois's life as well as his political and literary activities is provided at the back of *The Souls of Black Folk* (Vintage Books, 1990), from which the following selection has been excerpted. In the selection, Du Bois critiques what he refers to as "the Atlanta Compromise" of his contemporary and African American spokesman Booker T. Washington as well as Washington's positions on the situation of African Americans. Du Bois advocates more college-level study opportunities for academically able African American students and argues for the enforcement of the constitutional rights of all African Americans. He argues that the policies of Washington and some other leaders of the African American community in the early 1900s did not go nearly far enough in defending the civil liberties of African Americans. Du Bois accuses Washington of encouraging a policy of racial "accommodation" that led black people to give up the struggle for political power, civil rights, and the higher education of black youth. He also contends that the policies of Washington and his supporters led to the disenfranchisement of blacks, the legal creation of a distinct status of civil inferiority for African Americans, and "the steady withdrawal of aid from institutions for the higher training of the Negro."

Key Concept: critique of the "Atlanta Compromise"

From birth till death enslaved; in word, in deed, unmanned!
Hereditary bondsmen! Know ye not
Who would be free themselves must strike the blow?

—Byron.

Easily the most striking thing in the history of the American Negro since 1876 is the ascendancy of Mr. Booker T. Washington. It began at the time when war memories and ideals were rapidly passing; a day of astonishing commercial development was dawning; a sense of doubt and hesitation overtook the freedmen's sons,—then it was that his leading began. Mr. Washington came, with a simple definite programme, at the psychological moment when the nation was a little ashamed of having bestowed so much sentiment on Negroes, and was concentrating its energies on Dollars. His programme of industrial education, conciliation of the South, and submission and silence as to civil and political rights, was not wholly original; the Free Negroes from 1830 up to wartime had striven to build industrial schools, and the American Missionary Association had from the first taught various trades; and Price and others had sought a way of honorable alliance with the best of the Southerners. But Mr. Washington first indissolubly linked these things; he put enthusiasm, unlimited energy, and perfect faith into this programme, and changed it from a by-path into a veritable Way of Life. And the tale of the methods by which he did this is a fascinating study of human life.

It startled the nation to hear a Negro advocating such a programme after many decades of bitter complaint; it startled and won the applause of the South, it interested and won the admiration of the North; and after a confused murmur of protest, it silenced if it did not convert the Negroes themselves.

To gain the sympathy and coöperation of the various elements comprising the white South was Mr. Washington's first task; and this, at the time Tuskegee was founded, seemed, for a black man, well-nigh impossible. And yet ten years later it was done in the word spoken at Atlanta: "In all things purely social we can be as separate as the five fingers, and yet one as the hand in all things essential to mutual progress." This "Atlanta Compromise" is by all odds the most notable thing in Mr. Washington's career. The South interpreted it in different ways: the radicals received it as a complete surrender of the demand for civil and political equality; the conservatives, as a generously conceived working basis for mutual understanding. So both approved it, and to-day its author is certainly the most distinguished Southerner since Jefferson Davis, and the one with the largest personal following.

Next to this achievement comes Mr. Washington's work in gaining place and consideration in the North. Others less shrewd and tactful had formerly essayed to sit on these two stools and had fallen between them; but as Mr. Washington knew the heart of the South from birth and training, so by singular insight he intuitively grasped the spirit of the age which was dominating the North. And so thoroughly did he learn the speech and thought of triumphant commercialism, and the ideas of material prosperity, that the picture of a lone black boy poring over a French grammar amid the weeds and dirt of a neglected home soon seemed to him the acme of absurdities. One wonders that Socrates and St. Francis of Assisi would say to this.

And yet this very singleness of vision and thorough oneness with his age is a mark of the successful man. It is as though Nature must needs make men narrow in order to give them force. So Mr. Washington's cult has gained unquestioning followers, his work has wonderfully prospered, his friends are legion, and his enemies are confounded. To-day he stands as the one recognized spokesman of his ten million fellows, and one of the most notable figures in a nation of seventy millions. One hesitates, therefore, to criticise a life which, beginning with so little, has done so much. And yet the time is come when one may speak in all sincerity and utter courtesy of the mistakes and shortcomings of Mr. Washington's career, as well as of his triumphs, without being thought captious or envious, and without forgetting that it is easier to do ill than well in the world.

The criticism that has hitherto met Mr. Washington has not always been of this broad character. In the South especially has he had to walk warily to avoid the harshest judgments,—and naturally so, for he is dealing with the one subject of deepest sensitiveness to that section. Twice—once when at the Chicago celebration of the Spanish-American War he alluded to the color-prejudice that is "eating away the vitals of the South," and once when he dined with President Roosevelt—has the resulting Southern criticism been violent enough to threaten seriously his popularity. In the North the feeling has several times forced itself into words, that Mr. Washington's counsels of submission overlooked certain elements of true manhood, and that his educational programme was unnecessarily narrow. Usually, however, such criticism has not found open expression, although, too, the spiritual sons of the Abolitionists have not been prepared to acknowledge that the schools founded before Tuskegee, by men of broad ideals and self-sacrificing spirit, were wholly failures or worthy of ridicule. While, then, criticism has not failed to follow Mr. Washington, yet the prevailing public opinion of the land has been but too willing to deliver the solution of a wearisome problem into his hands, and say, "If that is all you and your race ask, take it."

Among his own people, however, Mr. Washington has encountered the strongest and most lasting opposition, amounting at times to bitterness, and even to-day continuing strong and insistent even though largely silenced in outward expression by the public opinion of the nation. Some of this opposition is, of course, mere envy; the disappointment of displaced demagogues and the spite of narrow minds. But aside from this, there is among educated and thoughtful colored men in all parts of the land a feeling of deep regret, sorrow, and apprehension at the wide currency and ascendancy which some of Mr. Washington's theories have gained. These same men admire his sincerity of purpose, and are willing to forgive much to honest endeavor which is doing something worth the doing. They coöperate with Mr. Washington as far as they conscientiously can; and, indeed, it is no ordinary tribute to this man's tact and power that, steering as he must between so many diverse interests and opinions, he so largely retains the respect of all.

But the hushing of the criticism of honest opponents is a dangerous thing. It leads some of the best of the critics to unfortunate silence and paralysis of effort, and others to burst into speech so passionately and intemperately as to lose listeners. Honest and earnest criticism from those whose interests are most nearly touched,—criticism of writers by readers, of government by those governed, of leaders by those led,—this is the soul of democracy and the safeguard of modern society. If the best of the American Negroes receive by outer pressure a leader whom they had not recognized before, manifestly there is here a certain palpable gain. Yet there is also irreparable loss,—a loss of that peculiarly valuable education which a group receives when by search and criticism it finds and commissions its own leaders. The way in which this is done is at once the most elementary and the nicest problem of social growth. History is but the record of such group-leadership; and yet how infinitely changeful is its type and character! And of all types and kinds, what can be more instructive than the leadership of a group within a group?—that curious double movement where real progress may be negative and actual advance be relative retrogression. All this is the social student's inspiration and despair.

Now in the past the American Negro has had instructive experience in the choosing of group leaders, founding thus a peculiar dynasty which in the light of present conditions is worth while studying. When sticks and stones and beasts form the sole environment of a people, their attitude is largely one of determined opposition to and conquest of natural forces. But when to earth and brute is added an environment of men and ideas, then the attitude of the imprisoned group may take three main forms,—a feeling of revolt and revenge; an attempt to adjust all thought and action to the will of the greater group; or, finally, a determined effort at self-realization and self-development despite environing opinion. The influence of all of these attitudes at various times can be traced in the history of the American Negro, and in the evolution of his successive leaders.

Before 1750, while the fire of African freedom still burned in the veins of the slaves, there was in all leadership or attempted leadership but the one motive of revolt and revenge,—typified in the terrible Maroons, the Danish blacks, and Cato of Stono, and veiling all the Americas in fear [of] insurrection. The liberalizing tendencies of the latter half of the eighteenth century brought, along with kindlier relations between black and white, thoughts of ultimate adjustment and assimilation. Such aspiration was especially voiced in the earnest sons of Phyllis, in the martyrdom of Attucks, the fighting of Salem and Poor, the intellectual accomplishments of Banneker and Derham, and the political demands of the Cuffes.

Stern financial and social stress after the war cooled much of the previous humanitarian ardor. The disappointment and impatience of the Negroes at the persistence of slavery and serfdom voiced itself in two movements. The slaves in the South, aroused undoubtedly by vague rumors of the Haytian revolt, made three fierce attempts at insurrection,—in 1800 under Gabriel in Virginia, in 1822 under Vesey in Carolina, and in 1831 again in Virginia under the terrible Nat Turner. In the Free States, on the other hand, a new and curious attempt at self-development was made. In Philadelphia and New York color-prescription led to a withdrawal of Negro communicants from white churches and the formation of a peculiar socio-religious institution among the Negroes known as the African Church,—an organization still living and controlling in its various branches over a million of men.

Walker's wild appeal against the trend of the times showed how the world was changing after the coming of the cotton-gin. By 1830 slavery seemed hopelessly fastened on the South, and the slaves thoroughly cowed into submission. The free Negroes of the North, inspired by the mulatto immigrants from the West Indies, began to change the basis of their demands; they recognized the slavery of slaves, but insisted that they themselves were freemen, and sought assimilation and amalgamation with the nation on the same terms with other men. Thus, Forten and Purvis of Philadelphia, Shad of Wilmington, Du Bois of New Haven, Barbadoes of Boston, and others, strove singly and together as men, they said, not as slaves; as "people of color," not as "Negroes." The trend of the times, however, refused them recognition save in individual and exceptional cases, considered them as one with all the despised blacks, and they soon found themselves striving to keep even the rights they formerly had of voting and working and moving as freemen. Schemes of migration and colonization arose among them; but these they refused to entertain, and they eventually turned to the Abolition movement as a final refuge.

Here, led by Remond, Nell, Wells-Brown, and Douglass, a new period of self-assertion and self-development dawned. To be sure, ultimate freedom and assimilation was the ideal before the leaders, but the assertion of the manhood rights of the Negro by himself was the main reliance, and John Brown's raid was the extreme of its logic. After the war and emancipation, the great form of Frederick Douglass, the greatest of American Negro leaders, still led the host. Self-assertion, especially in political lines, was the main programme, and behind Douglass came Elliot, Bruce, and Langston, and the Reconstruction politicians, and, less conspicuous but of greater social significance Alexander Crummell and Bishop Daniel Payne.

Then came the Revolution of 1876, the suppression of the Negro votes, the changing and shifting of ideas, and the seeking of new lights in the great night. Douglass, in his old age, still bravely stood for the ideas of his early manhood, —ultimate assimilation *through* self-assertion, and on no other terms. For a time Price arose as a new leader, destined, it seemed, not to give up, but to re-state the old ideals in a form less repugnant to the white South. But he passed away in his prime. Then came the new leader. Nearly all the former ones had become leaders by the silent suffrage of their fellows, had sought to lead their own people alone, and were usually, save Douglass, little known outside their race. But Booker T. Washington arose as essentially the leader not of one race but of two,—a compromiser between the South, the North, and the Negro. Naturally the Negroes resented, at first bitterly, signs of compromise which surrendered their civil and political rights, even though this was to be exchanged for larger chances of economic development. The rich and dominating North, however, was not only weary of the race problem, but was investing largely in Southern enterprises, and welcomed any method of peaceful coöperation. Thus, by national opinion, the Negroes began to recognize Mr. Washington's leadership; and the voice of criticism was hushed.

Mr. Washington represents in Negro thought the old attitude of adjustment and submission; but adjustment at such a peculiar time as to make his programme unique. This is an age of unusual economic development, and Mr. Washington's programme naturally takes an economic cast, becoming a gospel of Work and Money to such an extent as apparently almost completely to overshadow the higher aims of life. Moreover, this is an age when the more advanced races are coming in closer contact with the less developed races, and the race-feeling is therefore intensified; and Mr. Washington's programme practically accepts the alleged inferiority of the Negro races. Again, in our own land, the reaction from the sentiment of war time has given impetus to race-prejudice against Negroes, and Mr. Washington withdraws many of the high demands of Negroes as men and American citizens. In other periods of intensified prejudice all the Negro's tendency to self-assertion has been called forth; at this period a policy of submission is advocated. In the history of nearly all other races and peoples the doctrine preached at such crises has been that manly self-respect is worth more than lands and houses, and that a people who voluntarily surrender such respect, or cease striving for it, are not worth civilizing.

In answer to this, it has been claimed that the Negro can survive only through submission. Mr. Washington distinctly asks that black people give up, at least for the present, three things,—

- First, political power,
- Second, insistence on civil rights,
- Third, higher education of Negro youth,—

and concentrate all their energies on industrial education, the accumulation of wealth, and the conciliation of the South. This policy has been courageously and insistently advocated for over fifteen years, and has been triumphant for perhaps ten years. As a result of this tender of the palm-branch, what has been the return? In these years there have occurred:

1. The disfranchisement of the Negro.
2. The legal creation of a distinct status of civil inferiority for the Negro.
3. The steady withdrawal of aid from institutions for the higher training of the Negro.

These movements are not, to be sure, direct results of Mr. Washington's teachings; but his propaganda has, without a shadow of doubt, helped their speedier accomplishment. The question then comes: Is it possible, and probable, that nine millions of men can make effective progress in economic lines if they are deprived of political rights, made of servile caste, and allowed only the most meagre chance for developing their exceptional men? If history and reason give any distinct answer to these questions, it is an emphatic *No*. And Mr. Washington thus faces the triple paradox of his career:

1. He is striving nobly to make Negro artisans business men and property-owners; but it is utterly impossible, under modern competitive methods, for workingmen and property-owners to defend their rights and exist without the right of suffrage.

2. He insists on thrift and self-respect, but at the same time counsels a silent submission to civic inferiority such as is bound to sap the manhood of any race in the long run.
3. He advocates common-school and industrial training, and depreciates institutions of higher-learning; but neither the Negro common-schools, nor Tuskegee itself, could remain open a day were it not for teachers trained in Negro colleges, or trained by their graduates.

This triple paradox in Mr. Washington's position is the object of criticism by two classes of colored Americans. One class is spiritually descended from Toussaint the Savior, through Gabriel, Vesey, and Turner, and they represent the attitude of revolt and revenge; they hate the white South blindly and distrust the white race generally, and so far as they agree on definite action, think that the Negro's only hope lies in emigration beyond the borders of the United States. And yet, by the irony of fate, nothing has more effectually made this programme seem hopeless than the recent course of the United States toward weaker and darker peoples in the West Indies, Hawaii, and the Philippines,—for where in the world may we go and be safe from lying and brute force?

The other class of Negroes who cannot agree with Mr. Washington has hitherto said little aloud. They deprecate the sight of scattered counsels, of internal disagreement; and especially they dislike making their just criticism of a useful and earnest man an excuse for a general discharge of venom from small-minded opponents. Nevertheless, the questions involved are so fundamental and serious that it is difficult to see how men like the Grimkes, Kelly Miller, J. W. E. Bowen, and other representatives of this group, can much longer be silent. Such men feel in conscience bound to ask of this nation three things:

1. The right to vote.
2. Civic equality.
3. The education of youth according to ability.

They acknowledge Mr. Washington's invaluable service in counselling patience and courtesy in such demands; they do not ask that ignorant black men vote when ignorant whites are debarred, or that any reasonable restrictions in the suffrage should not be applied; they know that the low social level of the mass of the race is responsible for much discrimination against it, but they also know, and the nation knows, that relentless color-prejudice is more often a cause than a result of the Negro's degradation; they seek the abatement of this relic of barbarism, and not as systematic encouragement and pampering by all agencies of social power from the Associated Press to the Church of Christ. They advocate, with Mr. Washington, a broad system of Negro common schools supplemented by thorough industrial training; but they are surprised that a man of Mr. Washington's insight cannot see that no such educational system ever has rested or can rest on any other basis than that of the well-equipped college and university, and they insist that there is a demand for a few such institutions throughout the South to train the best of the Negro youth as teachers, professional men, and leaders.

This group of men honor Mr. Washington for his attitude of conciliation toward the white South; they accept the "Atlanta Compromise" in its broadest interpretation; they recognize, with him, many signs of promise, many men of high purpose and fair judgment, in this section; they know that no easy task has been laid upon a region already tottering under heavy burdens. But, nevertheless, they insist that the way to truth and right lies in straightforward honesty, not in indiscriminate flattery; in praising those of the South who do well and criticising uncompromisingly those who do ill; in taking advantage of the opportunities at hand and urging their fellows to do the same, but at the same time in remembering that only a firm adherence to their higher ideals and aspirations will every keep those ideals within the realm of possibility. They do not expect that the free right to vote, to enjoy civic rights, and to be educated, will come in a moment; they do not expect to see the bias and prejudices of years disappear at the blast of a trumpet; but they are absolutely certain that the way for a people to gain their reasonable rights is not by voluntarily throwing them away and insisting that they do not want them; that the way for a people to gain respect is not by continually belittling and ridiculing themselves; that, on the contrary, Negroes must insist continually, in season and out of season, that voting is necessary to modern manhood, that color discrimination is barbarism, and that black boys need education as well as white boys.

In failing thus to state plainly and unequivocally the legitimate demands of their people, even at the cost of opposing an honored leader, the thinking classes of American Negroes would shirk a heavy responsibility,—a responsibility to themselves, a responsibility to the struggling masses, a responsibility to the darker races of men whose future depends so largely on this American experiment, but especially a responsibility to this nation,—this common Fatherland. It is wrong to encourage a man or a people in evil-doing; it is wrong to aid and abet a national crime simply because it is unpopular not to do so. The growing spirit of kindliness and reconciliation between the North and South after the frightful differences of a generation ago ought to be a source of deep congratulation to all, and especially to those whose mistreatment caused the war; but if that reconciliation is to be marked by the industrial slavery and civic death of those same black men, with permanent legislation into a position of inferiority, then those black men, if they are really men, are called upon by every consideration of patriotism and loyalty to oppose such a course by all civilized methods, even though such opposition involves disagreement with Mr. Booker T. Washington. We have no right to sit silently by while the inevitable seeds are sown for a harvest of disaster to our children, black and white.

First, it is the duty of black men to judge the South discriminatingly. The present generation of Southerners are not responsible for the past, and they should not be blindly hated or blamed for it. Furthermore, to no class is the indiscriminate endorsement of the recent course of the South toward Negroes more nauseating than to the best thought of the South. The South is not "solid"; it is a land in the ferment of social change, wherein forces of all kinds are fighting for supremacy; and to praise the ill the South is to-day perpetrating is just as wrong as to condemn the good. Discriminating and broad-minded criticism is what the South needs,—needs it for the sake of her own white sons and daughters, and for the insurance of robust, healthy mental and moral development.

To-day even the attitude of the Southern whites toward the blacks is not, as so many assume, in all cases the same; the ignorant Southerner hates the Negro, the workingmen fear his competition, the money-makers wish to use him as a laborer, some of the educated see a menace in his upward development, while others—usually the sons of the masters—wish to help him to rise. National opinion has enabled this last class to maintain the Negro common schools, and to protect the Negro partially in property, life, and limb. Through the pressure of the money-makers, the Negro is in danger of being reduced to semi-slavery, especially in the country districts; the workingmen, and those of the educated who fear the Negro, have united to disfranchise him, and some have urged his deportation; while the passions of the ignorant are easily aroused to lynch and abuse any black man. To praise this intricate whirl of thought and prejudice is nonsense; to inveigh indiscriminately against "the South" is unjust; but to use the same breath in praising Governor Aycock, exposing Senator Morgan, arguing with Mr. Thomas Nelson Page, and denouncing Senator Ben Tillman, is not only sane, but the imperative duty of thinking black men.

It would be unjust to Mr. Washington not to acknowledge that in several instances he has opposed movements in the South which were unjust to the Negro; he sent memorials to the Louisiana and Alabama constitutional conventions, he has spoken against lynching, and in other ways has openly or silently set his influence against sinister schemes and unfortunate happenings. Notwithstanding this, it is equally true to assert that on the whole the distinct impression left by Mr. Washington's propaganda is, first, that the South is justified in its present attitude toward the Negro because of the Negro's degradation; secondly, that the prime cause of the Negro's failure to rise more quickly is his wrong education in the past; and, thirdly, that his future rise depends primarily on his own efforts. Each of these propositions is a dangerous half-truth. The supplementary truths must never be lost sight of: first, slavery and race-prejudice are potent if not sufficient causes of the Negro's position; second, industrial and common-school training were necessarily slow in planting because they had to await the black teachers trained by higher institutions,—it being extremely doubtful if any essentially different development was possible, and certainly a Tuskegee was unthinkable before 1880; and, third, while it is a great truth to say that the Negro must strive and strive mightily to help himself, it is equally true that unless his striving be not simply seconded, but rather aroused and encouraged, by the initiative of the richer and wiser environing group, he cannot hope for great success.

In his failure to realize and impress this last point, Mr. Washington is especially to be criticised. His doctrine has tended to make the whites, North and South, shift the burden of the Negro problem to the Negro's shoulders and stand aside as critical and rather pessimistic spectators; when in fact the burden belongs to the nation, and the hands of none of us are clean if we bend not our energies to righting these great wrongs.

The South ought to be led, by candid and honest criticism, to assert her better self and do her full duty to the race she has cruelly wronged and is still wronging. The North—her co-partner in guilt—cannot salve her conscience by plastering it with gold. We cannot settle this problem by diplomacy and suaveness, by "policy" alone. If worse come to worst, can the moral fibre of this country survive the slow throttling and murder of nine millions of men?

The black men of America have a duty to perform, a duty stern and delicate,—a forward movement to oppose a part of the work of their greatest leader. So far as Mr. Washington preaches Thrift, Patience, and Industrial Training for the masses, we must hold up his hands and strive with him, rejoicing in his honors and glorying in the strength of this Joshua called of God and of man to lead the headless host. But so far as Mr. Washington apologizes for injustice, North or South, does not rightly value the privilege and duty of voting, belittles the emasculating effects of caste distinctions, and opposes the higher training and ambition of our brighter minds,—so far as he, the South, or the Nation, does this,—we must unceasingly and firmly oppose them. By every civilized and peaceful method we must strive for the rights which the world accords to men, clinging unwaveringly to those great words which the sons of the Fathers would fain forget: "We hold these truths to be self-evident: That all men are created equal; that they are endowed by their Creator with certain unalienable rights; that among these are life, liberty, and the pursuit of happiness."

7.4 JAMES BALDWIN

A Talk to Teachers

James Baldwin (1924–1987) was a widely known twentieth-century African American essayist, novelist, and playwright. Born and raised in the Harlem ghettos in New York City, he became one of the most eloquent voices in the struggle for civil rights in the United States. His works, which reflect his own experience as a Black American writer and which focus on themes relating to the struggle for human rights, include *Go Tell It on the Mountain* (1953), his first novel and a best-seller; the play *The Amen Corner* (1965); and a collection of essays entitled *Notes of a Native Son* (1955), which attracted much critical attention and public acceptance in both Europe and America. In November 1962 he wrote a long essay on the Black Muslim separatist movement and the civil rights struggle in general; it was republished as a book under the title *The Fire Next Time* (1963).

On October 16, 1963, Baldwin agreed to give a talk to approximately 200 New York City teachers at one of their professional in-service meetings. The topic he chose to speak on was "The Negro Child—His Self Image." Baldwin delivered the talk extemporaneously, but he permitted it to be recorded. Because Baldwin was a major voice in the civil rights struggle at the time, his remarks were published in the December 21, 1963, edition of *Saturday Review* under the title "A Talk to Teachers." The following selection is from that talk.

Key Concept: a child's right to critically challenge social reality

*L*et's begin by saying that we are living through a very dangerous time.... We are in a revolutionary situation, no matter how unpopular that word has become in this country. The society in which we live is desperately menaced, not by Khrushchev [premier of the Soviet Union], but from within. So any citizen of this country who figures himself as responsible—and particularly those of you who deal with the minds and hearts of young people—must be prepared to "go for broke." Or to put it another way, you must understand that in the attempt to correct so many generations of bad faith and cruelty, when it is operating not only in the classroom but in society, you will meet the most fantastic, the most brutal, and the most determined resistance. There is no point in pretending that this won't happen.

Now,... I beg you to let me leave that and go back to what I think to be the entire purpose of education in the first place. It would seem to me that when a child is born, if I'm the child's parent, it is my obligation and my high duty to civilize that child. Man is a social animal. He cannot exist without a society. A society, in turn, depends on certain things which everyone within that society takes for granted. Now, the crucial paradox which confronts us here is that the whole process of education occurs within a social framework and is designed to perpetuate the aims of society. Thus, for example, the boys and girls who were born during the era of the Third Reich, when educated to the purposes of the Third Reich, became barbarians. The paradox of education is precisely this —that as one begins to become conscious one begins to examine the society in which he is being educated. The purpose of education, finally, is to create in a person the ability to look at the world for himself, to make his own decisions, to say to himself this is black or this is white, to decide for himself whether there is a God in heaven or not. To ask questions of the universe, and then learn to live with those questions, is the way he achieves his own identity. But no society is really anxious to have that kind of person around. What societies really, ideally, want is a citizenry which will simply obey the rules of society. If a society succeeds in this, that society is about to perish. The obligation of anyone who thinks of himself as responsible is to examine society and try to change it and to fight it—at no matter what risk. This is the only hope society has. This is the only way societies change.

Now, if what I have tried to sketch has any validity, it becomes thoroughly clear, at least to me, that any Negro who is born in this country and undergoes the American educational system runs the risk of becoming schizophrenic. On the one hand he is born in the shadow of the stars and stripes and he is assured it represents a nation which has never lost a war. He pledges allegiance to that flag which guarantees "liberty and justice for all." He is part of a country in which anyone can become President, and so forth. But on the other hand he is also assured by his country and his countrymen that he has never contributed anything to civilization—that his past is nothing more than a record of humiliations gladly endured. He is assured by the republic that he, his father, his mother, and his ancestors were happy, shiftless, watermelon-eating darkies who loved Mr. Charlie and Miss Ann, that the value he has as a black man is proven by one thing only—his devotion to white people. If you think I am exaggerating, examine the myths which proliferate in this country about Negroes.

Now all this enters the child's consciousness much sooner than we as adults would like to think it does. As adults, we are easily fooled because we are so anxious to be fooled. But children are very different. Children, not yet aware that it is dangerous to look too deeply at anything, look at everything, look at each other, and draw their own conclusions. They don't have the vocabulary to express what they see, and we, their elders, know how to intimidate them very easily and very soon. But a black child, looking at the world around him, though he cannot know quite what to make of it, is aware that there is a reason why his mother works so hard, why his father is always on edge. He is aware that there is some reason why, if he sits down in the front of the bus, his father or mother slaps him and drags him to the back of the bus. He is aware that there is some terrible weight on his parents' shoulders which menaces him. And it isn't long—in fact it begins when he is in school—before he discovers the shape of his oppression.

Let us say that the child is seven years old and I am his father, and I decide to take him to the zoo, or to Madison Square Garden, or to the U.N. Building, or to any of the tremendous monuments we find all over New York. We get into a bus and we go from where I live on 131st Street and Seventh Avenue downtown through the park and we get into New York City, which is not Harlem. Now, where the boy lives—even if it is a housing project—is in an undesirable neighborhood. If he lives in one of those housing projects of which everyone in New York is so proud, he has at the front door, if not closer, the pimps, the whores, the junkies—in a word, the danger of life in the ghetto. And the child knows this, though he doesn't know why.

I still remember my first sight of New York. It was really another city when I was born—where I was born. We looked down over the Park Avenue streetcar tracks. It was Park Avenue, but I didn't know what Park Avenue meant *downtown*. The Park Avenue I grew up on, which is still standing, is dark and dirty. No one would dream of opening a Tiffany's on that Park Avenue, and when you go downtown you discover that you are literally in the white world. It is rich —or at least it looks rich. It is clean—because they collect garbage downtown. There are doormen. People walk about as though they owned where they were —and indeed they do. And it's a great shock. It's very hard to relate yourself to this. You don't know what it means. You know—you know instinctively—that none of this is for you. You know this before you are told. And who is it for and who is paying for it? And why isn't it for you?

Later on when you become a grocery boy or messenger and you try to enter one of those buildings a man says, "Go to the back door." Still later, if you happen by some odd chance to have a friend in one of those buildings, the man says, "Where's your package?" Now this by no means is the core of the matter. What I'm trying to get at is that by this time the Negro child has had, effectively, almost all the doors of opportunity slammed in his face, and there are very few things he can do about it. He can more or less accept it with an absolutely inarticulate and dangerous rage inside—all the more dangerous because it is never expressed. It is precisely those silent people whom white people see every day of their lives—I mean your porter and your maid, who never say anything more than "Yes Sir" and "No Ma'am." They will tell you it's raining if that is what you want to hear, and they will tell you the sun is shining if *that* is what you want to hear. They really hate you—really hate you because in their eyes (and they're right) you stand between them and life. I want to come back to that in a moment. It is the most sinister of the facts, I think, which we now face.

There is something else the Negro child can do, too. Every street boy—and I was a street boy, so I know—looking at the society which has produced him, looking at the standards of that society which are not honored by anybody, looking at your churches and the government and the politicians, understands that this structure is operated for someone else's benefit—not for his. And there's no room in it for him. If he is really cunning, really ruthless, really strong—and many of us are—he becomes a kind of criminal. He becomes a kind of criminal because that's the only way he can live. Harlem and every ghetto in this city—

every ghetto in this country—is full of people who live outside the law. They wouldn't dream of calling a policeman. They wouldn't, for a moment, listen to any of those professions of which we are so proud on the Fourth of July. They have turned away from this country forever and totally. They live by their wits and really long to see the day when the entire structure comes down.

The point of all this is that black men were brought here as a source of cheap labor. They were indispensable to the economy. In order to justify the fact that men were treated as though they were animals, the white republic had to brainwash itself into believing that they were, indeed, animals and *deserved* to be treated like animals. Therefore it is almost impossible for any Negro child to discover anything about his actual history. The reason is that this "animal," once he suspects his own worth, once he starts believing that he is a man, has begun to attack the entire power structure. This is why America has spent such a long time keeping the Negro in his place. What I am trying to suggest to you is that it was not an accident, it was not an act of God, it was not done by well-meaning people muddling into something which they didn't understand. It was a deliberate policy hammered into place in order to make money from black flesh. And now, in 1963, because we have never faced this fact, we are in intolerable trouble.

The Reconstruction, as I read the evidence, was a bargain between the North and South to this effect: "We've liberated them from the land—and delivered them to the bosses." When we left Mississippi to come North we did not come to freedom. We came to the bottom of the labor market, and we are still there. Even the Depression of the 1930s failed to make a dent in Negroes' relationship to white workers in the labor unions. Even today, so brainwashed is this republic that people seriously ask in what they suppose to be good faith, "What does the Negro want?" I've heard a great many asinine questions in my life, but that is perhaps the most asinine and perhaps the most insulting. But the point here is that people who ask that question, thinking that they ask it in good faith, are really the victims of this conspiracy to make Negroes believe they are less than human.

In order for me to live, I decided very early that some mistake had been made somewhere. I was not a "nigger" even though you called me one. But if I was a "nigger" in your eyes, there was something about *you*—there was something *you* needed. I had to realize when I was very young that I was none of those things I was told I was. I was not, for example, happy. I never touched a watermelon for all kinds of reasons. I had been invented by white people, and I knew enough about life by this time to understand that whatever you invent, whatever you project, is you! So where we are now is that a whole country of people believe I'm a "nigger," and I *don't,* and the battle's on! Because if I am not what I've been told I am, then it means that *you're* not what you thought *you* were *either!* And that is the crisis.

It is not really a "Negro revolution" that is upsetting this country. What is upsetting the country is a sense of its own identity. If, for example, one managed to change the curriculum in all the schools so that Negroes learned more about themselves and their real contributions to this culture, you would be liberating not only Negroes, you'd be liberating white people who know nothing about their own history. And the reason is that if you are compelled to lie about one aspect of anybody's history, you must lie about it all. If you have to lie about my real role here, if you have to pretend that I hoed all that cotton just because I loved you, then you have done something to yourself. You are mad.

Now let's go back a minute. I talked earlier about those silent people—the porter and the maid—who, as I said, don't look up at the sky if you ask them if it is raining, but look into your face. My ancestors and I were very well trained. We understood very early that this was not a Christian nation. It didn't matter what you said or how often you went to church. My father and my mother and my grandfather and my grandmother knew that Christians didn't act this way. It was as simple as that. And if that was so there was no point in dealing with white people in terms of their own moral professions, for they were not going to honor them. What one did was to turn away, smiling all the time, and tell white people what they wanted to hear. But people always accuse you of reckless talk when you say this.

All this means that there are in this country tremendous reservoirs of bitterness which have never been able to find an outlet, but may find an outlet soon. It means that well-meaning white liberals place themselves in great danger when they try to deal with Negroes as though they were missionaries. It means, in brief, that a great price is demanded to liberate all those silent people so that they can breathe for the first time and *tell* you what they think of you. And a price is demanded to liberate all those white children—some of them near forty—who have never grown up, and who never will grow up, because they have no sense of their identity.

What passes for identity in America is a series of myths about one's heroic ancestors. It's astounding to me, for example, that so many people really appear to believe that the country was founded by a band of heroes who wanted to be free. That happens not to be true. What happened was that some people left Europe because they couldn't stay there any longer and had to go someplace else to make it. That's all. They were hungry, they were poor, they were convicts. Those who were making it in England, for example, did not get on the *Mayflower*. That's how the country was settled. Not by Gary Cooper. Yet we have a whole race of people, a whole republic, who believe the myths to the point where even today they select political representatives, as far as I can tell, by how closely they resemble Gary Cooper. Now this is dangerously infantile, and it shows in every level of national life. When I was living in Europe, for example, one of the worst revelations to me was the way Americans walked around Europe buying this and buying that and insulting everybody—not even out of malice, just because they didn't know any better. Well, that is the way they have always treated me. They weren't cruel, they just didn't know you were alive. They didn't know you had any feelings.

What I am trying to suggest here is that in the doing of all this for 100 years or more, it is the American white man who has long since lost his grip on reality. In some peculiar way, having created this myth about Negroes, and the myth about his own history, he created myths about the world so that, for example, he was astounded that some people could prefer Castro, astounded that there are people in the world who don't go into hiding when they hear the word "Communism," astounded that Communism is one of the realities of the twentieth century which we will not overcome by pretending that it does not exist. The political level in this country now, on the part of people who should know better, is abysmal.

The Bible says somewhere that where there is no vision the people perish. I don't think anyone can doubt that in this country today we are menaced— intolerably menaced—by a lack of vision.

It is inconceivable that a sovereign people should continue, as we do so abjectly, to say, "I can't do anything about it. It's the government." The government is the creation of the people. It is responsible to the people. And the people are responsible for it. No American has the right to allow the present government to say, when Negro children are being bombed and hosed and shot and beaten all over the deep South, that there is nothing we can do about it. There must have been a day in this country's life when the bombing of four children in Sunday School would have created a public uproar and endangered the life of a Governor Wallace. It happened here and there was no public uproar.

I began by saying that one of the paradoxes of education was that precisely at the point when you begin to develop a conscience, you must find yourself at war with your society. It is your responsibility to change society if you think of yourself as an educated person. And on the basis of the evidence—the moral and political evidence—one is compelled to say that this is a backward society. Now if I were a teacher in this school, or any Negro school, and I was dealing with Negro children, who were in my care only a few hours of every day and would then return to their homes and to the streets, children who have an apprehension of their future which with every hour grows grimmer and darker, I would try to teach them—I would try to make them know—that those streets, those houses, those dangers, those agonies by which they are surrounded, are criminal. I would try to make each child know that these things are the results of a criminal conspiracy to destroy him. I would teach him that if he intends to get to be a man, he must at once decide that he is stronger than this conspiracy and that he must never make his peace with it. And that one of his weapons for refusing to make his peace with it and for destroying it depends on what he decides he is worth. I would teach him that there are currently very few standards in this country which are worth a man's respect. That it is up to him to begin to change these standards for the sake of the life and the health of the country. I would suggest to him that the popular culture—as represented, for example, on television and in comic books and in movies—is based on fantasies created by very ill people, and he must be aware that these are fantasies that have nothing to do with reality. I would teach him that the press he reads is not as free as it says it is—and that he can do something about that, too. I would try to make him know that just as American history is longer, larger, more various, more beautiful, and more terrible than anything anyone has ever said about it, so is the world larger, more daring, more beautiful and more terrible, but principally larger—and that it belongs to him. I would teach him that he doesn't have to be bound by the expediencies of any given Administration, any given policy, any given time—that he has the right and the necessity to examine everything. I would try to show him that one has not learned anything about Castro when one says, "He is a Communist." This is a way of *not* learning something about

Castro, something about Cuba, something, in fact, about the world. I would suggest to him that he is living, at the moment, in an enormous province. America is not the world and if America is going to become a nation, she must find a way—and this child must help her to find a way—to use the tremendous potential and tremendous energy which this child represents. If this country does not find a way to use that energy, it will be destroyed by that energy.

James Baldwin

CHAPTER 8 Perspectives on the Struggle for Freedom in Education

8.1 PAULO FREIRE AND DONALDO MACEDO

Literacy and Critical Pedagogy

In the selection that follows, which is from *Literacy: Reading the Word and the World* (Bergin & Garvey, 1987), Paulo Freire and Donaldo Macedo demonstrate how achieving literacy is a political action and how people create the power to control their own lives through their own words—through their own expression of the contradictions and realities with which they have to deal in their cultural worlds. The authors argue that literacy "cannot be viewed as simply the development of skills aimed at acquiring the dominant standard language." They argue instead that a human being's decision to become literate is a choice to take power and control over his or her own life. They further state that literacy as a concept must be situated in the context of the struggle for human liberation from established systems of cultural reproduction. Literacy must involve the critical reexamination of all of a society's social arrangements and institutions on the part of those who choose to become literate.

Paulo Freire (1921–1997) was an educator in the Graduate Schools of Education at Harvard University. He also taught at the Catholic University of São Paulo, and he was a consultant to the World Council of Churches in

Geneva, Switzerland. A pioneer in critical pedagogy whose theories on the social forces that prevent people from fulfilling their potentials have inspired a vast critical literature in the field of education, Freire helped to establish the Institute of Cultural Action (IDAC), and he participated in adult literacy campaigns in several Third World countries.

Donaldo Macedo (b. 1950) is an associate professor of linguistics at the University of Massachusetts–Boston. The book that Macedo coauthored with Freire and from which the following selection comes is considered a critical contribution to the struggle for human freedom.

Key Concept: literacy and human liberation

Within the last decade, the issue of literacy has taken on a new importance among educators. Unfortunately, the debate that has emerged tends to recycle old assumptions and values regarding the meaning and usefulness of literacy. The notion that literacy is a matter of learning the standard language still informs the vast majority of literacy programs and manifests its logic in the renewed emphasis on technical reading and writing skills.

... [L]iteracy cannot be viewed as simply the development of skills aimed at acquiring the dominant standard language. This view sustains a notion of ideology that systematically negates rather than makes meaningful the cultural experiences of the subordinate linguistic groups who are, by and large, the objects of its policies. For the notion of literacy to become meaningful it has to be situated within a theory of cultural production and viewed as an integral part of the way in which people produce, transform, and reproduce meaning. Literacy must be seen as a medium that constitutes and affirms the historical and existential moments of lived experience that produce a subordinate or a lived culture. Hence, it is an eminently political phenomenon, and it must be analyzed within the context of a theory of power relations and an understanding of social and cultural reproduction and production. By "cultural reproduction" we refer to collective experiences that function in the interest of the dominant groups, rather than in the interest of the oppressed groups that are the object of its policies. We use "cultural production" to refer to specific groups of people producing, mediating, and confirming the mutual ideological elements that emerge from and reaffirm their daily lived experiences. In this case, such experiences are rooted in the interests of individual and collective self-determination.

This theoretical posture underlies our examination of how the public school systems in the ex-Portuguese colonies in Africa have developed educational policies aimed at stamping out the tremendously high illiteracy rate inherited from colonialist Portugal. These policies are designed to eradicate the colonial educational legacy, which had as its major tenet the total de-Africanization of these people. Education in these colonies was discriminatory, mediocre, and based on verbalism. It could not contribute anything to national reconstruction because it was not constituted for this purpose. Schooling was antidemocratic in its methods, in its content, and in its objectives. Divorced

194

*Chapter 8
Perspectives on
the Struggle for
Freedom in
Education*

from the reality of the country, it was, for this very reason, a school for a minority and thus against the majority.

Before the independence of these countries in 1975, schools functioned as political sites in which class, gender, and racial inequities were both produced and reproduced. In essence, the colonial educational structure served to inculcate the African[1] natives with myths and beliefs that denied and belittled their lived experiences, their history, their culture, and their language. The schools were seen as purifying fountains where Africans could be saved from their deep-rooted ignorance, their "savage" culture, and their bastardized language, which, according to some Portuguese scholars, was a corrupted form of Portuguese "without grammatical rules (they can't even be applied)."

This system could not help but reproduce in children and youth the profile that the colonial ideology itself had created for them, namely that of inferior beings, lacking in all ability.

On the one hand, schooling in these colonies served the purpose of deculturating the natives; on the other hand, it acculturated them into a predefined colonial model. Schools in this mold functioned "as part of an ideological state apparatus designed to secure the ideological and social reproduction of capital and its institutions, whose interests are rooted in the dynamics of capital accumulation and the reproduction of the labor force." This educated labor force in the ex-Portuguese colonies was composed mainly of low-level functionaries whose major tasks were the promotion and maintenance of the status quo. Their role took on a new and important dimension when they were used as intermediaries to further colonize Portuguese possessions in Africa. Thus, colonial schools were successful to the extent that they created a petit-bourgeois class of functionaries who had internalized the belief that they had become "white" or "black with white souls," and were therefore superior to African peasants, who still practiced what was viewed as barbaric culture.

This assimilation process penetrated the deepest level of consciousness, especially in the bourgeois class. For instance, with respect to becoming "white," we are reminded of an anecdote about a black Cape Verdian so preoccupied with his blackness that he paid a well-respected white Cape Verdian to issue him a decree proclaiming him white. The man jokingly wrote for him on a piece of paper "Dja'n branco dja," meaning "I have thereby been declared white."

After independence and in the reconstruction of a new society in these countries, schools have assumed as their major task the "decolonization of mentality," as it is termed by Aristides Pereira, and which Amilcar Cabral called the "re-Africanization of mentality." It is clear that both Pereira and Cabral were well aware of the need to create a school system in which a new mentality cleansed of all vestiges of colonialism would be formulated; a school system that would allow people to appropriate their history, their culture, and their language; a school system in which it was imperative to reformulate the programs of geography, history, and the Portuguese language, changing all the reading texts that were so heavily impregnated with colonialist ideology. It was an absolute priority that students should study their own geography and not that of Portugal, the inlets of the sea and not Rio Tejo. It was urgent that they study their history, the history of the resistance of their people to the invader and the struggle for their liberation, which gave them back the right to make their own history—not the history of the kings of Portugal and the intrigues of the court.

The proposal to incorporate a radical pedagogy in schools has met a lukewarm reception in these countries. We want to argue that the suspicion of many African educators is deeply rooted in the language issue (African versus Portuguese) and has led to the creation of a neocolonialist literacy campaign under the superficially radical slogan of eliminating illiteracy in the new republics. The difficulties of reappropriating African culture have been increased by the fact that the means for such struggle has been the language of the colonizer. As we will argue . . . , the present literacy campaign in these nations concerns itself mainly with the creation of functional literates in the Portuguese language. No longer based on the cultural capital of subordinate Africans, the program has fallen prey to positivistic and instrumental approaches to literacy concerned mainly with the mechanical acquisition of Portuguese language skills. . . .

APPROACHES TO LITERACY

Almost without exception, traditional approaches to literacy have been deeply ingrained in a positivistic method of inquiry. In effect, this has resulted in an epistemological stance in which scientific rigor and methodological refinement are celebrated, while "theory and knowledge are subordinated to the imperatives of efficiency and technical mastery, and history is reduced to a minor footnote in the priorities of 'empirical' scientific inquiry." In general, this approach abstracts methodological issues from their ideological contexts and consequently ignores the interrelationship between the sociopolitical structures of a society and the act of reading. In part, the exclusion of social and political dimensions from the practice of reading gives rise to an ideology of cultural reproduction, one that views readers as "objects." It is as though their conscious bodies were simply empty, waiting to be filled by that word from the teacher. Although it is important to analyze how ideologies inform various reading traditions, . . . we will limit our discussion to a brief analysis of the most important approaches to literacy, linking them to either cultural reproduction or cultural production.

The Academic Approach to Reading

The purpose assigned to reading in the academic tradition is twofold. First, the rationale for this approach "derives from classical definitions of the well-educated man—thoroughly grounded in the classics, articulate in spoken and written expression, actively engaged in intellectual pursuits." This approach to reading has primarily served the interests of the elite classes. In this case, reading is viewed as the acquisition of predefined forms of knowledge and is organized around the study of Latin and Greek and the mastery of the great classical works. Second, since it would be unrealistic to expect the vast majority of society to meet such high standards, reading was redefined as the

196

*Chapter 8
Perspectives on
the Struggle for
Freedom in
Education*

acquisition of reading skills, decoding skills, vocabulary development, and so on. This second rationale served to legitimize a dual approach to reading: one level for the ruling class and another for the dispossessed majority. According to Giroux (*Theory and Resistance*): "This second notion is geared primarily to working class students whose cultural capital is considered less compatible, and thus inferior in terms of complexity and value, with the knowledge and values of the dominant class."

This twofold academic approach to reading is inherently alienating in nature. On the one hand, it ignores the life experience, the history, and the language practice of students. On the other, it overemphasizes the mastery and understanding of classical literature and the use of literary materials as "vehicles for exercises in comprehension (literal and interpretative), vocabulary development, and word identification skills." Thus, literacy in this sense is stripped of its sociopolitical dimensions; it functions, in fact, to reproduce dominant values and meaning. It does not contribute in any meaningful way to the appropriation of working-class history, culture, and language.

The Utilitarian Approach to Reading

The major goal of the utilitarian approach is to produce readers who meet the basic reading requirements of contemporary society. In spite of its progressive appeal, such an approach emphasizes the mechanical learning of reading skills while sacrificing the critical analysis of the social and political order that generates the need for reading in the first place. This position has led to the development of "functional literates," groomed primarily to meet the requirements of our ever more complex technological society. Such a view is not simply characteristic of the advanced industrialized countries of the West; even within the Third World, utilitarian literacy has been championed as a vehicle for economic betterment, access to jobs, and increase of the productivity level. As it is clearly stated by UNESCO, "Literacy programs should preferably be linked with economic priorities. [They] must impart not only reading and writing, but also professional and technical knowledge, thereby leading to a fuller participation of adults in economic life."

This notion of literacy has been enthusiastically incorporated as a major goal by the back-to-basics proponents of reading. It has also contributed to the development of neatly packaged reading programs that are presented as the solution to difficulties students experience in reading job application forms, tax forms, advertisement literature, sales catalogs, labels, and the like. In general, the utilitarian approach views literacy as meeting the basic reading demand of an industrialized society. As Giroux points out:

> Literacy within this perspective is geared to make adults more productive workers and citizens within a given society. In spite of its appeal to economic mobility, functional literacy reduces the concept of literacy and the pedagogy in which it is suited to the pragmatic requirements of capital; consequently, the notions of critical thinking, culture and power disappear under the imperatives of the labor process and the need for capital accumulation.

*Paulo Freire
and Donaldo
Macedo*

While the academic and utilitarian approaches to reading emphasize the mastery of reading skills and view the readers as "objects," the cognitive development model stresses the construction of meaning whereby readers engage in a dialectical interaction between themselves and the objective world. Although the acquisition of literacy skills is viewed as an important task in this approach, the salient feature is how people construct meaning through problem-solving processes. Comprehension of the text is relegated to a position of lesser importance in favor of the development of new cognitive structures that can enable students to move from simple to highly complex reading tasks. This reading process is highly influenced by the early work of John Dewey and has been shaped in terms of the development of Piagetian cognitive structures. Under the cognitive development model, reading is seen as an intellectual process, "through a series of fixed, value-free, and universal stages of development."

The cognitive development model thus avoids criticism of the academic and utilitarian views of reading and fails to consider the content of what is read. Instead, it emphasizes a process that allows students to analyze and critique issues raised in the text with an increasing level of complexity. This approach, however, is rarely concerned with questions of cultural reproduction. Since students' cultural capital—i.e., their life experience, history, and language—is ignored, they are rarely able to engage in thorough critical reflection, regarding their own practical experience and the ends that motivate them in order, in the end, to organize the findings and thus replace mere opinion about facts with an increasingly rigorous understanding of their significance.

The Romantic Approach to Reading

Like the cognitive development model, the romantic approach is based on an interactionist approach with a major focus on the construction of meaning; however, the romantic approach views meaning as being generated by the reader and not occurring in the interaction between reader and author via text. The romantic mode greatly emphasizes the affective and sees reading as the fulfillment of self and a joyful experience. One writer praised "the intimate reliving of fresh views of personality and life implicit in the work (of literature); the pleasure and release of tensions that may flow from such an experience... ; the deepening and broadening of sensitivity to the sensuous quality and emotional impact of day-to-day living."

In essence, the romantic approach to reading presents a counterpoint to the authoritarian modes of pedagogy which view readers as "objects." However, this seemingly liberal approach to literacy fails to make problematic class conflict, gender, or racial inequalities. Furthermore, the romantic model completely ignores the cultural capital of subordinate groups and assumes that all people have the same access to reading, or that reading is part of the cultural capital of all people. This failure to address questions of cultural capital or various structural inequalities means that the romantic model tends to

198

Chapter 8
Perspectives on
the Struggle for
Freedom in
Education

reproduce the cultural capital of the dominant class, to which reading is intimately tied. It is presumptuous and naive to expect a student from the working class, confronted and victimized by myriad disadvantages, to find joy and self-affirmation through reading alone. But more important is the failure of the romantic tradition to link reading to the asymmetrical relations of power within the dominant society, relations of power that not only define and legitimate certain approaches to reading but also disempower certain groups by excluding them from such a process.

We have argued thus far that all of these approaches to literacy have failed to provide a theoretical model for empowering historical agents with the logic of individual and collective self-determination. While these approaches may differ in their basic assumptions about literacy, they all share one common feature: they all ignore the role of language as a major force in the construction of human subjectivities. That is, they ignore the way language may either confirm or deny the life histories and experiences of the people who use it. This becomes clearer in our analysis of the role of language in the literacy programs.

THE ROLE OF LANGUAGE IN LITERACY

... Educators must develop radical pedagogical structures that provide students with the opportunity to use their own reality as a basis of literacy. This includes, obviously, the language they bring to the classroom. To do otherwise is to deny students the rights that lie at the core of the notion of an emancipatory literacy. The failure to base a literacy program on the native language means that oppositional forces can neutralize the efforts of educators and political leaders to achieve decolonization of mind. Educators and political leaders must recognize that "language is inevitably one of the major preoccupations of a society which, liberating itself from colonialism and refusing to be drawn into neo-colonialism, searches for its own recreation. In the struggle to re-create a society, the reconquest by the people of their own world becomes a fundamental factor." It is of tantamount importance that the incorporation of the students' language as the primary language of instruction in literacy be given top priority. It is through their own language that they will be able to reconstruct their history and their culture.

In this sense, the students' language is the only means by which they can develop their own voice, a prerequisite to the development of a positive sense of self-worth. As Giroux elegantly states, the students' voice "is the discursive means to make themselves 'heard' and to define themselves as active authors of their world." The authorship of one's own world, which would also imply one's own language, means what Mikhail Bakhtin defines as "retelling a story in one's own words."

Although the concept of voice is fundamental in the development of an emancipatory literacy, the goal should never be to restrict students to their own vernacular. This linguistic constriction inevitably leads to a linguistic ghetto. Educators must understand fully the broader meaning of student's "empowerment." That is, empowerment should never be limited to what Arnowitz describes as "the process of appreciating and loving oneself." In addition to this process, empowerment should also be a means that enables students "to interrogate and selectively appropriate those aspects of the dominant culture that will provide them with the basis for defining and transforming, rather than merely serving, the wider social order." This means that educators should understand the value of mastering the standard dominant language of the wider society. It is through the full appropriation of the dominant standard language that students find themselves linguistically empowered to engage in dialogue with the various sectors of the wider society. What we would like to reiterate is that educators should never allow the students' voice to be silenced by a distorted legitimation of the standard language. The students' voice should never be sacrificed, since it is the only means through which they make sense of their own experience in the world.

... Educators must develop an emancipatory literacy program informed by a radical pedagogy so that the students' language will cease to provide its speakers the experience of subordination and, moreover, may be brandished as a weapon of resistance to the dominance of the standard language.

As we stated earlier, the linguistic issues raised [here] are not limited to [the] developing countries of Africa and Latin America. The asymmetrical power relations in reference to language use are also predominant in highly industrialized societies. For instance, the U.S. English movement in the United States headed by the ex-California senator S. I. Hayakawa points to a xenophobic culture that blindly negates the pluralistic nature of U.S. society and falsifies the empirical evidence in support of bilingual education, as has been amply documented. These educators... fail to understand that it is through multiple discourses that students generate meaning of their everyday social contexts. Without understanding the meaning of their immediate social reality, it is most difficult to comprehend their relations with the wider society.

By and large, U.S. English proponents base their criticism of bilingual education on quantitative evaluation results, which are "the product of a particular model of social structure that gear the theoretical concepts to the pragmatics of the society that devised the evaluation model to begin with." That is, if the results are presented as facts determined by a particular ideological framework, these facts cannot in themselves get us beyond that framework. We would warn educators that these evaluation models can provide answers that are correct and nevertheless without truth. A study that concludes that linguistic minority students in the United States perform way below other mainstream students in English is correct, but such an answer tells us very little about the material conditions with which these linguistic- and racial-minority students work in the struggle against racism, educational tracking, and the systematic negation of their histories....

We believe that the answer lies not in the technical questions of whether English is a more elaborate and viable language of instruction. This position would point to an assumption that English is in fact a superior language. We want to propose that the answer rests in a full understanding of the ideological elements that generate and sustain linguistic, racial, and sex discrimination....

The new literacy programs must be largely based on the notion of emancipatory literacy, in which literacy is viewed "as one of the major vehicles by

200

*Chapter 8
Perspectives on
the Struggle for
Freedom in
Education*

which 'oppressed' people are able to participate in the sociohistorical transformation of their society." In this view, literacy programs should be tied not only to mechanical learning of reading skills but, additionally, to a critical understanding of the overall goals for national reconstruction. Thus, the reader's development of a critical comprehension of the text, and the sociohistorical context to which it refers, becomes an important factor in our notion of literacy. The act of learning to read and write, in this instance, is a creative act that involves a critical comprehension of reality. The knowledge of earlier knowledge, gained by the learners as a result of analyzing praxis in its social context, opens to them the possibility of a new knowledge. The new knowledge reveals the reason for being that is behind the facts, thus demythologizing the false interpretations of these same facts. Thus, there is no longer any separation between thought-language and objective reality. The reading of a text now demands a reading within the social context to which it refers.

Literacy, in this sense, is grounded in a critical reflection on the cultural capital of the oppressed. It becomes a vehicle by which the oppressed are equipped with the necessary tools to reappropriate their history, culture, and language practices. It is, thus, a way to enable the oppressed to reclaim "those historical and existential experiences that are devalued in everyday life by the dominant culture in order to be both validated and critically understood."

NOTES

1. By African we mean to refer to African natives belonging to African countries that were colonized by Portugal. For the sake of economy of terms, we have selected this term, but we want to point out that we are aware of the great linguistic and cultural diversity that exists in Africa.

8.2 BENJAMIN R. BARBER

Radical Excesses and Post-Modernism

"Postmodernism" and "deconstructionism" are two leading concepts in the critical theoretical debate over the social purposes of education. The postmodernist movement was founded by Jacques Derrida and Michel Foucault. Derrida used the term *deconstruction* to make the point that all human knowledge is situated in a matrix, or web, of racial, cultural, gender, and social class relations. Postmodernists tend to believe that reason itself is politicized in such a matrix to the extent that people always reason from some politicized situation in life. Postmodernists also maintain that dominant social class, gender, and cultural forces in society exercise effective control over the lives of subordinate social groups, such as cultural minorities, women, and low-income or unemployed persons. When postmodernists turn to educational issues, they argue that teachers must play a socially transformative role in their classrooms by helping students to "deconstruct" the dominant group's vision of social reality and justice and to replace dominant conceptions of knowledge with visions of social reality based on their own experience of it.

In the following selection, Benjamin R. Barber explores the assumptions of critical theory and attacks them from a liberal perspective. Barber is concerned that postmodernism and deconstructionism may become new orthodoxies whose adherents will resist fundamental questioning of their theoretical framework. This selection illustrates the advantages of critical, reasoned analysis of ideas.

Barber (b. 1939) is the Walt Whitman Professor of Political Science and director of the Walt Whitman Center for the Culture and Politics of Democracy at Rutgers University. *An Aristocracy of Everyone: The Politics of Education and the Future of America* (Oxford University Press, 1992), from which the following selection is taken, is his eighth book.

Key Concept: a critique of pedagogical radicals and present-day progressive educators

Traditional orthodoxies have too often been replaced with new counter-orthodoxies, no less noxious for being novel, no less inimical to democracy for being offered on behalf of the powerless. Orthodoxy cannot be fought with

202

Chapter 8
Perspectives on
the Struggle for
Freedom in
Education

counterorthodoxy. The challenge is to overcome not to replace dogma, and this requires a critical spirit. I have argued that too many critics of political correctness have drawn a phony picture of neutrality that is oblivious to the realities of power in the modern school and university—particularly when seen from the perspective of the powerless. But pedagogical radicals at times outcaricature their critics and have themselves been oblivious to several of the most insidious modern sophistries, including a species of reductionism that lurks in their own "deconstruction" of traditional academic rationality. They have sometimes acceded to the temptation to intimidate, to suppress, and to silence not merely the powerful without but the doubtful within. They have been quick to assert as dogma convictions they do not wish to see subjected to critical questioning. And they have all too easily confounded their psychic longing for values with an actual argument on behalf of values.

Powerlessness is a justification for rebellion, but it is not a license for mindlessness. The reality of being without a voice can become part of a good argument, but it is not the same thing as a good argument; it certainly does not exempt the powerless and the voiceless from the obligation to offer good reasons. Indeed, this is precisely why there is both a need and a right to be heard—a right secured only through an education in liberty. This right, however, is not necessarily the same thing as the right to stop others from talking or the right to cease listening. Reason can be a smoke screen for interest, but the argument that it is a smoke screen itself depends on reason—or we are caught up in an endless regression in which each argument exposing the dependency of someone else's argument on arbitrariness and self-interest is in turn shown to be self-interested and arbitrary.

Let us consider the principal sins of the present generation of progressive educators justifiably concerned with the future of democracy—sins more of exaggeration than of attitude. Some of the problem is plain old silliness: the utterly serious and therefore utterly comical insistence on certain campuses that "seminars" be called "ovulars" or the caricatured transformation of Christopher Columbus from a silent movie saint into a silent movie villain, to be known henceforth exclusively as a torturer, plunderer, and proto-imperialist. The instinct of the sympathetic moderate here can only be to cry, "Whoa! Slow down!" In traversing the terra infirma of modern education, I have expressed a cautious solidarity with the progressives who have devoted themselves to institutionalizing in the schools the 1960s' critique of establishment education of the 1990s. Yet by trying to negotiate several sharp curves at too great a velocity, some seem in recent years to have skidded off the tracks. In their understandable haste to arrive at more democratic schools, their grasp on the meaning of democracy has sometimes looked shaky. In their devotion to a public education that can encompass a new and radically heterogenous American public, their feel for the public character of public education has been weakened. Impatience has prompted them to travel at reckless speeds; and so, at what we might fancifully call the curve of critical doubt, they have plunged into a gorge of hyperskepticism, where every argument turns relentlessly on itself and where the demand to ground values reasonably becomes a relativization of all values. At the sharp turn of difference, they have fallen into the ravine of hyperpluralism, where overdifferentiation destroys the possibility of integration and community.

I want to examine here these two perils of the current reform movement. Doubt is a powerful vehicle of learning, but moving at too high a speed can also undermine the process. Diversity is a condition of freedom for all, but when it runs off the rails it can rob the "all" of common identity and ultimately destroy the liberty of individuals.

HYPERSKEPTICISM: PRUDENT DOUBT OR FATAL NIHILISM?

All thoughtful inquiry, and hence all useful education, starts with questioning. All usable knowledge, and thus all practical science, starts with the provisional acceptance of answers. Education is a dialectic in moderation in which probing and accepting, questioning and answering, must achieve a delicate balance. Stories must be told, queried, retold, revised, questioned, and retold still again—much as the American story has been. In periods of rebellion, academic no less than social, when challenging authority means questioning answers, there is an understandable tendency toward skepticism, even cynicism. Michael Wood has characterized Jacques Derrida's approach to method as "a patient and intelligent suspicion," which is a useful description of one moment in a student's democratic education.

The methodologies deployed by critics of power and convention in the academy do not always find the dialectical center, however, and are subject to distortion by hyperbole. Sometimes they seem to call for all questions and no answers, all doubt and no provisional resting places. This radicalism has many virtues as scholarship, but as pedagogy far fewer. In its postmodern phase, where the merely modern is equated with something vaguely reactionary and post-modernism means a radical battering down of all certainty, this hyper-skeptical pedagogy can become self-defeating.

Skepticism is an essential but slippery and thus dangerously problematic teaching tool. It demystifies and decodes; it denies absolutes; it cuts through rationalization and hypocrisy. Yet it is a whirling blade, an obdurate reaper hard to switch off at will. It is not particularly discriminating. It doesn't necessarily understand the difference between rationalization and reason, since its effectiveness depends precisely on conflating them. It can lead to a refusal to judge or to take responsibility or to impose norms on conduct. If, as Derrida has insisted, "the concept of making a charge itself belongs to the structure of phallogocentrism" (the use of reason and language as forms of macho domination), there can be no responsibility, no autonomy, no morals, no freedom. Like a born killer who may be a hero in wartime but, unable to discriminate between war and peace, becomes a homocidal maniac when the war ends for everyone else, radical skepticism lacks a sense of time and place, a sense of elementary propriety.

The questions this poses for pedagogy are drawn in the recondite language of literary postmodernism and deconstruction, but are of the first importance for education. Does the art of criticism doom the object of critical

204

*Chapter 8
Perspectives on
the Struggle for
Freedom in
Education*

attention to displacement by the self-absorbed critic? In other words, does criticizing books replace reading them? Can the art of questioning be made self-limiting, or do critics always become skeptics? Are skeptics in turn doomed by their negative logic to be relativists? Must relativists melt down into nihilists? Conservatives have worried that this particularly slippery slope cannot be safely traversed at all, and thus have worried about a pedagogy that relies on a too-critical mode of radical questioning. They prefer to think of education as instilling the right values and teaching authoritative bodies of knowledge to compliant students for whom learning is primarily a matter of absorbing information. When these conservatives appeal to the ancients, it is the rationalist Plato to whom they turn, rather than the subversive Socrates.

Yet pedagogical progressives actually confirm the conservatives' fears when they themselves tumble happily down the slope, greasing it as they go with an epistemology that denies the possibility of any stopping place, any objectivity, any rationality, any criterion of reasonableness or universalism whatsoever. Asked to choose between dogma and nihilism, between affirming hegemonic authority and denying all authority, including the authority of reason, of science, and of open debate, what choice does the concerned teacher have but despair? Where she seeks a middling position, she is offered orthodoxy or nihilism. Where she seeks moderation in her students—a respect for rationality but an unwillingness to confound it with or measure it by somebody's power, or eloquence, or status—she is informed that all appeals to rationality are pretense....

There is little new or surprising in skepticism's consuming appetite. Cynicism has been a tendency of philosophy from the start, and its inclination to move from intelligent suspicion to wholesale paranoia is well documented. In *The Republic* Socrates had to contend with Thrasymachus, who saw behind every claim on behalf of truth or justice a sneaky rationalization of somebody's stealthily concealed interest. Socrates showed that Thrasymachus started with a prudent if furtive suspicion but ended as a moral bankrupt, a sellout to the brute argument of force, unable to defend any notion of virtue or justice. For many of the same reasons, the Sophists of ancient Athens who followed Thrasymachus were understood to be tireless interrogators who could ask, "Yes, but why?" until people with beliefs dropped of exhaustion or surrendered, running out of reasonable "becauses" long before their tormentors ran out of probing "whys."

From their earliest encounters with belief (the claims of subjectivity), knowledge (the claims of intersubjectivity), and truth (the claims of objectivity), pedagogy and scholarship have tried to balance the need to ask questions with the need to offer well-grounded if tentative answers. Since an answer is at least a provisional suspension of questioning, it interrupts the critical process and also suspends the critical element in learning. But unless questioning stops and is at some point provisionally satisfied, there is no knowledge worth the name—neither subjective beliefs, intersubjective values, nor objective truths (however small the *t* in truth).

The pedagogy of questioning naturally and properly takes the standpoint of suspicion. It looks behind appearances and beneath surfaces, and thus has a penchant for reductionism: turning the immediate into the mediated, turning the observed into the intuited, turning apparent universals into actual particulars, turning putative reasons into sham rationalizations, turning claims to truth into rationalizations of interest—looking always for a concealed reality behind *prima facie* events.... To reductionists, things are never quite what they seem. Suspicious of truth as an external "empirical" thing or an inherently meaningful text or an uncontested object, they reduce such entities to the conditions (psychological, historical, material) by which they are produced and the interests of those who produce them.

The author of a book, argues Foucault, a reductionist here who sees behind the smoke screen of "reason" a hundred hidden varieties of coercion, is not some vessel of art or creative genius but merely "an ideological product." A book is less a work of literature imbued with truth and beauty or with standards to which human conduct might be made to conform (the old-fashioned view) than a product of its readers or its critics; an emanation of the class, gender, and status of the background that produced the writer or his audience. As David Hume, skeptic and critic of objectivist ethics, said long before deconstruction seized on such arguments, a value is not a symbol for some objective right or eternal good, it is merely a token of someone's preference. To say "It is good" is merely a disguised way of saying "I like it." And whereas (when we allow that objective standards exist) we can presumably assess and argue rationally about human conduct, preferences are purely subjective, and all we can say about them is that at most they exist. The assertion "Cruelty is good" takes a form inviting debate and argument, and may elicit the counterassertion "No, it is evil," which can in turn be debated in historical, moral, and philosophical terms. On the other hand, the descriptive sentence "Cruelty feels good to me" cannot be contested at all other than in terms of its descriptive accuracy ("Does it *really* feel good to you?"). To someone who says "I like being cruel," neither "No, you don't" nor "But cruelty is evil" is an appropriate response. The reductive language of what philosophers call "noncognitivism" makes ethics radically subjective, and it soon vanishes as a subject of moral discourse....

Reducing supposed objective goods to subjective preferences and reducing claims about truth to statements about power and interest are two related forms of a very ancient and very useful but also very risky skepticism. For millennia, both skepticism and reductionism lived as parasites off the host philosophy—which, fortunately, had its own affirmative business to attend to (understanding human conduct in an often unintelligible cosmos). In the last hundred years or so, these two have more or less consumed the philosophical tradition that sustained them. The same thing has happened in literature, as the critic came first to deny the meaning of literature, then to displace it with the activities of the critics. Criticism is now seemingly severed from literature in many universities, leading an independent existence as literary theory in English departments that teach not literature and the art of reading, but theory and the art of criticism. Social scientists and humanists in many other departments, especially those understandably dissatisfied with traditional academe and its spurious appeals to neutrality and universalism, are taking their cue from literary theorists and deploying reductive post-modern critiques against the establishment. This has certain virtues as a tactic but ultimately is poor strategy and bad pedagogy.

206

Chapter 8
Perspectives on
the Struggle for
Freedom in
Education

... As Edmund Burke once noted, those who destroy everything are certain to remedy some grievance. The annihilation of all values will undoubtedly rid us of hypocritical ones or the ones misused by hypocrites. We can prevent the powerful from using reason to conceal their hegemony by burning the cloak—extirpating reason from political and moral discourse. However, those who come after can hardly complain that they feel naked or that their discourse, absent such terms as reason, legitimacy, and justice, seems incapable of establishing an affirmative pedagogy or a just politics.

Just how crucially such seemingly abstruse issues impact on actual college curricula is unpleasantly evident in this approving portrait of literature and culture in a recent issue of the *Bulletin of the American Association of University Professors:*

> Cultural studies moves away from "history of ideas" to a contested history of struggles for power and authority, to complicated relations between "center" and "margin," between dominant and minority positions. Literature is no longer investigated primarily as the masterworks of individual genius, but as a way of designating specialized practices of reading and writing and cultural production.... The renaming of "literature" as "culture" is thus not just a shift in vocabulary. It marks a rethinking of what is experienced as cultural materials... [including] media, MTV, popular culture, newspapers, magazines, advertising, textbooks, and advice materials. But the shift also marks the movement away from the study of an "object" to the study of a practice, the practice called "literary study" or "artistic production," the practice of criticism.

How slippery this particular slope has become! What begins as a sound attempt to show that art is produced by real men and women with agendas and interests attached to things like their gender, race, and economic status ends as the nihilistic denial of art as object. What beings as a pedagogically useful questioning of the power implications of truth ends as the cynical subverting of the very possibility of truth. What begins as a prudent unwillingness to accept at face value "objective" knowledge, which is understood to be, at least in part, socially constructed, ends as the absurd insistence that knowledge is exclusively social and can be reduced entirely to the power of those who produce it. What begins as an educationally provocative inquiry into the origins of literature in the practice of literary production ends in the educationally insidious annihilation of literature and its replacement by criticism—the practice, it turns out ever so conveniently, of those asking the questions! Thus does the whirling blade of skepticism's latest reductive manifestations, post-modernism and deconstruction, cut and cut and go on cutting until there is nothing left. Thus does·the amiable and pedagogically essential art of criticism somehow pass into carnage.

As epistemology, this is what post-moderns would, in their inimitable jargon, call logocidal—deadly to reason and discourse. As pedagogy it is suicidal, above all to those already deprived of power and voice by the social forms and educational strategies supposedly being deconstructed. It is hard to tell what service a teacher does a ninth grader just learning to read books when she informs him that there is no difference between Emily Dickinson and MTV, both being simply cultural products of interested artisans pushing their particular ideological interests. To make his point about the relativism of cultural values, Houston A. Baker, the current president of the Modern Language Association, tells us there is no more difference between high culture and pop culture than between a hoagie and a pizza. What he means is that there is no more difference between Shakespeare and Virginia Woolf than between Virginia Woolf and a pepperoni slice with extra cheese. This is to say, as John Stuart Mill quipped about Jeremy Bentham's reductionist utilitarianism, that there is no difference between pushpin and poetry.

These are more than theoretical points: Rutgers has offered social science courses not only on film but on MTV, and Duke University teaches Louis L'Amour alongside Shakespeare and George Eliot, not because popular writing deserves a place in the curriculum along with high culture (it does), but in the belief that the distinction between pop and high culture is spurious, an invention of elites trying to maintain their cultural hegemony. Yet without the aspiration to excellence, however contested the end products, "culture" loses its normative and directing power and becomes a cipher; no distinctions can be made between the "culture of pinball machines," "the drug culture," and "skinhead culture," on the one hand, and "Italian Renaissance culture," "the culture of Benin civilization," and "Harlem Renaissance culture," on the other. . . .

Like all fundamental political and social terms, culture is inherently and necessarily normative. That is why we argue about it, why it is contested. That is what makes multiculturalism worth debating. To annul the power of the word "culture" as a standard of human organization, aesthetic and intellectual evolution, and general excellence does nothing to enhance cultural pluralism or learning in the name of liberty and respect. On the contrary, it creates the impression that there are no standards of excellence whatsoever other than the bogus claims advanced by elites.

The confusion of multiculturalists on this question is evident in their ambivalence over whether to take some significant credit for Western civilization by showing its roots in Egyptian and African sources (thereby paying tribute to its many achievements), as does Martin Bernal in *Black Athena,* or to reject it altogether in favor of a radical "Afrocentric" view that celebrates Africa and subjects Western culture to a not so benign neglect, as scholars like Molefi Asante have done. If Western culture manifests certain virtues, if culture implies standards (however contested) and is more than just a collection of artifacts, then the sources of "Western" civilization are worth fighting over. If not, why bother contest their origins at all?

Sometimes multiculturalists want it both ways, sounding a little like the storied defense attorney who, without taking a breath, managed to argue, "My client is innocent, your honor; he never took the jewels, and besides, he didn't know they belonged to anyone, and anyway they were fake." With the same all-encompassing logic, the Afrocentric multiculturalist at times seems to say, "Western civilization is worthless, dangerous, a colonizing imperium with pretended virtues it never lives up to; and besides, it was originally *OUR* creation, a product of an Egypt we can prove was Black, and anyway Black Africa had a great culture of its own, which we can see reflected in the values of so-called Western civilization *IT* actually produced." Critics have suggested that Afro-

208

*Chapter 8
Perspectives on
the Struggle for
Freedom in
Education*

centrists are not really multiculturalists at all, but monocultural zealots of a civilization other than Europe's. Perhaps a response in keeping with the moderation offered earlier would be to see Afrocentrism as a stage on the way to a more genuine multiculturalism, itself a stage on the way to appreciating America as a culture defined precisely by its diversity and multiculturalism. This eliminates the harsh attack on Western culture, which is of more use to conservative critics looking to dismiss multiculturalism than to multicultured educators.

Conservatives (who surely have to be congratulating themselves privately on their good fortune in being tossed so splendid a provocation!) have repeatedly expressed their horror over the Stanford march led by the Reverend Jesse Jackson not so long ago in which students protesting traditional curricula chanted, "Hey, hey, ho, ho, Western Culture has got to go!" (although it was the course labeled as such rather than the generic entity they were protesting). As new expressions of anti-Western monocultural intolerance, such slogans are reprehensible. But they are also implicit in the reductionist perspective, which denies "culture" any status other than that of "ideological product." By transforming normative truths subject to rational debate that are embodied in the books, conventions, and institutions that constitute a civilization into an unwholesome product of vested interests, the skeptic undermines not civilization but civility, not rationalization but reason, not dogma but the possibility of consensus and thus community. Along the way, in impugning the inherent authority of the idea of culture, he also manages to impugn the authority of the non-Western civilizations to which his multiculturalism supposedly pays homage.

Questioning should challenge objectivity but also be capable of redeeming it. Criticism finds its pedagogical legitimacy in its powers of redemption: the power to save virtue from hypocrisy, truth from its counterfeits, reason from rationalization. Anything else pushes skepticism over the brink and gives to subjectivism the aspect of narcissism. In philosophy, this narcissism is called solipsism, a term suggesting a self so absorbed in the mysteries of its capacity to sense and make sense (or nonsense) of the world that it ceases to perceive anything but itself. This is a matter of the eye being distracted from the object to which the finger points to the finger itself, until the whole world resembles nothing so much as a finger.

... [A]dvocates of the new hyperskepticism... are genuine reformers struggling against the dogmas of what they see as a hypocritical establishment. They seek more equality, more justice, better education for all. They want not just to expose the hypocrisies of power, but to tame and equalize it. They want to reclaim true justice from its hypocritical abusers. They chase shadows in the valley of cynicism but trust they are on the path that leads to redemption.

Yet the instruments of revolution they have chosen are more suited to the philosophical terrorist than the pedagogical reformer. Radical skepticism, reductionism, solipsism, nihilism, subjectivism, and cynicism will not help American women gain a stronger voice in the classroom; will not lift Americans of color from the prison of ignorance and despair to which centuries of oppression, broken families, and ghettoized schools have relegated them; will not provide a firm value foundation for the young in equality, citizenship, and justice. How can such reformers think they will empower the voiceless by proving that voice is always a function of power? How can they believe the ignorant will be rescued from illiteracy by showing that literacy is an arbitrary form of cultural imperialism? How do they think the struggle for equality and justice can be waged with an epistemology that denies standing to reasons and normative rational terms such as justice and equality?

... [R]eason is an ideal that can teach us how to live in comity and free ourselves from the incivility that always attends reason's failure. When reason is polluted by interest and power, the remedy is not to jettison but to cleanse it. The remedy for hypocrisy is not less but more reason. Rationalization is evidence of reason abused, not proof that there is no reason. The object of questioning is to test and strengthen rather than to annihilate the idea of the rational.

Education is a training in the middle way between the dogmatic belief in absolutes and the cynical negation of all belief. On the fringes where dogma or nihilism prevail, force is always master. Well-taught students learn to suspect every claim to truth and then to redeem truth provisionally by its capacity to withstand pointed questioning. They learn that somewhere between Absolute Certainty and Permanent Doubt there is a point of balance that permits knowledge to be provisionally accepted and applied (science, modestly understood, for example) and allows conduct to be provisionally evaluated in a fashion that makes ethics, community, and democracy possible. There is much illusion in this fragile middle ground. Civilization, Yeats reminded us, is tied together by a hoop of illusion. It would be dangerous to pretend that the illusion is real, but it is fatal to dispense with it altogether. Justice and democracy are the illusions that permit us to live in comity. Truth and knowledge are the illusions that permit us to live commodiously. Art and literature are the illusions that make commodious living worthwhile. Deconstruction may rid us of all our illusions and thus seem a clever way to think, but it is no way at all to live.

The educator's art is to prompt questions that expose our illusions and at the same time to tether illusion to provisional moorings. The teacher must know how to arouse but also how to mollify the faculty of doubt. Her special art is moderation. She will question whether the statements "This is good! This is beautiful! This is justice!" mean something more than "I control the discourse! I define art! I am justice." But her aim will be to distinguish the counterfeit from the real rather than to expunge the very ideas of the good, the beautiful, and the right. There are illusions and there are illusions. "We the People" as a description of a slave-holding society is an illusion that needs to be exposed; "We the People" as an aspiration that permitted, even encouraged, the eventual abolition of slavery is an illusion worth keeping, even worth fighting for, along with such illusions as natural right and human reason on which the concept relies. The ability to discern the difference between these two forms of illusion is what good education teaches. Such judgment can come neither from inculcating fixed canons nor from deconstructing all canons.

The educator cannot teach when offered only the choice between dogma and nothingness; between orthodoxy and meaninglessness; between someone's covert value hegemony and the relativism of all values. The first business of educational reformers in schools and universities—multiculturalists,

210

*Chapter 8
Perspectives on
the Struggle for
Freedom in
Education*

feminists, progressives—ought to be to sever their alliance with esoteric post-modernism; with literary metatheory (theory about theory); with fun-loving, self-annihilating hyperskepticism. As pedagogy these intellectual practices court catastrophe.... They give to people whose very lives depend on the right choices a lesson in the impossibility of judgment. They tell emerging citizens looking to legitimize their preferences for democracy that there is no intellectually respectable way to ground political legitimacy.

CHAPTER 9

Women and Education

9.1 ELIZABETH CADY STANTON

Eighty Years and More (1815–1897): Reminiscences of Elizabeth Cady Stanton

Elizabeth Cady Stanton (1815–1902) was a leader in the fight for women's rights in the United States. Along with Lucretia Mott and others, Stanton led the call for the Seneca Falls (New York) Convention, which convened on July 19–20, 1848. This event is credited as being the official launching of the organized women's rights movement in the United States. Stanton read a "Declaration of Sentiments" before the Seneca Falls Convention, in which she listed the wrongs inflicted on women by then-existing laws and customs. She demanded suffrage and property rights for women as well as the right of women to divorce for good cause.

In the following selection from Stanton's autobiography, *Eighty Years and More (1815–1897): Reminiscences of Elizabeth Cady Stanton* (T. Fisher Unwin, 1898), we see the beginnings of her commitment as a girl and as a young woman to engage in the struggle for the rights of women. Her writing captures the spirit of her time and of her schooling.

Key Concept: education of girls in the nineteenth century

SCHOOL DAYS

When I was eleven years old, two events occurred which changed considerably the current of my life. My only brother, who had just graduated from Union College, came home to die. A young man of great talent and promise, he was the pride of my father's heart. We early felt that this son filled a larger place in our father's affections and future plans than the five daughters together. Well do I remember how tenderly he watched my brother in his last illness, the sighs and tears he gave vent to as he slowly walked up and down the hall, and, when the last sad moment came, and we were all assembled to say farewell in the silent chamber of death, how broken were his utterances as he knelt and prayed for comfort and support. I still recall, too, going into the large darkened parlor to see my brother, and finding the casket, mirrors, and pictures all draped in white, and my father seated by his side, pale and immovable. As he took no notice of me, after standing a long while, I climbed upon his knee, when he mechanically put his arm about me and, with my head resting against his beating heart, we both sat in silence, he thinking of the wreck of all his hopes in the loss of a dear son, and I wondering what could be said or done to fill the void in his breast. At length he heaved a deep sigh and said: "Oh, my daughter, I wish you were a boy!" Throwing my arms about his neck, I replied: "I will try to be all my brother was."

Then and there I resolved that I would not give so much time as heretofore to play, but would study and strive to be at the head of all my classes and thus delight my father's heart. All that day and far into the night I pondered the problem of boyhood. I thought that the chief thing to be done in order to equal boys was to be learned and courageous. So I decided to study Greek and learn to manage a horse. Having formed this conclusion I fell asleep. My resolutions, unlike many such made at night, did not vanish with the coming light. I arose early and hastened to put them into execution. They were resolutions never to be forgotten—destined to mold my character anew. As soon as I was dressed I hastened to our good pastor, Rev. Simon Hosack, who was always early at work in his garden.

"Doctor," said I, "which do you like best, boys or girls?"

"Why, girls, to be sure; I would not give you for all the boys in Christendom."

"My father," I replied, "prefers boys; he wishes I was one, and I intend to be as near like one as possible. I am going to ride on horseback and study Greek. Will you give me a Greek lesson now, doctor? I want to begin at once."

"Yes, child," said he, throwing down his hoe, "come into my library and we will begin without delay."

He entered fully into the feeling of suffering and sorrow which took possession of me when I discovered that a girl weighed less in the scale of being than a boy, and he praised my determination to prove the contrary. The old grammar which he had studied in the University of Glasgow was soon in my hands, and the Greek article was learned before breakfast.

Then came the sad pageantry of death, the weeping of friends, the dark rooms, the ghostly stillness, the exhortation to the living to prepare for death, the solemn prayer, the mournful chant, the funeral cortège, the solemn, tolling bell, the burial. How I suffered during those sad days! What strange undefined fears of the unknown took possession of me! For months afterward, at the twilight hour, I went with my father to the new-made grave. Near it stood two tall poplar trees, against one of which I leaned, while my father threw himself on the grave, with outstretched arms, as if to embrace his child. At last the frosts and storms of November came and threw a chilling barrier between the living and the dead, and we went there no more.

During all this time I kept up my lessons at the parsonage and made rapid progress. I surprised even my teacher, who thought me capable of doing anything. I learned to drive, and to leap a fence and ditch on horseback. I taxed every power, hoping some day to hear my father say: "Well, a girl is as good as a boy, after all." But he never said it. When the doctor came over to spend the evening with us, I would whisper in his ear: "Tell my father how fast I get on," and he would tell him, and was lavish in his praises. But my father only paced the room, sighed, and showed that he wished I were a boy; and I, not knowing why he felt thus, would hide my tears of vexation on the doctor's shoulder.

Soon after this I began to study Latin, Greek, and mathematics with a class of boys in the Academy, many of whom were much older than I. For three years one boy kept his place at the end of the class, and I always stood next. Two prizes were offered in Greek. I strove for one and took the second. How well I remember my joy in receiving that prize. There was no sentiment of ambition, rivalry, or triumph over my companions, nor feeling of satisfaction in receiving this honor in the presence of those assembled on the day of the exhibition. One thought alone filled my mind. "Now," said I, "my father will be satisfied with me." So, as soon as we were dismissed, I ran down the hill, rushed breathless into his office, laid the new Greek Testament, which was my prize, on his table and exclaimed: "There, I got it!" He took up the book, asked me some questions about the class, the teachers, the spectators, and, evidently pleased, handed it back to me. Then, while I stood looking and waiting for him to say something which would show that he recognized the equality of the daughter with the son, he kissed me on the forehead and exclaimed, with a sigh, "Ah, you should have been a boy!"

My joy was turned to sadness. I ran to my good doctor. He chased my bitter tears away, and soothed me with unbounded praises and visions of future success. He was then confined to the house with his last illness. He asked me that day if I would like to have, when he was gone, the old lexicon, Testament, and grammar that we had so often thumbed together. "Yes, but I would rather have you stay," I replied, "for what can I do when you are gone?" "Oh," said he tenderly, "I shall not be gone; my spirit will still be with you, watching you in all life's struggles." Noble, generous friend! He had but little on earth to bequeath to anyone, but when the last scene in his life was ended, and his will was opened, sure enough there was a clause saying: "My Greek lexicon, Testament, and grammar, and four volumes of Scott's commentaries, I will to Elizabeth Cady." I never look at these books without a feeling of thankfulness that in childhood I was blessed with such a friend and teacher....

An important event in our family circle was the marriage of my oldest sister, Tryphena, to Edward Bayard of Wilmington, Delaware. He was a graduate of Union College, a classmate of my brother, and frequently visited at my father's house. At the end of his college course, he came with his brother Henry to study law in Johnstown. A quiet, retired little village was thought to be a good place in which to sequester young men bent on completing their education, as they were there safe from the temptations and distracting influences of large cities. In addition to this consideration, my father's reputation made his office a desirable resort for students, who, furthermore, not only improved their opportunities by reading Blackstone, Kent, and Story, but also by making love to the Judge's daughters. We thus had the advantage of many pleasant acquaintances from the leading families in the country, and, in this way, it was that four of the sisters eventually selected most worthy husbands.

Though only twenty-one years of age when married, Edward Bayard was a tall, fully developed man, remarkably fine looking, with cultivated literary taste and a profound knowledge of human nature. Warm and affectionate, generous to a fault in giving and serving, he was soon a great favorite in the family, and gradually filled the void made in all our hearts by the loss of the brother and son.

My father was so fully occupied with the duties of his profession, which often called him from home, and my mother so weary with the cares of a large family, having had ten children, though only five survived at this time, that they were quite willing to shift their burdens to younger shoulders. Our eldest sister and her husband, therefore, soon became our counselors and advisers. They selected our clothing, books, schools, acquaintances, and directed our reading and amusements. Thus the reins of domestic government, little by little, passed into their hands, and the family arrangements were in a manner greatly improved in favor of greater liberty for the children.

The advent of Edward and Henry Bayard was an inestimable blessing to us. With them came an era of picnics, birthday parties, and endless amusements; the buying of pictures, fairy books, musical instruments and ponies, and frequent excursions with parties on horseback. Fresh from college, they made our lessons in Latin, Greek, and mathematics so easy that we studied with real pleasure and had more leisure for play. Henry Bayard's chief pleasures were walking, riding, and playing all manner of games, from jack-straws to chess, with the three younger sisters, and we have often said that the three years he passed in Johnstown were the most delightful of our girlhood....

As my father's office joined the house, I spent there much of my time, when out of school, listening to the clients stating their cases, talking with the students, and reading the laws in regard to woman. In our Scotch neighborhood many men still retained the old feudal ideas of women and property. Fathers, at their death, would will the bulk of their property to the eldest son, with the proviso that the mother was to have a home with him. Hence it was not unusual for the mother, who had brought all the property into the family, to be made an unhappy dependent on the bounty of an uncongenial daughter-in-law and a dissipated son. The tears and complaints of the women who came to my father for legal advice touched my heart and early drew my attention to the injustice and cruelty of the laws. As the practice of the law was my father's business, I could not exactly understand why he could not alleviate the sufferings of these women. So, in order to enlighten me, he would take down his books and show me the inexorable statutes. The students, observing my interest, would amuse themselves by reading to me all the worst laws they could find, over which I would laugh and cry by turns. One Christmas morning I went into the office to show them, among other of my presents, a new coral necklace and bracelets. They all admired the jewelry and then began to tease me with hypothetical cases of future ownership. "Now," said Henry Bayard, "if in due time you should be my wife, those ornaments would be mine; I could take them and lock them up, and you could never wear them except with my permission. I could even exchange them for a box of cigars, and you could watch them evaporate in smoke."

With this constant bantering from students and the sad complaints of the women, my mind was sorely perplexed. So when, from time to time, my attention was called to these odious laws, I would mark them with a pencil, and becoming more and more convinced of the necessity of taking some active measures against these unjust provisions, I resolved to seize the first opportunity, when alone in the office, to cut every one of them out of the books; supposing my father and his library were the beginning and the end of the law. However, this mutilation of his volumes was never accomplished, for dear old Flora Campbell, to whom I confided my plan for the amelioration of the wrongs of my unhappy sex, warned my father of what I proposed to do. Without letting me know that he had discovered my secret, he explained to me one evening how laws were made, the large number of lawyers and libraries there were all over the State, and that if his library should burn up it would make no difference in woman's condition. "When you are grown up, and able to prepare a speech," said he, "you must go down to Albany and talk to the legislators; tell them all you have seen in this office—the sufferings of these Scotchwomen, robbed of their inheritance and left dependent on their unworthy sons, and, if you can persuade them to pass new laws, the old ones will be a dead letter." Thus was the future object of my life foreshadowed and my duty plainly outlined by him who was most opposed to my public career when, in due time, I entered upon it.

Until I was sixteen years old, I was a faithful student in the Johnstown Academy with a class of boys. Though I was the only girl in the higher classes of mathematics and the languages, yet, in our plays, all the girls and boys mingled freely together. In running races, sliding downhill, and snowballing, we made no distinction of sex. True, the boys would carry the school books and pull the sleighs up hill for their favorite girls, but equality was the general basis of our school relations. I dare say the boys did not make their snowballs quite so hard when pelting the girls, nor wash their faces with the same vehemence as they did each other's, but there was no public evidence of partiality. However, if any boy was too rough or took advantage of a girl smaller than himself, he was promptly thrashed by his fellows. There was an unwritten law and public sentiment in that little Academy world that enabled us to study and play together with the greatest freedom and harmony.

From the academy the boys of my class went to Union College at Schenectady. When those with whom I had studied and contended for prizes for five years came to bid me good-by, and I learned of the barrier that prevented me from following in their footsteps—"no girls admitted here"—my vexation and mortification knew no bounds. I remember, now, how proud and handsome the boys looked in their new clothes, as they jumped into the old stage coach and drove off, and how lonely I felt when they were gone and I had nothing to do, for the plans for my future were yet undetermined. Again I felt more keenly than ever the humiliation of the distinctions made on the ground of sex.

My time was now occupied with riding on horseback, studying the game of chess, and continually squabbling with the law students over the rights of women. Something was always coming up in the experiences of everyday life, or in the books we were reading, to give us fresh topics for argument. They would read passages from the British classics quite as aggravating as the laws. They delighted in extract from Shakespeare, especially from "The Taming of the Shrew," an admirable satire in itself on the old common law of England. I hated Petruchio as if he were a real man. Young Bayard would recite with unction the famous reply of Milton's ideal woman to Adam: "God thy law, thou mine." The Bible, too, was brought into requisition. In fact it seemed to me that every book taught the "divinely ordained" headship of man; but my mind never yielded to this popular heresy.

GIRLHOOD

Mrs. Willard's Seminary at Troy was the fashionable school in my girlhood, and in the winter of 1830, with upward of a hundred other girls, I found myself an active participant in all the joys and sorrows of that institution. When in family council it was decided to send me to that intellectual Mecca, I did not receive the announcement with unmixed satisfaction, as I had fixed my mind on Union College. The thought of a school without boys, who had been to me such a stimulus both in study and play, seemed to my imagination dreary and profitless.

The one remarkable feature of my journey to Troy was the railroad from Schenectady to Albany, the first ever laid in this country. The manner of ascending a high hill going out of the city would now strike engineers as stupid to the last degree. The passenger cars were pulled up by a train, loaded with stones, descending the hill. The more rational way of tunneling through the hill or going around it had not yet dawned on our Dutch ancestors. At every step of my journey to Troy I felt that I was treading on my pride, and thus in a hopeless frame of mind I began my boarding-school career. I had already studied everything that was taught there except French, music, and dancing, so I devoted myself to these accomplishments. As I had a good voice I enjoyed singing, with a guitar accompaniment, and, having a good ear for time, I appreciated the harmony in music and motion and took great delight in dancing. The large house, the society of so many girls, the walks about the city, the novelty of everything made the new life more enjoyable than I had anticipated. To be sure I missed the boys, with whom I had grown up, played with for years, and later measured my intellectual powers with, but, as they became a novelty, there was new zest in occasionally seeing them. After I had been there a short time, I heard a call one day: "Heads out!" I ran with the rest and exclaimed, "What is it?" expecting to see a giraffe or some other wonder from Barnum's Museum. "Why, don't you see those boys?" said one. "Oh," I replied, "is that all? I have seen boys all my life." When visiting family friends in the city, we were in the way of making the acquaintance of their sons, and as all social relations were strictly forbidden, there was a new interest in seeing them. As they were not allowed to call upon us or write notes, unless they were brothers or cousins, we had, in time, a large number of kinsmen.

There was an intense interest to me now in writing notes, receiving calls, and joining the young men in the streets for a walk, such as I had never known when in constant association with them at school and in our daily amusements. Shut up with girls, most of them older than myself, I heard many subjects discussed of which I had never thought before, and in a manner it were better I had never heard. The healthful restraint always existing between boys and girls in conversation is apt to be relaxed with either sex alone. In all my intimate association with boys up to that period, I cannot recall one word or act for criticism, but I cannot say the same of the girls during the three years I passed at the seminary in Troy. My own experience proves to me that it is a grave mistake to send boys and girls to separate institutions of learning, especially at the most impressible age. The stimulus of sex promotes alike a healthy condition of the intellectual and the moral faculties and gives to both a development they never can acquire alone.

Mrs. Willard, having spent several months in Europe, did not return until I had been at the seminary some time. I well remember her arrival, and the joy with which she was greeted by the teachers and pupils who had known her before. She was a splendid-looking woman, then in her prime, and fully realized my idea of a queen. I doubt whether any royal personage in the Old World could have received her worshipers with more grace and dignity than did this far-famed daughter of the Republic. She was one of the remarkable women of that period, and did a great educational work for her sex. She gave free scholarships to a large number of promising girls, fitting them for teachers, with a proviso that, when the opportunity arose, they should, in turn, educate others. . . .

After the restraints of childhood at home and in school, what a period of irrepressible joy and freedom comes to us in girlhood with the first taste of liberty. Then is our individuality in a measure recognized and our feelings and opinions consulted; then we decide where and when we will come and go, what we will eat, drink, wear, and do. To suit one's own fancy in clothes, to buy what one likes, and wear what one chooses is a great privilege to most young people. To go out at pleasure, to walk, to ride, to drive, with no one to say us nay or question our right to liberty, this is indeed like a birth into a new world of happiness and freedom. This is the period, too, when the emotions rule us, and we idealize everything in life; when love and hope make the present an ecstasy and the future bright with anticipation.

Then comes that dream of bliss that for weeks and months throws a halo of glory round the most ordinary characters in every-day life, holding the strongest and most common-sense young men and women in a thraldom from which few mortals escape. The period when love, in soft silver tones, whispers his first words of adoration, painting our graces and virtues day by day in living colors in poetry and prose, stealthily punctuated ever and anon with a kiss or fond embrace. What dignity it adds to a young girl's estimate of herself when some strong man makes her feel that in her hands rest his future peace and happiness! Though these seasons of intoxication may come once to all, yet they are seldom repeated. How often in after life we long for one more such rapturous dream of bliss, one more season of supreme human love and passion!

After leaving school, until my marriage, I had the most pleasant years of my girlhood. With frequent visits to a large circle of friends and relatives in various towns and cities, the monotony of home life was sufficiently broken to make our simple country pleasures always delightful and enjoyable. An entirely new life now opened to me. The old bondage of fear of the visible and the invisible was broken and, no longer subject to absolute authority, I rejoiced in the dawn of a new day of freedom in thought and action.

My brother-in-law, Edward Bayard, ten years my senior, was an inestimable blessing to me at this time, especially as my mind was just then opening to the consideration of all the varied problems of life. To me and my sisters he was a companion in all our amusements, a teacher in the higher departments of knowledge, and a counselor in all our youthful trials and disappointments. He was of a metaphysical turn of mind, and in the pursuit of truth was in no way trammeled by popular superstitions. He took nothing for granted and, like Socrates, went about asking questions. Nothing pleased him more than to get a bevy of bright young girls about him and teach them how to think clearly and reason logically.

One great advantage of the years my sisters and myself spent at the Troy Seminary was the large number of pleasant acquaintances we made there, many of which ripened into lifelong friendships. From time to time many of our classmates visited us, and all alike enjoyed the intellectual fencing in which my brother-in-law drilled them. He discoursed with us on law, philosophy, political economy, history, and poetry, and together we read novels without number. The long winter evenings thus passed pleasantly, Mr. Bayard alternatively talking and reading aloud Scott, Bulwer, James, Cooper, and Dickens, whose works were just then coming out in numbers from week to week, always leaving us in suspense at the most critical point of the story. Our readings were varied with recitations, music, dancing, and games. . . .

As I had become sufficiently philosophical to talk over my religious experiences calmly with my classmates who had been with me through the Finney revival meetings, we all came to the same conclusion—that we had passed through no remarkable change and that we had not been born again, as they say, for we found our tastes and enjoyments the same as ever. My brother-in-law explained to us the nature of the delusion we had all experienced, the physical conditions, the mental processes, the church machinery by which such excitements are worked up, and the impositions to which credulous minds are necessarily subjected. As we had all been through that period of depression and humiliation, and had been oppressed at times with the feeling that all our professions were arrant hypocrisy and that our last state was worse than our first, he helped us to understand these workings of the human mind and reconciled us to the more rational condition in which we now found ourselves. He never grew weary of expounding principles to us and dissipating the fogs and mists that gather over young minds educated in an atmosphere of superstition.

We had a constant source of amusement and vexation in the students in my father's office. A succession of them was always coming fresh from college and full of conceit. Aching to try their powers of debate on graduates from the Troy Seminary, they politely questioned all our theories and assertions. However, with my brother-in-law's training in analysis and logic, we were a match for any of them. Nothing pleased me better than a long argument with them on woman's equality, which I tried to prove by a diligent study of the books they read and the games they played. I confess that I did not study so much for a love of the truth or my own development, in these days, as to make those young men recognize my equality. I soon noticed that, after losing a few games of chess, my opponent talked less of masculine superiority. Sister Madge would occasionally rush to the defense with an emphatic "Fudge for these laws, all made by men! I'll never obey one of them. And as to the students with their impertinent talk of superiority, all they need is such a shaking up as I gave the most disagreeable one yesterday. I invited him to take a ride on horseback. He accepted promptly, and said he would be most happy to go. Accordingly I told Peter to saddle the toughest-mouthed, hardest-trotting carriage horse in the stable. Mounted on my swift pony, I took a ten-mile canter as fast as I could go, with that superior being at my heels calling, as he found breath, for me to stop, which I did at last and left him in the hands of Peter, half dead at his hotel, where he will be laid out, with all his marvelous masculine virtues, for a week at least. Now do not waste your arguments on these prigs from Union College. Take each, in turn, the ten-miles' circuit on 'Old Boney' and they'll have no breath left to prate of woman's inferiority. You might argue with them all day, and you could not make them feel so small as I made that popinjay feel in one hour. I knew 'Old Boney' would keep up with me, if he died for it, and that my escort could neither stop nor dismount, except by throwing himself from the saddle."

"Oh, Madge!" I exclaimed; "what will you say when he meets you again?"

"If he complains, I will say 'the next time you ride see that you have a curb bit before starting.' Surely, a man ought to know what is necessary to manage a horse, and not expect a woman to tell him."

Our lives were still further varied and intensified by the usual number of flirtations, so called, more or less lasting or evanescent, from all of which I emerged, as from my religious experiences, in a more rational frame of mind. We had been too much in the society of boys and young gentlemen, and knew too well their real character, to idealize the sex in general. In addition to our own observations, we had the advantage of our brother-in-law's wisdom. Wishing to save us as long as possible from all matrimonial entanglements, he was continually unveiling those with whom he associated, and so critically portraying their intellectual and moral condition that it was quite impossible, in our most worshipful moods, to make gods of any of the sons of Adam.

However, in spite of all our own experiences and of all the warning words of wisdom from those who had seen life in its many phases, we entered the charmed circle at last, all but one marrying into the legal profession, with its odious statute laws and infamous decisions. And this, after reading Blackstone, Kent, and Story, and thoroughly understanding the status of the wife under the old common law of England, which was in force at that time in most of the States of the Union.

Childhood and Parenting in Children's Popular Culture and Childcare Magazines

The following selection is excerpted from an essay by Carmen Luke on the pedagogical influences of popular culture, parenting, and the impact of media on children. It is taken from Luke's edited book *Feminisms and Pedagogies of Everyday Life* (State University of New York Press, 1996). The author is a well-known, highly regarded scholar on feminist issues who is also well read in the literature of postmodernistic philosophy. Luke sees the importance of gender issues in a cultural context. She approaches pedagogical issues in the formation of human selves from a critical pedagogical perspective that attempts to demonstrate the influence of societal and cultural forces on the personal identity development of all people. This selection also reflects dialogues that continue to explore the socialization of women in general.

Luke understands that all social dialogue affects the power relations in society. She looks at the impact of all sorts of texts on the lives of children and represents the impact of all forms of visual media presentation on personal identity development. Luke notes that "visual representations such as cinematic texts, stylized illustrations, cartoons, video, or photographs, are part of the landscape of meaning that social subjects encounter in everyday life." She looks at how discourse on childhood and motherhood influences is affected by popular culture, and she explores the gendered organization of social space as one of the cultural vehicles for the socialization of girls and women. Luke cites as examples the organization of toy stores and the way in which magazines for children and parents present culturally induced messages to girls and women. She supports her theories with analyses of selected texts on parenting and mothering and argues that popular culture provides pedagogical learning experiences, which produce contradictory images of parenthood and childhood.

Key Concept: pedagogies of everyday life

CHILDREN'S POPULAR CULTURE AS PUBLIC PEDAGOGY

From infancy, most children are immersed in the texts of popular culture. The texts and artifacts of popular culture frame children's understanding of the world and of themselves, of narrative, heroes and heroines, gender and race relations, cultural symbols, values, and social power. How children negotiate and experience the messages of popular cultural texts is crucial to any understanding of the relationship among cultural texts, artifacts, social subjects, and practices. However, my concern in this [selection] is with the larger discourses —the rhetorical constructs—of childhood and parenthood in popular cultural representations.

Visual representations such as cinematic texts, stylized illustrations, cartoons, video, or photographs, are part of the landscape of meaning that social subjects encounter in everyday life. Television texts, the toy industry, and popular culture more generally teach powerful lessons about the social world which are variously reinforced by the discourses and pedagogies of home and school (Luke, 1990a,b,c; 1993). Together these discourses provide cultural meaning systems of concepts such as 'childhood', 'family', 'femininity', 'masculinity', 'race', and so forth.

I use the term discourse here following Foucault (1972) to define how theoretical and "commonsense" knowledges are produced historically and in specific sociocultural contexts. Self-other understandings, according to Foucault, are always contingent upon subjects' various positions within a range of discourses available at particular historical moments and in specific cultural locations. So, for instance, how one understands one's location within a class structure, racial, gender, or national identity is made possible through the symbolic meaning systems available to social agents. Cultural meaning systems are inscribed on social relations and innumerable texts, textual sites and practices (e.g., television, schools, play) which, in turn, give meaning to a range of gendered social and cultural identities and styles (Bourdieu, 1984). These, in turn, are made concrete through the social relations of lived experience in which variations of 'community', 'family', 'childhood', or 'gender' are enacted. Since contemporary Western culture is organized around a cult of the image (Ewen, 1988), then any analysis of mass cultural discourses must go beyond attention to the linguistic text and consider as well the representation of meaning encoded in images, objects and spaces (cf. Luke, 1994; 1996, in press). This is what I attempt here.

Foucault suggests that "discourse transmits and produces power": it is a product of and produces power relations (1981, 101). Western discourses of childhood and motherhood derive their power and "truth value" from a longstanding scientific history in disciplinary sociology, psychology, and social psychology. Variations of these discourses circulate through daytime talk shows, parenting self-help books and childcare magazines, mothercraft courses, in parent-child relationships, in daycare centres, schooling, and so on. These sites, texts, and social relations are the public forum in which specialized, disciplinary knowledges are transformed into public pedagogies and commonsense knowledges of everyday life.

As feminist scholarship has repeatedly shown, historically the author-authorities of theories of childhood, motherhood, and femininity have been men. From Aristotle to the social contract theorists to Freud, the relegation of women and symbolic femininity to nature and the private sphere, to identities of lack, inferiority, affect, and unreason, is testimony to the discursive production of femininity as both the product of historical power relations and the continuing (re)production of unequal real and symbolic power that structures gender relations from birth. Constructs of femininity and masculinity in the discourse of children's toys or parenting magazines attest to the remarkable historical consistency of such differential gender valuation. And, the power of discourse—in this case, that of childhood and motherhood—is sustained by its proliferation in popular cultural forms such as television, cinema, toys, videogames, lifestyle magazines and—paramount in late capitalist economies—by its ability to be transformed into consumer goods....

CHILDHOOD AND TOYWORLDS: GENDERED ORGANIZATION OF SPACE

The adult leisure market boomed in the 1980s and had a direct impact on the commercialisation of children's leisure (Butsch, 1990; Engelhardt, 1986; Kline, 1993). Advances in computer technology, refinements of niche marketing strategies, and the expansion of megamalls emerging as new micro-cities and revisioned "community" centres with safe play-zones and child-oriented events, all had direct spin-offs to the child market. Niche marketing to a "concept" and "identity" oriented generation of parents, meant the development and marketing of "quality" toys, children's designer clothing and shoes, alongside the hugely successful mass marketing of cross-linked toy, media, fast-food, and soft-drink product tie-ins. During the 1980s, retail toy chains expanded nationally and internationally, and the children's market entered an historically unprecedented retail profit boom (Kline, 1993; McNeal, 1987; Seiter, 1992).

A recent study by Seiter (1992) reveals some interesting insights about the gendered discourse underlying the organisation of space, color, and merchandise at Toys 'R' Us. As part of the postmodern globalisation and normalisation of experience, Toys 'R' Us, like McDonald's and other fast-food chains, has strict franchising requirements so that consumer experience is the same no matter where one shops or eats. In all stores, customers encounter high-tech toys and computer games first (marketed to boys and fathers) before moving on to licensed action figures and dolls. Moving from the high-tech "first encounter," boys' toys are available in the next sections, and towards the rear of the store are the girls' toys. What this means is that girls have to pass through the boys' section to get to the girls' ware, whereas boys can avoid the girls' merchandise altogether. All merchandise sectors are color-coded from signs to racks and packaging. The boys' section is coded in metallic, primary colors, whereas the girls' section consists of a riot of pinks and purples.

The girls' section is surrounded by arts and crafts goods, by preschooler instructional toys and gear, and the infant goods section. This arrangement suggests a natural connection between real baby bottles, infant gear, cribs, strollers, baby buggies, and "pretend play" baby toys. In one aisle merchandise for "real" babies is available paralleled in the next aisle by those same commodities at reduced size (and price). One sector for mothers, the adjacent sector for their girls. This gendered structural layout reproduces the domestication of femininity and functions as a silent pedagogy of gender differentiation—what Foucault calls social discipline and normalization through the organization of space.

The boys' sections, by contrast, are adjacent to sporting and outdoor and the computer and high-tech merchandise. The connection between "real" masculine interests such as sports, camping, or technology and "pretend" play is similarly assured. Yet there appears to be less of a disjunction between male adult leisure commodities and boys' toys since there are no reduced-size play replications of tents, bicycles, inflatable rafts, computer games, and so forth. In other words, unlike the girls' world of miniature household appliances and child-care paraphernalia, boys enter the world of male leisure interests earlier and more directly than girls.

Boys' toys are generally more expensive than girls' toys, and girls' toys keep them confined in more limited space compared to the spatial range enabled by boys' toys. Hot shots radical recoiler, radio-controlled vehicles, or cybertronic blaster guns keep boys on the move, whereas playing house requires less space, movement, and is far less action-oriented. One of the all-time best-selling toys "Supersoaker"—a watergun shaped like a handgun—en-genders different kinds of social and bodily behaviors than its equivalent of girls. "Flirt Squirts" waterguns for girls are shaped like compacts, lipsticks, and nailpolish bottles, all in fashion colors. Handgun action is oriented towards others, in pursuit of others, and structures social relations in conflict, opposition, and violence, whereas compacts and lipsticks are turned on the self in a discourse of self-adornment, not combat with others.

The gendered discourse in the toy industry's construction of childhood is not a subtext but a very explicit pedagogy of gendered identity. Marketers of childhood have produced an intensified dynamic between the cultural symbolic of television narratives and commodity "materiality" (Williams, 1980). Television programs and ads model the social narratives, the imaginary worlds of pretend and play, and the cultural goods of toyworlds enable and make concrete those play repertoires, and the shaping of identities and social relations. Corporate visions of 'childhood', 'gender', 'parenthood', or 'family' saturate the symbolic, spatial, material, and social environment to such an extent that, increasingly, we fail to take much note of them. How lessons on femininity and masculinity are constructed in the world of toys and toystores, or child-care magazines, are a case in point. I now turn to examine childcare magazines as one other discursive site in which particular visions of childhood and parenthood are inscribed.

CHILDHOOD AND PARENTING
IN CHILDCARE MAGAZINES

In liberal theory and modern or postmodern capitalism the child is situated in the social and economic unit of the idealized nuclear family and as the primary focus of labor for women. Childhood and motherhood are inseparable sociocultural and economic practices and discourses—theoretical and "commonsense." Put simply, mothering implies children, and children are reared primarily by women whether in nuclear, single-parent, extended family, daycare, or primary school contexts.

Women's magazines all feature editorials and advertisements which not only celebrate bourgeois notions of motherhood and the pampered child within a heterosexual and nuclear-family formation, but are implicitly based on theoretical narratives of moral, cognitive, social, and behavioral development (cf. Phoenix, Wollett, & Lloyd, 1991). Such implicit public pedagogies are intertextually linked to, for instance, Fisher-Price toy ads which "responsibly" mark their toys with age-appropriate labels, environment-friendly stickers, or guidelines on the kinds of psychomotor skills a particular toy claims to develop. And it is up to the informed consumer, most commonly mothers, to make the appropriate product choices. This section takes up these issues through a focus on constructs of childhood and motherhood in parenting magazines.

Most first-time mothers buy or are given pregnancy, childbirth, and baby-care books which they consult religiously (cf. Urwin, 1985). These texts, according to Urwin, help women learn about normative constructs of mothering, and about children's cognitive, behavioral, and physical development. Such texts are consulted by women both as a check on, and in anticipation of, expected development. Given the paucity of information many women receive from their doctors and clinics, and their reluctance to consult their doctors with questions they might find trivial (Todd, 1989; Waitzkin, 1991), women rely heavily on information exchanged with other mothers, books, television, and magazines. Unlike books, magazines are relatively cheap, the articles are usually short, written in nonmedical jargon and therefore easy to read, and the glossy illustrations provide appealing imageries of happy and good-looking mothers, babies, and toddlers.

Magazines offer visions of childhood and motherhood which both model and reinforce normative ideas of feminine desire located in idealized motherhood and childhood: of cute babies and stylishly dressed toddlers, of powerful emotional moments of bonding, tranquillity, and symbiotic identification which these texts and images consistently claim as intrinsic to the "most important time in a mother's and baby's life." Such visions of feminine destiny are socialized into girls early beginning with the toys parents buy to initiate girls into feminine discourses of nurture and domesticity. Toys come and go, but the "bread and butter" staples of girls' toys remain remarkably constant: from little ironing boards, miniature kitchens, stoves and toasters, to dolls, mini strollers, baby buggies, snugglipacks, and cribs. My analysis below suggests that parenting and childcare magazines both reinforce traditional gender values and experiences most women learned as girls, and prepare new mothers to reproduce those experiences with their own children.

I collected magazines on parenting and mothering over a six-month period in 1992. The total textual corpus consisted of twenty-three magazines of which six were analysed in detail for this study.[1] I had not purchased or read magazines about babies for some twenty years. My initial reading of these magazines for this study was radically different from how I think I first read those magazines as a young mother. Once I started reading issues of *Parents,* I became facinated with the discourse and quickly started gathering other magazines: American *Mothering, Parent's Digest* and *Parents,* and British *Practical Parenting.*[2] On a first glance through the magazines, three things became immediately apparent. First, without reading any of the (mostly redundant) articles, I was struck by the complete absence of women and children of color in Australian and British magazines. Secondly, I was also surprised at the overwhelming amount of advertising in American magazines compared with British and Australian ones. The construction of infancy and early childhood in the baby gadgets and world of instructional toys has produced ever finer distinctions within childhood by the increased segmentation of mothering activities, developmental stages, and mother and baby needs that the infant commodity discourse claims to cater to.

Finally, as I had anticipated, the concept of parenting by which most magazines identify their readership has very little to do with male parenting or fatherhood. All magazines address a woman who is implicitly assumed to be in a heterosexual relationship with a relatively comfortable male wage to support many of the commodity-based fantasies of motherhood. Men for the most part are excluded from the visual and textual discourse of these magazines. Their presence is token, stereotyped, disengaged from domestic and child care, and most often positioned in relation to articles on divorce, marriage problems, insurance or car ads, as celebrity endorsements or medical "experts."...

CONCLUSION: CONTRADICTORY IMAGES OF PARENTHOOD AND CHILDHOOD

I have here shown how the marketplace of childhood promotes highly gender-differentiated constructs of the child in the media and toy industries, and in parenting magazines. Whether in the toystore, on television, or in magazines—childhood and parenthood are made intelligible through a vast array of niche-marketed cultural goods, embedded in sexist and racist discourses. But cultural texts and markets are never simple either/or choices for "reader"-consumers, and there is a danger of viewing such texts as monoglossically or unproblematically pro- or anti-woman, pro- or anti-gay or particular cultures—as tends to happen in media, public and often academic debate over so-called "political correctness." I wish to conclude by highlighting the contradictory and often ambiguous status of such texts.

Within "mass access" public discourses of television, cinema, and lifestyle magazines, the social and economic restructuring of the Western family are being re-presented, albeit within ideologically disciplining limits. Starting in the

225

mid-1980s, "new age fathers" began to appear on television, in clothing and scent ads: the man of the moment was shown with laptop computer in one hand, a briefcase in the other, and a baby tucked in a "natural fibre" designer baby-backpack. American Calvin Klein ads were in the forefront of celebrating the new sexy male whose appeal and virility was constructed not only in relation to a sexy partner, a sculpted body, and good taste in clothes, but in relation to a new sexualized object—an infant or young child. The child in such ads functions as a culturally and ideologically significant prop in redefinitions of upscale 1990s female-male relationships, the politics of choice, sexual and social identity.

In the 1980s, the marketing of "new" visions of family and lifestyle choices emerged in television family sit-coms which brought us the postfeminist family (cf. Probyn, 1990), and in mainstream cinema which celebrated fatherhood (*Raising Arizona, Three Men and a Baby, Look Who's Talking*), and valorized motherhood over devastating career choices (*Fatal Attraction, Baby Boom*). Whereas television narratives and lifestyle magazine ads glamorize parenthood as a designer add-on to affluent, white, two-career couples and, indeed, can be read to signify the politics of choice, that vision disappears altogether in parenting and childcare magazines. In these discourses a far more traditional regime of femininity, motherhood, and domesticity is at work. Here, career, new age male partners, or sexuality are excluded from visions of feminine identity which are reconstructed solely around the pleasures of maternity and nurturing an other. Care of the self is displaced by care and nurture of a child which depends crucially on an implicit but assumed heterosexual marriage within a nuclear family.

Raising infants in this discourse is a lonely and isolated task. Daycare, friends, neighbors, and partners are absent from the pictographic and textual landscape. Women are on their own, most commonly shown inside the house, and engaged only in activities centred on a child. Her socially isolated relationship with an infant or toddler suggests that she is solely responsible for the early formation of a child's values and behaviors. She has sole moral responsibility for the upbringing of a new generation, and is thus positioned as the only candidate to blame for children's subsequent dysfunctional development.

The magazines' specialized sections map the stages not only of child development but normative expectations of a mother's psychological orientation and social responsibility in relation to those stages. These stages are invariably tied to the consumer products which claim to facilitate and enhance those stages. Advertising text exhorts women to become informed consumers in the best interests of their children's welfare. The importance of being well informed and one step ahead of her child's development in order to make the appropriate product choice (whether of snugglipacks, nappies, cereals, or medicines) is a recurring message for women. The lessons for women encourage them to study up on child development, to learn about product ranges, and to exercise informed consumer judgment in making correct product choices that match children's stage/age-related needs. The constructions of childhood, childcare, and motherhood as niche markets, and situating parent-child social bonds and familial relationships as crucially dependant on that market—product choices that guarantee "those special moments"—subtly provides women with the illusion of choice (cf. Knijin, 1994). The daily demands of childcare may not leave women much choice other than to respond to the child's immediate needs. Yet at the same time, the choice offered on the marketplace of childhood enables her to reclaim some measure of self-directed, albeit illusory, choice and agency.

The child in this discourse is an object of feminine desire, and yet it is a desiring and consuming subject in its own right. The child's maturing social and cognitive needs are intelligible primarily through the product ranges available to enhance and develop those needs: from Fisher-Price pedagogy to the tiny tots identity business of fashion offered by "Esprit," "Benetton," Reeboks' "Weeboks," or the latest McDonald's "McKids" designer wear (cf. Willis, 1991).

How-to and self-books and magazines can teach us lessons in manners, cooking, health and fitness, childcare, building construction, financial planning, car maintenance, or skills for career success. All of us have, at some time or another, taught ourselves from these books or magazines. Like television, books and magazines address us individually, but we nonetheless read and view collectively as mass readership or viewing audience. In staffrooms across the nation, people talk about last night's television programs or the weekend sports event. Kids enact media heroes or favorite programs in schoolyard play and interweave those texts in their written work. Women buy and share childcare magazines with other women, and they are also the primary purchasers of children's commodities. In short, popular cultural texts are indeed constitutive of "real" experience, and they do provide a mass cultural ideological framework which people variously dismiss, engage in, or buy into. Because public culture is woven into every crevice of everyday experience and cuts across traditional boundaries of class, ethnicity, age, and, certainly, nation and geography, the public texts of popular culture are probably a more powerful pedagogy than the generally decontextualized knowledge and skills taught in formal institutions of learning, disconnected as they are from what is referred to as "the real world."

Parenting magazines present only one version of motherhood. Yet specialized parenting magazines such as those analysed here provide a conservative and traditional vision of femininity, motherhood, and family. It is a vision which largely excludes women and children of color, single mothers, poor mothers, fathers, and nonheterosexual family formations. In contrast to "postfeminist" visions of family and parenthood in other mass media and cultural texts, the discourse of parenting magazines remains decidedly prefeminist.

How parents are to understand childhood and structure their children's experiences is today increasingly determined by the production of childhood as a market. And while many parents refuse or can't afford to buy into the system, the global expansion of commercialized childhood culture and massive profit returns, suggest that the majority of parents, indeed, *are* buying. What parents buy into, however, is a commodified cultural narrative that is highly gender segregated, almost exclusively white, middle-class, and heterosexual. Toys and toystores, movies and television, parenting books and magazines, or videogames and corporate mall playgrounds, weave a mass cultural construct of affluent Western childhood and parenthood, "winking" seductively at parents and kids. Many women at some point in their life trajectories will assume the positioning and practices of mothering: how the texts and artifacts of mainstream culture construct motherhood and childhood stands as a powerful normalising discipline with and against alternative and feminist constructs.

NOTES

An earlier version of this [selection] was originally published in the *Australian and New Zealand Journal of Sociology* (La Trobe University Press), 30(3) (1995).

1. One issue per magazine was selected for analysis on the basis of what I judged to be the most representative issue in a six-month period. Initially, my interest was in Australian *Mother & Baby* (AU $4.20) and *Parents* (AU $3.95), both published by the same company. The circulation staff of *Parents* advised that it has the highest exposure of all Australian childcare magazines with a monthly readership of 178,000, which includes household subscriptions, over the counter and a hospital/clinic sales, shared and/or exchanged magazines. *Mother and Baby* is a relatively expensive magazine and has a readership of 166,000. I also sought circulation figures from British *Practical Parenting*, (£1.20) and American *Mothering* (US $5.95), *Parents* (US $2.25), and *Parent's Digest* (US $2.95), but received a reply only from *Mothering*, which claims a circulation of 66,342 excluding shared or exchanged magazines.

2. I considered overseas magazines relevant for analysis because they are available on Australian news-stands and, clearly, women are buying them in volume.

PART FOUR

The American Constitutional Tradition and Education

On the Internet . . .

Sites appropriate to Part Four

On April 22, 1993, a forum for the *Woodstock Report* addressed the progress of African American education since *Brown v. Board of Education of Topeka*. This Web site presents edited and abridged versions of the talks as well as some of the questions that followed.

> http://www.georgetown.edu/centers/
> woodstock/report/r-fea34.htm

This is the home page of the American Association of University Women, a national organization that promotes education and equity for all women and girls.

> http://www.aauw.org/home.html

Articles on gender differences and gender equity in education can be found on this site. Topics include gender differences in academic achievement, gender equity in education, the value of single-sex schooling, and more.

> http://serendip.brynmawr.edu/sci_edu/
> education/genderdiff.html

CHAPTER 10

The Struggle for Civil Liberty in the Schools

10.1 U.S. SUPREME COURT

Brown v. Board of Education of Topeka, Kansas

In 1954 the United States Supreme Court issued a truly historic, constitutionally groundbreaking interpretation of the meaning of the "equal protection of the laws" clause of the Fourteenth Amendment to the Constitution of the United States. In the decision of *Brown v. Board of Education of Topeka, Kansas* (347 U.S. 483), from which the following selection is taken, the Court held that "in the field of public education the doctrine of 'separate but equal' has no place. Separate educational facilities are inherently unequal." Seventeen states had used the "separate but equal" principle first enunciated in *Plessy v. Ferguson* (1896) to pass laws requiring the segregation of students of differing racial backgrounds in the public schools of those states. The *Brown* decision declared such segregation unconstitutional. What gave even greater historical importance to *Brown* was that the Court found "for

Linda Brown and *all similarly situated persons*" (emphasis added by editor). This phrase made the decision a class action decision, the first time the "equal protection of the laws" clause was applied to all segregated persons.

In the years following the *Brown* decision, Hispanic Americans, Native Americans, Asian Americans, and all American women benefited from the powerful, clear finding for "Linda Brown and all similarly situated persons." Furthermore, during the 20 years after *Brown*, laws were passed by Congress that improved the educational opportunities of *all* Americans.

Key Concept: educational equality

Mr. Chief Justice Warren delivered the opinion of the Court.

These cases come to us from the States of Kansas, South Carolina, Virginia, and Delaware. They are premised on different facts and different local conditions, but a common legal question justifies their consideration together in this consolidated opinion.

In each of the cases, minors of the Negro race, through their legal representatives, seek the aid of the courts in obtaining admission to the public schools of their community on a nonsegregated basis. In each instance, they had been denied admission to schools attended by white children under laws requiring or permitting segregation according to race. This segregation was alleged to deprive the plaintiffs of the equal protection of the laws under the Fourteenth Amendment. In each of the cases other than the Delaware case, a three-judge federal district court denied relief to the plaintiffs on the so-called "separate but equal" doctrine announced by this Court in *Plessy* v. *Ferguson*.... Under that doctrine, equality of treatment is accorded when the races are provided substantially equal facilities even though these facilities be separate. In the Delaware case, the Supreme Court of Delaware adhered to that doctrine, but ordered that the plaintiffs be admitted to the white schools because of their superiority to the Negro schools.

The plaintiffs contend that segregated public schools are not "equal" and cannot be made "equal," and that hence they are deprived of the equal protection of the laws. Because of the obvious importance of the question presented, the Court took jurisdiction. Argument was heard in the 1952 Term, and reargument was heard this Term on certain questions propounded by the Court.

Reargument was largely devoted to the circumstances surrounding the adoption of the Fourteenth Amendment in 1868. It covered exhaustively consideration of the Amendment in Congress, ratification by the states, then existing practices in racial segregation, and the views of proponents and opponents of the Amendment. This discussion and our own investigation convince us that, although these sources cast some light, it is not enough to resolve the problem with which we are faced. At best, they are inconclusive. The most avid proponents of the post–War Amendments undoubtedly intended them to remove all legal distinctions among "all persons born or naturalized in the United States." Their opponents, just as certainly were antagonistic to both the letter and the spirit of the Amendments and wished them to have the most limited effect. What others in Congress and the state legislatures had in mind cannot be determined with any degree of certainty.

An additional reason for the inconclusive nature of the Amendment's history, with respect to segregated schools, is the status of public education at that time. In the South, the movement toward free common schools, supported by general taxation, had not yet taken hold. Education of white children was largely in the hands of private groups. Education of Negroes was almost nonexistent, and practically all of the race were illiterate. In fact, any education of Negroes was forbidden by law in some states. Today, in contrast, many Negroes have achieved outstanding success in the arts and sciences as well as in the business and professional world. It is true that public education had already advanced further in the North, but the effect of the Amendment on Northern States was generally ignored in the congressional debates. Even in the North, the conditions of public education did not approximate those existing today. The curriculum was usually rudimentary; ungraded schools were common in rural areas; the school term was but three months a year in many states; and compulsory school attendance was virtually unknown. As a consequence, it is not surprising that there should be so little in the history of the Fourteenth Amendment relating to its intended effect on public education.

In the first cases in this Court construing the Fourteenth Amendment, decided shortly after its adoption, the Court interpreted it as proscribing all state-imposed discriminations against the Negro race. The doctrine of "separate but equal" did not make its appearance in this court until 1896 in the case of *Plessy* v. *Ferguson, supra,* involving not education but transportation. American courts have since labored with the doctrine for over half a century. In this Court, there have been six cases involving the "separate but equal" doctrine in the field of public education. In *Cumming* v. *County Board of Education . . .* and *Gong Lum* v. *Rice . . .* , the validity of the doctrine itself was not challenged. In more recent cases, all on the graduate school level, inequality was found in that specific benefits enjoyed by white students were denied to Negro students of the same educational qualifications. *Missouri* ex rel. *Gaines* v. *Canada; Sipuel* v. *Oklahoma; Sweatt* v. *Painter; McLaurin* v. *Oklahoma State Regents.* In none of these cases was it necessary to reexamine the doctrine to grant relief to the Negro plaintiff. And in *Sweatt* v. *Painter, supra,* the Court expressly reserved decision on the question whether *Plessy* v. *Ferguson* should be held inapplicable to public education.

In the instant cases, that question is directly presented. Here, unlike *Sweatt* v. *Painter,* there are findings below that the Negro and white schools involved have been equalized, or are being equalized, with respect to buildings, curricula, qualifications and salaries of teachers, and other "tangible" factors. Our decision, therefore, cannot turn on merely a comparison of these tangible factors in the Negro and white schools involved in each of the cases. We must look instead to the effect of segregation itself on public education.

In approaching this problem, we cannot turn the clock back to 1868 when the Amendment was adopted, or even to 1896 when *Plessy* v. *Ferguson* was written. We must consider public education in the light of its full development and its present place in American life throughout the Nation. Only in this way can it be determined if segregation in public schools deprives these plaintiffs of the equal protection of the laws.

Today, education is perhaps the most important function of state and local governments. Compulsory school attendance laws and the great expenditures for education both demonstrate our recognition of the importance of education to our democratic society. It is required in the performance of our most basic public responsibilities, even service in the armed forces. It is the very foundation of good citizenship. Today it is a principal instrument in awakening the child to cultural values, in preparing him for later professional training, and in helping him to adjust normally to his environment. In these days, it is doubtful that any child may reasonably be expected to succeed in life if he is denied the opportunity of an education. Such an opportunity, where the state has undertaken to provide it, is a right which must be made available to all on equal terms.

We come then to the question presented: Does segregation of children in public schools solely on the basis of race, even though the physical facilities and other "tangible" factors may be equal, deprive the children of the minority group of equal educational opportunities? We believe that it does.

In *Sweatt* v. *Painter, supra,* in finding that a segregated law school for Negroes could not provide them equal educational opportunities, this Court relied in large part on "those qualities which are incapable of objective measurement but which make for greatness in a law school." In *McLaurin* v. *Oklahoma State Regents, supra,* the Court, in requiring that a Negro admitted to a white graduate school be treated like all other students, again resorted to intangible considerations: " . . . his ability to study, to engage in discussions and exchange views with other students, and, in general, to learn his profession." Such considerations apply with added force to children in grade and high schools. To separate them from others of similar age and qualifications solely because of their race generates a feeling of inferiority as to their status in the community that may affect their hearts and minds in a way unlikely ever to be undone. The effect of this separation on their educational opportunities was well stated by a finding in the Kansas case by a court which nevertheless felt compelled to rule against the Negro plaintiffs:

> Segregation of white and colored children in public schools has a detrimental effect upon the colored children. The impact is greater when it has the sanction of the law; for the policy of separating the races is usually interpreted as denoting the inferiority of the Negro group. A sense of inferiority affects the motivation of a child to learn. Segregation with the sanction of law, therefore, has a tendency to retard the educational and mental development of Negro children and to deprive them of some of the benefits they would receive in a racially integrated school system.

Whatever may have been the extent of psychological knowledge[1] at the time of *Plessy* v. *Ferguson,* this finding is amply supported by modern authority. Any language in *Plessy* v. *Ferguson* contrary to this finding is rejected.

We conclude that in the field of public education the doctrine of "separate but equal" has no place. Separate educational facilities are inherently unequal.

Therefore, we hold that the plaintiffs and others similarly situated for whom the actions have been brought are, by reason of the segregation complained of, deprived of the equal protection of the laws guaranteed by the Fourteenth Amendment. This disposition makes unnecessary any discussion whether such segregation also violates the Due Process Clause of the Fourteenth Amendment.

Because these are class actions, because of the wide applicability of this decision, and because of the great variety of local conditions, the formulation of decrees in these cases presents problems of considerable complexity. On re-argument, the consideration of appropriate relief was necessarily subordinated to the primary question—the constitutionality of segregation in public education. We have now announced that such segregation is a denial of the equal protection of the laws. In order that we may have the full assistance of the parties in formulating decrees, the cases will be restored to the docket, and the parties are requested to present further argument.

NOTES

1. The decision in *Brown* v. *Board of Education* was justified in part on psychological and sociological grounds. This line of argument helped Chief Justice Warren obtain a unanimous decision, but it did not provide the strongest legal foundation for attacking segregation.

A Better Chance to Learn: Bilingual-Bicultural Education

In May 1975 the United States Commission on Civil Rights issued a thoroughly documented, in-depth statement on the history of the education of language minority students in the United States and on how the struggle of language minority students to achieve equality of educational opportunity is linked to the broader struggle for equality in the field of education. The commission specifically discussed the direct relationship between the United States Supreme Court decision in *Brown v. Board of Education of Topeka, Kansas* (1954) and various federal court decisions involving the educational rights of limited English proficiency (LEP) students. The commission's document was distributed to all public school districts that had or were putting into place either bilingual educational programs or English as a Second Language programs for language minority children. This document, *A Better Chance to Learn: Bilingual-Bicultural Education* (Clearinghouse Publication 51, May 1975), is excerpted in the following selection. In it, the commission clarifies how the Supreme Court decision in *Lau v. Nichols* (1975) is based on Fourteenth Amendment "equal protection of the laws" precedents, which had led the Court to declare in *Brown* that segregated schools are "inherently unequal." The historical precedents for bilingual educational programs in the United States are also reviewed in the document.

Key Concept: bilingual education

INTRODUCTION

No public institution has a greater or more direct impact on future opportunity than the school. Between the ages of 6 and 16, American children spend much of their time in school. Early educational success or failure dictates to a large extent a student's expectations for the future, including whether he or she will seek postsecondary education and thus have a wide range of economic options available following formal schooling. The importance of an equal opportunity to public education was underscored in the case of *Brown* v. *Board of Education* and was followed in the 1960's by civil rights activity to end segregated schools. Similarly, much of the effort to overcome discrimination against limited or non-English speaking persons in the 1970's has been focused on schools.

The term "language minority" is used in this report to refer to persons in the United States who speak a non-English native language and who belong to an identifiable minority group of generally low socioeconomic status. Such language minority groups—including Mexican Americans, Puerto Ricans, Native Americans, and Asian Americans—have been subject to discrimination and limited opportunity. The emphasis given attainment of an education places them at a further disadvantage, since the public school does not appear to have met the needs of language minority groups.

Not only have many language minority children been subject to segregated education, low teacher expectations, cultural incompatibility with dominant culture-oriented curricula, and the educational neglect experienced by minority children in general, many also face a unique and equally severe form of discrimination which results from lack of proficiency in the language of instruction. In January 1974, the Supreme Court affirmed in *Lau* v. *Nichols* that school districts are compelled under Title VI of the Civil Rights Act of 1964 to provide children who speak little or no English with special language programs which will give them an equal opportunity to an education. The form such assistance should take is the subject of debate among educators, concerned language minority parents, and others.

There is little disagreement that learning English is essential to economic and social mobility in this monolingual English speaking society. The main controversy surrounds the issue of how language minority children can be taught English in a manner so that they do not fall so far behind in subject matter instruction that they cannot recover. Questions also have been raised concerning what methods are best for teaching English to language minority students; whether the learning of English alone will equalize educational opportunity and what role, if any, should be played by the native language and culture in the educational process.

Bilingual bicultural education is instruction using the native language and culture as a basis for learning subjects until second language skills have been developed sufficiently; it is the most widely discussed of approaches to providing language minority children with an equal educational opportunity. On the one hand, it has been hailed as a sound educational approach that overcomes the incompatibility between language minority students and the monolingual English public school. On the other, it has been criticized as failing to provide language minority students with sufficient English skills and as fostering ethnic separateness.

In this report, the Commission examines the extent to which bilingual bicultural education is an effective educational approach for increasing the opportunity of language minority students. In undertaking this study, the Commission assessed the educational principles behind bilingual bicultural education but did not analyze findings from existing bilingual bicultural programs, since few reliable evaluation data are available.

Because of the Commission's civil rights jurisdiction, this report concentrates primarily on bilingual bicultural education as a means for overcoming a denial of equal educational opportunity. However, another valuable objective of bilingual bicultural education is the enrichment of the education of children of all socioeconomic levels and racial/ethnic groups through learning two languages and two cultures....

THE NEED TODAY

Although the height of immigration has long since passed, a large proportion of Americans still have a native language that is other than English. According to the 1970 census, 33.2 million Americans, or roughly 16 percent of the population, speak a language other than English as a native tongue. Spanish, German, and Italian speakers are the most numerous, in that order. Spanish is the only one of the three which has experienced substantial growth in the number of speakers since 1940, largely owing to increased immigration from Latin America.

Although persons of Mexican origin are native to the Southwest, the number of Spanish speaking persons in this country has grown noticeably since 1920. In the 1920's two factors contributed to a major influx of Mexican immigrants: a socially disruptive revolution in Mexico and the agricultural development of the Southwest United States and the subsequent need for labor. Between 1920 and 1973, 1,480,887 or more than 60 percent of all Mexican immigrants came to the United States.

Similarly, since 1920, Puerto Ricans have migrated in greater numbers, stimulated by the crowded living and bad economic conditions of Puerto Rico and the need in urban areas for low-paid, unskilled workers. The Puerto Rican migration swelled from 7,000 in 1920 to 852,061 in 1970.

Between 1920 and 1973, 215,778 Central Americans and 487,925 South Americans immigrated to this country. By 1973, Spanish origin persons numbered 9,072,602 nationwide and constituted the second largest minority group in the United States at roughly 4.4 percent of the total American population.

Immigration continues to be a major source for increasing the size of American language minority communities. Asian groups, for example, have experienced rapid increases in size since restrictive legislation barring or limiting their entry was repealed. In the less than 10 years since 1965, when all immigration quotas were liberalized, 654,736 or more than one-third of all Asian immigrants since 1820 have entered the United States. In 1973 more Asians immigrated than any other group. Other language minority groups, including Italians, Greeks, French Canadians, and Portuguese, have been part of a steady stream of language minorities coming to this country.

The 1970 census estimates that 31 percent of the 760,572 Native Americans counted speak a Native American tongue as their first language. Unlike the other groups, the survival of Native American languages is primarily the result of their continued use by existing groups and geographic isolation, rather than of replenishment through immigration.

Although precise data are not available on the numbers of limited or non-English speaking children currently in school, at the present time, the U.S. Office of Education estimates that at least 5 million need special language programs. The Census Bureau reports that 4.5 million Spanish speaking children under 20 years of age speak Spanish at home. An estimated 259,830 Asian American children speak little or no English, and some 56,493 Native American children speak a Native American language as a first language.

Unlike earlier non-English speaking children in this country, these children face an increasingly technical, skills-oriented society. There has been a shift in jobs from manual labor to skilled occupations. Although there is no direct correlation between years of schooling and ability to perform many jobs, educational level has become one frequently employed means of differentiating job applicants from one another.

Educators have known for many years that language minority children have difficulty succeeding in English monolingual schools. As early as 1930 it was documented that, in Texas, overageness and dropout rates were higher for Mexican American children than for either black or white students, and that most Mexican American children never progressed beyond third grade. In addition, while approximately 95 percent of Anglo children were enrolled in schools, only 50 percent of Mexican American children were. The causes were considered at the time to include lack of English language knowledge, low socioeconomic status, and inaccurate measuring instruments.

Although some scattered attempts were made to improve the education of Mexican American children from 1920–1940, no large scale effort was undertaken to alter the effects of education on them. A number of questions were raised about the education of non-English speaking children, including whether children would suffer less language handicap in school if first instruction in reading were in their native language. In the 1940's one researcher called for action to be taken by the Texas Department of Education, teacher training institutions, and schools to better meet the needs of Spanish speaking students. In 1946, the First Regional Conference on the Education of Spanish-speaking People in the Southwest was held in Austin, Texas. Recommendations included an end to segregated schools for Spanish speaking children, improved teacher training, and more efficiency in teaching English.

That public education continued to neglect the needs of language minority students for another 20 years is evident in the fact that recommendations of the 1964 Orange County Conference on the Education of Spanish Speaking Children and Youth were almost identical to those developed 18 years before. Nearly three decades after the First Regional Conference on the Education of Spanish-speaking People compiled information on the difficulties experienced by Mexican American students, the U.S. Commission on Civil Rights conducted a five-year Mexican American education study. It revealed that problems of segregation, teacher training, and language difficulty are still severe for Mexican American students in the five Southwestern States. In addition, the Commission's State Advisory Committees have examined the problems of Puerto Ricans, Native Americans, and Asian Americans. All of these studies document the continuing failure of public schools to provide language minority children with a meaningful education.

Compared with the median number of 12.0 school years completed for whites, the median is 8.1 for Mexican Americans, 8.6 for Puerto Ricans, 9.8 for Native Americans, and 12.4 for Asian Americans. The Commission's Mexican American Education Study shows that 40 percent of Mexican Americans who enter first grade never complete high school. As of 1972, the drop out rate for Puerto Ricans in New York City from 10th grade to graduation was 57 percent. In New England, 25 percent of the Spanish speaking student population had been retained in grade for at least 3 years; 50 percent, for at least 2 years. Only 12 percent were found to be in the correct grade for their age group. The dropout rate for Native Americans in the Southwest between grades 9 and 12 is 30.6 percent. For Navajos, the largest Native American tribe, the median educational level achieved is fifth grade.

Academic achievement scores recorded for language minority groups in the 1966 Coleman report show that they lag significantly behind majority group Americans. By the 12th grade the Mexican American student is 4.1 years behind the national norm in math achievement; 3.5, in verbal ability; and 3.3, in reading. The Puerto Rican student is 4.8 years behind the national norm in math; 3.6, in verbal ability; and 3.2, in reading. The Asian American student is 0.9 years behind the norm in math; 1.6, in verbal ability; and 1.6, in reading. Studies indicate that the longer language minority students stay in school the further they fall behind their classmates in grade level achievements. On tests of general information—including humanities, social sciences, and natural sciences—the median 12th grade score is 43.3 for Mexican Americans, 41.7 for Puerto Ricans, 44.7 for Native Americans, and 49.0 for Asian Americans as compared to a median score of 52.2 for whites.

In the 1960's there was a growing recognition that language minority children needed some manner of special assistance if they were to have an opportunity to succeed in school. Where efforts were made to provide such assistance, they usually took the form of supplemental English language development, or what is commonly known as the English as a Second Language (ESL) approach. In 1968, the Bilingual Education Act provided funds to support a few bilingual programs, which were to use the children's native language and culture for instruction while they were learning English. Since 1971, Massachusetts, Texas, Illinois, and New Jersey have enacted mandatory bilingual education laws.

The first expression of Executive policy in the area of equal educational opportunity for language minority students came in 1970 when the Department of Health, Education, and Welfare (HEW) issued its May 25 memorandum, which required federally-funded school districts to provide assistance for language minority children. The memorandum indicated that failure to provide such assistance, where needed, would be considered a violation of Title VI of the Civil Rights Act of 1964.

In *Lau* v. *Nichols,* the Supreme Court affirmed that interpretation of Title VI's scope, stating:

> Under these state-imposed standards there is no equality of treatment merely by providing students with the same facilities, textbooks, teachers, and curriculum; for students who do not understand English are effectively foreclosed from any meaningful education.

Basic English skills are at the very core of what these public schools teach. Imposition of a requirement that, before a child can effectively participate in the educational program, he must already have acquired those basic skills is to make a mockery of public education. We know that those who do not understand English are certain to find their classroom experiences wholly incomprehensible and in no way meaningful.

... It seems obvious that the Chinese-speaking minority receives less benefits than the English-speaking majority from respondents' school system which denies them a meaningful opportunity to participate in the educational program ...

Both HEW and the Supreme Court declined to prescribe for school districts the type of assistance program which would provide language minority children with equal benefits in the attainment of an education, leaving the ultimate decision to the local districts themselves. Many school districts are faced with determining what constitutes that equality of educational opportunity. If we assume that the goal of public education is to provide basic skills and knowledge needed for participation in American society, then equal educational opportunity means that all students should have the same chance to acquire those skills and knowledge. In considering ESL and bilingual bicultural education— the two major approaches to meeting the needs of language minority children— it is important, therefore, to examine their overall potential for providing such an education.

CONCLUSION

The Commission's basic conclusion is that bilingual bicultural education is the program of instruction which currently offers the best vehicle for large numbers of language minority students who experience language difficulty in our schools.

Many language minority children, including Mexican Americans, Puerto Ricans, Native Americans, and Asian Americans, face two obstacles in attaining an education. Not only may they be the target of discrimination because they belong to identifiable minority groups, they also may not understand English well enough to keep up with their English speaking counterparts.

Under *Lau* v. *Nichols,* the Supreme Court has held that school districts receiving Federal funds cannot discriminate against children of limited or non-English speaking ability by denying them the language training they need for meaningful participation in the educational process. In this report, the Commission has examined whether the bilingual bicultural education approach is an effective means of providing that opportunity. Primary emphasis was placed on the educational principles which support the use of the native language in educating children, in nurturing positive self concept, and in developing proficiency in English. However, consideration was also given the effect on successful learning of the attitudes toward language minority groups in this country.

How Schools Shortchange Girls

The American Association of University Women (AAUW) is an organization of college and university graduates that was founded in 1881 to work for the advancement of women. In 1990 the AAUW Educational Foundation's Eleanor Roosevelt Fund commissioned the Wellesley College Center for Research on Women to do an in-depth study and to report on the treatment of girls from early childhood through grade 12. The completed study, which is based on the analysis of several years of empirical research on the status of girls in American schools, was published in 1992. *The AAUW Report: How Schools Shortchange Girls* will be a major source of reliable information on how girls are treated in school for several years to come. The data in the report are to be used to help advise educators and government policymakers on educational policy issues relating to equality of educational opportunities for girls and young women in school.

The selection that follows is from the AAUW's executive summary of their findings, and it includes the association's recommendations for action to improve the quality of opportunities for girls and young women in school. There are many implications for educational policymakers and for classroom teachers in the findings of the AAUW report. The call for gender fairness in the education of all American children is in earnest. The report's recommendations, such as that girls be taught assertive and affiliative skills as well as verbal and mathematical skills, cover several areas of concern.

Key Concept: gender equity in the schools

*F*or those who believe that equitable education for all young Americans is the greatest source of a nation's strength, The AAUW Report: How Schools Shortchange Girls, will not be reassuring. Commissioned by the AAUW Educational Foundation and developed by the Wellesley College Center for Research on Women, the study challenges the common assumption that girls and boys are treated equally in our public schools.

Ironically, AAUW's first national study—undertaken in 1885—was initiated to dispel the commonly accepted myth that higher education was harmful to women's *health. This latest report presents the truth behind another myth—that girls and boys receive equal education.*

While most of us are painfully aware of the crisis in American education, few understand or acknowledge the inequities that occur daily in classrooms across the country. Didn't we address that problem in Title IX of the 1972 Education Amendments, which prohibits discrimination in educational institutions receiving federal funds? Many of us worked hard to ensure that this legislation would be passed. Its passage, however, did not solve the problem.

This report is a synthesis of all the available research on the subject of girls in school. It presents compelling evidence that girls are not receiving the same quality, or even quantity, of education as their brothers.

The implications of the report's findings are enormous. Women and children are swelling the ranks of the poor, at great cost to society. Yet our education policymakers are failing to address the relationship between education and the cycle of poverty. The shortchanging of girls is not even mentioned in the current educational restructuring debate.

A well-educated work force is essential to the country's economic development, yet girls are systematically discouraged from courses of study essential to their future employability and economic well-being. Girls are being steered away from the very courses required for their productive participation in the future of America, and we as a nation are losing more than one-half of our human potential. By the turn of the century, two out of three new entrants into the work force will be women and minorities. This work force will have fewer and fewer decently paid openings for the unskilled. It will require strength in science, mathematics, and technology—subjects girls are still being told are not suitable for them.

The AAUW Report presents a base for a new and enlightened education policy —a policy that will ensure that this nation will provide the best possible education for all its children. It provides policymakers with impartial data on the ways in which our school system is failing to meet the needs of girls and with specific strategies that can be used to effect change. The wealth of statistical evidence must convince even the most skeptical that gender bias in our schools is shortchanging girls—and compromising our country.

The AAUW Educational Foundation is proud to present The AAUW Report: How Schools Shortchange Girls, *made possible through the generosity of the many supporters of the Eleanor Roosevelt Fund. This report is destined to add a new dimension to the education debate. The evidence is in, and the picture is clear: shortchanging girls—the women of tomorrow—shortchanges America.*

—Alice McKee, President
AAUW Educational Foundation

WHY A REPORT ON GIRLS?

The invisibility of girls in the current education debate suggests that girls and boys have identical educational experiences in school. Nothing could be further from the truth. Whether one looks at achievement scores, curriculum design, or teacher-student interaction, it is clear that sex and gender make a difference in the nation's public elementary and secondary schools.

The educational system is not meeting girls' needs. Girls and boys enter school roughly equal in measured ability. Twelve years later, girls have fallen behind their male classmates in key areas such as higher-level mathematics and measures of self-esteem. Yet gender equity is still not a part of the national debate on educational reform.

Neither the *National Education Goals* issued by the National Governors Association in 1990 nor *America 2000*, the 1991 plan of the President and the U.S. Department of Education to "move every community in America toward these goals," makes any mention of providing girls equitable opportunities in the nation's public schools. Girls continue to be left out of the debate—despite the fact that for more than two decades researchers have identified gender bias as a major problem at all levels of schooling.

Schools must prepare both girls and boys for full and active roles in the family, the community, and the work force. Whether we look at the issues from an economic, political, or social perspective, girls are one-half of our future. We must move them from the sidelines to the center of the education-reform debate.

A critical step in correcting educational inequities is identifying them publicly. The *AAUW Report: How Schools Shortchange Girls* provides a comprehensive assessment of the status of girls in public education today. It exposes myths about girls and learning, and it supports the work of the many teachers who have struggled to define and combat gender bias in their schools. The report challenges us all—policymakers, educators, administrators, parents, and citizens—to rethink old assumptions and act now to stop schools from shortchanging girls.

Our public education system is plagued by numerous failings that affect boys as negatively as girls. But in many respects girls are put at a disadvantage simply because they are girls. *The AAUW Report* documents this in hundreds of cited studies.

When our schools become more gender-fair, education will improve for all our students—boys as well as girls—because excellence in education cannot be achieved without equity in education. By studying what happens to girls in school, we can gain valuable insights about what has to change in order for each student, every girl and every boy, to do as well as she or he can.

WHAT THE RESEARCH REVEALS

What Happens in the Classroom?

- Girls receive significantly less attention from classroom teachers than do boys.

- African American girls have fewer interactions with teachers than do white girls, despite evidence that they attempt to initiate interactions more frequently.
- Sexual harassment of girls by boys—from innuendo to actual assault—in our nation's schools is increasing.

A large body of research indicates that teachers give more classroom attention and more esteem-building encouragement to boys. In a study conducted by Myra and David Sadker, boys in elementary and middle school called out answers eight times more often than girls. When boys called out, teachers listened. But when girls called out, they were told to "raise your hand if you want to speak." Even when boys do not volunteer, teachers are more likely to encourage them to give an answer or an opinion than they are to encourage girls.

Research reveals a tendency, beginning at the preschool level, for educators to choose classroom activities that appeal to boys' interests and to select presentation formats in which boys excel. The teacher-student interaction patterns in science classes are often particularly biased. Even in math classes, where less-biased patterns are found, psychologist Jacquelynne Eccles reports that select boys in each math class she studied received particular attention to the exclusion of all other students, female and male.

Teaching methods that foster competition are still standard, although a considerable body of research has demonstrated that girls—and many boys as well—learn better when they undertake projects and activities cooperatively rather than competitively.

Researchers, including Sandra Damico, Elois Scott, and Linda Grant, report that African American girls have fewer interactions with teachers than do white girls, even though they attempt to initiate interactions more often. Furthermore, when African American girls do as well as white boys in school, teachers often attribute their success to hard work while assuming that the white boys are not working up to their potential.

Girls do not emerge from our schools with the same degree of confidence and self-esteem as boys. The 1990 AAUW poll, *Shortchanging Girls, Shortchanging America,* documents a loss of self-confidence in girls that is twice that for boys as they move from childhood to adolescence. Schools play a crucial role in challenging and changing gender-role expectations that undermine the self-confidence and achievement of girls.

Reports of boys sexually harassing girls in schools are increasing at an alarming rate. When sexual harassment is treated casually, as in "boys will be boys," both girls and boys get a dangerous, damaging message: "girls are not worthy of respect; appropriate behavior for boys includes exerting power over girls."

What Do We Teach Our Students?

- The contributions and experiences of girls and women are still marginalized or ignored in many of the textbooks used in our nation's schools.

- Schools, for the most part, provide inadequate education on sexuality and healthy development despite national concern about teen pregnancy, the AIDS crisis, and the increase of sexually transmitted diseases among adolescents.

- Incest, rape, and other physical violence severely compromise the lives of girls and women all across the country. These realities are rarely, if ever, discussed in schools.

Curriculum delivers the central message of education. It can strengthen or decrease student motivation for engagement, effort, growth, and development through the images it gives to students about themselves and the world. When the curriculum does not reflect the diversity of students' lives and cultures, it delivers an incomplete message.

Studies have shown that multicultural readings produced markedly more favorable attitudes toward nondominant groups than did the traditional reading lists, that academic achievement for all students was linked to use of nonsexist and multicultural materials, and that sex-role stereotyping was reduced in students whose curriculum portrayed males and females in nonstereotypical roles. Yet during the 1980s, federal support for reform regarding sex and race equity dropped, and a 1989 study showed that of the ten books most frequently assigned in public high school English courses only one was written by a woman and none by members of minority groups.

The "evaded" curriculum is a term coined in this report to refer to matters central to the lives of students that are touched on only briefly, if at all, in most schools. The United States has the highest rate of teenage childbearing in the Western industrialized world. Syphilis rates are now equal for girls and boys, and more teenage girls than boys contract gonorrhea. Although in the adult population AIDS is nine times more prevalent in men than in women, the same is not true for young people. In a District of Columbia study, the rate of HIV infection for girls was almost three times that for boys. Despite all of this, adequate sex and health education is the exception rather than the rule.

Adolescence is a difficult period for all young people, but it is particularly difficult for girls, who are far more likely to develop eating disorders and experience depression. Adolescent girls attempt suicide four to five times as often as boys (although boys, who choose more lethal methods, are more likely to be successful in their attempts).

Perhaps the most evaded of all topics in schools is the issue of gender and power. As girls mature they confront a culture that both idealizes and exploits the sexuality of young women while assigning them roles that are clearly less valued than male roles. If we do not begin to discuss more openly the ways in which ascribed power—whether on the basis of race, sex, class, sexual orientation, or religion—affects individual lives, we cannot truly prepare our students for responsible citizenship.

How Do Race/Ethnicity and Socioeconomic Status Affect Achievement in School?

247

American Association of University Women

- Girls from low-income families face particularly severe obstacles. Socioeconomic status, more than any other variable, affects access to school resources and educational outcomes.
- Test scores of low-socioeconomic-status girls are somewhat better than for boys from the same background in the lower grades, but by high school these differences disappear. Among high-socioeconomic-status students, boys generally outperform girls regardless of race/ethnicity.
- Too little information is available on differences among various groups of girls. While African Americans are compared to whites, or boys to girls, relatively few studies or published data examine differences by sex *and* race/ethnicity.

All girls confront barriers to equal participation in school and society. But minority girls, who must confront racism as well as sexism, and girls from low-income families face particular severe obstacles. These obstacles can include poor schools in dangerous neighborhoods, low teacher expectations, and inadequate nutrition and health care.

Few studies focus on issues affecting low-income girls and girls from minority groups—unless they are pregnant or drop out of school. In order to develop effective policies and programs, a wide range of issues—from course-taking patterns to academic self-esteem—require further examination by sex, race/ethnicity, and socioeconomic status.

How Are Girls Doing in Math and Science?

- Differences between girls and boys in math achievement are small and declining. Yet in high school, girls are still less likely than boys to take the most advanced courses and be in the top-scoring math groups.
- The gender gap in science, however, is *not* decreasing and may, in fact, be increasing.
- Even girls who are highly competent in math and science are much less likely to pursue scientific or technological careers than are their male classmates.

Girls who see math as "something men do" do less well in math than girls who do not hold this view. In their classic study, Elizabeth Fennema and Julia Sherman reported a drop in both girls' math confidence and their achievement in the middle school years. The drop in confidence *preceded* the decline in achievement.

Researcher Jane Kahle found that boys come to science classes with more out-of-school familiarity and experience with the subject matter. This advantage is furthered in the classroom. One study of science classrooms found that 79 percent of all student-assisted science demonstrations were carried out by boys.

We can no longer afford to disregard half our potential scientists and science-literate citizens of the next generation. Even when girls take math and science courses and do well in them, they do not receive the encouragement they need to pursue scientific careers. A study of high school seniors found that 64 percent of the boys who had taken physics and calculus were planning to major in science and engineering in college, compared to only 18.6 percent of the girls who had taken the same subjects. Support from teachers can make a big difference. Studies report that girls rate teacher support as an important factor in decisions to pursue scientific and technological careers.

Tests: Stepping Stones or Stop Signs?

- Test scores can provide an inaccurate picture of girls' and boys' abilities. Other factors such as grades, portfolios of student work, and out-of-school achievements must be considered in addition to test scores when making judgments about girls' and boys' skills and abilities.
- When scholarships are given based on the Scholastic Aptitude Test (SAT) scores, boys are more apt to receive scholarships than are girls who get equal or slightly better high school grades.
- Girls and boys with the same Math SAT scores do not do equally well in college—girls do better.

In most cases tests reflect rather than cause inequities in American education. The fact that groups score differently on a test does not necessarily mean that the test is biased. If, however, the score differences are related to the validity of the test—for example, if girls and boys know about the same amount of math but boys' test scores are consistently and significantly higher—then the test is biased.

A number of aspects of a test—beyond that which is being tested—can affect the score. For example, girls tend to score better than boys on essay tests, boys better than girls on multiple-choice items. Even today many girls and boys come to a testing situation with different interests and experiences. Thus a reading-comprehension passage that focuses on baseball scores will tend to favor boys, while a question testing the same skills that focuses on child care will tend to favor girls.

Why Do Girls Drop Out and What Are the Consequences?

- Pregnancy is not the only reason girls drop out of school. In fact, less than half the girls who leave school give pregnancy as the reason.
- Dropout rates for Hispanic girls vary considerably by national origin: Puerto Rican and Cuban American girls are more likely to drop out than are boys from the same cultures or other Hispanic girls.
- Childhood poverty is almost inescapable in single-parent families headed by women without a high school diploma: 77 percent for whites and 87 percent for African Americans.

In a recent study, 37 percent of the female dropouts compared to only 5 percent of the male dropouts cited "family-related problems" as the reason they left high school. Traditional gender roles place greater family responsibilities on adolescent girls than on their brothers. Girls are often expected to "help out" with caretaking responsibilities; boys rarely encounter this expectation.

However, girls as well as boys also drop out of school simply because they do not consider school pleasant or worthwhile. Asked what a worthwhile school experience would be, a group of teenage girls responded, "School would be fun. Our teachers would be excited and lively, not bored. They would act caring and take time to understand how students feel.... Boys would treat us with respect. If they run by and grab your tits, they would get into trouble."

Women and children are the most impoverished members of our society. Inadequate education not only limits opportunities for women but jeopardizes their children's—and the nation's—future.

PART FIVE

Perspectives From the Behavioral Sciences

On the Internet . . .

Sites appropriate to Part Five

This site contains lists of categories, Internet resources, and literature pertaining to Benjamin S. Bloom's Taxonomy of Educational Objectives. The three types of learning—cognitive, affective, and psychomotor—are discussed. Also included is a page with study questions.

> http://faculty.washington.edu/krumme/
> guides/bloom.html

Design Based Education: K–12, a project of the Graduate Program in Industrial Design and the Art Education Department of the University of Arts in Philadelphia, is presented on this site. Read about the project's goals, results, and more.

> http://www.uarts.edu/proj/dk12/index.html

This page contains a paper entitled, "Teaching Thinking and Dispositions: From Transmission to Enculturation." The teaching of thinking is a very important part of the educational process and this paper outlines a dispositional view, rather than simply a skills-centered view, to teach students how to think.

> http://learnweb.harvard.edu/alps/thinking/
> docs/article2.html

CHAPTER 11 Testing and the Critical Response to It

11.1 B. F. SKINNER

Why Teachers Fail

B. F. Skinner, whose work is known all over the world, was one of the leading behavioral psychologists of the twentieth century. His ideas on teaching and learning had great influence on American teachers for several decades of the past century. The selection that follows is from his book *The Technology of Teaching* (Appleton-Century-Crofts, 1968) and is taken from the last part of the chapter on why teachers fail. In it, Skinner is critical of aversive (punitive) teacher behavior and argues for positive (rewarding) approaches by teachers to encourage students to want to learn. He looks at and critiques several models of teacher behavior. Skinner responds to advocates of therapeutic models of schooling, to very permissive models of schooling, and to the Socratic approach to schooling.

Skinner argues that many people probably approve of aversive methods of reinforcing student behavior because these methods are compatible with dominant philosophies of government and religion. He goes on to say that it is not only the teacher who punishes the student "justly" when he or she fails. Skinner argues that students do not learn simply by being shown or told; good teaching is more than telling students things. He contends that students do learn by listening to their peers, significant other adults, and the media, but that effective classroom learning involves more than this. Skinner consistently argues for noncoercive methods of classroom instruction.

"Positive reinforcement" of projected behavioral goals teaches students to respond positively, he believes, but it does not punish them aversively. He uses the metaphor of the "idols of the school" (the idol of the good teacher and the idol of the good student) to reinforce his argument. Skinner concludes that the concept of teaching may be seen as an organized set of "contingencies of reinforcement" under which behavioral changes can occur without aversive methods.

Key Concept: teaching

*P*roposals to add requirements and raise standards are usually part of an aversive pattern. A well-known educator has written:

> We must stiffen the work of our schools ... we have every reason to concentrate on [certain subjects] and be unflagging in our insistence that they be really learned.... Senior year [in high school] ought to be the hardest.... [We should give] students work that is both difficult and important, and [insist] that it be well done.... We should demand more of our students.

These expressions were probably intended to be synonymous with "students should learn more" or possibly "teachers should teach more." There may be good reasons why students should take more mathematics or learn a modern language more thoroughly or be better prepared for college or graduate school, but they are not reasons for intensifying aversive pressures. A standard is a level of achievement; only under a particular philosophy of education is it a criterion upon which some form of punishment is contingent.

It is not difficult to explain the use of aversive control. The teacher can easily arrange aversive contingencies; his culture has already taught him how to do so. In any case, since the immediate effects are clear-cut, effective techniques are easily learned. When the control begins early and is maintained consistently, and particularly when it takes the moderate form of "gentle admonition," by-products are minimized. Systems which are basically aversive have produced well-disciplined, obedient, industrious, and eventually informed and skilled students sometimes to the envy of teachers who cannot skillfully use the same techniques. Even the students themselves may be impressed and may return years later to thank their teachers for having beaten or ridiculed them.

Aversive control can be defended as "nature's way." In learning to turn a hand spring, a child improves by avoiding bumps and bruises. The natural environment teaches a person to act in ways which resolve puzzlement or reduce the threat of not knowing. Why should the teacher not imitate nature and arrange comparable aversive contingencies, such as puzzling the student to induce him to think or making him curious to induce him to explore. But nature ... is not always an admirable teacher. Its aversive contingencies are not a model to be copied but a standard to be excelled.

Aversive contingencies also provide an opportunity for the student to learn to adjust to the unpleasant and painful, to act effectively when threatened, to submit to pain, but they are usually not well designed for that purpose. As Rousseau pointed out, a child may be taught to cope with aversive stimulation, but the required contingencies are not easily combined with contingencies designed to teach other things.

Aversive control is no doubt sanctioned in part because it is compatible with prevailing philosophies of government and religion. It is not only the teacher who holds the student responsible for doing what he ought to do or punishes him "justly" when he fails. It is not only the failing student who is told that "ignorance is no excuse." Schools and colleges must, of course, share in the ethical and legal control of the societies which support them and of which they are a part, and they have comparable problems of their own to which aversive control has always seemed relevant, but ... alternative courses of action should be considered. Existing systems with their unfortunate by-products cannot be defended as necessary evils until we are sure that other solutions cannot be found.

Most teachers are humane and well disposed. They do not want to threaten their students yet they find themselves doing so. They want to help but their offers are often declined. Most students are well disposed. They want an education, yet they cannot force themselves to study, and they know they are wasting time. For reasons which they have probably not correctly identified, many are in revolt. Why should education continue to use the aversive techniques to which all this is so obviously due? Evidently because effective alternatives have not been found. It is not enough simply to abandon aversive measures.... [B]y withholding punishment teachers may help students who have been badly treated elsewhere and prepare them to be taught, but something else is needed. Tolstoy soon abandoned the school for the children of his serfs in which no child was obliged to go to school or, when in school, to pay attention, and similar experiments by the anarchists and one by Bertrand Russell also failed.

TELLING AND SHOWING

A child sees things and talks about them accurately afterward. He listens to news and gossip and passes it along. He recounts in great detail the plot of a movie he has seen or a book he has read. He seems to have a "natural curiosity," a "love of knowledge," an "inherent wish to learn." Why not take advantage of these natural endowments and simply bring the student into contact with the world he is to learn about? There are practical problems, of course. Only a small part of the real world can be brought into the classroom even with the aid of films, tape recorders, and television, and only a small part of what remains can be visited outside. Words are easily imported, but the verbal excesses of classical education have shown how easily this fact may lead to dangerous overemphasis. Within reasonable limits, however, is it not possible to teach simply by giving the student an opportunity to learn in a natural way?

Unfortunately, a student does not learn simply when he is shown or told. Something essential to his natural curiosity or wish to learn is missing from the classroom. What is missing, technically speaking, is "positive reinforcement." In daily life the student looks, listens, and remembers because certain consequences then follow. He learns to look and listen in those special ways which encourage remembering because he is reinforced for recalling what he has seen and heard, just as a newspaper reporter notes and remembers things he sees because he is paid for reporting them. Consequences of this sort are lacking when a teacher simply shows a student something or tells him something.

Rousseau was the great advocate of natural learning. Émile was to be taught by the world of things. His teacher was to draw his attention to that world; but otherwise his education was to be negative. There were to be no arranged consequences. But Émile was an imaginary student with imaginary learning processes. When Rousseau's disciple, Pestalozzi, tried the methods on his own flesh-and-blood son, he ran into trouble. His diary is one of the most pathetic documents in the history of education. As he walked with his young son beside a stream, Pestalozzi would repeat several times, "Water flows downhill." He would show the boy that "wood swims in water and... stones sink." Whether the child was learning anything or not, he was not unhappy, and Pestalozzi could believe that at least he was using the right method. But when the world of things had to be left behind, failure could no longer be concealed. "I could only get him to read with difficulty; he has a thousand ways of getting out of it, and never loses an opportunity of doing something else." He could make the boy sit still at his lessons by first making him "run and play out of doors in the cold," but Pestalozzi himself was then exhausted. Inevitably, of course, he returned to aversive measures: "He was soon tired of learning to read, but as I had decided that he should work at it regularly every day, whether he liked it or not, I determined to make him feel the necessity of doing so, from the very first, by showing him there was no choice between this work and my displeasure, which I made him feel by keeping him in ."[1]

GETTING ATTENTION

The failure of "showing and telling" is sometimes attributed to lack of attention. We are often aware that we ourselves are not listening or looking carefully. If we are not to punish the student for not looking and listening, how can we make him concentrate? One possibility is to make sure that there is nothing else to be seen or heard. The schoolroom is isolated and freed of distractions. Silence is often the rule. Physical constraints are helpful. Earphones reassure the teacher that only what is to be heard is going into the student's ears. The TV screen is praised for its isolation and hypnotic effect. A piece of equipment has been proposed which achieves concentration in the following desperate way: the student faces a brightly lighted text, framed by walls which operate on the principle of the blinders once worn by carriage horses. His ears are between earphones. He reads part of the text aloud and then listens to his recorded voice as he reads it again. If he does not learn what he reads, it is certainly not because he has not seen it!

A less coercive practice is to make what is to be seen or heard attractive and attention-compelling. The advertiser faces the same problem as the teacher, and his techniques have been widely copied in the design of textbooks, films, and classroom practices. Bright colors, variety, sudden change, big type, animated sequences—all these have at least a temporary effect in inducing the student to look and listen. They do not, however, *teach* the student to look and listen, because they occur at the wrong time. A similar weakness is seen in making school itself pleasant. Attractive architecture, colorful interiors, comfortable furniture, congenial social arrangements, naturally interesting subjects—these are all reinforcing, but they reinforce only the behaviors they are contingent upon. An attractive school building reinforces the behavior of coming in sight of it. A colorful and comfortable classroom reinforces the behavior of entering it. Roughly speaking, these things could be said to strengthen a positive attitude toward school. But they provide merely the setting for instruction. They do not teach what students are in school to learn.

In the same way audio-visual aids usually come at the wrong time to strengthen the forms of behavior which are the principal concern of the teacher. An interesting page printed in four colors reinforces the student simply for opening the book and looking at it. It does not reinforce reading the page or even examining it closely; certainly it does not reinforce those activities which result in effective recall of what is seen. An interesting lecturer holds his listeners in the sense that they look at and listen to him, just as an interesting demonstration film reinforces the behavior of watching it, but neither the lecture nor the film necessarily reinforces listening or listening in those special ways which further recall. In good instruction interesting things should happen *after* the student has read a page or listened or looked with care. The four-color picture should *become* interesting when the text which accompanies it has been read. One stage in a lecture or film should be interesting only if earlier stages have been carefully examined and remembered. In general, naturally attractive and interesting things further the primary goals of education only when they enter into much more subtle contingencies of reinforcement than are usually represented by audio-visual aids.

MAKING MATERIAL EASY TO REMEMBER

It is possible that students may be induced to learn by making material not only attractive but memorable. An obvious example is making material easy. The child first learns to write in manuscript because it resembles the text he is learning to read; he may learn to read material printed in a phonetic alphabet; he may learn to spell only words he will actually use; if he cannot read he can listen to recorded speech. This sort of simplification shows a lack of confidence in methods of teaching and often merely postpones the teacher's task, but it is sometimes a useful strategy. Material which is well organized is also, of course, easier to learn.

Some current psychological theories suggest that material may be made memorable in another way. Various laws of perception imply that an observer cannot help seeing things in certain ways. The stimulus seems to force itself upon the organism. Optical illusions are often cited as examples. These laws suggest the possibility that material may be presented in a form in which it is irresistibly learned. Material is to be so "structured" that it is readily—and almost necessarily—"grasped." Instructional examples are, however, far less persuasive than the demonstrations offered in support of them. In trying to assign an important function to the material to be learned, it is particularly easy to overlook other conditions under which learning actually occurs.

THE TEACHER AS MIDWIFE

No matter how attractive, interesting, and well structured material may be, the discouraging fact is that it is often not learned. Rather than continue to ask why, many educational theorists have concluded that the teacher cannot really teach at all but can only help the student learn. The dominant metaphor goes back to Plato. As Emile Bréhier puts it, "Socrates... possessed no other art but maieutics, his mother Phaenarete's art of delivering; he drew out from souls what they have in them...." The student already knows the truth; the teacher simply shows him that he knows. As we have seen, however, there is no evidence that the boy in the scene from the *Meno* learned anything. He could not have reconstructed the theorem by himself when Socrates had finished, and Socrates says as much later in the dialogue: "If someone will keep asking him these same questions often and in various forms, you can be sure that in the end he will know about them as accurately as anybody." (Socrates was a frequency theorist!)[2]

It must be admitted that the assignment was difficult. The boy was starting from scratch. When [George] Polya uses the same technique in presiding at the birth of the formula for the diagonal of a parallelepiped his students make a more positive contribution because they have already had some geometry, but any success due to previous teaching weakens the claim for maieutics. And Polya's promptings and questionings give more help than he wants to admit.

It is only because mathematical proofs seem to arise from the nature of things that they can be said in some sense to be "known by everyone" and simply waiting to be drawn out. Even Socrates could not argue that the soul knows the facts of history or a second language. Impregnation must precede parturition. But is it not possible that a presentation which has not seemed to be learned is the seed from which knowledge grows to be delivered by the teacher? Perhaps the intellectual midwife is to show the student that he remembers what he has already been shown or told. In *The Idea of a University* Cardinal Newman gave an example of the maieutic method applied to acquired knowledge. It will stir painful memories in many teachers. A tutor is talking with a candidate about a bit of history—a bit of history, in fact, in which Plato's Menon lost his life.

T: It is the *Anabasis* you take up?... What is the meaning of the word *Anabasis*?

C: *is silent.*

T: You know very well; take your time, and don't be alarmed. Anabasis means...

C: An ascent....

T: *Who* ascended?

C: The Greeks, Xenophon.

T: Very well: Xenophon and the Greeks; the Greeks ascended. To what did they ascend?

C: Against the Persian king: they ascended to fight the Persian king.

T: That is right... an ascent; but I thought we called it a descent when a foreign army carried war into a country?

C: *is silent.*

T: Don't we talk of a descent of barbarians?

C: Yes.

T: Why then are the Greeks said to go *up*?

C: They went up to fight the Persian king.

T: Yes; but why *up*... why not *down*?

C: They came *down* afterwards, when they retreated back to Greece.

T: Perfectly right; they did... but could you give no reason why they are said to go *up* to Persia, not *down*?

C: They went *up* to Persia.

T: Why do you not say they went *down*?

C: *pauses, then,...* They went *down* to Persia.

T: You have misunderstood me.

Newman warned his reader that the Candidate is "deficient to a great extent... not such as it is likely that a respectable school would turn out." He recognized a poor student, but not a poor method. Thousands of teachers have wasted years of their lives in exchanges which have been no more profitable— and all to the greater glory of maieutics and out of a conviction that telling and showing are not only inadequate but wrong.

Although the soul has perhaps not always known the truth nor ever been confronted with it in a half-forgotten experience, it may still *seek* it. If the student can be taught to learn from the world of things, nothing else will ever have to be taught. This is the method of discovery. It is designed to absolve the teacher from a sense of failure by making instruction unnecessary. The teacher arranges the environment in which discovery is to take place, he suggests lines of inquiry, he keeps the student within bounds. The important thing is that he should tell him nothing.

The human organism does, of course, learn without being taught. It is a good thing that this is so, and it would no doubt be a good thing if more could be learned in that way. Students are naturally interested in what they learn by themselves because they would not learn if they were not, and for the same reason they are more likely to remember what they learn in that way. There are reinforcing elements of surprise and accomplishment in personal discovery which are welcome alternatives to traditional aversive consequences.[3] But discovery is no solution to the problems of education. A culture is no stronger than its capacity to transmit itself. It must impart an accumulation of skills, knowledge, and social and ethical practices to its new members. The institution of education is designed to serve this purpose. It is quite impossible for the student to discover for himself any substantial part of the wisdom of his culture, and no philosophy of education really proposes that he should. Great thinkers build upon the past, they do not waste time in rediscovering it. It is dangerous to suggest to the student that it is beneath his dignity to learn what others already know, that there is something ignoble (and even destructive of "rational powers") in memorizing facts, codes, formulae, or passages from literary works, and that to be admired he must think in original ways. It is equally dangerous to forgo teaching important facts and principles in order to give the student a chance to discover them for himself. Only a teacher who is unaware of his effects on his students can believe that children actually discover mathematics, that (as one teacher has written) in group discussions they "can and do figure out all of the relationships, facts, and procedures that comprise a full program in math."

There are other difficulties. The position of the teacher who encourages discovery is ambiguous. Is he to pretend that he himself does not know? (Socrates said Yes. In Socratic irony those who know enjoy a laugh at the expense of those who do not.) Or, for the sake of encouraging a joint venture in discovery, is the teacher to choose to teach only those things which he himself has not yet learned? Or is he frankly to say, "I know, but you must find out" and accept the consequences for his relations with his students?

Still another difficulty arises when it is necessary to teach a whole class. How are a few good students to be prevented from making all the discoveries? When that happens, other members of the class not only miss the excitement of discovery but are left to learn material presented in a slow and particularly confusing way. Students should, of course, be encouraged to explore, to ask questions, to study by themselves, to be "creative." When properly analyzed... the kinds of behavior referred to in such expressions can be taught. It does not follow, however, that they must be taught by the method of discovery.

THE IDOLS OF THE SCHOOL

Effective instructional practices threaten the conception of teaching as a form of maieutics. If we suppose that the student is to "exercise his rational powers," to "develop his mind," or to learn through "intuition or insight," then it may indeed be true that the teacher cannot teach but can only help the student learn. But these goals can be restated in terms of explicit changes in behavior, and effective methods of instruction can then be designed.

In his famous four idols, Francis Bacon formulated some of the reasons why men arrive at false ideas. He might have added two special Idols of the School which affect those who want to improve teaching. The Idol of the Good Teacher is the belief that what a good teacher can do, any teacher can do. Some teachers are, of course, unusually effective. They are naturally interesting people, who make things interesting to their students. They are skillful in handling students, as they are skillful in handling people in general. They can formulate facts and principles and communicate them to others in effective ways. Possibly their skills and talents will someday be better understood and successfully imparted to new teachers. At the moment, however, they are true exceptions. The fact that a method proves successful in their hands does not mean that it will solve important problems in education.

The Idol of the Good Student is the belief that what a good student can learn, any student can learn. Because they have superior ability or have been exposed to fortunate early environments, some students learn without being taught. It is quite possible that they learn more effectively when they are not taught. Possibly we shall someday produce more of them. At the moment, however, the fact that a method works with good students does not mean that it will work with all. It is possible that we shall progress more rapidly toward effective education by leaving the good teacher and the good student out of account altogether. They will not suffer, because they do not need our help. We may then devote ourselves to the discovery of practices which are appropriate to the remaining—what?—ninety-five percent of teachers and students.

The Idols of the School explain some of the breathless excitement with which educational theorists return again and again to a few standard solutions. Perhaps we should regard them as merely two special cases of a more general source of error, the belief that personal experience in the classroom is the primary source of pedagogical wisdom. It is actually very difficult for teachers to profit from experience. They almost never learn about their long-term successes or failures, and their short-term effects are not easily traced to the practices from which they presumably arose. Few teachers have time to reflect on such matters, and traditional educational research has given them little help. A much more effective kind of research is now becoming possible. Teaching may be defined as an arrangement of contingencies of reinforcement under which behavior changes. Relevant contingencies can be most successfully analyzed in studying the behavior of one student at a time under carefully controlled conditions. Few educators are aware of the extent to which human behavior is being examined in arrangements of this sort, but a true technology of teaching is imminent. It is beginning to suggest effective alternatives to the aversive practices which have caused so much trouble.

NOTES

1. A contemporary of Pestalozzi's, Thomas Day, author of *Sandford and Merton,* a book for children, "died from a kick by a horse which he was trying to break in on Rousseau's principles, a martyr to Reason and Nature."

2. It is astonishing how seriously the scene from the *Meno* has been taken. Karl Popper has recently written: "For Meno's slave is helped by Socrates' judicious questions to remember or recapture the forgotten knowledge which his soul possessed in its antenatal state of omniscience. It is, I believe, this famous Socratic method, called in the Theaetetus the art of midwifery or maieutic, to which Aristotle alluded when he said that Socrates was the inventor of the method of induction."

3. As Pascal pointed out, "Reasons which one has discovered oneself are usually more persuasive than those which have turned up in the thinking of others"—but not because the reasons are proprietary; one discovers a rule describing contingencies of reinforcement only after having been exposed to the contingencies. The rule seems to the discoverer particularly apropos because it is supported by the variables it describes.

The Nature and Development of the Taxonomy

Benjamin S. Bloom (b. 1913) was a pioneer in the development of the categorization of educational objectives. During his long career at the University of Chicago, he conducted ongoing research on mastery learning with children and young adults. His work became the basis for behavioral objectives in instruction. Bloom has published a number of works on learning, including *Every Kid Can: Learning for Mastery* (College/University Press, 1973) and *Handbook on Formative and Summative Evaluation of Student Learning* (McGraw-Hill, 1971), coedited with J. Thomas Hastings and George F. Madaus. Bloom's work on mastery learning as well as his taxonomy of educational objectives in the cognitive domain have had an enormous impact on the testing and measurement of school learning in the United States.

Bloom worked with a committee composed of members of the American Educational Research Association to produce *Taxonomy of Educational Objectives, Handbook I: Cognitive Domain* (David McKay, 1956). This became the conceptual basis for the development of behavioral objectives in American curriculum and instruction in the 1970s and 1980s. Although this taxonomy was first published in 1956, its use in the development of instructional objectives really did not begin to achieve widespread acceptance by American educators until the late 1960s. The following selection, which is from *Taxonomy of Educational Objectives, Handbook I,* introduces the reader to the overall structure of the taxonomy in the cognitive domain.

Key Concept: cognitive objectives of instruction and evaluation

THE TAXONOMY AS A CLASSIFICATION DEVICE

The major purpose in constructing a taxonomy of educational objectives is to facilitate communication. In our original consideration of the project we conceived of it as a method of improving the exchange of ideas and materials among test workers, as well as other persons concerned with educational research and curriculum development. For instance, the use of the taxonomy as an aid in developing a precise definition and classification of such vaguely defined terms as "thinking" and "problem solving" would enable a group of schools to discern the similarities and differences among the goals of their different instructional programs. They could compare and exchange tests and other evaluative devices intended to determine the effectiveness of these programs. They could, therefore, begin to understand more completely the relation between the learning experiences provided by these various programs and the changes which take place in their students.

Set at this level, the task of producing a taxonomy, that is, a classification of educational outcomes, is quite analogous to the development of a plan for classifying books in a library. Or, put more abstractly, it is like establishing symbols for designating classes of objects where the members of a class have something in common. In a library these symbols might be the words "fiction" and "nonfiction" and would apply to classes of books having something in common. If the problem is essentially one of finding new symbols for the classes, any set of symbols, numbers, nonsense syllables, or words could be used. Thus, we could have used the symbols "F" and "NF" for fiction and nonfiction. Further, since the symbols selected are not intended to convey that one class is of a higher order than another or that there is any particular relationship between the classes, they can be selected in very arbitrary fashion. The labels "fiction" and "nonfiction" do not imply that the one class of book is better, more abstract, or more complex than the other kind.

Of course, such a classification procedure cannot be a private fantasy since it is of value only if used by the workers who wish to communicate with each other. Thus, the classifications "fiction" and "nonfiction" are of value only if librarians use them. Acceptance of such classifications by potential users is likely to be facilitated if the class names are terms which are reasonably familiar to them and if these terms are given precise and usable definitions. Thus, one might expect more ready acceptance of a library classification scheme if he took such a term as "fiction," which is already in use, and defined it so that any competent librarian would easily be able to determine which books fit the classification.

In summary then, the major task in setting up any kind of taxonomy is that of selecting appropriate symbols, giving them precise and usable definitions, and securing the consensus of the group which is to use them. Similarly, developing a classification of educational objectives requires the selection of an appropriate list of symbols to represent all the major types of educational outcomes. Next, there is the task of defining these symbols with sufficient precision to permit and facilitate communication about these phenomena among teachers, administrators, curriculum workers, testers, educational research workers, and others who are likely to use the taxonomy. Finally, there is the task of trying the classification and securing the consensus of the educational workers who wish to use the taxonomy.

Before one can build a classification scheme, it must be clear what it is that is to be classified. This is not much of a problem when one is classifying books. But descriptions of curricula are set up on such different bases as descriptions of teacher behavior, descriptions of instructional methods, and descriptions of intended pupil behaviors. As achievement testers and educational research workers, the major phenomena with which we are concerned are the changes produced in individuals as a result of educational experiences. Such changes may be represented by the global statements of the educational objectives of an educational unit, or they may be represented by the actual description of the student behaviors which are regarded as appropriate or relevant to the objectives. Objectives may also be inferred from the tasks, problems, and observations used to test or evaluate the presence of these behaviors.

We are of the opinion that although the objectives and test materials and techniques may be specified in an almost unlimited number of ways, the student behaviors involved in these objectives can be represented by a relatively small number of classes. Therefore, the taxonomy is designed to be a classification of the student behaviors which represent the intended outcomes of the educational process. It is assumed that essentially the same classes of behavior may be observed in the usual range of subject-matter content, at different levels of education (elementary, high school, college), and in different schools. Thus, a single set of classifications should be applicable in all these instances.

It should be noted that we are not attempting to classify the instructional methods used by teachers, the ways in which teachers relate themselves to students, or the different kinds of instructional materials they use. We are not attempting to classify the particular subject matter or content. What we are classifying is the *intended behavior* of students—the ways in which individuals are to act, think, or feel as the result of participating in some unit of instruction. (Only such of these intended behaviors as are related to mental acts or thinking are included in the part of the taxonomy developed in this Handbook.)

It is recognized that the *actual behaviors* of the students after they have completed the unit of instruction may differ in degree as well as in kind from the *intended behaviors* specified by the objectives. That is, the effects of instruction may be such that the students do not learn a given skill to the desired level of perfection; or, for that matter, they may not develop the intended skill to any degree. This is a matter of grading or evaluating the goodness of the performance. The emphasis in the Handbook is on obtaining evidence on the extent to which desired and intended behaviors have been learned by the student. It is outside the scope of the task we set ourselves to properly treat the matter of determining the appropriate value to be placed on the different degrees of achievement of the objectives of instruction.

It should also be noted that the intended behaviors specified by educational objectives do not include many of the behaviors which psychologists are interested in classifying and studying. One reason is that the intended behaviors represent the social goals imposed upon youngsters by their society or culture. Thus, the intended or desired behaviors included in educational objectives usually do not include undesirable or abnormal behaviors which are socially disapproved. Similarly, certain natural or unsocialized behaviors which might be of interest to psychologists may fall outside the categories of the taxonomy.

Our present studies of the affective area have indicated that the selective nature of intended behaviors will be even more apparent there than in the cognitive domain. The fact that we include objectives which specify social and emotional adjustment as a part of the affective domain points up this fact.

GUIDING PRINCIPLES

Since the determination of classes and their titles is in some ways arbitrary, there could be an almost infinite number of ways of dividing and naming the domains of educational outcomes. To guide us in our selection of a single classification system and to make the product more readily understood and used, we established certain guiding principles. First, since the taxonomy is to be used in regard to existing educational units and programs, we are of the opinion that the major distinctions between classes should reflect, in large part, the distinctions teachers make among student behaviors. These distinctions are revealed in the ways teachers state educational objectives. They are also found in their curricular plans, their instructional material, and their instructional methods. To the extent it was possible, the subdivisions of the taxonomy are intended to recognize these distinctions.

A second principle is that the taxonomy should be logically developed and internally consistent. Thus, each term should be defined and used in a consistent way throughout the taxonomy. In addition, each category should permit logical subdivisions which can be clearly defined and further subdivided to the extent that appears necessary and useful.

A third principle is that the taxonomy should be consistent with our present understanding of psychological phenomena. Those distinctions which are psychologically untenable, even though regularly made by teachers, would be avoided. Further, distinctions which seem psychologically important, even though not frequently made in educational objectives, would be favorably considered for inclusion. Perhaps it should be reiterated that, since the taxonomy deals only with educationally intended behavior, it falls considerably short of being a classification scheme for all psychological phenomena.

A fourth principle is that the classification should be a purely descriptive scheme in which every type of educational goal can be represented in a relatively neutral fashion. Thus, the Dewey decimal classification system for libraries describes all the classes of books. It does not indicate the value or quality of one class as compared with another, nor does it specify the number and kind of books any particular library should possess. Similarly, to avoid partiality to one view of education as opposed to another, we have attempted to make the taxonomy neutral by avoiding terms which implicitly convey value judgments and by making the taxonomy as inclusive as possible. This means that the kinds of behavioral changes emphasized by *any* institution, educational unit, or educational philosophy can be represented in the classification. Another way of saying this is that any objective which describes an intended behavior should be classifiable in this system. On the other hand, the taxonomy will probably include a greater variety of behaviors than those emphasized by any one school, course, or educational philosophy. Thus, one course might have objectives classifiable in four of the categories, another in only three of the categories, and so on.

In one sense, however, the taxonomy is not completely neutral. This stems from the already-noted fact that it is a classification of intended behaviors. It cannot be used to classify educational plans which are made in such a way that either the student behaviors cannot be specified or only a single (unanalyzed) term or phrase such as "understanding," or "desirable citizen," is used to describe the outcomes. Only those educational programs which can be specified in terms of intended student behaviors can be classified.

DEVELOPING THE TAXONOMY

Keeping in mind the aforementioned principles, we began work by gathering a large list of educational objectives from our own institutions and the literature. We determined which part of the objective stated the behavior intended and which stated the content or object of the behavior. We then attempted to find divisions or groups into which the behaviors could be placed. We initially limited ourselves to those objectives commonly referred to as knowledge, intellectual abilities, and intellectual skills. (This area, which we named the cognitive domain, may also be described as including the behaviors: remembering; reasoning; problem solving; concept formation; and, to a limited extent, creative thinking.) We proceeded to divide the cognitive objectives into subdivisions from the simplest behavior to the most complex. We then attempted to find ways of defining these subdivisions in such a way that all of us working with the material could communicate with each other about the specific objectives as well as the testing procedures to be included.

We have not succeeded in finding a method of classification which would permit complete and sharp distinctions among behaviors.... There are two basic views. First, we were again made aware of what any teacher knows—two boys may appear to be doing the same thing; but if we analyze the situation, we find they are not. For example, two students solve an algebra problem. One student may be solving it from memory, having had the identical problem in class previously. The other student has never met the problem before and must reason out the solution by applying general principles. We can only distinguish between their behaviors as we analyze the relation between the problem and each student's background of experience. This then introduces a new aspect of the classification problem, namely, the experiential backgrounds of the students to whom the objective is to apply.... [T]his may be a very important factor in using the taxonomy to classify test exercises.

A second difficulty in classification results from the fact that the more complex behaviors include the simpler behaviors. If we view statements of educational objectives as intended behaviors which the student shall display at the end of some period of education, we can then view the process of one of change. As teachers we intend the learning experiences to change the student's behavior from a simpler type to another more complex one which in some ways at least will include the first type.

One may take the Gestalt point of view that the complex behavior is more than the sum of the simpler behaviors, or one may view the complex behavior as being completely analyzable into simpler components. But either way, so long as the simpler behaviors may be viewed as components of the more complex behaviors, we can view the educational process as one of building on the simpler behavior. Thus, a particular behavior which is classified in one way at a given time may develop and become integrated with other behaviors to form a more complex behavior which is classified in a different way. In order to find a single place for each type of behavior, the taxonomy must be organized from simple to complex classes of behavior. Furthermore, for consistency in classification, a rule of procedure may be adopted such that a particular behavior is placed in the most complex class which is appropriate and relevant.

But, having specified that the classes shall be arranged from simple to complex, we have exceeded the simple classification scheme which called primarily for a series of categories without order or rank. The next section addresses itself to this problem.

THE PROBLEM OF A HIERARCHY— CLASSIFICATION VERSUS TAXONOMY

We have so far used the terms "classification" and "taxonomy" more or less interchangeably. It is necessary, however, that we examine the relationship between these terms because, strictly speaking, they are not interchangeable. Taxonomies, particularly Aristotelian taxonomies, have certain structural rules which exceed in complexity the rules of a classification system. While a classification scheme may have many arbitrary elements, a taxonomy scheme may not. A taxonomy must be so constructed that the order of the terms must correspond to some "real" order among the phenomena represented by the terms. A classification scheme may be validated by reference to the criteria of communicability, usefulness, and suggestiveness; while a taxonomy must be validated by demonstrating its consistency with the theoretical views in research findings of the field it attempts to order.

As educators and specialists in research, we are interested in a long-term inquiry into the nature of the phenomena with which we deal, and no simple set of terms and definitions by itself really is a satisfactory tool in making this inquiry. We need a method of ordering phenomena such that the method of ordering reveals significant relationships among the phenomena. This is the basic problem of a taxonomy—to order phenomena in ways which will reveal some of their essential properties as well as the interrelationships among them. Members of the taxonomy group spent considerable time in attempting to find a psychological theory which would provide a sound basis for ordering the categories of the taxonomy. We reviewed theories of personality and learning but were unable to find a single view which, in our opinion, accounted for the varieties of behaviors represented in the educational objectives we attempted to classify. We were reluctantly forced to agree with Hilgard[1] that each theory of learning accounts for some phenomena very well but is less adequate in accounting for others. What is needed is a larger synthetic theory of learning than at present seems to be available. We are of the opinion that our method of ordering educational outcomes will make it possible to define the range of phenomena for which such a theory must account. The taxonomy also uses an order consistent with research findings and it should provide some clues as to the nature of the theory which may be developed. This is an extremely complex problem; and although it has probably not been solved completely satisfactorily, it is the opinion of the writers that we have made some progress toward a solution.

As the taxonomy is now organized, it contains six major classes:

1.00 Knowledge

2.00 Comprehension

3.00 Application

4.00 Analysis

5.00 Synthesis

6.00 Evaluation

The classes of Bloom's taxonomy are defined in an appendix in the original source. The following are abbreviated definitions of the six classes:

1.00 Knowledge: *the recall of specifics and universals, the recall of methods and processes, or the recall of a pattern, structure, or setting.*

2.00 Comprehension: *the lowest level of understanding, in which the individual has a basic understanding or apprehension such that he or she knows what is being communicated without necessarily relating it to other material or seeing its fullest implications.*

3.00 Application: *the use of abstractions in particular and concrete situations; abstractions may be in the form of general ideas, rules of procedures, generalized methods, or technical principles, ideas, and theories that must be remembered and applied.*

4.00 Analysis: *the breakdown of a communication into its constituent elements or parts such that the relative hierarchy of ideas is made clear or the relations between the ideas expressed are made explicit.*

5.00 Synthesis: *the putting together of elements and parts so as to form a whole; this involves the process of working with pieces, parts, elements, etc., and arranging and combining them in such a way as to constitute a pattern or structure that was not clearly there before.*

6.00 Evaluation: *judgments about the value of material and methods for given purposes; quantitative and qualitative judgments about the extent to which material and methods satisfy criteria, which could be provided for the student*

Although it is possible to conceive of these major classes in several different arrangements, the present one appears to us to represent something of the hierarchical order of the different classes of objectives. As we have defined them, the objectives in one class are likely to make use of and be built on the behaviors found in the preceding classes in this list....

Our attempt to arrange educational behaviors from simple to complex was based on the idea that a particular simple behavior may become integrated with other equally simple behaviors to form a more complex behavior. Thus our classifications may be said to be in the form where behaviors of type A form one class, behaviors of type AB form another class, while behaviors of type ABC form still another class. If this is the real order from simple to complex, it should be related to an order of difficulty such that problems requiring behavior A alone should be answered correctly more frequently than problems requiring AB. We have studied a large number of problems occurring in our comprehensive examinations and have found some evidence to support this hypothesis. Thus, problems requiring knowledge of specific facts are generally answered correctly more frequently than problems requiring a knowledge of the universals and abstractions in a field. Problems requiring knowledge of principles and concepts are correctly answered more frequently than problems requiring both knowledge of the principle and some ability to apply it in new situations. Problems requiring analysis and synthesis are more difficult than problems requiring comprehension. Scatter plots of the performances of individuals on one test composed of items at a simple level in the taxonomy against their performances on another test composed of items at a more complex level in the taxonomy show that it is more common to find that individuals have low scores on complex problems and high scores on the less complex problems than the reverse. Our evidence on this is not entirely satisfactory, but there is an unmistakable trend pointing toward a hierarchy of classes of behavior which is in accordance with our present tentative classification of these behaviors.

While we have been primarily concerned with the cognitive domain, we have done some thinking about the classification versus taxonomy problem as it applies to all the domains. The arrangement of behaviors from simple to complex and the differentiation of behaviors into three domains—the cognitive, the psychomotor, and the affective—were made primarily from an educational viewpoint. That is, these are the distinctions which teachers make in the development of curriculum and teaching procedures. We as educational testers also make similar distinctions. As we examine the classification system so far developed, however, we note an additional dimension not usually considered in educational and teaching procedures. One of the major threads running through all the taxonomy appears to be a scale of consciousness or awareness. Thus, the behaviors in the cognitive domain are largely characterized by a rather high degree of consciousness on the part of the individual exhibiting the behavior, while the behaviors in the affective domain are much more frequently exhibited with a low level of awareness on the part of the individual. Further, in the cognitive domain especially, it appears that as the behaviors become more complex, the individual is more aware of their existence. We are of the opinion that this applies to the other domains as well. Clearly there is no precise scale of consciousness which may be used to test these speculations. However, some of our research on the thought processes involved in problem solving[2] indicates that students are able to give more complete reports of their attack on a problem as the problem becomes more complex, that is, as the problem is classified in the more complex classes of intellectual abilities and skills.

If the level of consciousness can be demonstrated to be an important dimension in the classification of behavior, it would pose a great range of problems and point to a whole new set of relationships which would be of interest to researchers in the field of educational psychology. One might hope that it would provide a basis for explaining why behaviors which are initially displayed with a high level of consciousness become, after some time and repetition, automatic or are accompanied by a low level of consciousness. Perhaps this would provide a partial basis for explaining why some learning, especially of the affective behaviors, is so difficult. Perhaps it will also help to explain the extraordinary retention of some learning—especially of the psychomotor skills.

NOTES

1. Hilgard, E. R., *Theories of Learning* (Century Psychology Series), New York: Appleton-Century-Crofts, 1948.
2. Bloom, B. S., and Broder, Lois, *Problem-solving processes of college students* (A Supplementary Educational Monograph), Chicago: University of Chicago Press, Summer, 1950.

11.3 DAVID R. KRATHWOHL, BENJAMIN S. BLOOM, AND BERTRAM B. MASIA

Affective Domain

David R. Krathwohl, in collaboration with Benjamin S. Bloom and Bertram B. Masia, developed a classification scheme for educational objectives in the affective (emotional) domain. In the following selection from *Taxonomy of Educational Objectives, Handbook II: Affective Domain* (David McKay, 1964), which presents a section from the book's very important fourth chapter, Krathwohl, Bloom, and Masia discuss the relationships between the cognitive and the affective domains of human behavior and how these interrelationships impact on the task of preparing or evaluating affective behavior. The authors emphasize that the cognitive and affective domains are linked, not autonomous (independent) dimensions of behavior.

Krathwohl, currently a professor emeritus at Syracuse University in Syracuse, New York, was teaching at Michigan State University when *Taxonomy of Educational Objectives, Handbook II* was published. Bloom and Masia both held academic appointments at the University of Chicago at that time.

Key Concept: affective educational objectives

Internalization as It Appears in the Taxonomy Structure

The process of internalization can be described by summarizing the continuum at successive levels as they appear in the *Affective Domain Taxonomy*. The process begins when the attention of the student is captured by some phenomenon, characteristic, or value. As he pays attention to the phenomenon, characteristic, or value, he differentiates it from the others present in the perceptual field. With differentiation comes a seeking out of the phenomenon as he gradually attaches emotional significance to it and comes to value it. As the process unfolds he relates this phenomenon to other phenomena to which he responds that also have value. This responding is sufficiently frequent so that he comes to react regularly, almost automatically, to it and to other things like it. Finally the values are interrelated in a structure or view of the world, which he brings as a "set" to new problems.

Even from this abstract description it can be seen that the internalization process represents a continuous modification of behavior from the individual's being aware of a phenomenon to a pervasive outlook on life that influences all his actions.

While this description of the process seemed reasonably satisfactory, if a hierarchical structure was to be provided and more adequate description of the process developed, it was clear that the continuum needed to be divided into steps or stages. In so far as possible, when this was done, the breaking points between steps were located where there appeared to be some kind of transition, such as the addition of a new component or kind of activity. Since the boundaries of the categories are completely arbitrary and can be defended only on pragmatic grounds, it is possible that later work may suggest that other breaking points would be more satisfactory. The divisions between major categories have proved quite useful in the analysis of objectives. We feel more sure of the major divisions than of the subcategories, some of which appear to be easier to delineate than others.

The steps in the process and their description... are reviewed here to acquaint the reader with them and to show the parallel between the description of internalization which has been developed and the steps and levels into which it has been arbitrarily divided.

We begin with the individuals being aware of the stimuli which initiate the affective behavior and which form the context in which the affective behavior occurs. Thus, the lowest category is 1.0 *Receiving*. It is subdivided into three categories. At the 1.1 *Awareness* level, the individual merely has his attention attracted to the stimuli (e.g., he develops some consciousness of the use of shading to portray depth and lighting in a picture).[1] The second subcategory, 1.2 *Willingness to receive*, describes the state in which he has differentiated the stimuli from others and is willing to give it his attention (e.g., he develops a tolerance for bizarre uses of shading in modern art). At 1.3 *Controlled or selected attention* the student looks for the stimuli (e.g., he is on the alert for instances where shading has been used both to create a sense of three-dimensional depth and to indicate the lighting of the picture; or he looks for picturesque words in reading).

At the next level, 2.0 *Responding*, the individual is perceived as responding regularly to the affective stimuli. At the lowest level of responding, 2.1 *Acquiescence in responding*, he is merely complying with expectations (e.g., at the request of his teacher, he hangs reproductions of famous paintings in his dormitory room; he is obedient to traffic rules). At the next higher level, 2.2 *Willingness to respond*, he responds increasingly to an inner compulsion (e.g., voluntarily looks for instances of good art where shading, perspective, color, and design have been well used, or has an interest in social problems broader than those of the local community). At 2.3 *Satisfaction in response* he responds emotionally as well (e.g., works with clay, especially in making pottery for personal pleasure). Up to this point he has differentiated the affective stimuli; he has begun to seek them out and to attach emotional significance and value to them.

As the process unfolds, the next levels of 3.0 *Valuing* describe increasing internalization, as the person's behavior is sufficiently consistent that he comes to hold a value: 3.1 *Acceptance of a value* (e.g., continuing desire to develop the ability to write effectively and hold it more strongly), 3.2 *Preference for a value* (e.g., seeks out examples of good art for enjoyment of them to the level where he behaves so as to further this impression actively), and 3.3 *Commitment* (e.g., faith in the power of reason and the method of experimentation).

As the learner successively internalizes values he encounters situations for which more than one value is relevant. This necessitates organizing the values into a system, 4.0 *Organization.* And since a prerequisite to interrelating values is their conceptualization in a form which permits organization, this level is divided in two: 4.1 *Conceptualization of a value* (e.g., desires to evaluate works of art which are appreciated, or to find out and crystallize the basic assumptions which underlie codes of ethics) and 4.2 *Organization of a value system* (e.g., acceptance of the place of art in one's life as one of dominant value, or weighs alternative social policies and practices against the standards of public welfare).

Finally, the internalization and the organization processes reach a point where the individual responds very consistently to value-laden situations with an interrelated set of values, a structure, a view of the world. The *Taxonomy* category that describes this behavior is 5.0 *Characterization by a value or value complex,* and it includes the categories 5.1 *Generalized set* (e.g., views all problems in terms of their aesthetic aspects, or readiness to revise judgments and to change behavior in the light of evidence) and 5.2 *Characterization* (e.g., develops a consistent philosophy of life).

Stripped of their definitions, the category and subcategory titles appear in sequence as follows:

    1.0 Receiving (attending)
        1.1 Awareness
        1.2 Willingness to receive
        1.3 Controlled or selected attention
    2.0 Responding
        2.1 Acquiescence in responding
        2.2 Willingness to respond
        2.3 Satisfaction in response
    3.0 Valuing
        3.1 Acceptance of a value
        3.2 Preference for a value
        3.3 Commitment (conviction)
    4.0 Organization
        4.1 Conceptualization of a value
        4.2 Organization of a value system
    5.0 Characterization by a value or value complex
        5.1 Generalized set
        5.2 Characterization

Relation of the Affective-Domain Structure to Common Affective Terms

. . . [T]he analysis of such commonly used terms as interest, attitude, appreciation, and value showed each of them to have a wide range of meanings. When we examined the range of meanings for any one term and compared this range to the *Taxonomy* structure we found that each term generally took on meanings over a section of the internalization continuum. Figure 1 illustrates this.

Thus, objectives were found where interpretation of the term "interest" ranged all the way from the student's being aware that a phenomenon exists to

FIGURE 1

*The Range of Meaning Typical of Commonly Used Affective Terms
Measured Against the Taxonomy Continuum*

*David R.
Krathwohl et al.*

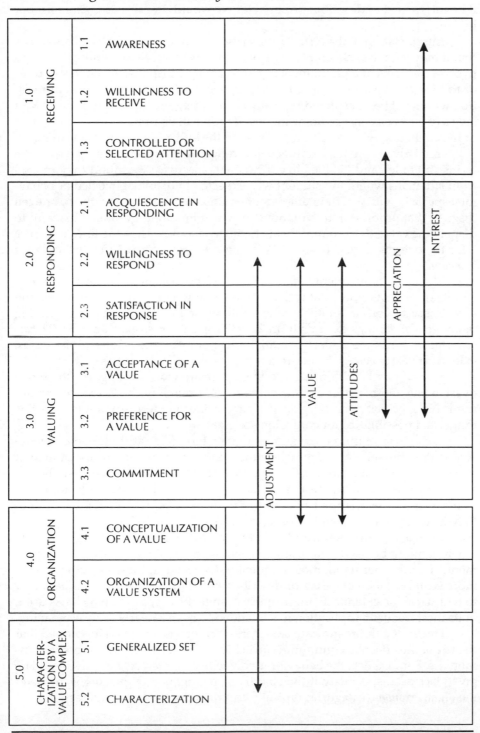

the behavior of avidly seeking a phenomenon. This is shown in Figure 1 by the line marked "Interest" extending from the *Taxonomy* category of 1.1 *Awareness* to 3.2 *Preference for a value.* Apparently the term "interest" typically describes behavior that would be classified at the lower levels of the *Taxonomy.* Rarely would it be interpreted as describing a behavior we would describe as *Commitment* or higher.

Interpretation of the term "appreciation" as it appears in objectives shows that it may refer to such simple behavior as the person's being willing to attend to certain aspects of a phenomenon, to his feeling a response to some stimulus, or to his showing a preference for certain behavior or stimuli. Thus, appreciation would not be interpreted typically as including the behaviors at the lowest levels of the *Taxonomy* nor at the highest. The line in Figure 1 shows the segment of the continuum which appears to include the bulk of its range of meanings.[2]

Similarly when we examined the range of interpretations given to the terms "attitude" and "value" in educational objectives, we found they ranged from situations where the student was expected to display a particular behavior, especially with a certain amount of emotion (enthusiasm, warmth, or even disgust, if appropriate), to situations in which he might go out of his way to display the value or to communicate to others about it. Thus the lines in Figure 1 for these terms extend from 2.2 *Willingness to respond* to 4.1 *Conceptualization of a value.*

The term "adjustment" appeared to take on a range of meanings, from a simple display of appropriate behavior in social interaction to the interrelation of one aspect of self to another—one's outlook on life. Thus, the line indicating its range of meanings extends from 2.2 *Willingness to respond* through 5.2 *Characterization.* It has the widest potential range of meanings of any of the terms, extending nearly across the entire range of taxonomic categories.

Several points with respect to this figure are worth noting. All the terms overlap one another in meaning in the middle range of the *Taxonomy* continuum. No specificity can be gained by replacing one term by another in this range, and possibilities for confusion are great.

A corollary of this observation is that no term (e.g., attitude) uniquely describes its entire segment of the continuum. Every term is overlapped by at least one other term for a major portion of that part of the continuum it describes.

Only the terms "interest" and "adjustment," at the lower and upper extremes, are not overlapped by another term for a portion of the continuum they include. In the objectives we have analyzed, "interest" appears to be used more often to describe behavior toward the middle range of the continuum than where it might be used with unique meaning, at the lowest extreme. "Adjustment," on the other hand, most frequently does refer in these objectives to the more complex kinds of behavior described in the upper levels of the *Taxonomy* to which it alone extends. In this respect, despite the range over which it is used, in its most frequent application it is intended to have a nearly unique meaning.

Finally, the figure indicates the increase in precision which it is hoped that the use of the affective continuum can achieve if its terms replace those in common use. For instance, the behavior involved in an "interest" objective could be given increased specificity if the objective were defined by placing it in one of the eight *Taxonomy* categories typically embraced by the term "interest." . . .

THE RELATION OF THE AFFECTIVE TO THE COGNITIVE DOMAIN

There has been much research on and logical analysis of the relation of cognitive to affective behavior, particularly the attainment of affective goals by cognitive means. We hope that the development of the *Affective Domain Taxonomy* will stimulate further research and thought on the relation between it and the cognitive domain....

The Fundamental Unity of the Organism

The fact that we attempt to analyze the affective area separately from the cognitive is not intended to suggest that there is a fundamental separation. There is none. As Scheerer puts it, "... behavior may be conceptualized as being embedded in a cognitive-emotional-motivational matrix in which no true separation is possible. No matter how we slice behavior, the ingredients of motivation-emotion-cognition are present in one order or another" (Scheerer, 1954, p. 123)....

Thus James, a forerunner of modern psychology, admits a fundamental unity of affective and cognitive behavior but proceeds to a fragmenting analysis showing how one is involved in the other. That this kind of reasoning continues is indicated by Rokeach, a contemporary psychologist who, also realizing the unity, shows how the one domain is involved in the other. This is what we, too, have done in developing the *Taxonomy*. Our problem has been (recognizing the arbitrariness of our conceptualization) to gain a perspective of our task essential to the formulating of a useful framework.

The Arbitrariness of Classification Schemes

Every classification scheme is an abstraction which arbitrarily makes divisions among phenomena solely for the convenience of the user, more particularly to emphasize some special characteristic of the phenomena of importance to the user. Some of these divisions seem "natural," since they correspond to differences which are readily perceived in the phenomena categorized. In other instances, the differences may be much more difficult to perceive and thus seem more arbitrary. One may find both "natural" and quite arbitrary classifications within the same framework, depending upon the nature of the phenomenon to be classified and what is important to the person using the framework. To the biochemist, the dichotomy between the physical and the biological sciences is extremely arbitrary, and there is nothing "natural" about it, though this division may be highly useful and "natural" to the administrators of a large university.

The arbitrariness of the *Taxonomy* structure is at once apparent in, among other things,[3] its division of the realm of educational goals into three domains: cognitive, affective, and psychomotor. These seem to be "natural" divisions, since teachers and educators have more or less traditionally divided their objectives into these categories, either explicitly or implicitly. It is hoped that the divisions within each of the domains will also seem "natural," once the reader is familiar with them. We have tried to make the breaks between categories at what appeared to be the "natural" places without attempting to force a correspondence between domains. Whether this permits the most useful and meaningful analysis remains for the user to judge.... The increasing use of the *Taxonomy's* already published portion encourages us to believe that this kind of analysis has proved useful and meaningful and that this second portion may prove to be of worth as well.

With full recognition of the arbitrariness of the *Taxonomy's* division between cognitive and affective behavior, we may find it helpful to examine the way teachers' statements of objectives split cognitive from affective behavior, and then how the cognitive domain is related to the affective in terms of the particular categories used in this taxonomic analysis.

The Affective Component of Cognitive Objectives

The "garden variety" of objectives concentrates on specifying behavior in only one domain at a time. No doubt this results from the customarily analytic approaches to building curricula. Only occasionally do we find a statement like "The student should learn to analyze a good argument with pleasure." Such a statement suggests not only the cognitive behavior but also the affective aspect that accompanies it. In spite of the lack of explicit formulation, however, nearly all cognitive objectives have an affective component if we search for it. Most instructors hope that their students will develop a continuing interest in the subject matter taught. They hope that their students will have learned certain attitudes toward the phenomena dealt with or toward the way in which problems are approached. But they leave these goals unspecified. This means that many of the objectives which are classified in the cognitive domain have an implicit but unspecified affective component that could be concurrently classified in the affective domain. Where such an attitude or interest objective refers, as it most often does, to the content of the course as a whole or at least to a sizable segment of it, it may be most convenient to specify it as a separate objective. Many such affective objectives—the interest objective, for example—become the affective components of all or most of the cognitive objectives in the course. The affective domain is useful in emphasizing the fact that affective components exist and in analyzing their nature. Perhaps by its very existence it will encourage greater development of affective components of cognitive objectives.

It is possible that a different affective objective accompanies every cognitive objective in a course.[4] Were this a common situation, the present form of the *Taxonomy* would be unwieldy, for it would require a dual categorization of each objective. While the present state of the art of curriculum development suggests that the latter concern is by no means immediate, this is not a possibility to be discarded.

The relation of cognitive to affective objectives as conceived by teachers is mirrored in the relations of the taxonomies of the two domains. We turn next to this matter.

When one looks for relations between the subcategories of the two domains one finds that they clearly overlap. This overlap is implicit in [Table 1, which presents] descriptions of roughly parallel steps in the two continua. The terms set in italic are used as heads of divisions in the *Taxonomy* of the cognitive or affective domains. Their category numbers are given in parentheses.

David R.
Krathwohl et al.

TABLE 1

1. The cognitive continuum begins with the student's recall and recognition of *Knowledge* (1.0),	1. The affective continuum begins with the student's merely *Receiving* (1.0) stimuli and passively attending to it. It extends through his more actively attending to it,
2. it extends through his *Comprehension* (2.0) of the knowledge,	2. his *Responding* (2.0) to stimuli on request, willingly responding to these stimuli, and taking satisfaction in this responding,
3. his skill *Application* (3.0) of the knowledge that he comprehends,	3. his *Valuing* (3.0) the phenomenon or activity so that he voluntarily responds and seeks out ways to respond,
4. His skill in *Analysis* (4.0) of situations involving this knowledge, his skill in *Synthesis* (5.0) of this knowledge into new organizations,	4. his *Conceptualization* (4.1) of each value responded to,
5. his skill in *Evaluation* (6.0) in that area of knowledge to judge the value of material and methods for given purposes.	5. his *Organization* (4.2) of these values into systems and finally organizing the value complex into a single whole, a *Characterization* (5.0) of the individual.

The most apparent places at which the affective domain meets the cognitive domain in this description are at steps 1, 4, and 5. Setting the two domains parallel, as we have done to facilitate the examination of the relationship, suggests a much closer level-to-level correspondence than actually exists, however. Let us examine this correspondence, taking steps 1, 4, and 5, and 2 and 3 in that order.

STEP 1.   The first point of close parallelism between the domains is at step 1, where "receiving" a phenomenon, or attending to it to some extent, corresponds to having "knowledge" of the phenomenon. But the emphasis in 1.0

Receiving is different from that in 1.0 *Knowledge* in that we are less concerned with memory and retrieval on demand. There is a relation, however, for certainly attending to a phenomenon is prerequisite to knowing about it. Further, only as one is willing to attend to a phenomenon will he learn about it.

On first glance, one might assume that "receiving" would always refer to awareness of certain information, and thus its parallel in the cognitive domain would always be the *Knowledge* category (e.g., the simple awareness of the way perspective is portrayed in a painting). While frequently true, this is not necessarily the case. Thus, *Receiving* includes the objective "Listens to music with some discrimination as to its mood and meaning and with some recognition of the contributions of various musical elements and instruments to the total effect." This certainly involves 2.0 *Comprehension*, the second category of the cognitive continuum, and probably 3.0 *Application* and 4.0 *Analysis*, the third and fourth levels of it. On looking over the objectives in the lowest levels of the affective domain, however, this is about as high a level in the cognitive continuum as one finds implied by the cognitive concomitants of these affective objectives.

But whatever the behavior specified in the lowest level in the affective domain, it is almost a certainty that one could interpret the objective so that, except for the fact that it is a building stone for more complex affective objectives, the objective might be restated so as to be classified in the cognitive domain. Some of our critics have argued that we should have begun the affective domain with 2.0 *Responding*, because of the heavily cognitive nature of this bottom category. But the fact that this behavior is a necessary first step to building objectives higher in the affective-domain hierarchy is the reason—an important one—for its being included as the bottom rung in the affective domain. Further, the emphasis in "receiving" is different from that of "knowledge," stressing, as is proper for an affective category, the volitional aspects of the knowing act.

STEPS 4 AND 5.   A second point of apparent close contact between the affective and cognitive domains is the correspondence in the upper levels of the two continua at steps 4 and 5. Here the behavior described by the affective domain is at least in part cognitive, as the student conceptualizes a value to which he has been responding, and this value is in turn integrated and organized into a system of values which comes eventually to characterize the individual. Such objectives would appear to require, at the very least, the ability to 2.0 *Comprehend*, for the student must translate his behavior into a set of verbal terms describing the value involved. In some instances this might call for the student to 4.0 *Analyze* the common value element from a series of activities or situations in which he has been involved and to 5.0 *Synthesize* this commonality into a value which encompasses all of them. The ability to organize and interrelate values into systems must certainly call for the ability to 4.0 *Analyze*, as it is described in the cognitive domain, and the development of new value complexes also most likely involves the ability to 5.0 *Synthesize*. Further, the ability to balance values against one another, which is implied by the very highest affective categories, implies capability for 6.0 *Evaluation* as it is defined in the cognitive domain. For example, "Judges problems and issues in terms of situations, issues, purposes, and consequences involved rather than in terms of fixed, dogmatic precepts or emotionally wishful thinking" (Part II, p. 184).

It is possible, however, that in everyday behavior much of this balancing of values is at a semiconscious intuitive level rather than at the rational, objective, conscious, level implied by 6.0 *Evaluation* in the cognitive domain. Such semiconscious behavior is described in the affective domain by category 5.1 *Generalized Set*, where the behavior is so internalized that it is displayed almost automatically, without conscious consideration. On the surface, this makes the affective domain appear to extend further than the cognitive in the sense that it describes a behavior so deeply internalized that it is automatic. No such behavior appears in the cognitive continuum.

But one could argue that some cognitive evaluation behavior ought also to be that well learned. Indeed, one may question whether such regularity of behavior is not implicit in most cognitive and affective objects at all *Taxonomy* levels. In general, in both the cognitive and affective domains the regularity of behavior is measured, not in terms of the *Taxonomy* level of behavior, but as such regularity affects the test score. Given a test which includes a variety of situations in which the observed behavior should be displayed if learned or internalized, the regularity with which it is displayed across these situations is reflected in the person's score. At the top level of the affective domain we happen to have specified a level of behavior which is so well learned, so deeply internalized, that it is automatic.

In this sense, at the 5.1 *Generalized Set* level we have described a kind of behavior which can be attained only with complete regularity, and the level of performance required in scoring is implicit in the behavior description. (This is the only category in the *Taxonomy* which so specifies the score performance for achievement of that level.) It was included because affective objectives were found which described this regularity of the behavior. Certain affective objectives have made explicit a complete regularity and automaticity of response which may also be implied in many cognitive objectives. Thus a discrepancy wherein the affective domain appears to extend beyond the cognitive domain can be reconciled on careful examination. The overlap between the two domains at this level appears to be real.

STEPS 2 AND 3. In the middle portions of the affective continuum the individual begins to respond to the stimuli, at first on request (2.1 *Acquiescence in responding*), then increasingly on his own volition to the point where he is actively seeking instances in which he may respond (3.3 *Commitment*). These are not unrelated to the cognitive domain, but the nature of the relation is much less easily specified. The range of cognitive behavior corresponding to this portion of the affective continuum appears to cover a wide portion of the cognitive domain. But in all the affective behavior the cognitive element is present and implied. For example, in the lowest level of this portion, in the subcategory 2.1 *Acquiescence in responding*, we find the objective "Willingness to comply with health regulations." This objective implies that at least there is comprehension of these regulations and the ability to apply them to new situations; both of these are cognitive behaviors. At the highest level of this middle range of the continuum, in the subcategory 3.3 *Commitment*, we find the objective "Devotion to those ideas and ideals which are the foundation of democracy." This objective in turn implies cognitive behaviors such as the ability to analyze situations in order to determine how the ideas and ideals apply in a given situation.

It can be noted that throughout this analysis of the five steps there is some tendency for the cognitive counterpart of a low-level objective to come from the lower levels of the affective continuum and for objectives at the upper level of the affective continuum to have upper-level cognitive counterparts.

From the analysis above it appears that at all levels of the affective domain, affective objectives have a cognitive component, and one can find affective components for cognitive objectives. But lest this relationship appear more obvious than it really is, it should be noted that the examples of objectives in the preceding discussion were chosen so as to make the relation clear. We could have chosen affective-domain objectives for which the cognitive component is much more obscure; for instance, "Enjoyment of worship" or "Responds emotionally to a work of art." While we could recognize a cognitive component in such objectives, we should clearly be less certain to secure agreement among educators about the most appropriate cognitive behavior to accompany the affective behavior. Though undoubtedly there is some cognitive component in every affective objective, its nature is much more easily seen in some instances than in others.

Other Relationships Between the Cognitive and Affective Domains...

Cognitive Objectives as Means to Affective Goals.   The fact that our learning research and theories focus largely on cognitive behavior is an indication that we feel we know better how to handle the cognitive domain. Moving from the cognitive domain to the affective thus tends to be the preferred orientation. Attitudes, and even feelings, for example, tend to be defined in cognitive terms. James, in the quotation cited earlier in this chapter, defined feeling as a kind of knowing. Asch (1952) stated that an "attitude contains a more or less coherent ordering of data... an organization of experience and data with reference to an object" (p. 580). Rhine (1958) surveyed the definitions of attitudes by outstanding psychologists and concluded that the common element is the essence of what is generally meant by a concept. He therefore defined an attitude as a concept with an evaluative component and proceeded to explain attitude formation in the cognitive terms usually reserved for concept formation. As he pointed out, this approach could make attitudes more amenable to laboratory scrutiny, one indication of why this approach to the affective domain is preferred.

Rokeach, as already noted, saw a basic congruence between the cognitive and affective systems. He stated further, "... although our approach to belief systems, including esthetic ones, is a purely cognitive one... if the assumption is correct that every emotion has its cognitive counterpart, then we should be able to reach down into the complexities of man's emotional life via a study of his cognitive processes.... If we know something about the way a person relates himself to the world of ideas we may also be able to say in what way he relates himself to the world of people and to authority" (Rokeach, 1960, p. 8).

Similarly, Rosenberg (1956) examined attitudes in terms of cognitive structure. Noting the relations between cognitive and affective components, he argued that a tendency to respond to an object with positive or negative affect is "accompanied by a cognitive structure made up of beliefs about the potentialities of that object for attaining or blocking the realization of valued states" (p. 367). He further argued that both the direction of the affect—whether it is positive or negative with reference to the object—and the strength of the affect are correlated with the content of the associated cognitive structure. Here again we see the affective component made a function of cognitive components which are more easily dealt with, thus permitting manipulation of the affective by the cognitive.

Festinger (1957) and Heider (1958), among others, have propounded so-called "balance theories" which provide another approach to the study of affective changes as a result of cognitive behavior. Festinger, in his theory of cognitive dissonance, described the motivating effect of disharmonious or dissonant states in cognition. He defined cognition so broadly as to include affectively tinged states such as opinions and beliefs as well as cognitive states of knowledge. Thus his theory easily bridges the cognitive-affective distinction and cannot be seen as one which manipulates cognitive behavior (in its usual sense) alone. But Festinger did describe the effects of changes in knowledge on affective behavior, and this represents one kind of approach to affective behavior through cognition.

The careful observer of the classroom can see that the wise teacher as well as the psychological theorist uses cognitive behavior and the achievement of cognitive goals to attain affective goals. In many instances she does so more intuitively than consciously. In fact, a large part of what we call "good teaching" is the teachers' ability to attain affective objectives through challenging the students' fixed beliefs and getting them to discuss issues.

In some instances teachers use cognitive behavior not just as a means to affective behavior but as a kind of prerequisite. Thus appreciation objectives are often approached cognitively by having the student analyze a work of art so that he will come to understand the way in which certain effects are produced —the nuances of shading to produce depth, color to produce emotional tone, etc. Such analysis on a cognitive level, when mastered, may be seen as learning necessary for "truly" appreciating a work of art.

In other instances teachers use cognitive behavior and cognitive goals as a means to multiple affective ends. This occurs especially in areas where the problem of indoctrination arises. Cognitive behavior may be used to indoctrinate points of view and to build attitudes and values. Indeed, we do this shamelessly in the aesthetic fields, where we want our students to learn to recognize "good" poetry, painting, architecture, sculpture, music, and so on. But in most areas of the curriculum we have a horror of indoctrinating the student with any but our most basic core values (we cannot always agree on the nature of these core values, the court cases on religion in the schools are an example). In most instances where indoctrination is avoided, we seek to have the student take his own position with respect to the issue. Thus a discussion may result in the development of a variety of "correct" positions and attitudes with respect to the area of concern, rather than in a single type of behavioral outcome as when a cognitive objective has been achieved. This also occurs where there are conflicts in values within our own culture. For example, the problems of honesty vs. dishonesty vs. "white lies," or of competition vs. cooperation, usually result in a variety of acceptable solutions, each a function of the situation in which such a conflict arises.

There are some instances where the cognitive route to affective achievement has resulted in learning just the opposite of that intended. Thus the infamous example of the careful and detailed study of "good" English classics, which was intended to imbue us with a love of deathless prose, has in many instances alienated us from it instead. Emphasis on very high mastery of one domain may in some instances be gained at the expense of the other.

Similarly, ... emphasis on one domain may tend to drive out the other. New courses often start with a careful analysis of both cognitive and affective objectives. But we feel more comfortable in teaching for cognitive than for affective objectives. Our drive for subject-matter mastery and the ever-increasing amount of knowledge available gives us more and more subject matter to cover. Further, our preference for approaching affective achievement through the attainment of cognitive objectives tends to focus attention on these cognitive goals as ends in themselves without our determining whether they are actually serving as means to an affective end. Over time the emphasis in most courses tends more and more to concentrate on the cognitive objectives at the expense of the affective ones. This erosion may be inevitable, but it could be lessened or stopped if we were conscious of its action. One of the major uses of *Handbook I: Cognitive Domain* has been to provide a basis for showing the current overwhelming emphasis on knowledge objectives at the expense of the development of skills and abilities in using that knowledge. Similarly, the development of *Handbook II: Affective Domain* should help to highlight the current emphasis on cognitive objectives at the expense of the affective.

Affective Objectives as Means to Cognitive Goals. From the previous discussion it seems clear that the cognitive approach to affective objectives is a frequently traveled route. What about the reverse? One of the main kinds of affective-domain objectives which are sought as means to cognitive ends is the development of interest or motivation. As viewed from the cognitive pole, the student may be treated as an analytic machine, a "computer" that solves problems. In contrast, viewed from the affective pole, we take greater cognizance of the motivation, drives, and emotions that are the factors bringing about achievement of cognitive behavior.

Obviously motivation is critical to learning and thus is one of the major ways in which the affective domain is used as a means to the cognitive. The large number of interest objectives indicates the importance of this aspect of the learning situation. The influence of hedonic tone on memory and learning is also important: children are more likely to learn and remember material for which they have a positive feeling. Note for instance the prevalence of girls who dislike mathematics and so cannot learn it, as well as boys who dislike school in general and do poorly. Though these "likes" may be produced by role expectancies, it is the internalized preferences which produce the effect.

Where educational objectives are involved we are almost always concerned with positive affect, with leading rather than driving the student into learning. But there are some school situations where negative affect is used to prevent certain behaviors from occurring and to facilitate cognitive learning. Such is the use of negative affect (fear of punishment, for instance) rather than the attempt to attain affective objectives as means to cognitive ends. In some instances social pressure may be exerted to change a student's position or viewpoint. We recognized that occasionally the school will have affective goals of this kind when we provided category 2.1 *Acquiescence in responding* but noted that this was a rarely used category.

Both the theoretical and experimental literature suggest that this is not an easy route to cognitive change. Both Kelman's (1958) model and Jahoda (1956) point to the likelihood that persons may outwardly comply under such situations but inwardly remain unchanged. Festinger's (1957) theory of cognitive dissonance posits that severe external threat or pressure represents a justification to the individual for engaging in behavior contrary to his beliefs, so that there is less need to reduce the dissonance caused by his engaging in this behavior under the threat conditions. Where the threat is mild, there is less justification for engaging in the behavior, and we can thus expect more change in private opinion to reduce the dissonance. Experimentation by Festinger and Carlsmith (1959) backs up this theoretical prediction. It appears that certain threatening school climates could actually defeat teachers' attempts to bring about both cognitive and affective learning.

But, as already noted, more often our motivation results from positive affect. Increasingly this is taking the form of building upon the method of self-discovery as a means of fostering interest in learning material. In thus enhancing curiosity and exploratory activity we may be building upon a basic drive. White (1959), giving careful consideration to previous literature on motivation and to recent experimentation on curiosity and the attractiveness of novel stimuli, posits a drive for competency, a need for a feeling of efficacy. He suggests that curiosity, exploratory behavior, manipulation, and general activity bring man in contact with his environment and make him more competent to deal with it. White's competency drive underlies these and similar activities. Few of us have recognized that with discovery-type objectives we may have been building on a basic drive.

Discovery-type material, such as that going into the University of Illinois School Mathematics Program, uses the affective effects of self-discovery as a means of simultaneously achieving the goals of mastery of the material and developing interest in it. This corresponds to what Bruner (1960) points to as an important goal in our new curricula. He suggests that we must increase "the inherent interest of the materials taught, giving the student a sense of discovery, translating what we say into thought forms appropriate to the child and so on. What this amounts to is developing in the child an interest in what he is learning and with it an appropriate set of attitudes and values about intellectual activities in general" (p. 73). This suggestion, that we build in a set of attitudes toward learning and the value of learning, represents another of the all-encompassing goals of most curricula. It is another common way in which attainment of the affective goal is a means to the facilitation of cognitive learning.

Simultaneous Achievement of Cognitive and Affective Goals. In some instances it is impossible to tell whether the affective goal is being used as a means to a cognitive goal or vice versa. It is a chicken and egg proposition. Perhaps it is fairest to say they are both being sought simultaneously....

In some instances the joint seeking of affective and cognitive goals results in curricula which use one domain as the means to the other on a closely-knit alternating basis. Thus a cognitive skill is built and then used in rewarding situations so that affective interest in the task is built up to permit the next cognitive task to be achieved, and so on. Perhaps it is analogous to a man scaling a wall using two step ladders side by side, each with rungs too wide apart to be conveniently reached in a single step. One ladder represents the cognitive behaviors and objectives, the other the affective. The ladders are so constructed that the rungs of one ladder fall between the rungs of the other. The attainment of some complex goal is made possible by alternately climbing a rung on one ladder, which brings the next rung of the other ladder within reach. Thus alternating between affective and cognitive domains, one may seek a cognitive goal using the attainment of a cognitive goal to raise interest (an affective goal). This permits achievement of a higher cognitive goal, and so on....

Summary

This really only scratches the surface of what is undoubtedly a very complex relationship between the cognitive and affective domains. We still have much to learn about it. But the fact should be clear that the two domains are tightly intertwined. Each affective behavior has a cognitive-behavior counterpart of some kind and vice versa. An objective in one domain has a counterpart in the opposite domain, though often we do not take cognizance of it. There is some correlation between the *Taxonomy* levels of an affective objective and its cognitive counterpart. Each domain is sometimes used as a means to the other, though the more common route is from the cognitive to the affective. Theory statements exist which permit us to express one in terms of the other and vice versa.

Our split between the affective and cognitive domains is for analytical purposes and is quite arbitrary. Hopefully the analysis of the two domains will have heuristic value so that we may better understand the nature of each as well as the relationship of one to the other.

NOTES

1. This same objective is successively modified to carry it through many of the levels of the continuum.
2. Appreciation is sometimes interpreted to mean that the student can describe that aspect of a phenomenon (e.g., a dance) that he appreciates. In this respect the line should extend to 4.1 *Conceptualization of a value.* Yet, rarely does an appreciation objective connote a commitment to a value.

3. We could, for example, cite as arbitrary the insistence that educational goals are most meaningfully stated as student behaviors rather than teacher activities. But this aspect is less relevant to the chapter topic.

4. This is not to imply that the full range from 1.1 to 5.2 of affective behaviors would apply to every cognitive objective, however. This matter is explored further in the next section.

*David R.
Krathwohl et al.*

CHAPTER 12 The Cognitive Revolution in Learning

12.1 ANN L. BROWN ET AL.

Learning, Remembering, and Understanding

The selection that follows explores two foundational concepts in the cognitivist tradition in the psychology of learning and human development: metacognition and self-regulation. Metacognition deals with how we acquire strategies for learning, remembering, understanding, and problem solving. The concept of self-regulation is important in understanding how we learn to master strategies for achieving "executive" (self) control over those cognitive processes whereby we learn how to apply old and newly acquired knowledge to the problems that we encounter in life.

The following selection is an excerpt from chapter 2, "Learning, Remembering, and Understanding," of Paul H. Mussen, ed., *Handbook of Child Psychology, vol. 3: Cognitive Development,* 4th ed. (John Wiley, 1983). The chapter represents the efforts of Ann L. Brown and her colleagues to summarize the development of research on human learning, remembering, and understanding that had taken place since the 1960s. This source has had a very extensive impact on thought regarding human learning from a cognitive perspective. The authors of this selection are prominent cognitive researchers. The senior author, Brown, developed her ideas and understandings of metacognition so that she could inquire into how students can learn to become consciously aware of learning strategies they can use and practice to meet the challenges of school learning and to remember and use what they learn.

Brown grew up in England and studied psychology at the University of London. Although she was schooled in the behaviorist tradition, she began to study the cognitive approach to the psychology of learning and human development after moving to the United States in 1968. She did research on the teaching of reading and developed her pioneering insight into the concept of metacognition. She currently teaches and performs research on student learning in schools at the University of California, Berkeley. She has also held teaching positions at the University of Sussex in England and at the University of Illinois, and in 1994 she gave the Presidential Address before the annual meeting of the American Education Research Association (AERA).

Key Concept: metacognition and self-regulation

A TETRAHEDRAL FRAMEWORK FOR EXPLORING PROBLEMS OF LEARNING

The majority of developmental memory research conducted in the late 1960s and throughout the 1970s led to the establishment of a fairly detailed picture of how the child becomes a school expert, that is, how the young learner acquires academic skills and comes to know how to learn deliberately. To illustrate the current state of our knowledge, we would like to introduce the diagram in Figure 1. At first glance this seems like a simple model, particularly in comparison with the elaborate flow diagrams favored by modern cognitive psychologists, who were imprinted on the computer in their formative years. Unfortunately, as is often the case in psychology, the simple model becomes more complex on closer examination. It does, however, provide a useful aid to help us remember the major factors that should be taken into account when considering any aspect of learning. We would like to stress that not only should we, the psychologists, consider the tetrahedral nature of the learning process but also that this is exactly what expert learners come to consider when they design their own plans for learning (Flavell & Wellman, 1977; also see *Metacognition, Executive Control . . .*).

There are a minimum of four factors that comprise the learner-in-context, and these factors interact in nontrivial ways. The four factors are: (1) the learner's activity, (2) the characteristics of the learner, (3) the nature of the materials to be learned, and (4) the criterial task. Because of the sheer weight of empirical evidence, we will give only a few illustrations of the types of factors that have been considered under each of these rubrics and then provide selected examples of the essentially interactive nature of the model.

Learning Activities

The activities that the learner engages in are a prime determinant of efficiency. Some systematic activities that learners use are referred to as strategies, although what is strategic and what is not has not been made particularly clear in the literature. . . .

Strategies are part of the knowledge base and, therefore, could be classified as a characteristic of the learner within the model. But the learner's activities are not necessarily synonymous with the strategies available in the knowledge base. Learners can access strategies or any other form of knowledge to help learning, but they need not. Having knowledge, of any kind, does not necessitate using it effectively. . . .

FIGURE 1

*An Organizational Framework for Exploring
Questions About Learning*

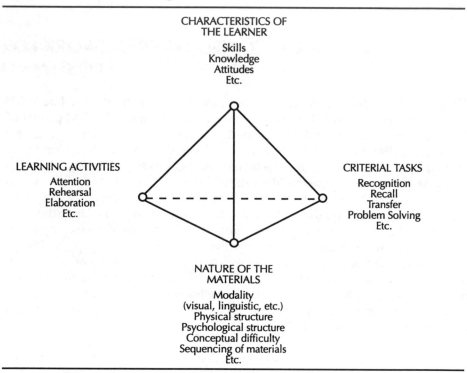

CHARACTERISTICS OF
THE LEARNER

Skills
Knowledge
Attitudes
Etc.

LEARNING ACTIVITIES

Attention
Rehearsal
Elaboration
Etc.

CRITERIAL TASKS

Recognition
Recall
Transfer
Problem Solving
Etc.

NATURE OF THE
MATERIALS

Modality
(visual, linguistic, etc.)
Physical structure
Psychological structure
Conceptual difficulty
Sequencing of materials
Etc.

Adapted from Jenkins, 1979, and Bransford, 1979.

One of the most established facts is the active strategic nature of a great deal of learning in older children. During the 1960s and 1970s, developmental psychologists provided a rich picture of the development of strategies for learning and remembering as well as quite convincing evidence that efficient performance in a wide variety of tasks is in large part dependent on the appropriate activities the subject engages in, either on his own volition when trained to do so or even when tricked into doing so by means of a cunning incidental orienting task. As children mature, they gradually acquire a basic repertoire of strategies, first as isolated task-dependent actions, but gradually these may evolve into flexible, and to some extent generalizable, skills. With extensive use, strategic intervention may become so dominant that it takes on many of the characteristics of automatic and unconscious processing (Shiffrin & Schneider, 1977). Under instructions to remember, the mature learner employs a variety of acquisition and retrieval strategies that are not readily available to the developmentally less mature individual....

METACOGNITION, EXECUTIVE CONTROL, SELF-REGULATION, AND OTHER EVEN MORE MYSTERIOUS MECHANISMS[1]

What Is Metacognition?

In this section, we will describe some of the historical roots and discuss the current status of the fashionable but complex concept of metacognition and other topics with which it shares a family resemblance. Various forms of metacognition have appeared in the literature and some of these instantiations are puzzling and mysterious. For example, Marshall and Morton (1978) refer to the mechanism that permits the detection and correction of errors in speech production as an EMMA—even more mysterious apparatus; it is a mechanism that could be an optional extra. We will argue that far from being an optional extra, the processes that have recently earned the title metacognitive are central to learning....

Knowledge about cognition refers to the relatively stable, statable, often fallible, and late-developing information that human thinkers have about their own cognitive processes and those of others (Flavell & Wellman, 1977). This form of knowledge is relatively *stable*. One would expect that knowledge of pertinent facts about a domain, for example, memory (that it is fallible, that it is severely limited for short-term verbatim retention, etc.), would be a permanent part of one's naive theory on the topic. This form of knowledge is often *statable*, in that one can reflect on the cognitive processes involved and discuss them with others. Of course, this form of knowledge is often *fallible*, in that the child (or adult for that matter) can perfectly well know certain facts about cognition that are not true. Naive psychology is not always empirically supportable. Finally, this type of knowledge is usually assumed to be *late developing*, in that it requires that learners step back and consider their own cognitive processes as objects of thought and reflection (Flavell & Wellman, 1977).

The second cluster of activities dubbed metacognitive in the developmental literature consists of those used to regulate and oversee learning. These processes include *planning* activities prior to undertaking a problem (predicting outcomes, scheduling strategies, various forms of vicarious trial and error, etc.), *monitoring* activities during learning (testing, revising, rescheduling one's strategies for learning), and *checking* outcomes (evaluating the outcome of any strategic actions against criteria of efficiency and effectiveness). It has been assumed that these activities are not necessarily statable, somewhat unstable, and relatively age independent, that is, task and situation dependent (Brown, 1978, 1980, in press-a).

Although knowledge and regulation of cognition are incestuously related, the two forms of activity have quite different roots and quite different attendant problems. The tension generated by the use of the same term, metacognition, for the two types of behavior is well illustrated by the fact that even the leading proponents in the field tend to answer questions about the nature of metacognition with, "It depends." Is metacognition late developing? It depends on the type of knowledge or process to which one refers. Is metacognition conscious? It depends....

Self-Regulation

Any active learning process involves continuous adjustments and fine tuning of action by means of self-regulating processes and "other even more mysterious" mechanisms (Marshall & Morton, 1978). Psychologists interested in mechanisms of growth and change have traditionally been concerned with such self-regulating processes. Of course, substantial contributions are made by external agents.... But even without external pressure, human thinkers "play" with thinking (Gardner, 1978), that is, subject their own thought processes to examination and treat their own thinking as an object of thought. Similarly, learners regulate and refine their own actions, sometimes in response to feedback concerning errors, but often in the absence of such feedback. Indeed, even if the system with which one is experimenting is adequate, active learners will improve upon their original production (Karmiloff-Smith, 1979a, 1979b).

Recently, the term metacognition has been extended to encompass such regulatory functions as error detection and correction (Brown & DeLoache, 1978; Clark, in press), but the historical roots of such concepts can be found in most of the major developmental theories....

Given space limitations, we will concentrate here primarily on relatively recent Genevan research on self-regulatory mechanisms in children's thinking and on the growing emphases in developmental psycholinguistics on error correction, systematization, and metalinguistic awareness.

PIAGET'S THEORY OF REGULATION.   In the latter part of his career, the transformational period (Riegel, 1975), Piaget became more and more interested in mechanisms of learning and the influence of both conscious and unconscious regulatory functions in promoting conceptual change. Again, owing to space restrictions, we cannot begin to describe the complex theory of Piaget's latter years.... Briefly (and probably too simplistically), Piaget distinguished between three primary types of self-regulation: autonomous, active, and conscious.

Autonomous regulation is an inherent part of any knowing act; learners continually regulate their performance, fine tuning and modulating actions, however small the learner and however simple the action (Bruner, 1973; Koslowski & Bruner, 1972). *Active regulation* is more akin to trial and error, where the learner is engaged in constructing and testing theories-in-action (Karmiloff-Smith & Inhelder, 1974/1975). Under the guidance of a powerful theory-in-action, the learner tests a current theory via concrete actions that produce tangible results. Not until a much later stage can the learner mentally construct and reflect upon the hypothetical situations that would confirm or refute a current theory without the need for active regulation. *Conscious regulation* involves the mental formulation of hypotheses capable of being tested via imaginary counterexamples or confirmatory evidence.

Consciousness first emerges as the child becomes capable of reflecting upon her own actions in the presence of the actual event. At this initial stage, consciousness is tied to concrete action but does not direct it. The child's "reactions remain elementary, the subject is likely to distort conceptualizations of what he observes, instead of recording it without modification." Such distortion can be quite dramatic. For example, having witnessed an event that is contrary to a tenaciously held belief, the "subject contests the unexpected evidence of his own eyes and thinks that he sees what he predicted would happen" (Piaget, 1976, p. 340).

At the most mature level, which Piaget would prefer to restrict to the stage of formal operations, the entire thinking process can be carried out on the mental plane. The learner can consciously invent, test, modify, and generalize theories and discuss these operations with others....

In brief, the developmental progression is from unconscious autonomous regulation to active regulation but in the absence of anything more than a "fleeting consciousness." The beginning of conscious reflection occurs when the child is capable of considering her actions and describing them to others, albeit sometimes erroneously. The mature level of reflected abstraction, however, is characterized by conscious processes that can be carried out exclusively on the mental plane. Mature learners can create imaginary worlds and theories to explain actions and reactions within them. Such theories can be confirmed or refuted by means of the further construction of mental tests, conflict trials, or thought experiments that extend the limits of generality of the theory. This is the essence of scientific reasoning and the end state for a Piagetian development progression of "child as scientist."...

METAPROCEDURAL REORGANIZATION AND SYSTEMATIZATION. Piaget's colleagues, Inhelder and Karmiloff-Smith, have introduced another concept relevant to this discussion of self-regulation, that of *metaprocedural reorganization* (Karmiloff-Smith, 1979a; Karmiloff-Smith & Inhelder, 1974/1975). The basic idea is that learning within a domain follows a predictable sequence that is characterized by internal pressure to systematize, consolidate, and generalize knowledge. The prototypical microgenetic sequence is that the child first works on developing an adequate partial theory for a salient aspect of the problem space; the partial theory is practiced and perfected until it is fully operational. Only when the partial theory is consolidated and functioning efficiently can the child step back and consider the system as a whole. Typically, the child will develop several juxtaposed theories adequate for various parts of the problem space, each theory operating in isolation from the other. Once the procedures are functioning well, the next stage of development is possible and the child "steps up" and reconsiders the problem-space metaprocedurally. Once children become aware of the discrepancies or contradictions resulting from the simultaneous existence of several different partial theories, they begin attempts to reconcile the differences and obviate contradictions resulting from the juxtaposition (Inhelder et al., 1974).

A concrete example might help to clarify this complicated theoretical notion. Karmiloff-Smith and Inhelder (1974/1975) asked 4- to 9-year-old children to balance rectangular wooden blocks on a narrow metal rod fixed to a larger piece of wood. Length blocks had their weight evenly distributed, and the correct solution was to balance the blocks at the geometric center. With weight blocks, the weight of each "side" varied either conspicuously (by gluing a large square block to one end of the base rectangular block) or inconspicuously (by inserting a hidden weight into a cavity on one end of the rectangular block).

At first, the children made the blocks balance by brute trial and error, using proprioceptive information to guide action. Behavior was purely directed at the goal of balancing. This ploy was obviously successful; the children balanced each block in turn. There was no attempt to examine the properties of the objects that led to balance and no attempt to subject each block to a test of a unified theory.

This early errorless, but unanalyzed, phase was supplanted by the emergence of strong theories-in-action. These theories were directed at uncovering the rules governing balance in the miniature world of these particular blocks. Unfortunately, they were incomplete rules that produced errors. A common early theory developed by the children was to concentrate exclusively on the geometric center and attempt to balance all blocks in this fashion. This works for unweighted blocks. When the theory did not result in balance, the blocks involved were discarded as exceptions ("impossible to balance").

After this theory was well established and working well for length blocks, the children became discomforted by the number of, and regularity of, the errors. A new juxtaposed theory was then developed for the conspicuous weight blocks. For these, the children compensated for the weight that was obviously added to one end and adjusted the point of balance accordingly. For a time, however, length and weight were considered independently. Length blocks were solved by the geometric center rule and conspicuous weight blocks were solved by the rule of estimate weight first and then compensate. Inconspicuous weight problems still generated errors; they looked identical to the unweighted blocks and were, therefore, subjected to the dominant geometric center rule. When they did not conform to the theory they were discarded as anomalies that were "impossible to balance." The children's verbal responses reflected these juxtaposed solutions, with exclusively length justifications given for unweighted blocks and weight justifications given for conspicuously weighted blocks.

Gradually and reluctantly, the children entered the period of metaprocedural reorganization, which was only possible when both their juxtaposed procedures were working smoothly. Now, the young theorists were made uncomfortable by the remaining exceptions to their own rules and began to seek a rule for them. In so doing, a metaprocedural reorganization was induced that resulted in a single rule for all blocks. The children abandoned the simple theories and reorganized the problem space so that a single unifying theory predominated. Now, the children paused before balancing any block and roughly assessed the point of balance. Verbal responses reflected their consideration of both length and weight, for example, "You have to be careful, sometimes it's just as heavy on each side and so the middle is right, and sometimes it's heavier on one side." *After* inferring the probable point of balance, and only then, did the child place the block on the bar.

There are three main points to note about this example: first, there is the finding of a developmental lull or even a seemingly retrogressive stage when errors predominate. Initially, the children made no errors; all blocks were balanced. But, during the quest for a comprehensive theory of balance, the children generated partially adequate procedures that resulted in errors. Only when the unifying theory was discovered did the children revert to perfect performance. If errors alone formed the data base, a U-shaped developmental growth curve would be apparent (Strauss & Stavey, in press). Actually, what was happening was that the children were analyzing the problem space to generate a theory that would incorporate all the blocks. In so doing, they made what looked like errors but what were often tests of the existing partial theory.

A second main point is that metaprocedural reorganization leading to a "stepping up" in theory complexity is only possible when the partially adequate, juxtaposed systems are well established (see also Siegler, 1981). It is essential that the child gain control of simple theories in her quest for a more complex and more adequate theory. Karmiloff-Smith and Inhelder refer to this as creative simplification:

> The construction of false theories or the over-generalization of limited ones are in effect productive processes. Overgeneralization, a sometimes derogatory term, can be looked upon as the *creative simplification* of a problem by ignoring some of the complicating factors (such as weight in our study). This is implicit in the young child's behavior but could be intentional in the scientist's. Overgeneralization is not just a means to simplify but also to unify; it is then not surprising that the child and the scientist often refuse counterexamples since they complicate the unification process. However, to be capable of unifying positive examples implies that one is equally capable of attempting to find a unifying principle to cover counterexamples... [there is] a general tendency to construct a powerful, yet often inappropriate hypothesis which [learners] try to verify rather than refute. This temporarily blinds the [learner] to counterexamples which should actually suffice to have them reject their hypothesis immediately. (Karmiloff-Smith & Inhelder, 1974/1975, p. 209)

Progress comes only when the inadequate partial theory is well established and the learner is free to attempt to extend the theory to other phenomena. In this way, the theorists, be they children or scientists, are able to discover new properties that, in turn, make it possible for new theories to be constructed.

The third main point is that metaprocedural reorganization is not solely a response to external pressure or failure but rather occurs spontaneously when the child has developed well-functioning procedures that are incomplete but adequate for the task at hand. It is not failure that directs the change but success, success that the child wishes to extend throughout the system....

LEVELS OF SELF-REGULATION.   In this brief and oversimplified synopsis of latter-day Genevan psychology and language-acquisition data, a central place in theoretical speculation is afforded to the concept of self-regulation; there is basic agreement that self-regulatory functions are integral to learning and are central mechanisms of growth and change. Similarly, in the emergent field of metacognition, the notion of self-regulatory mechanisms has a central place (Brown & DeLoache, 1978).

All agree that there are many degrees of self-regulation and that self-regulation is essential for any knowing act. It is important to note, however, that a sharp distinction is made in both theories of language acquisition and in Genevan psychology, a sharp distinction that has not been made as clearly in the metacognitive literature. The distinction is between conscious awareness and direction of thought versus self-correction and regulation that can proceed below this level.

Piaget (1976, 1978) distinguishes sharply between active regulation as part of any knowing act and conscious regulation and direction of thought, the keystone of formal operations. The first process is age independent, even the young learner succeeds in action by regulating, correcting, and refining his current theories. Some form of error correction must be part of any active learning attempt, even very young children are capable of regulating their activities by means of a systematic procedure of error detection and correction. For example, in a recent study, DeLoache, Sugarman, and Brown (1981) observed young children (24 to 42 months) as they attempted to assemble a set of nesting cups. Children in this age range did not differ in the likelihood of their attempting to correct a set of nonseriated cups. They did, however, differ in their strategies for correction.

The most primitive strategy, used frequently by children below 30 months, was brute force. When a large cup was placed on a smaller one, the children would press down hard on the nonfitting cup. Variants of brute pressure were twisting and banging, but the same principle held—the selected cup will fit if only one can press hard enough. Older children also used the brute-force approach, but only after an unsuccessful series of maneuvers; for them, it appeared to be a last resort.

A second strategy initiated by some of the younger subjects was that of trying an alternative. After placing two nonfitting cups together, the child removed the top cup and did one of two things. He either looked for an alternative base for the nonfitting cup or he tried an alternative top for the original base. Both ploys involve minimal restructuring and necessitate considering the relation between only two cups at any one time. The third characteristic ploy of children below 30 months was to respond to a cup that would not fit into a partially completed set of cups by dismantling the entire set and starting again.

Older children (30 to 42 months) faced with a nonfitting cup engaged in strategies that involved consideration of the entire set of relations in the stack. For example, one sophisticated strategy was insertion; the children took apart the stack at a point that enabled them to insert the new cup in its correct position. A second strategy, reversal, was also shown by older children. After placing two nonfitting cups together, the child would *immediately* reverse the relation between them (5/4 immediately switched to 4/5).

The rapidly executed reversal strategy was not shown by the younger group. Some young children would repeatedly assemble, for example, cups 4 to 1, starting with 4 as a base and then inserting 3, 2, and 1. Then, they encountered

When we do begin to understand how to apply cognitive neuroscience in instructional contexts, it is likely that it will first be of most help in addressing the educational needs of special populations. Cognitive psychology allows us to understand how learning and instruction support the acquisition of culturally transmitted skills like numeracy and literacy. Cognitive psychology in combination with brain imaging and recording technologies also allows us to see how learning and instruction alter brain circuitry. It opens the possibility of being able to see and to compare these learning-related changes in normal-versus-special learning populations. Such comparative studies might yield insights into specific learning problems and, more importantly, into alternative, compensatory strategies, representations, and neural circuits that children with learning disabilities might exploit. These insights could in turn help us develop better instructional interventions to address specific learning problems.

CONCLUSION

The brain does and should fascinate all of us, and we should find advances in neuroscience exciting. As educators, we should also be interested in how basic research might contribute to and improve educational practice. However, we should be wary of claims that neuroscience has much to tell us about education, particularly if those claims derive from the neuroscience and education argument. The neuroscience and education argument attempts to link learning, particularly early childhood learning, with what neuroscience has discovered about neural development and synaptic change. Neuroscience has discovered a great deal about neurons and synapses, but not nearly enough to guide educational practice. Currently, the span between brain and learning cannot support much of a load. Too many people marching in step across it could be dangerous.

If we are looking for a basic science to help guide educational practice and policy, cognitive psychology is a much better bet. It already is helping us solve educational problems and design better instructional tools. Cognitive psychology, in the hands of cognitive neuroscientists, is also fundamental to our emerging understanding of how neural structures support and implement cognition functions. If, in the future, brain research does contribute to educational practice, it will most likely do so via the indirect, two-bridge route, not the direct one espoused in the neuroscience and education argument.

Looking to the future, we should attempt to develop an interactive, recursive relationship among research programs in education, cognitive psychology, and systems neuroscience. Such interaction would allow us to extend and apply our understanding of how mind and brain support learning. In the meantime, we should remain skeptical about brain-based educational practice and policy, but look more carefully at what behavioral science already can tell us about teaching, learning, and cognitive development.[3]

NOTES

1. In addition to the cited references, other prominent mentions of the neuroscience and education argument include:

   Caine, R. & G. (1996). Making connections. *Wingspread Journal, 18*(3), The Johnson Foundation.

   Carnegie Task Force. (1994). *Starting points: Meeting the needs of our youngest children.* New York: Carnegie Corporation of New York.

   Clinton, B. (1997, February 4). *President Clinton's 1997 State of the Union Address.*

   The Johnson Foundation. (1997, February 3). How a child's brain develops. *Time.*

   Marchese, T. (1996). The search for next-century learning. *Wingspread Journal, 18*(3). The Johnson Foundation.

   Public Radio International. *Gray matters: The developing brain.* Available at `http://www.dana.org/dana/gray.html`.

   Shanker, A. (1996, October 27). Building brains. *New York Times Week in Review,* p. 7.

   Shore, K. (1997). *Rethinking the brain.* New York: Families and Work Institute.

   White House Conference. (1997, April 17). *Early childhood development and learning: What new research on the brain tells us about our youngest children.*

   Your child. (1997). Special edition of *Newsweek.*

2. Despite this demonstrated success, parents and teachers recently asked Case why one should bother teaching number sense. Wouldn't it be more effective and beneficial, they suggested, to exploit the Mozart effect? These parents and teachers had read about the contributions of brain science to education. (See Begley, 1996; Jones, 1995.) The Mozart effect is the claim that when children exercise cortical neurons by listening to classical music (unfortunately not R&B or heavy metal), they are also strengthening brain circuits used for mathematics. So the neuroscience and education articles do have an audience and do have repercussions for instruction and research.

3. The author thanks the editors and reviewers of *Educational Researcher* for their many constructive comments and criticisms on earlier versions of this article.

PART SIX

Society, Culture, and Education

On the Internet . . .

Sites appropriate to Part Six

New Horizons for Learning offers resources for learning organizations and also for translating research and theory into workable solutions for contemporary learning organizations. This site focuses on the theory of multiple intelligences.

```
http://www.newhorizons.org/bibmishelf.html
```

Harvard Project Zero, a research group at the Harvard Graduate School of Education, has investigated the development of learning processes in children and adults for 30 years. Today, Project Zero is building on this research to help create communities of reflective, independent learners; to enhance deep understanding within disciplines; and to promote critical and creative thinking.

```
http://pzweb.harvard.edu/History/
   History.html
```

In this interview from *TECHNOS Quarterly*, Jonathan Kozol discusses educational inequality between the suburbs and the inner city, the underprivileged children he has worked with, and the people who have been major influences in his life.

```
http://www.technos.net/journal/volume7/
   3kozol.htm
```

CHAPTER 13 Social Change

13.1 JOHN DEWEY

Education and Social Change

The Social Frontier was a very important publishing forum for the ideas of progressive-liberal scholars in American education from 1934 to 1944. During its brief history, *The Social Frontier* published many important essays by William Heard Kilpatrick, Goodwin Watson, Harold Rugg, and many other prominent liberal scholars in the fields of teacher education and social foundations of education. John Dewey was a regular contributor to this journal. Dewey's view was that schools have an important role in forging any society's future.

In the following selection, which is from "Education and Social Change," *The Social Frontier* (May 1937), Dewey uses one of his favorite rhetorical techniques: He gives the reader three clearly different arguments; he then phrases two of them so as to lead the reader to support the one he prefers. Dewey delivers in this essay a stirring defense of democracy as well as of freedom of information and communication in schools as a way to better prepare students for social change.

Dewey (1859–1952) was a professor of philosophy at Columbia University. His many publications include *Democracy and Education: An Introduction to the Philosophy of Education* (Macmillan, 1916) and *How We Think: A Restatement of the Relation of Reflective Thinking to the Educative Process* (D. C. Heath, 1933).

Key Concept: schools and social change

*U*pon certain aspects of my theme there is nothing new to be said. Attention has been continually called of late to the fact that society is in process of change, and that the schools tend to lag behind. We are all familiar with the pleas that are urged to bring education in the schools into closer relation with the forces that are producing social change and with the needs that arise from these changes. Probably no question has received so much attention in educational discussion during the last few years as the problem of integration of the schools with social life. Upon these general matters, I could hardly do more than reiterate what has often been said.

Nevertheless, there is as yet little consensus of opinion as to what the schools can do in relation to the forces of social change and how they should do it. There are those who assert in effect that the schools must simply reflect social changes that have already occurred, as best they may. Some would go so far as to make the work of schools virtually parasitic. Others hold that the schools should take an active part in *directing* social change, and share in the construction of a new social order. Even among the latter there is, however, marked difference of attitude. Some think the schools should assume this directive role by means of indoctrination; others oppose this method. Even if there were more unity of thought than exists, there would still be the practical problem of overcoming institutional inertia so as to realize in fact an agreed-upon program.

There is, accordingly, no need to justify further discussion of the problem of the relation of education to social change. I shall do what I can, then, to indicate the factors that seem to me to enter into the problem, together with some of the reasons that prove that the schools do have a role—and an important one —in *production* of social change.

SCHOOLS REFLECT THE SOCIAL ORDER

One factor inherent in the situation is that schools *do* follow and reflect the social "order" that exists. I do not make this statement as a grudging admission, nor yet in order to argue that they should *not* do so. I make it rather as a statement of a *conditioning* factor which supports the conclusion that the schools thereby do take part in the determination of a future social order; and that, accordingly, the problem is not whether the schools *should* participate in the production of a future society (since they do so anyway) but whether they should do it blindly and irresponsibly or with the maximum possible of courageous intelligence and responsibility.

The grounds that lead me to make this statement are as follows: The existing state of society, which the schools reflect, is not something fixed and uniform. The idea that such is the case is a self-imposed hallucination. Social conditions are not only in process of change, but the changes going on are in different directions, so different as to produce social confusion and conflict. There is no single and clear-cut pattern that pervades and holds together in a unified way the social conditions and forces that operate. It would be easy to cite highly

respectable authorities who have stated, as matter of historic fact and not on account of some doctrinal conclusion to be drawn, that social conditions in all
that affects the relations of human beings to one another have changed more
in the last one hundred and fifty years than in all previous time, and that the
process of change is still going on. It requires a good deal of either ignorance or
intellectual naiveté to suppose that these changes have all been tending to one
coherent social outcome. The plaint of the conservative about the imperiling of
old and time-tried values and truths, and the efforts of reactionaries to stem the
tide of changes that occur, are sufficient evidence, if evidence be needed to the
contrary.

Of course the schools have mirrored the social changes that take place.
The efforts of Horace Mann and others a century ago to establish a public, free,
common school system were a reflection primarily of the social conditions that
followed the war by the colonies for political independence and the establishment of republican institutions. The evidential force of this outstanding instance
would be confirmed in detail if we went through the list of changes that have
taken place in (1) the kind of schools that have been established, (2) the new
courses that have been introduced, (3) the shifts in subject-matter that have occurred, and (4) the changes in methods of instruction and discipline that have
occurred in intervening years. The notion that the educational system has been
static is too absurd for notice; it has been and still is in a state of flux.

The fact that it is possible to argue about the desirability of many of the
changes that have occurred, and to give valid reasons for deploring aspects
of the flux, is not relevant to the main point. For the stronger the arguments
brought forth on these points, and the greater the amount of evidence produced
to show that the educational system is in a state of disorder and confusion, the
greater is the proof that the schools have responded to, and have reflected, social
conditions which are themselves in a state of confusion and conflict.

INCONSISTENT CONSERVATISM

Do those who hold the idea that the schools should not attempt to give direction to social change accept complacently the confusion that exists, because the
schools *have* followed in the track of one social change after another? They certainly do not, although the logic of their position demands it. For the most part
they are severe critics of the existing state of education. They are as a rule opposed to the studies called modern and the methods called progressive. They
tend to favor return to older types of studies and to strenuous "disciplinary"
methods. What does this attitude mean? Does it not show that its advocates
in reality adopt the position that the schools can do something to affect positively and constructively social conditions? For they hold in effect that the
school should discriminate with respect to the social forces that play upon it;
that instead of accepting the latter *in toto*, education should select and organize
in a given direction. The adherents of this view can hardly believe that the effect
of selection and organization will stop at the doors of school rooms. They must

expect some ordering and healing influence to be exerted sooner or later upon the structure and movement of life outside. What they are really doing when they deny directive social effect to education is to express their opposition to some of the directions social change is actually taking, and their choice of other social forces as those with which education should throw in its lot so as to promote as far as may be their victory in the strife of forces. They are conservatives in education because they are socially conservative and vice-versa.

ALTERNATIVE COURSES

This is as it should be in the interest of clearness and consistency of thought and action. If these conservatives in education were more aware of what is involved in their position, and franker in stating its implications, they would help bring out the real issue. It is not whether the schools shall or shall not influence the course of future social life, but in what direction they shall do so and how. In some fashion or other, the schools will influence social life anyway. But they can exercise such influence in different ways and to different ends, and the important thing is to become conscious of these different ways and ends, so that an intelligent choice may be made, and so that if opposed choices are made, the further conflict may at least be carried on with understanding of what is at stake, and not in the dark.

There are three possible directions of choice. Educators may act so as to perpetuate the present confusion and possibly increase it. That will be the result of drift, and under present conditions to drift is in the end to make a choice. Or they may select the newer scientific, technological, and cultural forces that are producing change in the old order; may estimate the direction in which they are moving and their outcome if they are given freer play, and see what can be done to make the schools their ally. Or, educators may become intelligently conservative and strive to make the schools a force in maintaining the old order intact against the impact of new forces.

If the second course is chosen—as of course I believe it should be—the problem will be other than merely that of accelerating the rate of the change that is going on. The problem will be to develop the insight and understanding that will enable the youth who go forth from the schools to take part in the great work of construction and organization that will have to be done, and to equip them with the attitudes and habits of action that will make their understanding and insight practically effective.

DRIFT OR INTELLIGENT CHOICE?

There is much that can be said for an intelligent conservatism. I do not know anything that can be said for perpetuation of a wavering, uncertain, confused condition of social life and education. Nevertheless, the easiest thing is to refrain from fundamental thinking and let things go on drifting. Upon the basis of any other policy than drift—which after all is a policy, though a blind one—every special issue and problem, whether that of selection and organization of subject-matter of study, or methods of teaching, of school buildings and equipment, of school administration, is a special phase of the inclusive and fundamental problem: What movement of social forces, economic, political, religious, cultural, shall the school take to be controlling in its aims and methods, and with which forces shall the school align itself?

Failure to discuss educational problems from this point of view but intensifies the existing confusion. Apart from this background, and outside of this perspective, educational questions have to be settled *ad hoc* and are speedily unsettled. What is suggested does not mean that the schools shall throw themselves into the political and economic arena and take sides with some party there. I am not talking about parties; I am talking about social forces and their movement. In spite of absolute claims that are made for this party or that, it is altogether probable that existing parties and sects themselves suffer from existing confusions and conflicts, so that the understanding, the ideas, and attitudes that control their policies, need re-education and re-orientation. I know that there are some who think that the implications of what I have said point to abstinence and futility; that they negate the stand first taken. But I am surprised when educators adopt this position, for it shows a profound lack of faith in their own calling. It assumes that education as education has nothing or next to nothing to contribute; that formation of understanding and disposition counts for nothing; that only immediate overt action counts and that it can count equally whether or not it has been modified by education.

NEUTRALITY AIDS REACTION

Before leaving this aspect of the subject, I wish to recur to the utopian nature of the idea that the schools can be completely neutral. This idea sets up an end incapable of accomplishment. So far as it is acted upon, it has a definite social effect, but that effect is, as I have said, perpetuation of disorder and increase of blind because unintelligent conflict. Practically, moreover, the weight of such action falls upon the reactionary side. Perhaps the most effective way of re-inforcing reaction under the name of neutrality, consists in keeping the on-coming generation ignorant of the conditions in which they live and the issues they have to face. This effect is the more pronounced because it is subtle and indirect; because neither teachers nor those taught are aware of what they are doing and what is being done to them. Clarity can develop only in the extent to which there is frank acknowledgment of the basic issue: Where shall the social emphasis of school life and work fall, and what are the educational policies which correspond to this emphasis?

REVOLUTIONARY RADICALS BELIEVE
EDUCATION IMPOTENT

So far I have spoken of those who assert, in terms of the views of a conservative group, the doctrine of complete impotence of education. But it is an old story that politics makes strange bedfellows. There is another group which holds the schools are completely impotent; that they so necessarily reflect the dominant economic and political regime, that they are committed, root and branch, to its support. This conclusion is based upon the belief that the organization of a given society is fixed by the control exercised by a particular economic class, so that the school, like every other social institution, is of necessity the subservient tool of a dominant class. This viewpoint takes literally the doctrine that the school can only reflect the existing social order. Hence the conclusion in effect that it is a waste of energy and time to bother with the schools. The only way, according to advocates of this theory, to change education in any important respect is first to overthrow the existing class-order of society and transfer power to another class. Then the needed change in education will follow automatically and will be genuine and thorough-going.

This point of view serves to call attention to another factor in the general issue being discussed. I shall not here take up in detail the basic premise of this school of social thought, namely the doctrine of domination of social organization by a single rather solidly-unified class; a domination so complete and pervasive that it can be thrown off only by the violent revolutionary action of another distinct unified class. It will be gathered, however, from what has been said that I believe the existing situation is so composite and so marked by conflicting criss-cross tendencies that this premise represents an exaggeration of actual conditions so extreme as to be a caricature. Yet I do recognize that so far as any general characterization of the situation can be made, it is on the basis of a conflict of older and newer forces—forces cultural, religious, scientific, philosophic, economic, and political.

But suppose it is admitted for the sake of argument that a social revolution is going on, and that it will culminate in a transfer of power effected by violent action. The notion that schools are completely impotent under existing conditions then has disastrous consequences. The schools, according to the theory, are engaged in shaping as far as in them lies a mentality, a type of belief, desire, and purpose that is consonant with the present class-capitalist system. It is evident that if such be the case, any revolution that is brought about is going to be badly compromised and even undermined. It will carry with it the seeds, the vital seeds, of counter-revolutions. There is no basis whatever, save doctrinaire absolutism, for the belief that a complete economic change will produce of itself the mental, moral, and cultural changes that are necessary for its enduring success. The fact is practically recognized by the school of thought under discussion in that part of their doctrine which asserts that no genuine revolution can occur until the old system has passed away in everything but external political power, while within its shell a new economic system has grown to maturity. What is ignored is that the new system cannot grow to maturity without an accompanying widespread change of habits of belief, desire, and purpose.

John Dewey

IS INDOCTRINATION THE WAY OUT?

It is unrealistic, in my opinion, to suppose that the schools can be a *main* agency in producing the intellectual and moral changes, the changes in attitudes and disposition of thought and purpose, which are necessary for the creation of a new social order. Any such view ignores the constant operation of powerful forces outside the school which shape mind and character. It ignores the fact that school education is but one educational agency out of many, and at the best is in some respects a minor educational force. Nevertheless, while the school is not a sufficient condition, it is a necessary condition of forming the understanding and the dispositions that are required to maintain a genuinely changed social order. No social change is more than external unless it is attended by and rooted in the attitudes of those who bring it about and of those who are affected by it. In a genuine sense, social change is accidental unless it has also a psychological and moral foundation. For it is then at the mercy of currents that veer and shift. The utmost that can be meant by those who hold that schools are impotent is that education in the form of *systematic indoctrination* can only come about when some government is sufficiently established to make schools undertake the task of single-minded inculcation in a single direction.

The discussion has thus reached the point in which it is advisable to say a few words about indoctrination. The word is not free from ambiguity. One definition of the dictionary makes it a synonym for teaching. In order that there may be a definite point to consider, I shall take indoctrination to mean the systematic use of every possible means to impress upon the minds of pupils a particular set of political and economic views to the exclusion of every other. This meaning is suggested by the word "inculcation," whose original signification was "to stamp in with the heel." This signification is too physical to be carried over literally. But the idea of stamping in is involved, and upon occasion does include physical measures. I shall discuss this view only as far as to state, in the first place, that indoctrination so conceived is something very different from education, for the latter involves, as I understand it, the active participation of students in reaching conclusions and forming attributes. Even in the case of something as settled and agreed upon as the multiplication table, I should say if it is taught educatively, and not as a form of animal training, the active participation, the interest, reflection, and understanding of those taught are necessary.

The upholders of indoctrination rest their adherence to the theory in part upon the fact that there is a great deal of indoctrination now going on in the schools, especially with reference to narrow nationalism under the name of patriotism, and with reference to the dominant economic regime. These facts unfortunately *are* facts. But they do not prove that the right course is to seize upon the method of indoctrination and reverse its objective.

DEMOCRACY AS A FRAME OF REFERENCE

A much stronger argument is that unless education has some frame of reference it is bound to be aimless, lacking a unified objective. The necessity for a frame of reference must be admitted. There exists in this country such a unified frame. It is called democracy. I do not claim for a moment that the significance of democracy as a mode of life is so settled that there can be no disagreement as to its significance. The moment we leave glittering generalities and come to concrete details, there is great divergence. I certainly do not mean either that our political institutions as they have come to be, our parties, legislatures, laws, and courts constitute a model upon which a clear idea of democracy can be based. But there is a tradition and an idea which we can put in opposition to the very much that is undemocratic in our institutions. The idea and ideal involve at least the necessity of personal and voluntary participation in reaching decisions and executing them—in so far it is the contrary of the idea of indoctrination. And I, for one, am profoundly sceptical of the notion that because we now have a rather poor embodiment of democracy we can ultimately produce a genuine democracy by sweeping away what we have left of one.

The positive point, however, is that the democratic ideal, in its human significance, provides us with a frame of reference. The frame is not filled in, either in society at large or in its significance for education. I am not implying that it is so clear and definite that we can look at it as a traveler can look at a map and tell where to go from hour to hour. Rather the point I would make is that the *problem* of education in its relation to direction of social change is all one with the *problem* of finding out what democracy means in its total range of concrete applications; economic, domestic, international, religious, cultural, economic, *and* political.

I cannot wish for anything better to happen for, and in, our schools than that this problem should become the chief theme for consideration until we have attained clarity concerning the concrete significance of democracy—which like everything concrete means its application in living action, individual and collective. The trouble, at least one great trouble, is that we have taken democracy for granted; we have thought and acted as if our forefathers had founded it once for all. We have forgotten that it has to be enacted anew in every generation, in every year and day, in the living relations of person to person in all social forms and institutions. Forgetting this, we have allowed our economic and hence our political institutions to drift away from democracy; we have been negligent even in creating a school that should be the constant nurse of democracy.

I conclude by saying that there is at least one thing in which the idea of democracy is not dim, however far short we have come from striving to make it reality. Our public school system was founded in the name of equality of opportunity for all, independent of birth, economic status, race, creed, or color. The school cannot by itself alone create or embody this idea. But the least it can do is to create individuals who understand the concrete meaning of the idea with their minds, who cherish it warmly in their hearts, and who are equipped to battle in its behalf in their actions.

Democracy also means voluntary choice, based on an intelligence that is the outcome of free association and communication with others. It means a way of living together in which mutual and free consultation rule instead of force, and in which cooperation instead of brutal competition is the law of life; a social order in which all the forces that make for friendship, beauty, and knowledge are cherished in order that each individual may become what he, and he alone, is capable of becoming. These things at least give a point of departure for the filling in of the democratic idea and aim as a frame of reference. If a sufficient number of educators devote themselves to striving courageously and with full sincerity to find the answers to the concrete questions which the idea and the aim put to us, I believe that the question of the relation of the schools to direction of social change will cease to be a question, and will become a moving answer in action.

John Dewey

Conflicting Theories of Education

I. L. Kandel (1881–1965), a professor of education, is considered the father of the study of comparative and international education in the United States. He founded the Center for International Studies of Education at Teachers College, Columbia University, in the 1930s and edited more than 20 of the yearbooks on world education published by the center. He published lengthy studies on the educational systems in Germany, France, and several other nations as well as on issues in American education. He wrote one of the first textbooks on comparative education and one of the first critiques of the Nazi educational program in Germany, *The Making of Nazis* (Teachers College Press, 1935).

Kandel saw a threat to democratic nation-states in the 1930s. What he had to say about it is as relevant for our time as it was for his. The selection that follows is from *Conflicting Theories of Education* (Macmillan, 1938). In it, Kandel discusses the role of education in defense of freedom of thought, and he addresses the issue of education and social change. He argues that educational processes do not take place in a social or cultural vacuum; schools are institutions created by societies to achieve certain specific purposes. He maintains that students should be taught to understand the world in which they live. Here he discusses teachers' responsibilities in dealing with social controversies. He says that there is no choice but to bring conflicting social issues into the classroom.

Key Concept: education and social change

*E*ducation does not . . . take place in a vacuum. The school is an agency established by society to achieve certain ends. These ends will differ according to the form of each society. Totalitarian states have adopted fixed patterns into which the individual is to be molded. Democracies will fail if they attempt to adopt a type of education which ignores any values but those chosen by each individual to suit the needs of the moment. The mystical, irrational notion that freedom is synonymous with the right to follow inner drives ignores both the history and the meaning of freedom.

That freedom is a conquest has been as true of the progress of humanity as it is of the growth of the individual. The whole history of humanity has been —despite aberrations in recent years—the history of the emancipation from external controls and, at the same time, of the ways in which man has learned to control himself. This history has been one of the emancipation of man from servitude to fears—fears of nature, slavery, political tyranny, and external controls and coercion over life. Man's struggle for personal freedom, freedom of movement, freedom of thought and expression, freedom of worship, justice, tolerance, and equality of opportunity has been painfully slow and is not yet ended. But in emerging successfully from the struggle, man did so by learning that he must accept certain limitations on his freedom, by recognizing his responsibility and duty to others. It was only as man learned to appreciate the moral consequence of his actions that he became free.

What has been true of the history of civilization applies equally to the education of the individual—freedom is not an inherent right (totalitarian states have proved how easily it may be lost) but a privilege to be won. And it is in confusing freedom with noninterference and in failing to stress social and moral obligations adequately that those who have most loudly urged freedom in education have erred. The slogan of self-expression, for example, failed to recognize that the true self can be realized only in and through a social milieu. Hence, the fundamental issue is the extent to which such realization of the self can be free and yet result in a personality enriched through and by a consciousness of social values. Here again the answer will be found in the principle that freedom is a right which, like all other rights, must be won, and that all rights imply a corresponding responsibility in their use, no matter what the field of activity may be.

A free society cannot divest itself of the obligation of handing on to new generations those common traditions, loyalties, and interests which make community life possible, but it can and should avoid that claim to omniscience and infallibility which must in the long run spell stagnation and failure to permit adaptation to changing conditions. If this is accepted, then the only thing that a free society should indoctrinate is faith in freedom and in free inquiry. But the essence of freedom and free inquiry is the recognition of responsibility. Not until the concept of responsibility is incorporated in the discussion of education in a free society, can education be expected to make its rightful contribution to a troubled world. For such a discussion Santayana's description of English liberty may well furnish the text, for in it may be found the answer of a free society to the criticisms of the totalitarian: "It moves by a series of checks, mutual concessions, and limited satisfactions; it counts on chivalry, sportsmanship, brotherly love, and on that rarest and least lucrative of virtues, fair-mindedness; it is a broad-based, stupid, blind adventure, groping towards an unknown goal."

And this, in essence, is the definition of liberal education, which has unfortunately acquired a connotation in terms of familiarity with certain subjects. But a liberal education implies more than a knowledge of classical or modern languages, science and mathematics. It implies breadth of interests, knowledge and information, standards of taste and appreciation, and the possession of certain moral and social qualities. It should result in tolerance and open-mindedness, in ability to meet new situations because one has knowledge and insight, and in readiness to co-operate because of a refined sense of responsibility. All these are social values, values which make the existence of a free society possible and which cannot be acquired incidentally as and when the pupil feels the need of them.

... And if a free society is to accept the challenge and meet the charges of totalitarianism it will be only as it realizes that there must be common agreement, common social faith, and common values as a foundation for that freedom upon which it is based. It is upon these common elements, consciously and deliberately recognized and defined, that education can build a free personality. To set up the child as an idol and to worship his inner drives, urges, and impulses is to encourage chaos; to set up the ideal of a free personality implies a vision of social purposes which alone can give meaning to education and save the rising generation from immersion in the destructive element which sees no values in the past, no meaning in the present, and no hope in the future. In this task of defining the meaning of freedom in education the English-speaking peoples can find a field of common endeavor—England with her reverence for traditional values and deliberate and cautious acceptance of change, the United States with her buoyant optimism and preference for change at the cost of traditions, and the Dominions rooted in British traditions but with the vigor and vision of youthful pioneers. Democratic institutions may safely be entrusted to them, but only as these nations become conscious of the significance of these institutions for humanity and the part to be played by education in their preservation....

EDUCATION AND SOCIAL CHANGE

The general social and cultural unrest which can be traced back to the beginnings of the modern scientific movement and the consequent technological changes, an unrest which has grown in intensity since the War, has had its repercussions on educational thought. This has, indeed, been the history of education, for education has been most vigorous and vital in periods of great social changes, as, for example, in Athens, during the Renaissance and the Reformation, at the time of the early scientific movement of the seventeenth century, and at the beginning of the nineteenth century following the Industrial Revolution and the consolidation of nation-states. The period through which the world is passing in the present era is probably one of those nodal periods in which old ideas and ideals, standards and loyalties, are being questioned and modified, if not revolutionized. Science is remaking the world and bringing an economic upheaval in its train; political institutions are being questioned or overturned; a war of ideas is going on in every field that concerns human relationships. The conflicts are more profound and more widespread than those which have always existed between the older and younger generations.

Under these conditions unrest in education is inevitable, but in the discussions on education and social change it is not clear whether a formula is being sought whereby the rising generation shall be acquainted with the social changes going on about it or whether it is proposed that the school itself should be made an instrument for the reconstruction of society. These alternatives can be answered only in the light of the purposes for which society establishes schools.

The earliest and most persistent reason for the establishment of schools as formal agencies of education is the desire on the part of a group, society, or state to conserve and transmit its culture and heritage to the younger generation and to equip this generation with those habits, skills, knowledges, and ideals that will enable it to take its place in a society and contribute to the stability and perpetuation of that society. This purpose is based on faith in the possibilities of formal education during the formative and plastic period of childhood and adolescence. This is the principle in Plato's statement that the effectual functioning of the state depends upon the proper training of the young, and in Aristotle's insistence that the stability of systems of government has its basis in the adaptation of education to the form of government.

Education does not proceed in a vacuum; its character is determined by the group culture, and schools are institutions created by society to attain certain specific ends. These ends began to be defined when the national states at the beginning of the nineteenth century undertook to establish systems of education to initiate their future citizens into the national culture. Stability was to be secured by instructing the pupils in the schools in a common language, common history, common government and political ideals, common economic and social ideas and ideals, and common objects of social allegiance in order that there might emerge a common group, or national, self-consciousness. If the younger generation is to enter into meaningful partnership in and responsibility for its heritage the first function of the school is to initiate it into its common culture. Society is, in fact, prior to the individual, and the school is an agency for promoting stability and adapting the individual to the environment in which he lives. Without entering into other considerations which justify the transmission of the social heritage or the experiences of the race as a basis for understanding the present, it will be generally agreed that the function here described has received wide acceptance from the days of Plato down to modern times.

If, however, the school stops with the performance of this function, then a society either stagnates, as was the case in China, or its progress is determined by the will of the few who lead the rest, trained through the school to habits of duty, discipline, quiescent obedience, and uncritical acceptance of authority. The method of such a school is that of direct indoctrination and education becomes indistinguishable from propaganda. This was already the trend in authoritarian states of the last century; it is the principle definitely accepted in the totalitarian states of the present, in which education is directed by and to a common ideology. The social changes wrought by revolutions have produced patterns which know no compromise and are not open to question or criticism. Education has become adjustment to a fixed and unchanging environment, and national culture is something that is colored by a particular ideology and controlled by organizations created to prevent changes in it.

The situation is different in those countries in which culture is accepted as the spontaneous expression of individuals and the free interplay among individuals or groups. It is at this point that education and social change begin to be clothed with meaning and to challenge traditional practices. The procedure in the past was to impart a body of content, knowledge, and information representing selections from the group culture designed primarily to "train the mind." It tended to become stereotyped and formal and rarely came to grips with the present. The school was a cloistered institution which eschewed any contact with the environment into which the pupil was soon to pass. It must be remembered, however, that even this type of procedure did not ignore the changing environment and was not designed to maintain a static society, but it was conducted with the conviction that a mind trained by "academic" or "scholastic" material would have no difficulty in dealing with the realities of life. Nor was the procedure in the education of the masses differentiated from the procedure in the education of the potential leaders.

These practices were not accepted without protest. Since the days of Seneca educators have urged that education must be for life and not for the school, but it was not until the beginning of the present century that widespread efforts began to be made to bring school and society together. A better understanding of the process of child growth, a new interpretation of the concept of interest, a clearer realization of the meaning of democracy and the part to be played by the individual in it, and the rapid changes in the culture, due in the main to the progress of science—all these forces and many others contributed to the spread of the theory that if education is a social process, it must contribute to an understanding of the society which it serves. The influence of John Dewey's philosophy in bringing about the change of outlook not only in the United States but in other parts of the world is too well known to need further discussion. The vast body of educational literature which has grown up in the United States in the past three decades speaks eloquently of this influence. The educational trend in Germany during the period of the short-lived Republic was rooted in *Bodenständigkeit*, the relation of education to the environment. In England the latest edition of the *Handbook of Suggestions for Teachers* is inspired by the same principle, as is illustrated by a statement in the general introduction that "we feel more deeply the need of relating what is taught in the schools to what is happening in the world outside."

The new theory of education, in insisting that the work of the school must be related to the environment in which and for which its pupils are being educated, contains in its definition the suggestion that discussions of social change are implicit in the curriculum. It means that pupils should be taught to understand the world in which they live. Up to this point the problem is fairly simple. Difficulties arise, however, when it is suggested that change is the characteristic note of the present world—and change not merely in its material but in its ideational aspects. To what extent should or can the school concern itself with political and economic conflicts, with changes in the attitudes to authority, or with the general atmosphere that questions all traditions?

Changes in the material world are facts; political and economic theories are matters of opinion. If the teacher is an agent of the state, to what extent is he free to introduce controversial issues into the classroom? It is not necessary here to state that the issues should be relevant to the stage of development and the maturity of the pupils concerned and to the subject of instruction. But if the function of education is to develop an understanding of the problems of the environment in which the learner lives, the opportunity of discussing controversial issues in the school cannot be ignored. Indeed, one may argue that it is essential to train the pupil in recognizing the importance of accurate knowledge before reaching an opinion.

If the doors of the school are to be closed to the discussion of controversial issues, it might well be asked what the alternative would be; in a period of change the schools would be guilty of turning pupils out into the world ignorant of the problems that will confront them. There is, in fact, no choice but to bring those elements of conflict into the classroom. To adopt an ostrichlike attitude and ignore the existence of such issues, to deny the right to mention even the existence of what may be regarded as subversive ideas, is to follow the old practice of ignoring the existence of sex. Carried to its logical conclusion, such a policy could be used to justify the suppression of a free press and of freedom of opinion, and the arrest of anyone suspected of "harboring dangerous thoughts."

Any reference to the introduction of controversial issues in politics and economics arouses the fear that pupils will be exposed to the bias of the teachers. It may be true that no teacher can successfully conduct a discussion of controversial issues without the pupils' detecting his bias. Nevertheless, pupils pass through the hands of a large number of teachers during their school careers; to suspect that all teachers have the same bias has no justification in fact; nor are teachers the only educational influences that play upon the growing youth. The choice is whether the rising generation is to receive its political and economic education through informal agencies or through methods that are truly educative; whether the young are to be enlightened and trained through the scientific study of facts or whether they are to be exposed to deliberate propaganda without the support of accurate information on both sides of an issue. If the relationship between school and society or education and the environment means anything, then the schools must, at the appropriate stage, impart the realities of society. And if that society is in process of change, then all that the school can do is to place the pupils in possession of full knowledge of the facts in the issues involved and to give them that training which will enable them to make up their own minds on the basis of that knowledge.

The emphasis in this argument is on training in methods of thinking through issues that are real. There is some truth in the objection that solutions cannot be given to contemporary controversial issues; this objection is, however, not a valid argument for their exclusion from the schools. Neither the issues nor the solutions are likely to be the same when pupils now in school take their places in life as adult citizens; the detailed facts of an issue and the knowledge requisite to its solution will inevitably be different, but unless some training is given in the schools in the patterns of thinking with which a problem is to be approached, the intellectual equipment necessary to recognize even the existence of problems will have been withheld. If democracy depends for its survival upon the intelligence and understanding of the ordinary man, it is the function of the school to equip him in advance with the necessary knowledge and powers of clear thinking to discharge his duties as a citizen.

It is only in this sense that education and social change can be discussed. Education must go beyond its task of imparting a knowledge and appreciation of the common interests, or what Dewey has called the objects of that social allegiance which makes common social understanding and consciousness of group membership possible. It must help men and women to think for themselves, unless they are to succumb to the will of an authority which claims omniscience and infallibility.

There has, however, been injected into discussions of education and social change the suggestion that schools should, in a period of change, educate for a new social order, and that teachers should ally themselves with some political group and use their classrooms to propagate certain doctrines. Schools and teachers should, in other words, participate more directly and vitally in projecting particular ideas or patterns of social change and in their execution. The whole history of education emphasizes the impossibility of this idea, for society establishes schools to provide a firm basis for itself and to sustain the common interest. Schools are a part of the environment which they serve; they are not autonomous or insulated against the social forces and influences around them; nor can teachers on the basis of a guess as to the active forces of the day help to build a new social order. Society changes first and schools follow.

It is, however, becoming increasingly important that teachers should be more alive than they have been in the past and better informed about the environment in and for which they are educating their pupils. Only in this way can they give meaning to the subjects for which they are responsible, for subjects, if they are to have any significance, must be saturated with social meaning. To attempt to instill ready-made ideas on controversial issues or to influence pupils to accept one doctrine rather than another is to adopt the methods of totalitarian states and to confuse education with propaganda.

In a democracy the only acceptable aim in bringing the school and society more closely together is to develop the knowledge and understanding that make for enlightened citizenship. But the acquisition of knowledge, facts, and information about the environment in all those aspects that concern the conduct of the citizen is not the sole end of education; such an acquisition must be made the vehicle for training in scientific methods of thinking and for cultivating free and disciplined minds. To educate for a new social order is to close the minds of the pupils, for, in a society in transition, no one can have a final answer concerning the issues that are involved. True education would help to put the pupils in a position to appreciate the urgent necessity of acquiring knowledge, to discriminate between facts and prejudices, to weigh and judge evidence, to reach conclusions warranted by the information secured, and to recognize the issues involved in a period of social transition or crisis. If this end is to be achieved, if the aim of education is to develop free and enlightened citizens, then the teachers who are to be entrusted with carrying out this aim must themselves be enlightened and free. The problem, like all other problems in education, becomes one of teacher preparation and of the status of teachers. In the words of a former president of the English Board of Education, "The standards of the teaching profession itself are the only sure protection" against the abuse of the teachers' positions in discussing educational and social change.

The problem of education and social change solves itself if education is defined as the process of bringing pupils to an understanding of the environment in and for which they are being educated. That environment is a constantly expanding one; to concentrate on change alone is to deal only with the immediate present and to avoid the development of an understanding of the rich heritage which the environment carries with it. But understanding must lead to conduct, and if democracy is to survive, the schools must cultivate in their pupils ideals of freedom, tolerance, and open-mindedness, a critical attitude and intellectual sensitiveness based on ascertained facts and knowledge, a spirit of inquiry and insight, and those emotional qualities in addition which make for a sense of responsibility and cooperation. For democracy, in the words of Santayana, is a blind, groping adventure which implies openmindedness and sensitiveness to the need of flexibility and adaptation of social institutions. These are the qualities which education can cultivate as the basis of social change....

I. L. Kandel

EDUCATION AND THE CHALLENGE TO DEMOCRACY

In the war of ideas which is raging between totalitarianism and democracy the special responsibility which falls on education in a democracy is too frequently ignored. This is in part due to failure to recognize the challenge to democratic ideals; it is due also to the basic difference between the two groups of ideas—totalitarianism because it is built on a set body of doctrines dominated by acceptance of the supremacy of the state has by far the simpler task in education, while democracy as an ideal is a way of life based on the freedom and responsibility of the individual. The democratic state depends upon the collective will of the individuals who make it up and exists to guarantee the rights of individuals and to maintain justice between them; though too frequently the free citizen of a democracy is more conscious of his rights than he is of his duties. The totalitarian state insists upon the co-ordination of all individuals so that all think and behave like all other individuals, and how they may think and behave is determined by a dictator or a party. The essence of democracy is that each individual thinks for himself and behaves as his conscience dictates, provided that he does not encroach on the right of others to do the same. In the one case the individual must be "in the right line"; in the other the individual has a right to his own opinions.

The totalitarian state has recognized more clearly than the democratic the axiom already enunciated by Plato and Aristotle that education and the form of government are closely interdependent, that education, in other words, is an instrument of social control employed to perpetuate society and to advance social progress. Whether education is defined as a process of molding all individuals to the same pattern or of promoting progress through the enlightenment of all individuals depends upon the nature of the state and its form of government. Here is to be found the explanation of the interest shown in the provision of education by the nation states in the nineteenth century as well as the insistence of George Washington on the enlightenment of public opinion through "institutions for the general diffusion of knowledge."

The Passions of Pluralism: Multiculturalism and the Expanding Community

Maxine Greene's career in philosophy of education has brought her widespread scholarly recognition. Her books and essays are widely read, and she is a past president of the American Educational Research Association. In the following selection from "The Passions of Pluralism: Multiculturalism and the Expanding Community," *Educational Researcher* (January–February 1993), she reviews the dialogue in American society related to the recognition of all of the voices to be heard in the nation's multicultural reality. Greene speaks to the need to champion the right of all citizens to be heard. She notes the changing cultural demographics of the American experience, and, recognizing America's increasing cultural diversity, she stresses the need to revisit John Dewey's conception of American society as a "Great Community." The author calls for the rediscovery—or, for some, the discovery for the first time—of their uniqueness as individuals and their right to be heard and recognized in the national community.

Greene takes a multifaceted, interdisciplinary approach to establishing her case, using sources from philosophy, history, and literature. She says that it is time to repair the social damage done in the past by the exclusion of women and cultural minorities from America's national dialogue on what it means to be a citizen of the nation. Greene supports a pluralistic conceptualization of what it should be like to build a truly democratic national sense of "communion" among all citizens. She represents feminist concerns as well as those of all the cultures that have had to struggle in American society. Greene argues that in order to open up our experience to our existential possibilities as persons, to possibilities of many kinds, we must extend and deepen, and we must further develop our understanding of what it means to be brothers and sisters in a great national community.

Key Concept: community, voice, inclusion, cultural pluralism, and multiculturalism

*T*here have always been newcomers in this country; there have always been strangers. There have always been young persons in our classrooms we did not, could not see or hear. In recent years, however, invisibility has been refused on many sides. Old silences have been shattered; long-repressed voices are making themselves heard. Yes, we are in search of what John Dewey called "the Great Community" (1954, pp. 143ff), but, at once, we are challenged as never before to confront plurality and multiplicity. Unable to deny or obscure the facts of pluralism, we are asked to choose ourselves with respect to unimaginable diversities. To speak of passions in such a context is not to refer to the strong feelings aroused by what strikes many as a confusion and a cacophony. Rather, it is to have in mind the central sphere for the operation of the passions: "the realm of face-to-face relationships" (Unger, 1984, p. 107). It seems clear that the more continuous and authentic personal encounters can be, the less likely it will be that categorizing and distancing will take place. People are less likely to be treated instrumentally, to be made "other" by those around. I want to speak of pluralism and multiculturalism with concrete engagements in mind, actual and imagined: engagements with persons, young persons and older persons, some suffering from exclusion, some from powerlessness, some from poverty, some from ignorance, some from boredom. Also, I want to speak with imagination in mind, and metaphor, and art. Cynthia Ozick writes:

> Through metaphor, the past has the capacity to imagine us, and we it. Through metaphorical concentration, doctors can imagine what it is to be their patients. Those who have no pain can imagine those who suffer. Those at the center can imagine what it is to be outside. The strong can imagine the weak. Illuminated lives can imagine the dark. Poets in their twilight can imagine the borders of stellar fire. We strangers can imagine the familiar hearts of strangers. (1989, p. 283)

TOWARDS A COMMUNITY OF PERSONS

Passions, then, engagements, and imagining: I want to find a way of speaking of community, an expanding community, taking shape when diverse people, speaking as *who* and not *what* they are, come together in speech and action, as Hannah Arendt puts it, to constitute something in common among themselves. She writes: "Plurality is the condition of human action because we are all the same, that is, human, in such a way that nobody is ever the same as anyone else who ever lived, lives, or will live" (1958, p. 57). For her, those present on a common ground have different locations on that ground; and each one "sees or hears from a different position." An object—a classroom, a neighborhood street, a field of flowers—shows itself differently when encountered by a variety of spectators. The reality of that object (or classroom, or neighborhood, or field of flowers) arises out of the sum total of its appearances. Thinking of those spectators as participants in an ongoing dialogue, each one speaking out of a distinct perspective and yet open to those around, I find a kind of paradigm for what I have in mind. I discover another in the work of Henry Louis Gates, Jr., who writes about the fact that "the challenge facing America in the next century will be the shaping, at long last, of a truly common public culture, one responsive to the long-silenced cultures of color" (1991, p. 712). (It is not long, it will be remembered, since the same Professor Gates asked in a *New York Times* article, "Whose canon is it anyway?" See Gates, 1992.) More recently, he has evoked the philosopher Michael Oakeshott and his notion of a conversation with different voices. Education, Gates suggests, might be "an invitation into the art of this conversation in which we learn to recognize the voices, each conditioned by a different perception of the world." Then Gates adds: "Common sense says that you don't bracket out 90% of the world's cultural heritage if you really want to learn about the world" (1991, p. 712).

For many, what is common sense for Gates represents an attack on the coherence of what we think of as our heritage, our canon. The notion of different voices conditioned by different perspectives summons up the spectre of relativism; and relativism, according to Clifford Geertz, is the "intellectualist Grande Peur." It makes people uneasy, because it appears to subvert authority; it eats away at what is conceived of as objectively real. "If thought is so much out in the world as this," Geertz asks, as the uneasy might ask, "what is to guarantee its generality, its objectivity, its efficacy, or its truth?" (1983, p. 153). There is irony in Geertz's voice, since he knows and has said: "For our time and forward, the image of a general orientation, perspective, *Weltanschauung*, growing out of humanistic studies (or, for that matter, out of scientific ones) and shaping the direction of the culture is a chimera." He speaks of the "radical variousness of the way we think now" and suggests that the problem of integrating cultural life becomes one of "making it possible for people inhabiting different worlds to have a genuine, and reciprocal, impact upon one another" (p. 161). This is troubling for people seeking assurances, seeking certainties. And yet they, like the rest of us, keep experiencing attacks on what is familiar, what James Clifford calls "the irruption of otherness, the unexpected" (1988, p. 13). It may well be that our ability to tolerate the unexpected relates to our tolerance for multiculturalism, for the very idea of expansion and the notion of plurality.

We are well aware, for all that, that Arthur Schlesinger, Jr., who must be taken seriously, sees a "disuniting of America" in the making if shared commitments shatter, if we lose touch with the democratic idea (1992). Proponents of what is called "civism" (Pratte, 1988, pp. 104–107) are concerned that pluralism threatens the existence of a democratic ethos intended to transcend all differences. The ethos encompasses the principles of freedom, equality, and justice, as well as regard for human rights, and there is fear that the new relativism and particularism will subvert the common faith. And there are those like E. D. Hirsch, Jr., who see the concept of "background knowledge" and the shared content it ensures undermined by "variousness" and the multicultural emphases that distract from the common. What they call "cultural literacy" is undermined as a result, and the national community itself is eroded (Hirsch, 1987). At the extreme, of course, are those on the far right who find a conspiracy in challenges to the so-called Eurocentric canon and in what they construct as "politically correct," signifying a new orthodoxy built out of oversensitivity to multicultural concerns (D'Sousa, 1991, p. 239). As for the religious fundamentalist right, says Robert Hughes (writing in *The New York Review of Books*), one of the motives driving men like Jesse Helms is to establish themselves as defenders of what they define as the "American way" now (as Hughes puts it) "that their original crusade against the Red Menace has been rendered null and void" (1992, p. 21). Not only do they argue for their construct against the National Endowment for the Arts' grants to avant garde artists; they attack such deviations as multiculturalism. It is important to hold this in mind as we try to work through a conception of pluralism to an affirmation of the struggle to attain the life of "free and enriching communion" John Dewey identified with democracy.

The seer of the life of communion, according to Dewey, was Walt Whitman. Whitman wrote about the many shapes arising in 'the country in his time, "the shapes of doors giving many exits and entrances" and "shapes of democracy... ever projecting other shapes." In "Song of Myself" (in total contradiction in the fundamentalist version of the "American way") he wrote:

> Through me many long dumb voices,
> Voices of the interminable generations of prisoners and slaves,
> Voices of the diseas'd and despairing and of thieves and dwarfs,
> Voices of cycles of preparation and accretion,
> And of the threads that connect the stars, and of wombs and of the
>   father-stuff,
> And of the rights of them the others are down upon....
> Through me forbidden voices.... (Whitman, 1931, p. 53)

He was, from all appearances, the seer of a communion arising out of "many shapes," out of multiplicity. There is no suggestion of a melting pot here, nor is there a dread of plurality.

SILENCE AND INVISIBILITY:
THE NEED TO REPAIR

For some of us, just beginning to feel our own stories are worth telling, the reminders of the "long dumb voices," the talk of "the rights of them the others are down upon" cannot but draw attention to the absences and silences that are as much a part of our history as the articulate voices, the shimmering faces, the images of emergence and success. Bartleby, the clerk who "prefers not to" in Herman Melville's story (1986), may suddenly become exemplary. What of those who said no, who found no place, who made no mark? Do they not say something about a society that closed too many doors, that allowed people to be abandoned like "wreckage in the mid-Atlantic" (Melville, 1986, p. 121)? What of those like Tod Clifton in Ralph Ellison's *Invisible Man?* A former youth leader in the so-called Brotherhood, he ends up selling Sambo dolls in front of the public library. When the police try to dislodge him, he protests; and they kill him. The narrator, watching, wonders:

> Why did he choose to plunge into nothingness, into the void of faceless faces, of soundless voices, lying outside history? . . . All things, it is said, are duly recorded —all things of importance, that is. But not quite; for actually it is only the known, the seen, the heard, and only those events that the recorder regards as important are put down. . . . But the cop would be Clifton's historian, his judge, his witness, his executioner, and I was the only brother in the watching crowd. (1952, p. 379)

The many who ended up "lying outside history" diminished the community, left an empty space on the common ground, left undefined an aspect of reality.

It is true that we cannot know all the absent ones, but they must be present somehow in their absence. Absence, after all, suggests an emptiness, a void to be filled, a wound to be healed, a flaw to be repaired. I think of E. L. Doctorow painting a landscape of denial at the beginning of *Ragtime*, appealing to both wonder and indignation, demanding a kind of repair. He is writing about New Rochelle in 1906 but he is presenting a past that reaches into the present, into *our* present, whether or not we ride trolleys anymore.

> Teddy Roosevelt was President. The population customarily gathered in great numbers either out of doors for parades, public concerts, fish fries, political picnics, social outings, or indoors in meeting halls, vaudeville theatres, operas, ballrooms. There seemed to be no entertainment that did not involve great swarms of people. Trains and steamers and trolleys moved them from one place to another. That was the style; that was the way people lived. Women were stouter then. They visited the fleet carrying white parasols. Everyone wore white in summer. There was alot of sexual fainting. There were no Negroes. There were no immigrants. (1975, pp. 3–4)

The story has focally to do with a decent, intelligent Black man named Coalhouse Walker, who is cheated, never acknowledged, never understood, scarcely *seen*, and who begins his own fated strategy of vengeance which ends when promises are broken and he is shot down in cold blood. Why is he unseen?

Why were there no Negroes, no immigrants? More than likely because of the condition of the minds of those in power, those in charge. Ellison may explain it when he attributes invisibility to "a peculiar disposition of the eyes of those with whom I come in contact. A matter of the construction of their inner eyes, those eyes with which they look through their physical eyes upon reality" (1952, p. 7). But that disposition must itself have been partly due to the play of power in discourse as well as in social arrangements. We may wonder even now what the assimilation or initiation sought by so many educators signified when there were so many blanked out spaces—"no Negroes . . . no immigrants," oftentimes no full-grown women.

Looking back at the gaps in our own lived experiences, we might think of silences like those Tillie Olsen had in mind when she spoke of literary history "dark with silences," of the "unnatural silences" of women who worked too hard or were too embarrassed to express themselves (1978, p. 6), of others who did not have the words or had not mastered the proper "ways of knowing" (Belenky, Clinchy, Goldberger, & Tarule, 1986). We might ponder the plight of young island women, like Jamaica Kincaid's Lucy from Antigua, forced to be "two-faced" in a post-colonial school: "Outside, I seemed one way, inside I was another; outside false, inside true" (1990, p. 18). For years we knew no more about people like her (who saw "sorrow and bitterness" in the face of daffodils because of the Wordsworth poem she had been forced to learn) than we did about the Barbadians Paule Marshall has described, people living their fragmented lives in Brooklyn. There was little consciousness of what Gloria Anzaldua calls *Borderlands/La Frontera* on which so many Latinos live (1987), or of the Cuban immigrants like the musicians in Oscar Hijuelos's *The Mambo Kings Sing Songs of Love* (1989). Who of us truly wondered about the builders of the railroads, those Maxine Hong Kingston calls "China Men," chopping trees in the Sandalwood and Sierra Nevada Mountains? Who of us could fill the gaps left by such a person as Ah Goong, whose "existence was outlawed by the Chinese Exclusion Acts"? His family, writes Kingston,

> did not understand his accomplishments as an American ancestor, a holding, homing ancestor of this place. He'd gotten the legal or illegal papers burned in the San Francisco earthquake and fire; he appeared in America in time to be a citizen and to father citizens. He had also been seen carrying a child out of the fire, a child of his own in spite of the laws against marrying. He had built a railroad out of sweat, why not have an American child out of longing? (1989, p. 151)

Did we pay heed to a person like Michelle Clift, an Afro-Caribbean woman who felt that speaking in words that were not her own was a form of speechlessness? Or to a child like Pecola Breedlove in Toni Morrison's (1972) *The Bluest Eye*, the unloved Black child who wanted to look like Shirley Temple so she could be included in the human reality? Or to a Mary Crow Dog, who finds her own way of saying in the autobiography, *Lakota Woman*? How many of us have been willing to suffer the experiences most recently rendered in Art Spiegelman's two-volume comic book called *Maus*? He tells about his father, the ill-tempered Vladek, a survivor of Auschwitz, and his resentful sharing of his Holocaust memories with his son. Every character in the book is an animal: the Jews, mice;

the Germans, cats; the Poles, pigs. It is a reminder, not simply of a particular culture's dissolution. ("Anja's parents, the grandparents, her big sister Tosha, little Bibi, and our Richieu.... All what is left, it's the photos"; 1991, p. 115). It is a reminder of the need to recognize that everything is possible, something normal people (including school people) either do not know or do not want to know.

To open up our experience (and, yes, our curricula) to existential possibilities of multiple kinds is to extend and deepen what we think of when we speak of a community. If we break through and even disrupt surface equilibrium and uniformity, this does not mean that particular ethnic or racial traditions ought to replace our own. Toni Morrison writes of pursuing her freedom as a writer in a "genderized, sexualized, wholly racialized world," but this does not keep her from developing a critical project "unencumbered by dreams of subversion or rallying gestures at fortress walls" (1992, pp. 4–5). In her case, the project involves exploring the ways in which what we think of as our Americanness is in many ways a response to an Africanist presence far too long denied. She is not interested in replacing one domination by another; she is interested in showing us what she sees from her own perspective—and, in showing us, enriching our understanding not only of our own culture, but of ourselves. She speaks of themes familiar to us all: "individualism, masculinity, social engagement versus historical isolation; acute and ambiguous moral problematics; the thematics of innocence coupled with an obsession with figurations of death and hell." Then she goes on to query what Americans are alienated from, innocent of, different from. "As for absolute power, over whom is this power held, from whom withheld, to whom distributed? Answers to these questions lie in the potent and ego-reinforcing presence of an Africanist population" (1992, p. 45). Even as Americans once defined their moral selves against the wilderness, they began to define their whiteness against what Melville called "the power of blackness"; they understood their achievement of freedom against slavery. Whether we choose to see our history that way or not, she is introducing a vision only she could create, and it offers us alternative vantage points on our world. Indeed, the tension with regard to multiculturalism may be partially due to the suspicion that we have often defined ourselves against some unknown, some darkness, some "otherness" we chose to thrust away, to master, not to understand. In this regard, Morrison says something that seems to me unanswerable: "My project is an effort to avert the critical gaze from the racial object to the racial subject; from the described and imagined to the describers and imaginers; from the serving to the served" (1992, p. 45).

To take this view is not to suggest that curricula should be tailored to the measure of specific cultural groups of young people. Nor is it to suggest, as the Afrocentrists do, that emphasis should be laid on the unique experiences, culture and perspectives of Afro-Americans and their link to African roots. There is no question that what history has overlooked or distorted must be restored —whether it has to do with Afro-Americans, Hispanics, Asians, women, Jews, Native Americans, the Irish, or Poles; but the exclusions and the deformations have not kept artists like Morrison, Ellison, James Baldwin from plunging into and learning from Western literary works, anymore than it has prevented scholars like Gates and Cornel West and Alain Locke from working for more and richer interchanges between Afro-American and Euro-American cultures. Morrison begins her new book with a verse from Eliot and goes on to pay tribute to Homer, Dostoevsky, Faulkner, James, Flaubert, Melville, and Mary Shelley. It is difficult to forget James Baldwin reading Dostoevsky and haunting the public library, to turn attention from West's critiques of Emerson, to ignore Ellison writing about Melville and Hemingway, even as he drew attention to what he called "the Negro stereotype" that was "really an image of the irrational, unorganized forces in American life" (Ellison, 1964, p. 55). We might think of Maya Angelou as well, of her years of self-imposed silence as a child and the reading she did through those years. We might recall Alice Walker engaging with Muriel Rukeyser and Flannery O'Connor, drawing energy from them, even as she went in search of Zora Neale Hurston and Bessie Smith and Sojourner Truth and Gwendolyn Brooks. ("I also loved Ovid and Catullus... the poems of E.E. Cummings and William Carlos Williams"; Walker, 1983, p. 257). And we are aware that, as time goes on, more and more Afro-American literature and women's literature and Hispanic-American literature are diversifying our experience, changing our ideas of time and life and birth and relationship and memory.

REPRESENTATION AND OWNERSHIP

My point has to do with openness and variety as well as with inclusion. It has to do with the avoidance of fixities, of stereotypes, even the stereotypes linked to multiculturalism. To view a person as in some sense "representative" of Asian culture (too frequently grouping together human beings as diverse as Japanese, Koreans, Chinese, and Vietnamese) or Hispanic culture or Afro-American culture is to presume an objective reality called "culture," a homogeneous and fixed presence that *can* be adequately represented by existing subjects. (Do Amy Tan's maternal characters embody the same reality as does Maxine Hong Kingston's "woman warrior"? Does Richard Wright's Bigger Thomas stand for the same thing as Miss Celie stands for in Alice Walker's *The Color Purple*?) We do not *know* the person in the front row of our classroom, or the one sharing the raft, or the one drinking next to us at the bar by her/his cultural or ethnic affiliation.

Cultural background surely plays a part in shaping identity, but it does not determine identity. It may well create differences that must be honored; it may occasion styles and orientations that must be understood; it may give rise to tastes, values, even prejudices that must be taken into account. It is important to know, for example, without embarrassing or exoticizing her, why Jamaica Kincaid's Antiguan Lucy feels so alienated from a Wordsworth poem, and whether or not (and against what norms) it is necessary to argue her out of her distaste for daffodils. It is important to realize why (as in Bharaka Mukherjee's *Jasmine*, 1990) Hindus and Sikhs are so at odds with one another, even in this country, and to seek out ways in which (consulting what we believe to be the Western principle of justice) they can be persuaded to set aside hostility. Or perhaps, striving to sympathize with what they feel, we can communicate our own caring for their well-being in such a fashion as to move them provisionally to reconceive each other's reality. Paulo Freire makes the point that every person ought, on some level, to cherish her or his culture; but he says it should never be absolutized. When it is absolutized, when a person is closed against the new culture surrounding her or him, "you would," Freire says, "even find it hard to learn new things which, placed alongside your personal history, can be meaningful" (Freire & Macedo, 1987, p. 126).

There has, however, to be a feeling of ownership of one's personal history. In this culture, because of its brutal and persistent racism, it has been painfully difficult for Afro-American young people to affirm and be proud of what they choose as personal history. Poverty, hopelessness, the disruption of families and communities, the ubiquity of media images, all make it difficult to place new things against a past too often made to appear a past of victimization, shadows, and shame. To make it worse, the mystification that proceeds on all sides gives rise to a metanarrative of what it means to be respectable and successful in America—a metanarrative that too often seems to doom minorities to life on the outermost borders, or as Toni Morrison writes in *The Bluest Eye*, "outdoors" where there is no place to go. ("Outdoors," she writes, "is the end of something, an irrevocable, physical fact, defining and complementing our metaphysical condition. Being a minority in both caste and class, we moved about anyway on the hem of life, struggling to consolidate our weaknesses and hang on, or to creep singly up into the major folds of the garment"; 1972, p. 18).

LIFE STORIES AND POSSIBILITY

It happens that *The Bluest Eye*, because of its use of the first paragraph of the basal reader *Dick and Jane*, dramatizes (as few works do) the coercive and deforming effect of the culture's official story, the metanarrative of secure suburban family life. As the novel plays itself out, everything that occurs is the obverse of the basal reader's story with its themes of pretty house, loving family, play, laughter, friendship, cat, and dog. The narrator of the main story, Pecola Breedlove's story, is young Claudia—also black and poor, but with a supporting family, a sister, a mother who loves her even as she complains and scolds. A short preface, ostensibly written after Pecola's baby and her rapist father have died, after the seeds would not flower, after Pecola went mad, ends with Claudia saying: "There is really nothing more to say—except why. But since *why* is difficult to handle, one must take refuge in *how*" (1972, p. 9). When very young and then a little older, Claudia tells the story and, in the telling, orders the materials of her own life, her own helplessness, her own longings. She does that in relation to Pecola, whom she could not help, and in relation to the seeds that would not flower and those around her "on the hem of life." She weaves her narrative in such a fashion that she establishes an important connection to the past and (telling about Pecola and her family and her pain) reinterprets her own ethnicity in part through what Michael Fischer calls "the arts of memory." Whatever meaning she can draw from this feeds into an ethic that may be meaningful in the future, an ethic that takes her beyond her own guilt at watching Pecola search the garbage:

> I talk about how I did *not* plant the seeds too deeply, how it was the fault of the earth, the land, of our town. I even think now that the land of the entire country was hostile to marigolds that year.... Certain seeds it will not nurture, certain fruit it will not bear, and when the land kills of its own volition, we acquiesce and say the victim had no right to live. We are wrong, of course, but it doesn't matter. It's too late. (1972, p. 160)

As Charles Taylor and Alasdair MacIntyre have written, we understand our lives in narrative form, as a quest. Taylor writes: "because we have to determine our place in relation to the good, therefore we cannot be without an orientation to it, and hence must see our life in stories" (1989, p. 51). Clearly, there are different stories connected by the same need to make sense, to make meaning, to find a direction.

To help the Claudias we know, the diverse students we know, articulate their stories is not only to help them pursue the meanings of their lives—to find out *how* things are happening, to keep posing questions about the why. It is to move them to learn the "new things" Freire spoke of, to reach out for the proficiencies and capacities, the craft required to be fully participant in this society, and to do so without losing the consciousness of who they are. That is not all. Stories like the one Claudia tells must break through into what we think of as our tradition or our heritage. They should with what Cornel West has in mind when he speaks about the importance of acknowledging the "distinctive cultural and political practices of oppressed people" without highlighting their marginality in such a way as to further marginalize them. Not only does he call attention to the resistance of Afro-Americans and that of other long-silenced people. He writes of the need to look at Afro-Americans' multiple contributions to the culture over the generations. We might think of the music, Gospel, jazz, ragtime; we might think of the Black churches; we might summon up the Civil Rights movement and the philosophies, the dreams that informed it; we might ponder—looking back, looking around—the images of courage, the images of survival. West goes on to say:

> Black cultural practices emerge out of a reality they cannot *not* know—the ragged edges of the real, of necessity; a reality historically constructed by white supremacist practices in North America.... These ragged edges—of not being able to eat, not to have shelter, not to have health care—all this is infused into the strategies and styles of black cultural practices. (1989, p. 23)

Viewed in connection with the idea of multiculturalism, this does not mean that Afro-American culture in all its variousness can be defined mainly in terms of oppression and discrimination. One of the many reasons for opening spaces in which Afro-Americans can tell their own stories is that they, far more than those from other cultures, can explain the ways in which poverty and exclusion have mediated their own sense of the past. It is true that experiences of pain and abandonment have led to a search for roots and, on occasion, for a revision of recorded history. What is crucial is the provision of opportunities for telling all the diverse stories, for interpreting membership as well as ethnicity, for making inescapable the braids of experience woven into the fabric of America's plurality.

In the presence of an increasingly potent Third World, against the sounds of increasingly eloquent postcolonial (and, now, posttotalitarian) voices, we can no longer pretend that the "ragged edges" are an exception. We can no longer talk in terms of seamless totalities under rubrics like "free world," "free market," "equality," or even "democracy." Like the "wreckage in the mid-Atlantic," like the "faceless faces," like the "unnatural silences," the lacks and deprivations have to be made aspects of our plurality as well as of our cultural identity. Publics, after all, take shape in response to unmet needs and broken promises. Human beings are prone to take action in response to the sense of injustice or to the imagination's capacity to look at things as if they could be otherwise. The democratic community, always a community in the making, depends not so much on what has been achieved and funded in the past. It is kept alive; it is energized and radiated by an awareness of future possibility. To develop a vision of such possibility, a vision of what might and ought to be, is very often to be made aware of present deficiencies and present flaws. The seeds did not flower; Pecola and her baby could not be saved. But more and more persons, paying heed, may move beyond acquiescence. They may say, as Claudia does, "We are wrong, of course . . ." but go on to overcome the "doesn't matter." At that moment, they may reach beyond themselves, choose themselves as who they are and reach out to the common to repair.

CONCLUSION

Learning to look through multiple perspectives, young people may be helped to build bridges among themselves; attending to a range of human stories, they may be provoked to heal and to transform. Of course there will be difficulties in affirming plurality and difference and, at once, working to create community. Since the days of De Tocqueville, Americans have wondered how to deal with the conflicts between individualism and the drive to conform. They have wondered how to reconcile the impassioned voices of cultures not yet part of the whole with the requirements of conformity, how not to lose the integrity of those voices in the process, how not to allow the drive to conformity determine what happens at the end. But the community many of us hope for now is not to be identified with conformity. As in Whitman's way of saying, it is a community attentive to difference, open to the idea of plurality. Something life-affirming in diversity must be discovered and rediscovered, as what is held in common becomes always more many-faceted—open and inclusive, drawn to untapped possibility.

No one can predict precisely the common world of possibility, nor can we absolutely justify one kind of community over another. Many of us, however, for all the tensions and disagreements around us, would reaffirm the value of principles like justice and equality and freedom and commitment to human rights since, without these, we cannot even argue for the decency of welcoming. Only if more and more persons incarnate such principles, we might say, and choose to live by them and engage in dialogue in accord with them, are we likely to bring about a democratic pluralism and not fly apart in violence and disorder. Unable to provide an objective ground for such hopes and claims, all we can do is speak with others as eloquently and passionately as we can about justice and caring and love and trust. Like Richard Rorty and those he calls pragmatists, we can only articulate our desire for as much intersubjective agreement as possible, "the desire to extend the reference of 'us' as far as we can" (1991, p. 23). But, as we do so, we have to remain aware of the distinctive members of the plurality, appearing before one another with their own perspectives on the common, their own stories entering the culture's story, altering it as it moves through time. We want our classrooms to be just and caring, full of various conceptions of the good. We want them to be articulate, with the dialogue involving as many persons as possible, opening to one another, opening to the world. And we want them to be concerned for one another, as we learn to be concerned for them. We want them to achieve friendships among one another, as each one moves to a heightened sense of craft and wide-awakeness, to a renewed consciousness of worth and possibility.

With voices in mind and the need for visibility, I want to end with a call for human solidarity by Muriel Rukeyser, who—like many of us—wanted to "widen the lens and see/standing over the land myths of identity, new signals, processes." And then:

> Carry abroad the urgent need, the scene,
> to photograph and to extend the voice,
> to speak this meaning.
> Voices to speak to us directly. As we move.
> As we enrich, growing in larger motion,
> this word, this power. (Rukeyser, 1938, p. 71)

This power, yes, the unexplored power of pluralism, and the wonder of an expanding community.

Savage Inequalities: Children in America's Schools

Jonathan Kozol first came to national attention in 1967 with the publication of *Death at an Early Age,* which documents his experiences as a substitute teacher in a Boston elementary school. Since then, Kozol has written seven more books that examine the social context of education. He has traveled all over the United States observing schools and the conditions of the lives of children and their parents. He has conducted an in-depth study of the educational system in revolutionary Cuba, and he has studied the lives of teachers, parents, and students who confront savagely complex circumstances. He has frequently testified before congressional committees and lectured to groups of educators.

The following selection is from *Savage Inequalities: Children in America's Schools* (Crown Publishers, 1991). In *Savage Inequalities,* Kozol argues that America's schools are even more segregated than they were in 1954. He bases his conclusions on two years of observation in public schools and on conversations with parents, educators, and students. Many of the anecdotes from his interviews and observations are poignant reminders of how much needs to be done in the area of public education in the United States.

Key Concept: life in urban public schools

*I*t was a long time since I'd been with children in the public schools.

I had begun to teach in 1964 in Boston in a segregated school so crowded and so poor that it could not provide my fourth grade children with a classroom. We shared an auditorium with another fourth grade and the choir and a group that was rehearsing, starting in October, for a Christmas play that, somehow, never was produced. In the spring I was shifted to another fourth grade that had had a string of substitutes all year. The 35 children in the class hadn't had a permanent teacher since they entered kindergarten. That year, I was their thirteenth teacher.

The results were seen in the first tests I gave. In April, most were reading at the second grade level. Their math ability was at the first grade level.

In an effort to resuscitate their interest, I began to read them poetry I liked. They were drawn especially to poems of Robert Frost and Langston Hughes. One of the most embittered children in the class began to cry when she first heard the words of Langston Hughes.

> *What happens to a dream deferred?*
> *Does it dry up*
> *like a raisin in the sun?*

She went home and memorized the lines.

The next day, I was fired. There was, it turned out, a list of "fourth grade poems" that teachers were obliged to follow but which, like most first-year teachers, I had never seen. According to school officials, Robert Frost and Langston Hughes were "too advanced" for children of this age. Hughes, moreover, was regarded as "inflammatory."

I was soon recruited to teach in a suburban system west of Boston. The shock of going from one of the poorest schools to one of the wealthiest cannot be overstated. I now had 21 children in a cheerful building with a principal who welcomed innovation.

After teaching for several years, I became involved with other interests —the health and education of farmworkers in New Mexico and Arizona, the problems of adult illiterates in several states, the lives of homeless families in New York. It wasn't until 1988, when I returned to Massachusetts after a long stay in New York City, that I realized how far I'd been drawn away from my original concerns. I found that I missed being with schoolchildren, and I felt a longing to spend time in public schools again. So, in the fall of 1988, I set off on another journey.

During the next two years I visited schools and spoke with children in approximately 30 neighborhoods from Illinois to Washington, D.C., and from New York to San Antonio. Wherever possible, I also met with children in their homes. There was no special logic in the choice of cities that I visited. I went where I was welcomed or knew teachers or school principals or ministers of churches.

What startled me most—although it puzzles me that I was not prepared for this—was the remarkable degree of racial segregation that persisted almost everywhere. Like most Americans, I knew that segregation was still common in the public schools, but I did not know how much it had intensified. The Supreme Court decision in *Brown v. Board of Education* 37 years ago, in which the court had found that segregated education was unconstitutional because it was "inherently unequal," did not seem to have changed very much for children in the schools I saw, not, at least, outside of the Deep South. Most of the urban schools I visited were 95 to 99 percent nonwhite. In no school that I saw anywhere in the United States were nonwhite children in large numbers truly intermingled with white children.

Moreover, in most cities, influential people that I met showed little inclination to address this matter and were sometimes even puzzled when I brought it up. Many people seemed to view the segregation issue as "a past injustice" that had been sufficiently addressed. Others took it as an unresolved injustice that no longer held sufficient national attention to be worth contesting. In all cases, I was given the distinct impression that my inquiries about this matter were not welcome.

None of the national reports I saw made even passing references to inequality or segregation. Low reading scores, high dropout rates, poor motivation—symptomatic matters—seemed to dominate discussion. In three cities —Baltimore, Milwaukee and Detroit—separate schools or separate classes for black males had been proposed. Other cities—Washington, D.C., New York and Philadelphia among them—were considering the same approach. Black parents or black school officials sometimes seemed to favor this idea. Booker T. Washington was cited with increasing frequency, Du Bois never, and Martin Luther King only with cautious selectivity. He was treated as an icon, but his vision of a nation in which black and white kids went to school together seemed to be effaced almost entirely. Dutiful references to "The Dream" were often seen in school brochures and on wall posters during February, when "Black History" was celebrated in the public schools, but the content of the dream was treated as a closed box that could not be opened without ruining the celebration.

For anyone who came of age during the years from 1954 to 1968, these revelations could not fail to be disheartening. What seems unmistakable, but, oddly enough, is rarely said in public settings nowadays, is that the nation, for all practice and intent, has turned its back upon the moral implications, if not yet the legal ramifications, of the *Brown* decision. The struggle being waged today, where there is any struggle being waged at all, is closer to the one that was addressed in 1896 in *Plessy v. Ferguson,* in which the court accepted segregated institutions for black people, stipulating only that they must be equal to those open to white people. The dual society, at least in public education, seems in general to be unquestioned.

To the extent that school reforms such as "restructuring" are advocated for the inner cities, few of these reforms have reached the schools that I have seen. In each of the larger cities there is usually one school or one subdistrict which is highly publicized as an example of "restructured" education; but the changes rarely reach beyond this one example. Even in those schools where some "restructuring" has taken place, the fact of racial segregation has been, and continues to be, largely uncontested. In many cities, what is termed "restructuring" struck me as very little more than moving around the same old furniture within the house of poverty. The perceived objective was a more "efficient" ghetto school or one with greater "input" from the ghetto parents or more "choices" for the ghetto children. The fact of ghetto education as a permanent American reality appeared to be accepted.

Liberal critics of the Reagan era sometimes note that social policy in the United States, to the extent that it concerns black children and poor children, has been turned back several decades. But this assertion, which is accurate as a description of some setbacks in the areas of housing, health and welfare, is not adequate to speak about the present-day reality in public education. In public schooling, social policy has been turned back almost one hundred years.

These, then, are a few of the impressions that remained with me after re-visiting the public schools from which I had been absent for a quarter-century. My deepest impression, however, was less theoretical and more immediate. It was simply the impression that these urban schools were, by and large, extraordinarily unhappy places. With few exceptions, they reminded me of "garrisons" or "outposts" in a foreign nation. Housing projects, bleak and tall, surrounded by perimeter walls lined with barbed wire, often stood adjacent to the schools I visited. The schools were surrounded frequently by signs that indicated DRUG-FREE ZONE. Their doors were guarded. Police sometimes patrolled the halls. The windows of the schools were often covered with steel grates. Taxi drivers flatly refused to take me to some of these schools and would deposit me a dozen blocks away, in border areas beyond which they refused to go. I'd walk the last half-mile on my own. Once, in the Bronx, a woman stopped her car, told me I should not be walking there, insisted I get in, and drove me to the school. I was dismayed to walk or ride for blocks and blocks through neighborhoods where every face was black, where there were simply *no white people anywhere.*

In Boston, the press referred to areas like these as "death zones"—a specific reference to the rate of infant death in ghetto neighborhoods—but the feeling of the "death zone" often seemed to permeate the schools themselves. Looking around some of these inner-city schools, where filth and disrepair were worse than anything I'd seen in 1964, I often wondered why we would agree to let our children go to school in places where no politician, school board president, or business CEO would dream of working. Children seemed to wrestle with these kinds of questions too. Some of their observations were, indeed, so trenchant that a teacher sometimes would step back and raise her eyebrows and then nod to me across the children's heads, as if to say, "Well, there it is! They know what's going on around them, don't they?"

It occurred to me that we had not been listening much to children in these recent years of "summit conferences" on education, of severe reports and ominous prescriptions. The voices of children, frankly, had been missing from the whole discussion.

This seems especially unfortunate because the children often are more interesting and perceptive than the grown-ups are about the day-to-day realities of life in school. For this reason, I decided, early in my journey, to attempt to listen very carefully to children and, whenever possible, to let their voices and their judgments and their longings find a place within this book—and maybe, too, within the nation's dialogue about their destinies. I hope that, in this effort, I have done them justice.

East St. Louis—which the local press refers to as "an inner city without an outer city"—has some of the sickest children in America. Of 66 cities in Illinois, East St. Louis ranks first in fetal death, first in premature birth, and third in infant death. Among the negative factors listed by the city's health director are the sewage running in the streets, air that has been fouled by the local plants, the high lead levels noted in the soil, poverty, lack of education, crime, dilapidated housing, insufficient health care, unemployment. Hospital care is deficient too. There is no place to have a baby in East St. Louis. The maternity ward at the city's Catholic hospital, a 100-year-old structure, was shut down some years ago. The only other hospital in town was forced by lack of funds to close in 1990. The closest obstetrics service open to the women here is seven miles away. The infant death rate is still rising.

As in New York City's poorest neighborhoods, dental problems also plague the children here. Although dental problems don't command the instant fears associated with low birth weight, fetal death or cholera, they do have the consequence of wearing down the stamina of children and defeating their ambitions. Bleeding gums, impacted teeth and rotting teeth are routine matters for the children I have interviewed in the South Bronx. Children get used to feeling constant pain. They go to sleep with it. They go to school with it. Sometimes their teachers are alarmed and try to get them to a clinic. But it's all so slow and heavily encumbered with red tape and waiting lists and missing, lost or canceled welfare cards, that dental care is often long delayed. Children live for months with pain that grown-ups would find unendurable. The gradual attrition of accepted pain erodes their energy and aspiration. I have seen children in New York with teeth that look like brownish, broken sticks. I have also seen teen-agers who were missing half their teeth. But, to me, most shocking is to see a child with an abscess that has been inflamed for weeks and that he has simply lived with and accepts as part of the routine of life. Many teachers in the urban schools have seen this. It is almost commonplace.

Compounding these problems is the poor nutrition of the children here —average daily food expenditure in East St. Louis is $2.40 for one child—and the underimmunization of young children. Of every 100 children recently surveyed in East St. Louis, 55 were incompletely immunized for polio, diphtheria, measles and whooping cough. In this context, health officials look with all the more uneasiness at those lagoons of sewage outside public housing....

A 16-year-old student in the South Bronx tells me that he went to English class for two months in the fall of 1989 before the school supplied him with a textbook. He spent the entire year without a science text. "My mother offered to help me with my science, which was hard for me," he says, "but I could not bring home a book."

In May of 1990 he is facing final exams, but, because the school requires students to pass in their textbooks one week prior to the end of the semester, he is forced to study without math and English texts.

He wants to go to college and he knows that math and English are important, but he's feeling overwhelmed, especially in math. He asked his teacher if he could come in for extra help, but she informed him that she didn't have the time. He asked if he could come to school an hour early, when she might have time to help him, but security precautions at the school made this impossible.

Sitting in his kitchen, I attempt to help him with his math and English. In math, according to a practice test he has been given, he is asked to solve the following equation: "$2x - 2 = 14$. What is x?" He finds this baffling. In English, he is told he'll have to know the parts of speech. In the sentence "Jack walks to the store," he is unable to identify the verb.

He is in a dark mood, worried about this and other problems. His mother has recently been diagnosed as having cancer. We leave the apartment and walk downstairs to the street. He's a full-grown young man, tall and quiet and strong-looking; but out on the street, when it is time to say good-bye, his eyes fill up with tears.

In the fall of the year, he phones me at my home. "There are 42 students in my science class, 40 in my English class—45 in my home room. When all the kids show up, five of us have to stand in back."

A first-year English teacher at another high school in the Bronx calls me two nights later: "I've got five classes—42 in each! We have no textbooks yet. I'm using my old textbook from the seventh grade. They're doing construction all around me so the noise is quite amazing. They're actually *drilling* in the hall outside my room. I have more kids than desks in all five classes.

"A student came in today whom I had never seen. I said, 'We'll have to wait and see if someone doesn't come so you can have a chair.' She looked at me and said, 'I'm leaving.'"

The other teachers tell her that the problem will resolve itself. "Half the students will be gone by Christmastime, they say. It's awful when you realize that the school is *counting* on the failure of one half my class. If they didn't count on it, perhaps it wouldn't happen. If I *begun* with 20 students in a class, I'd have lots more time to spend with each of them. I'd have a chance to track them down, go to their homes, see them on the weekends.... I don't understand why people in New York permit this."

One of the students in her class, she says, wrote this two-line poem for Martin Luther King:

He tried to help the white and black.
Now that he's dead he can't do jack.

Another student wrote these lines:

America the beautiful,
Who are you beautiful for?

"Frequently," says a teacher at another crowded high school in New York, "a student may be in the wrong class for a term and never know it." With only one counselor to 700 students system-wide in New York City, there is little help available to those who feel confused. It is not surprising, says the teacher, "that many find the experience so cold, impersonal and disheartening that they decide to stay home by the sad warmth of the TV set." ...

I stopped in Cincinnati on the way home so that I could visit in a school to which I'd been invited by some friends. It was, I thought, a truly dreadful school and, although I met a number of good teachers there, the place left me disheartened. The children were poor, but with a kind of poverty I'd never seen before. Most were not minority children but the children of poor Appalachian whites who'd settled in this part of Cincinnati years before and led their lives in virtual isolation from the city that surrounded them.

The neighborhood in which they lived is known as Lower Price Hill. Farther up the hill, there is a middle-income neighborhood and, at the top, an upper-income area—the three communities being located at successive levels of the same steep rise. The bottom of the hill, which stands beside the banks of the Ohio River, is the poorest area. The middle of the hill is occupied by working families that are somewhat better off. At the top of the hill there is a luxury development, which has a splendid view of Cincinnati, and a gourmet restaurant. The division of neighborhoods along this hill, with an apportionment of different scales of economics, domicile and social station to each level, reminded me of a painting by Giotto: a medieval setting in which peasants, burghers, lords and ladies lead their separate lives within a single frame.

To get to the neighborhood you have to drive from the center of the city through the West Side, which is mainly black, and then along a stretch of railroad tracks, until you come to the Ohio River. Lower Price Hill is on the north side of the river.

Some indication of the poverty within the neighborhood may be derived from demographics. Only 27 percent of adults in the area have finished high school. Welfare dependence is common, but, because the people here identify the welfare system with black people, many will not turn to welfare and rely on menial jobs; better-paying jobs are quite beyond their reach because of their low education levels.

The neighborhood is industrial, although some of the plants are boarded up. Most of the factories (metal-treatment plants and paint and chemical manufacturers) are still in operation and the smoke and chemical pollutants from these installations cloud the air close to the river. Prostitutes stand in a ragged line along the street as I approach the school. Many of the wood-frame houses are in disrepair. Graffiti... decorates the wall of an abandoned building near the corner of Hatmaker Street and State.

The wilted-looking kids who live here, says Bob Moore, an organizer who has worked with parents in the neighborhood for several years, have "by far the lowest skills in math and reading in the city." There is some concern, he says, about "developmental retardation" as a consequence perhaps of their continual exposure to the chemical pollutants, but this, he says, is only speculation. "That these kids are damaged is quite clear. We don't know exactly why."

Oyler Elementary School, unlike so many of the schools I've seen in poor black neighborhoods, is not so much intense and crowded as it is depleted, bleak and bare. The eyes of the children, many of whom have white-blond hair and almost all of whom seem rather pale and gaunt, appear depleted too. During several hours in the school I rarely saw a child with a good big smile.

Bleakness was the order of the day in fifth grade science. The children were studying plant biology when I came in, but not with lab equipment. There was none. There was a single sink that may have worked but was not being used, a couple of test tubes locked up in a cupboard, and a skeleton also locked behind glass windows. The nearly total blankness of the walls was interrupted only by a fire safety poster. The window shades were badly torn. The only textbook I could find (*Mathematics in Our World*) had been published by Addison-Wesley in 1973. A chart of "The Elements" on the wall behind the teacher listed no elements discovered in the past four decades.

"A lot of these kids have behavior problems," the science teacher said. He spoke of kids with little initiative whose "study habits," he said, "are poor." Much of what they learn, he said, "is gotten from the streets." Asked if more supplies, a cheerier classroom or a better lab would make a difference, he replied that he was "not sure money is the answer."

The class was studying a worksheet. He asked a question: "What is photosynthesis?"

After a long wait, someone answered: "Light."

"This is the least academic group I have," he told me after they were gone.

Children who attend this school, according to a school official, have the second-highest dropout rate in Cincinnati. Of young people age 16 to 21 in this community, 59.6 percent are high school dropouts. Some 85 percent of Oyler's students are below the national median in reading. The school spends $3,180 for each pupil.

The remedial reading program, funded by a federal grant, has only one instructor. "I see 45 children in a day," she says. "Only first and second graders —and, if I can fit them in, a few third graders. I have a waiting list of third grade children. We don't have sufficient funds to help the older kids at all."

There are four computers in the school, which holds almost 600 children.

The younger children seem to have a bit more fire than those in the science class. In a second grade class, I meet a boy with deep brown eyes and long blond hair who talks very fast and has some strong opinions: "I hate this school. I hate my teacher. I like the principal but she does not like me." In the morning, he says, he likes to watch his father shave his beard.

"My mother and father sleep in the bedroom," he goes on. "I sleep in the living room. I have a dog named Joe. I have a bird who takes her bath with me. I can count to 140. My mother says that I do numbers in my sleep."

Three girls in the class tell me their names: Brandy, Jessica, Miranda. They are dressed poorly and are much too thin, but they are friendly and seem glad to have a visitor in class and even act a little silly for my benefit.

Before I leave, I spend part of an hour in a class of industrial arts. The teacher is superb, a painter and an artisan, who obviously likes children. But the class is reserved for upper-level kids and, by the time they get here, many are worn down and seem to lack the spark of merriment that Jessica and Brandy and their classmates had. It does seem a pity that the best instruction in the school should be essentially vocational, not academic.

Next year, I'm told, the children of this school will enter a cross-busing program that will mix them with the children of the black schools on the West Side. Middle-class white neighborhoods, like Rose Lawn for example, will not be included in the busing plan. Nor will very wealthy neighborhoods, like Hyde Park, be included.

I ask a teacher why Hyde Park, where friends of mine reside, won't be included in desegregation.

"That," he tells me, "is a question you don't want to ask in Cincinnati."

Cincinnati, like Chicago, has a two-tier system. Among the city's magnet and selective schools are some remarkable institutions—such as Walnut Hills, a famous high school that my hosts compared to "a *de facto* private school" within the public system. It is not known if a child from Lower Price Hill has ever been admitted there. Few of these children, in any case, would have the preparation to compete effectively on the exams that they would have to take in order to get in. Long before they leave this school, most of their academic options are foreclosed.

From the top of the hill, which I returned to visit the next day, you can see across the city, which looks beautiful from here. You also have a good view of the river. The horizon is so wide and open, and so different from the narrow view of life to be surmised from the mean streets around the school—one wonders what might happen to the spirits of these children if they had the chance to breathe this air and stretch their arms and see so far. Might they feel the power or the longing to become inheritors of some of this remarkable vast nation?

Standing here by the Ohio River, watching it drift west into the edge of the horizon, picturing it as it flows onward to the place three hundred miles from here where it will pour into the Mississippi, one is struck by the sheer beauty of this country, of its goodness and unrealized goodness, of the limitless potential that it holds to render life rewarding and the spirit clean. Surely there is enough for everyone within this country. It is a tragedy that these good things are not more widely shared. All our children ought to be allowed a stake in the enormous richness of America. Whether they were born to poor white Appalachians or to wealthy Texans, to poor black people in the Bronx or to rich people in Manhasset or Winnetka, they are all quite wonderful and innocent when they are small. We soil them needlessly.

14.3 JONATHAN KOZOL

Amazing Grace

The following selection is from *Amazing Grace: The Lives of Children and the Conscience of a Nation* (Crown Publishers, 1995). In that book, Jonathan Kozol powerfully portrays the spirit of young life in the South Bronx in New York City. He paints a portrait of children who live amidst poverty and social chaos yet cling to hope and love. Kozol lived with the children of the impoverished South Bronx for more than a year, and he dedicates *Amazing Grace* to them. Although wounded by the social chaos and poverty amidst which they live, Kozol tells us that the children are not hardened; they are full of hope and love and are open to welcome life. Kozol interviews many children in *Amazing Grace*, along with some of their teachers, psychologists, and clergy. His interviews with the children reveal their hope for the future in the midst of social despair. Kozol asks important questions: Why doesn't America care about the children of the poor? Why are they neglected? Don't they have the right to the same educational opportunities as the children of wealthy suburbs? Why do we shun them? How can the children of the South Bronx still pray? What gives them hope? Kozol makes a powerful appeal to the conscience of the American people. He describes how AIDS has reached almost pandemic proportions in the South Bronx, and he reports that many of the children with whom he talked have lost loved ones to this dread scourge on the neighborhood.

Kozol offers a particularly pertinent observation regarding the social isolation and neglect of the children of the urban poor: "Whatever good things may happen for the children of another generation are, in any case, of little solace to those who are children now and will not have their childhood to live a second time in the next century." He goes on to say that this is particularly true for those children who are losing their loved ones to AIDS.

Key Concept: America's unwanted children

*T*he Number 6 train from Manhattan to the South Bronx makes nine stops in the 18-minute ride between East 59th Street and Brook Avenue. When you enter the train, you are in the seventh richest congressional district in the nation. When you leave, you are in the poorest.

The 600,000 people who live here and the 450,000 people who live in Washington Heights and Harlem, which are separated from the South Bronx by a narrow river, make up one of the largest racially segregated concentrations of poor people in our nation.

Brook Avenue, which is the tenth stop on the local, lies in the center of Mott Haven, whose 48,000 people are the poorest in the South Bronx. Two thirds are Hispanic, one third black. Thirty-five percent are children. In 1991, the median household income of the area, according to the *New York Times*, was $7,600.

St. Ann's Church, on St. Ann's Avenue, is three blocks from the subway station. The children who come to this small Episcopal church for food and comfort and to play, and the mothers and fathers who come here for prayer, are said to be the poorest people in New York. "More than 95 percent are poor," the pastor says—"the poorest of the poor, poor by any standard I can think of."

At the elementary school that serves the neighborhood across the avenue, only seven of 800 children do not qualify for free school lunches. "Five of those seven," says the principal, "get reduced-price lunches, because they are classified as only 'poor,' not 'destitute.'"

In some cities, the public reputation of a ghetto neighborhood bears little connection to the world that you discover when you walk the streets with children and listen to their words. In Mott Haven, this is not the case. By and large, the words of the children in the streets and schools and houses that surround St. Ann's more than justify the grimness in the words of journalists who have described the area.

Crack-cocaine addiction and the intravenous use of heroin, which children I have met here call "the needle drug," are woven into the texture of existence in Mott Haven. Nearly 4,000 heroin injectors, many of whom are HIV-infected, live here. Virtually every child at St. Ann's knows someone, a relative or neighbor, who has died of AIDS, and most children here know many others who are dying now of the disease. One quarter of the women of Mott Haven who are tested in obstetric wards are positive for HIV. Rates of pediatric AIDS, therefore, are high.

Depression is common among children in Mott Haven. Many cry a great deal but cannot explain exactly why.

Fear and anxiety are common. Many cannot sleep.

Asthma is the most common illness among children here. Many have to struggle to take in a good deep breath. Some mothers keep oxygen tanks, which children describe as "breathing machines," next to their children's beds.

The houses in which these children live, two thirds of which are owned by the City of New York, are often as squalid as the houses of the poorest children I have visited in rural Mississippi, but there is none of the greenness and the healing sweetness of the Mississippi countryside outside their windows, which are often barred and bolted as protection against thieves.

Some of these houses are freezing in the winter. In dangerously cold weather, the city sometimes distributes electric blankets and space heaters to its tenants. In emergency conditions, if space heaters can't be used, because substandard wiring is overloaded, the city's practice is to pass out sleeping bags.

"You just cover up... and hope you wake up the next morning," says a father of four children, one of them an infant one month old, as they prepare to climb into their sleeping bags in hats and coats on a December night.

Jonathan Kozol

In humid summer weather, roaches crawl on virtually every surface of the houses in which many of the children live. Rats emerge from holes in bedroom walls, terrorizing infants in their cribs. In the streets outside, the restlessness and anger that are present in all seasons frequently intensify under the stress of heat.

In speaking of rates of homicide in New York City neighborhoods, the *Times* refers to the streets around St. Ann's as "the deadliest blocks" in "the deadliest precinct" of the city. If there is a deadlier place in the United States, I don't know where it is.

In 1991, 84 people, more than half of whom were 21 or younger, were murdered in the precinct. A year later, ten people were shot dead on a street called Beekman Avenue, where many of the children I have come to know reside. On Valentine's Day of 1993, three more children and three adults were shot dead on the living room floor of an apartment six blocks from the run-down park that serves the area.

In early July of 1993, shortly before the first time that I visited the neighborhood, three more people were shot in 30 minutes in three unrelated murders in the South Bronx, one of them only a block from St. Ann's Avenue. A week later, a mother was murdered and her baby wounded by a bullet in the stomach while they were standing on a South Bronx corner. Three weeks after that, a minister and elderly parishioner were shot outside the front door of their church, while another South Bronx resident was discovered in his bathtub with his head cut off. In subsequent days, a man was shot in both his eyes and a ten-year-old was critically wounded in the brain.

What is it like for children to grow up here? What do they think the world has done to them? Do they believe that they are being shunned or hidden by society? If so, do they think that they deserve this? What is it that enables some of them to pray? When they pray, what do they say to God?...

No matter how final a visit seems, I keep on going back to the same places—Beekman Avenue, and St. Ann's Avenue, and Cypress, and East Tremont, and the area around the Hunts Point Market, then to Featherbed Lane and Shakespeare Avenue, and back to St. Ann's Church. Thinking often of a teacher I had met some months before at P.S. 65, who had wondered whether the kinds of questions I was asking could be answered by a teacher and whether they were "better asked to priests or theologians," I go back again and again to talk with ministers and priests in almost every neighborhood, to Gregory Groover in Hunts Point, to the priest of St. Luke's Church, near P.S. 65, in which Bernardo Rodriguez had been baptized and in which a memorial mass was held upon his death, and to the ministers of several of the storefront churches on Brook Avenue. I also talk with a number of the nuns from several different Catholic orders who work at the clinics and food pantries of the area.

Each time, the conversation starts with something quite specific—AIDS or education, welfare rules or housing or lead poison or the flight of jobs—but ends with talk of personal pain, anxiety about the future of the children, the search for faith in almost anyone or anything that offers strength, sometimes with talk of God.

The specifics of each issue—dump-sites, asthma, or waste burners, or whatever else—soon begin to seem almost beside the point. The search for explanations of the sadness heard in many of the voices of the people I have met is not answered by the factual questions one might ask about "environment" or "health care" or "the public schools." The questions that need asking seem to go beyond these concrete matters. One wants instead to know how certain people hold up under terrible ordeal, how many more do not, how human beings devalue other people's lives, how numbness and destructiveness are universalized, how human pity is at length extinguished and the shunning of the vulnerable can come in time to be perceived as natural behavior. "The poor frighten me," a rich lady told St. Vincent. "The poor are frightening," he answered, "as frightening as God's justice." What do we do to those who frighten us? Do we put them off, as far away as possible, and hope, as one of the students said to me during the previous summer, that they'll either die or disappear? How does a nation deal with those whom it has cursed?

One day in the spring, when Reverend Overall is driving with me from Manhattan to the Bronx, she stops her car at 96th Street, then drives one block more to 97th Street, in order to enable me to see the cutoff point between the races in this section of New York.

The sharpness of the demarcation line, which I have never seen before at the street level, is more dramatic and extreme than I anticipated. To the south, along Park Avenue, impressive buildings stand on both sides of the street, pedestrian islands with well-tended grass and flower plantings in the center. In the other direction, to the north, a railroad line, submerged beneath Park Avenue up to this point, appears from under 97th Street and splits the avenue in two. The trains, from this point on, run along the street for several blocks until Park Avenue dips slightly and the tracks are elevated on a large stone viaduct that shadows children playing in the sun of afternoon.

The significance of 96th Street in New York is inescapable and comes up time and again in conversations and in the newspapers. Luxury grocers advertise their willingness to make deliveries only south of 96th Street, and even liberal papers such as the *Observer* print these ads. McDonald's announces "home delivery" from 40 of its outlets in New York, but none of them north of this point on the East Side....

"The next ten years will see a new South Bronx," said South Bronx congressman Herman Badillo in 1972, in reference to ... signs of progress.

Visitors to Lincoln Hospital or Beekman Avenue today may have an opportunity to judge to what degree the optimism of those years was justified. The new public schools of the South Bronx, with stilts or without stilts, have proven, with a few remarkable exceptions, to be sad repositories for the disappointed dreams of children of dark skin. The newly built Lincoln Hospital has proven to be another terrifying and chaotic monument to medical apartheid. The wiring in many of those "sparkling new apartment houses" along Beekman Avenue has long since been eaten through by rats. The new plumbing of 22 years ago sprays scalding steam at mothers and their infants. . . .

"If there is one thing more destructive and demoralizing to poor people than to live in desolation," Reverend Overall observes, "it is to have these false hopes reawakened at these routine intervals. Do that to me enough times and I'll never hope again. It's like shooting someone up with drugs. This is how you turn poor people into zombies."

There is another, entirely different issue that is being raised about these promises of reconstruction and renewal. Even if the efforts under way today should prove, unlike those of the past, to be enduring, and even if they ever reach the St. Ann's neighborhood, many of the poorest residents believe that they are not the people who will benefit. They are convinced that those who benefit will be "the least poor of the poor," for whom the city or a nonprofit corporation may provide unusual security and private sanitation, so that the immediate environs may become an island of protected, if ephemeral, wholesomeness within a sea of suffering and sickness. And, if the South Bronx as a whole should ever become a truly pleasant place to live, many here feel certain that the very poor will simply be pushed off into another squalid quarter somewhere else, perhaps one of the deeply troubled, segregated suburbs that are now proliferating on all sides of New York City.

No one in New York, in any case, expects the racial isolation of these neighborhoods to lessen in the years ahead. A demographic forecast by the city's planning agency predicts that the population of the Bronx—both North and South—half of which was white in 1970, and nearly a quarter of which was white in 1990, will be entirely black and Hispanic by the early years of the next century, outside of a handful of de facto segregated enclaves of white people and a few essentially detached communities like parts of Riverdale. By that time, the Bronx and Harlem and Washington Heights will make up a vast and virtually uninterrupted ghetto with a population close to that of Houston, Texas, which is America's fourth-largest city.

Despite these demographic probabilities, the Bronx borough president, Fernando Ferrer, with whom I've talked at length about the health and education problems of the families here, manages to be contagiously enthusiastic. He is a likable person and seems genuinely dedicated to the people whom he represents; it is, of course, his job to be enthusiastic. I have met politicians equally dedicated and enthusiastic in Detroit and East St. Louis, but their energy and dedication could not bring back life-sustaining jobs or first-class schools or anything like modern health care to a population viewed as economically and socially superfluous; nor, of course, could they reverse the flight of most white people from those cities. There are neighborhoods with handsome houses in Detroit and East St. Louis too. Both these cities have their periodic episodes of neighborhood renewal also.

Perhaps something is truly different this time in the Bronx. Perhaps the skepticism of the people I have talked with in Mott Haven is misplaced. Perhaps the predictions of the city's planning agency will prove to be in error too. Perhaps the children of the children who are growing up today in the South Bronx will someday live in attractive houses on the same nice streets as middle-class and working-class homeowners of all races. It is tempting to imagine this, but it is only honest to report that no one I have met here holds such expectations.

Whatever good things may happen for the children of another generation are, in any case, of little solace to those who are children now and will not have their childhood to live a second time in the next century. This is particularly the case for those, especially the very young, who are about to lose, or have already lost, their mothers or their fathers to the epidemic that now stalks the neighborhood.

The rapid emergence in New York of thousands of black and Hispanic children of low income who have lost their parents to the plague of AIDS is, says the director of an organization called the Orphans Project, a catastrophe that has no real analogy within our nation in this century. "Only the great influenza pandemic of 1918 ... offers a partial analogy from diseases of the twentieth century. ... We are only at the beginning of this phenomenon. We do not yet know its duration."

Already in 1993, when I began to visit in the South Bronx, some 10,000 children in New York had lost their mothers to the epidemic. As many as 2,000 of these children were believed to live in the Mott Haven area and in three or four adjacent sections of the Bronx. The Orphans Project estimated that, between then and the year 2000, HIV-infected mothers in New York would "give birth to between 32,000 and 38,000 HIV-infected babies" and more than twice as many babies who would not have been infected. If these projections prove to be correct, and if the city continues with its present policy of channeling its sickest and most troubled families, often addicted and quite frequently infected, into housing in this area, it is likely that entire blocks will soon be home to mourning orphans, many of whom will follow their own parents to an early grave.

"The viral path" of AIDS, says *Newsday*, "has crept through the family tree" in many South Bronx neighborhoods, "breaking branch after branch." By the spring of 1993, 1,381 women in the area and 3,428 men had been diagnosed. But thousands of people in the South Bronx "have no personal physician. ... Infected women still go undiagnosed, their lifespans significantly reduced" because they get no early treatment.

A specialist in pediatric AIDS says he's "seeing things medically that I've never seen before and never thought I would ever see." Speaking of people with "rampant TB and three other types of infection at the same time" waiting at hospitals as long as three days for a bed, he says, "It's like the Middle Ages."

"Right now at Bronx-Lebanon," says Mrs. Washington's doctor, "a quarter of all our *general* admissions—not just on obstetric wards—are known to be positive for HIV." The area served by the hospital, according to a study of blood samples tested at the hospital, "apparently has one of the highest AIDS rates in the world."

According to the city's health officials, 91 percent of children in New York who are born with AIDS are black or Hispanic, as are 84 percent of women who have AIDS. So the racial demographics of Mott Haven, as well as the prevalence of intravenous drug use in the area and an apparent increase in the rate of HIV infection among adolescents here, tend to justify the somber language used by doctors in Mott Haven as they look into the future.

At a walk-in center in Mott Haven, run by the Dominican Sisters, which offers medical help and other services to families with AIDS, a social worker who does "anticipatory grieving" with the children of AIDS patients speaks of a 15-year-old girl who is infected "but is afraid to tell her mother, because her mother is already dying." The girl's ten-year-old sister has AIDS also, says the social worker, "presumably because she was infected perinatally," in which case it is remarkable that she has lived this long. But, she says, "with a ten-year-old you can't be sure exactly *how* she was infected."

The incubation period for development of AIDS in infants is, she tells me, generally shorter than in adults—an average of three years. Most subsequently die in 18 months. Only about five percent live to be 12 years old.

In another family in the neighborhood, she says, the father died two years ago and the mother is about to die. The four soon-to-be-orphaned children are being cared for by their 75-year-old grandmother. "One of the children, a nine-year-old, is sick with full-blown AIDS. Another child, seven years old, is less sick but he's been getting IV blood infusions. The six-year-old may be okay. But it's the 13-year-old girl, who *isn't* sick, who's causing the most worries. She's staying out all night, defying her grandmother. She started to do this at 11, when her father died. Recently, this girl had an abortion."

"Thirteen years old?"

"Yes," she replies. "Thirteen years old. You can imagine the risks that child must be taking...."

All of the families she's described, she tells me, live in approximately a 12-block radius of St. Ann's Church, and, she adds, "we're barely scratching the surface of the families in the neighborhood who need our help."

How do children living in this medieval landscape face the losses that they must expect? How do they confront the process of bereavement?...

Amazing grace! How sweet the sound
That saved a wretch like me.
I once was lost and now am found
Was blind but now I see.

...[T]he organ becomes louder and the congregation rises and the verse that Reverend Groover spoke is turned to music and the whole room sings. They end with the hopeful words of the fourth verse that I have read now several times at home. But reading it in Massachusetts and hearing it sung by people in Hunts Point are not the same.

When the service ends, people turn to those around them and shake hands and say, "God bless you." The woman beside me says, "God bless you" to her baby and then turns and says the same to me, but I am afraid to say it in return.

Reverend Groover invites me to have lunch upstairs with members of the church. After lunch, a couple who grew up here but now live out in the suburbs offer me a ride back to Mott Haven. I sit for the rest of the afternoon in the garden of St. Ann's and think for a long time of the sermon I have heard.

The preacher told the mothers of the church to tell their sons in prison, "I am a woman! One day the God I see, you shall see also!" She told the mothers, "I want you to know there is a song for *you*.... Your children may be drowning in despair today but they will rise in glory!"

I write this question on the back of the church program: "Then where is He? What is He waiting for? Come on, Jehovah! Let's get moving. Where's your sword?"

As soon as I write this down, I feel embarrassed by these thoughts. The words of the gospel songs I heard in church, like a stern reprimand, keep going through my mind.

There are children in the garden. Their playfulness is like a reprimand as well. The sweetness of the hour and the voices of the children soon dispel the feeling of irreverence I had fallen into. Their voices are like summer songs, not songs of pain. Several boys are walking single-file on the top rung of a wooden structure, daring one another to go all the way to a small platform at the end. Precariously balanced, they shout challenges to one another. How long will they be content to stay within this garden?

When it gets dark, I fish in my pocket for two quarters and go out on St. Ann's Avenue and buy an icie and walk up to Beekman Avenue,... but see no children there and head off finally to Brook Avenue, then to the train and the hotel, then to the Delta terminal, and then the plane. As the plane takes off, I try to get a look at Rikers Island, but I'm on the wrong side of the plane and it climbs fast into the clouds.

I look at my notes as the plane crosses Connecticut. I'm looking forward to getting home and sitting at my desk and trying to make sense of everything I've learned. But I don't really think I will make sense of anything and I don't expect that I'll be able to construct a little list of "answers" and "solutions," as my editor would like. I have done this many times before; so have dozens of other writers; so have hundreds of committees and foundations and commissions. The time for lists like that now seems long past.

Will the people Reverend Groover called "the principalities and powers" look into their hearts one day in church or synagogue and feel the grace of God and, as he put it, "be transformed"? Will they become ashamed of what they've done, or what they have accepted? Will they decide they do not need to quarantine the outcasts of their ingenuity and will they then use all their wisdom and their skills to build a new society and new economy in which no human being will be superfluous? I wish I could believe that, but I don't think it is likely. I think it is more likely that they'll write more stories about "Hope Within the Ashes" and then pile on more ashes and then change the subject to the opening of the ballet or a review of a new restaurant. And the children of disappointment will keep dying.

I think that Mrs. Washington is right to view the years before us with foreboding. I have never lived through a time as cold as this in the United States. Many men and women in the Bronx believe that it is going to get worse. I don't know what can change this.

ACKNOWLEDGMENTS

1.1 From Theodore R. Sizer, *Horace's Hope: What Works for the American High School* (Houghton Mifflin, 1996). Copyright © 1996 by Theodore R. Sizer. Reprinted by permission of Houghton Mifflin Company. All rights reserved. Notes omitted.

1.2 From E. D. Hirsch, Jr., *Cultural Literacy: What Every American Needs to Know* (Houghton Mifflin, 1987). Copyright © 1987 by Houghton Mifflin Company. Reprinted by permission. All rights reserved. Notes omitted.

1.3 From Diane Ravitch, *The Troubled Crusade: American Education, 1945–1980* (Basic Books, 1983). Copyright © 1983 by Diane Ravitch. Reprinted by permission of Basic Books, a member of Perseus Books, LLC. Notes omitted.

1.4 From Mortimer Adler, "The Paideia Proposal: Rediscovering the Essence of Education," *The American School Board Journal* (July 1982). Copyright © 1982 by The National School Boards Association. Reprinted by permission. All rights reserved.

2.1 From John Dewey, *Democracy and Education: An Introduction to the Philosophy of Education* (Macmillan, 1916). Notes omitted.

2.2 From William Heard Kilpatrick, "The Project Method," *Teachers College Record*, vol. 19, no. 4 (September 1918).

2.3 From Maria Montessori, *The Montessori Method* (Robert Bentley, 1965).

2.4 From C. H. Patterson, *Humanistic Education* (Prentice-Hall, 1973). Copyright © 1973 by Prentice-Hall, Inc. Reprinted by permission of Allyn & Bacon.

3.1 From Joel Spring, *Deculturalization and the Struggle for Equality: A Brief History of the Education of Dominated Cultures in the United States*, 2d ed. (McGraw-Hill, 1997). Copyright © 1994, 1997 by The McGraw-Hill Companies, Inc. Reprinted by permission.

3.2 From Henry A. Giroux, "Culture, Power and Transformation in the Work of Paulo Freire: Toward a Politics of Education," in Henry A. Giroux, *Teachers as Intellectuals: Toward a Critical Pedagogy of Learning* (Bergin & Garvey, 1988). Copyright © 1988 by Bergin & Garvey Publishers, Inc. Reprinted by permission of Greenwood Publishing Group, Inc., Westport, CT.

3.3 From Paulo Freire, *Pedagogy of the Oppressed*, rev. ed., trans. Myra Bergman Ramos (Continuum, 1993). Copyright © 1970, 1993 by Paulo Freire. Reprinted by permission of The Continuum International Publishing Group, Inc.

3.4 From Ivan Illich, *Deschooling Society* (Harper & Row, 1971), pp. 10–12, 25–33. Copyright © 1971 by Ivan Illich and Valentina Borremans. Reprinted by permission.

4.1 From Herbert R. Kohl, *The Open Classroom: A Practical Guide to a New Way of Teaching* (New York Review, 1969). Copyright © 1969 by Herbert R. Kohl. Reprinted by permission of *The New York Review of Books*.

4.2 From Katherine Camp Mayhew and Anna Camp Edwards, *The Dewey School: The Laboratory School of the University of Chicago, 1896–1903* (D. Appleton-Century, 1936). Notes omitted.

5.1 From Hilda Taba, *Curriculum Development: Theory and Practice* (Harcourt, Brace & World, 1962), under the general editorship of Willard B. Spalding. Copyright © 1962 by Harcourt Brace & Company. Copyright renewed 1990 by Margaret A. Spalding. Reprinted by permission of Harcourt Brace & Company. Notes and references omitted.

11.3 From David R. Krathwohl, Benjamin S. Bloom, and Bertram B. Masia, *Taxonomy of Educational Objectives, Handbook II: Affective Domain* (David McKay, 1964). Copyright © 1964 by Longman, Inc. Reprinted by permission of Addison-Wesley Educational Publishers, Inc. Some notes omitted.

12.1 From Ann L. Brown, John D. Bransford, Roberta A. Ferrara, and Joseph C. Campione, "Learning, Remembering, and Understanding," in Paul H. Mussen, ed., *Handbook of Child Psychology, vol. 3: Cognitive Development*, 4th ed. (John Wiley, 1983). Copyright © 1946, 1954, 1970, and 1983 by John Wiley & Sons, Inc. Reprinted by permission. Notes and references omitted.

12.2 From John Bransford, Robert Sherwood, Nancy Vye, and John Rieser, "Teaching Thinking and Problem Solving," *American Psychologist*, vol. 41, no. 10 (October 1986), pp. 1078, 1083–1086. Copyright © 1986 by The American Psychological Association. Reprinted by permission. References omitted.

12.3 From Howard Gardner and Joseph Walters, "A Rounded Version," in Howard Gardner, *Multiple Intelligences: The Theory in Practice* (Basic Books, 1993). Copyright © 1993 by Howard Gardner. Reprinted by permission of Basic Books, a member of Perseus Books, LLC. References omitted.

12.4 From John T. Bruer, "Education and the Brain: A Bridge Too Far," *Educational Researcher*, vol. 26, no. 8 (November 1997). Copyright © 1997 by The American Educational Research Association. Reprinted by permission. References omitted.

13.1 From John Dewey, "Education and Social Change," *The Social Frontier*, vol. 3, no. 26 (May 1937). Copyright © 1937 by The Center for Dewey Studies, Southern Illinois University, Carbondale, IL. Reprinted by permission.

13.2 From I. L. Kandel, *Conflicting Theories of Education* (Macmillan, 1938).

14.1 From Maxine Greene, "The Passions of Pluralism: Multiculturalism and the Expanding Community," *Educational Researcher*, vol. 22, no. 1 (January-February 1993). Copyright © 1993 by The American Educational Research Association. Reprinted by permission. References omitted.

14.2 From Jonathan Kozol, *Savage Inequalities: Children in America's Schools* (Crown, 1991). Copyright © 1991 by Jonathan Kozol. Reprinted by permission of Crown Publishers, a division of Random House, Inc.

14.3 From Jonathan Kozol, *Amazing Grace: The Lives of Children and the Conscience of a Nation* (Crown, 1995). Copyright © 1995 by Jonathan Kozol. Reprinted by permission of Crown Publishers, a division of Random House, Inc.

Index

*Notable
Selections in
Education*

DATE DUE

AG 15 08			
APR 0 0 2009			
AUG 2 3 2009			

DEMCO 38-296

Please remember that this is a library book,
and that it belongs only temporarily to each
person who uses it. Be considerate. Do
not write in this, or any, library book.